Dynamics of Virtual Work

Series Editors
Ursula Huws
Hertfordshire Business School
Hatfield, UK

Rosalind Gill
Department of Sociology
City, University of London
London, UK

Technological change has transformed where people work, when and how. Digitisation of information has altered labour processes out of all recognition whilst telecommunications have enabled jobs to be relocated globally. ICTs have also enabled the creation of entirely new types of 'digital' or 'virtual' labour, both paid and unpaid, shifting the borderline between 'play' and 'work' and creating new types of unpaid labour connected with the consumption and co-creation of goods and services. This affects private life as well as transforming the nature of work and people experience the impacts differently depending on their gender, their age, where they live and what work they do. Aspects of these changes have been studied separately by many different academic experts however up till now a cohesive overarching analytical framework has been lacking. Drawing on a major, high-profile COST Action (European Cooperation in Science and Technology) Dynamics of Virtual Work, this series will bring together leading international experts from a wide range of disciplines including political economy, labour sociology, economic geography, communications studies, technology, gender studies, social psychology, organisation studies, industrial relations and development studies to explore the transformation of work and labour in the Internet Age. The series will allow researchers to speak across disciplinary boundaries, national borders, theoretical and political vocabularies, and different languages to understand and make sense of contemporary transformations in work and social life more broadly. The book series will build on and extend this, offering a new, important and intellectually exciting intervention into debates about work and labour, social theory, digital culture, gender, class, globalisation and economic, social and political change.

More information about this series at
http://www.palgrave.com/gp/series/14954

Rosalind Gill · Andy C. Pratt
Tarek E. Virani
Editors

Creative Hubs
in Question

Place, Space and Work
in the Creative Economy

Editors
Rosalind Gill
City, University of London
London, UK

Andy C. Pratt
City, University of London
London, UK

Tarek E. Virani
Queen Mary University of London
London, UK

Dynamics of Virtual Work
ISBN 978-3-030-10652-2   ISBN 978-3-030-10653-9   (eBook)
https://doi.org/10.1007/978-3-030-10653-9

Library of Congress Control Number: 2018965779

This Palgrave Macmillan imprint is published by the registered company Springer Nature Switzerland AG
The registered company address is: Gewerbestrasse 11, 6330 Cham, Switzerland

This book is dedicated to our beloved colleague and friend Debbie Dickinson, who passed away as it was going to press in March 2019. Debbie's warmth, generosity and commitment to music, the arts and cultural life were an inspiration to many of the contributors to this book, and to numerous others. We will miss her, and cherish her memory.

Contents

Notes on Contributors

Daniel Ashton is Associate Professor of Cultural and Creative Industries at Winchester School of Art, University of Southampton. His research focuses on creative careers, and he is the co-editor of *Cultural Work and Higher Education*. He is currently undertaking research with arts and cultural organizations exploring cultural value.

Vasilis Avdikos is Assistant Professor at the Department of Economic and Regional Development, Panteion University, Athens and a member of the Regional Development Institute. He has published several papers on urban and regional development issues and on creative and cultural industries.

Carolina Bandinelli has conducted research on emerging forms of subjectivities in neoliberal societies, with a focus on entrepreneurship and self-branding in the creative industries. Currently, she is undertaking a research project on the digital culture of love. She is a lecturer in Media at the University of Lincoln.

Boukje Cnossen currently works as a postdoctoral researcher at the Institute of Sociology and Cultural Organization at Leuphana University of Lüneburg (Germany), where she investigates organizing practices in the arts, with a specific focus on materiality and discourse. Her work has been published in *Human Relations and European Journal of Cultural Studies*, among other outlets.

Roberta Comunian is Reader in Creative Economy at the Department of Culture, Media and Creative Industries at King's College London. Her research focuses on the relationship between creative industries, cultural policy and public-supported art institutions. She has also undertaken research on knowledge transfer and creative industries investigating the career opportunities and patterns of creative graduates.

Marianna d'Ovidio at present works as Assistant Professor in economic sociology at the University of Bari, and her research interests include the cultural economy, creativity, and social and cultural innovation, in particular their interactions with local development and urban transformations. d'Ovidio has published extensively on the analysis of creative and cultural industries in the local development of urban regions.

Cecilia Dinardi is Senior Lecturer in Cultural Policy at Goldsmiths, University of London (Institute for Creative and Cultural Entrepreneurship). Her background is in cultural and urban sociology (Ph.D./M.Sc., LSE) with an expertise in cities and culture-led urban regeneration, cultural policies, grass-roots interventions and the informal creative economy in Latin America.

Alessandro Gandini is a sociologist and a senior researcher at the Department of Social and Political Sciences, University of Milan. Previously, he was a lecturer in the Department of Digital Humanities, King's College, London. His research interests include the transformation of work, social relations and research methods in the digital society. He is the author of *The Reputation Economy* (Palgrave, 2016), the co-author of *Qualitative Research in Digital Environments* (Routledge, 2017) and a co-editor of *Unboxing the Sharing Economy*, part of *The Sociological Review Monograph Series* (2018).

Rosalind Gill is Professor of Social and Cultural Analysis at City, University of London. She is author or editor of ten books including *Gender and Creative Labour* (with Bridget Conor and Stephanie Taylor, 2015), *Aesthetic Labour: Beauty Politics in Neoliberalism* (with Ana Elias and Christina Scharff, 2016) and *Mediated Intimacy: Sex Advice in Media Culture* (with Meg-John Barker and Laura Harvey, 2018). Her work is animated by questions about power and social justice and the relationship between subjectivity and culture. She has worked extensively on the topic of inequalities in the creative economy.

Tom Gill is a policy analyst working in London regional government, with a background in social research. His research interests are broad and include the night time economy, affordable housing and sexualities.

Eirini Iliopoulou is an Architect–Urbanist and holds a Doctor of Engineering degree, awarded by the Technical University of Berlin. She is currently a postdoctoral researcher at the Regional Development Institute, Panteion University, and a freelance urban planning consultant. Her interests focus on community engagement and civic participation practices, urban co-production, socio-spatial conflicts, cultural/creative industries.

David Lee is an Associate Professor in Media and Communication, University of Leeds, UK. His books include *Independent Television Production in the UK: From Cottage Industry to Big Business* (2018), and as co-author, *Culture, Economy and Politics: The Case of New Labour* (2015). He has published widely on cultural work, media industries and cultural policy.

Jo Littler is a Reader in the Department of Sociology at City, University of London. Her books include *Radical Consumption? Shopping for Change in Contemporary Culture; The Politics of Heritage: The Legacies of 'Race'*, co-edited with Roshi Naidoo, and most recently *Against Meritocracy: Culture, Power and Myths of Mobility*.

Paul Long is Professor of Media and Cultural History in the Birmingham Centre for Media and Cultural Research, Birmingham City University. He researches popular music history, heritage and archives as well as histories of creative industries. He is currently writing

Memorialising Popular Music Culture: History, Heritage and the Archive (Rowman and Littlefield) for publication in 2020.

Janet Merkel is an urban sociologist (Ph.D., Humboldt University Berlin). She works as a senior researcher at the Institute of Urban and Regional Planning at Technical University Berlin. Her research interests include creative industries, cultural policy and new forms of work organization in cities.

Ceren Mert is a part-time lecturer at the Faculty of Social Sciences at Özyeğin University in Istanbul, Turkey. Having completed her undergraduate and master's degrees in the Sociology Department of Middle East Technical University, Ankara, Turkey, she has gained her Ph.D. in the field of Sociology from Mimar Sinan Fine Arts University, Istanbul. She works on interdisciplinary fields, which crosscuts the subject areas of popular music and culture, creative and cultural industries, urban studies, digital sociology and media studies.

George Morgan is Associate Professor at the Institute for Culture and Society at Western Sydney University. His recent research deals with creative skills, and in particular, the obstacles encountered by young people from disadvantaged/minority backgrounds in building creative careers. His book *The Creativity Hoax: Precarious Work and the New Economy* (Anthem Press), co-authored with Pariece Nelligan was published in 2018.

Annette Naudin is Senior Lecturer in media and cultural entrepreneurship. Naudin's current research is concerned with gender and BAME cultural workers as a focus for an interrogation of cultural policy. Naudin recently published *Cultural Entrepreneurship: The Cultural Worker's Experience of Entrepreneurship* (2018) exploring entrepreneurship studies, cultural policy and cultural work.

Øyvind Økland is an Associate Professor in Intercultural Studies at NLA University College in Norway. He teaches intercultural communication and media studies. His research focuses on communication in a global and cultural perspective, as well as health issues. He has worked especially with youth in different cultures, in Norway, Ghana and

Kenya. He has written several chapters in books and edited a book and young Somali immigrants and their media usage.

Valentina Pacetti currently works as Associate Professor in economic sociology at the University of Milano-Bicocca. Pacetti's field of research includes local governance, regulation and economic development. Pacetti has published extensively on organizations and their socio-economic embeddedness.

Andy C. Pratt is Professor of Cultural Economy at City, University of London, and Director of the Centre for Culture and the Creative Industries. He has previously taught at UCL, LSE, KCL and City University in London. He has been researching and teaching all aspects of the cultural economy, in London and globally for the last 25 years. He has both published extensively on the topic and advised public agencies worldwide.

Marisol Sandoval is a Senior Lecturer in the Department of Sociology at City, University of London. Her research critically deals with questions of power, ideology and resistance in the global culture industries. Currently, she is working on a project that explores the politics of worker co-operatives in the cultural sector.

Michael Seman is the Director of Creative Industries Research and Policy at the University of Colorado Denver's College of Arts & Media. He holds a doctorate in urban planning and public policy, and his work primarily examines how the creative economy, entrepreneurship and economic development intersect on the urban landscape.

Nicola J. Thomas is Associate Professor in Cultural and Historical Geography at the University of Exeter. She has developed a body of work around craft geographies, situating contemporary and twentieth-century craft practice within the broader creative economy. Her approach addresses the intersection of material, historical, cultural, social, political and economic contexts through an exploration of craft makers' livelihoods and the spatial dimension of their labour. Her research always attends to the historicity of cultural production and consumption, bringing a historical sensitivity to critical understandings of the cultural and creative economy. She has a particular interest in co-creating practice led routes within her research working with practitioners to develop collaborative practice project which support makers' well-being and livelihoods.

Tarek E. Virani is Lecturer of Creative Industries at the School of Business and Management at Queen Mary University of London, UK. He is also Deputy Director of Network: Queen Mary's Centre for the Creative and Cultural Economy. His research interests include: the role of knowledge in the cultural economy, urban policy and local creative economies, new workspaces in the creative and cultural economy, and the role of higher education in regional creative clusters.

James Woodriff is a research assistant at the Institute for Culture and Society, School of Humanities and Communication Arts Western Sydney University, and the principal of the Ponderance Collective, a research and design agency.

List of Figures

List of Tables

1

Introduction

Andy C. Pratt, Tarek E. Virani and Rosalind Gill

Over the last fifteen years, the term 'hub' has captured the imagination of policy makers, urban planners and politicians. Tied to a broader hyperbole about creativity, creative hubs have come to be presented as unquestionably a 'Good Thing', a panacea for all economic ills. No longer do urban areas simply want to rebrand themselves as 'creative cities', now, in a seemingly unstoppable global trend, they want to become—or to host—creative hubs—districts, clusters or spaces that

A. C. Pratt (✉) · R. Gill
Department of Sociology, City, University of London,
London, UK
e-mail: andy.pratt.1@city.ac.uk

R. Gill
e-mail: Rosalind.gill.2@city.ac.uk

T. E. Virani
School of Business and Management,
Queen Mary University of London, London, UK
e-mail: t.virani@qmul.ac.uk

© The Author(s) 2019
R. Gill et al. (eds.), *Creative Hubs in Question*, Dynamics of Virtual Work,
https://doi.org/10.1007/978-3-030-10653-9_1

1

will concentrate the kismet of 'creatives', as well as offering attractive, buzzy locales.

Since the beginning of the twenty-first century, the growth and proliferation of these types of largely urban industrial agglomeration have been exponential. From San Francisco to Moscow and from Durban to Hanoi, creative hubs have really taken off. Yet they have done so with very little scrutiny or research and with hardly any shared understanding of what hubs are, what they do and how—or indeed if—they work. Academic work on creative hubs is surprisingly scarce. Instead, there exists a kind of unquestioned faith in hubs—despite—or more tellingly perhaps *because*—their meaning is not always clear.

Hubs have variously been understood as co-working spaces, as studios, as incubators, as accelerators, as districts, quarters or zones and/or a mix of all of the above. The lack of clarity—let alone consensus—is particularly troubling given that policy makers, research councils, consultants and governments have been so quick to promote and endorse the value of creative hubs as a catalyst for innovation and growth in local creative and cultural economies, as well as for producing urban regeneration.

In this book our aim is to look critically at creative hubs from interdisciplinary perspectives including Sociology, Geography, Economics, Media and Communications, Culture and Creative Industries and Critical Policy studies. We are interested in 'pressing pause' on the celebratory discourses about creative hubs to ask how they are best conceptualised, who they include or exclude, whether they make for 'good' workplaces, and what diverse forms they take across different places and contexts.

From our perspective, one of the most important 'hidden' aspects of hubs that find little expression in the writings about them are the voices of those that work there. This oversight is all the more critical given the transformation of all work, and in particular work in the creative and cultural economy, in recent years which has highlighted, first, the structural and, second, the organisation changes (evidenced by micro-enterprises and freelance work) and, third, the particular affective conditions of cultural labour. The first two factors in part explain a demand for hubs, but the latter concerns the ways that hubs operate, and the conditions within then: in both senses, these are particular to the cultural economy.

Cultural labour requires the engagement of aesthetics and values, and the unique interplay between the economy and art. Often, cultural workers choose to or are forced to do things in unique ways. This is in part because the risk of failure is great, but also because normal economic and bureaucratic systems assume a reality that is different from that of the cultural economy. These conditions, and the experiences of cultural workers, have generated a substantial debate in academic fields that has slowly found its way into the political sphere largely through concern with 'precarious work'. However, our concern goes further, to address the experiences and aspirations that cultural workers bring to these question: how do they use, and share, knowledges, skills, practices and aspirations; what sort of situated 'solutions' do they achieve; and furthermore do creative hubs help or hinder these actions.

As our contributors argue, creative hubs are seldom amenable to binary divisions between competition and cooperation, the formal and informal, and the for-profit and its alternatives. To accept such binary thinking endangers the creative economy being imprisoned not only in the physical structures of the industrial revolution, but also the thinking of mass manufacture. Debates are not reducible to 'flexible workspaces' that are assumed to accommodate new, or rapidly changing, organisational forms that are associated with project work, collective and individual work. Rather, the concerns of cultural workers include balancing material and cognitive (or immaterial) labour, and the moral economy of work, materials and organisation; they also concern questions about how they can connect with their audiences and markets for both inspiration and social validation. We hope that this collection causes readers to question how, and why, hubs operate as they do, as well as attending to the communities that they are part of, and the workers and their aspirations and motivations.

Creative Hubs in Question: Space, Place and Work in the Creative Economy

Hubs in general and creative hubs in particular have become since the early 2000s a contemporary meme in the policy fields of culture/creativity; urban, regional and national development; industrial and innovation (Pratt and Jeffcutt 2009b). A Google Search on the term 'creative hub' shows peaks in search occurrences in 2005 and 2017; the latest high point being dominated by searches in Asia.[1] Even companies such as Facebook and Ikea are promoting versions of a hub as part of their business activities. Like many ideas before them, hubs have become a 'go to' solution that rests on a common-sense understanding of concentration and intensity of activities (more must be better), and the implicit facility to connect firms and creatives, and to distribute those benefits locally. Whilst notions of the 'death of distance' (Cairncross 1998) were one popular response to the growth of the Internet and digital culture, hubs represent the inverse: an appreciation of proximity and co-location (Pratt 2000).

The generic notion of the hub relies on a number of questionable assumptions. The popularity and general understanding of hubs has led to a political favour. The translation of this general idea into practice has usually taken the form of a designated building or space that is branded a hub. The promoters and supporters of hubs commonly assume that by facilitating co-location (by provision of space that was not previously available) that economies of aggregation and knowledge transfer will inevitably follow. Whilst the idea of hubs (or clusters, or districts) has been a popular topic for industrial strategy and economics, those empirical analyses that have been carried out are characterised in macro-scale studies using secondary data.[2] Little empirical

---

[1]See https://trends.google.com/trends/explore?date=all&q=creative%20hub (August 20, 2018).

[2]The notion of hubs and clusters of economic activities has been promoted by Michael Porter and his consultancy activities. Porter's (1998) work builds on a wide range of work on industrial co-location in economics and geography. It is relevant that Porter's work comes from a business and management studies perspective, and hubs and clusters are viewed as part of the (internal) 'value chain' of the production company: the bottom line is efficiency and cost.

work has either focused on particular industrial sectors, or explored detailed analysis of product or information exchange: that is, what goes on inside or within hubs. The research deficit regarding hubs is most acute in the field of the creative economy.

The lack of detailed research and the understanding of creative hubs is surprising. The term creative hub appears in urban regeneration policies and in creative economy strategies; also it has occurred in a number of public research funding calls. The relatively small body of research that has been carried out on hubs can be broken down into three types: first, perhaps the most popular are pragmatic accounts of 'how to set up a hub'; inevitably, these tend to stress the positive or aspirational agenda of the agency promoting the hub. Implicitly, they highlight that the process is not quite as easily achieved by a supply of 'hubs' based on a logic of 'build it and they will come'; incorrectly assuming that the 'demand' from a nascent creative economy would look after itself. Second, the main body of academic research on creative hubs is of a policy-descriptive variety: whilst much of it is critical, it offers little in the way of evaluation or understanding of either the actual practices, or the gap between the observed and expected outcomes (Evans 2001, 2009; Pratt 2004a; Bagwell 2008). Finally, a strand of work that attempts to offer a robust evaluation of hubs is closely bound by economic assumptions and use of secondary data to test their economic impact on wider regions (Chapain et al. 2010).

There are number of weaknesses in this economic field of research. First, the gap between what was expected or proposed in hubs and what actually occurred. Second, most of the insight is gained from secondary aggregate data such that it is unclear which firms or creatives are included in a spatial unit. Third, there is a lack of explicit statement on testing the objectives for hubs (often because there were not clear for policy makers); in the exceptional cases where they are stated by policy makers (rather than implied by researchers from assumptions based on economy theory), they tend to relate to property management. Fourth, where data is collected on firms and creatives, it focuses on the numbers of workers employed rather than their experiences. Overall, there exists a blind spot in relation to what actually goes on within hubs. This question relates to the management and organisation of the hub, how they are governed, and what the character of the relationships is between the various users of hubs are (internal and external): are they material, or immaterial; formal, or informal, relationships? Moreover, in the field of culture and creativity, the question of values is an important one; this may be apparent in the set of questions above, or expressed as a moral or ethical position. Aesthetic and political judgements may, for some participants, be more important than profit generation per se.

Arguably, one important forerunner of the idea of a creative hub was that which was developed at St Katherine's Dock in London by SPACE in 1968 (see Harding 2018). The acronym SPACE stands for Space Provision Artistic Cultural and Educational and reflected an ambitious attempt to provide space for artists run by artists,[3] and a new way of working across boundaries: professional, social, political, cultural and philosophically, between artist and audiences, and artist and materials going beyond sites of individualistic expression (Wilson 2018). This innovative initiative was clearly driven by a deep concern for the quality and nature of art that was produced and the practices whereby it was produced, not simply the economic bottom line, although this had to be satisfied too. We present this manifestation of SPACE as a counter-point to the outlier cases of generic workspaces provision that occasionally carry the label 'creative hub'.

The example of SPACE alerts us to the live questions of ethics and values that underpin all work, but particularly creative and cultural work. It highlights the fact that there is an alternative to the 'isolated studio' that commonly makes up much hub provision (echoing standard workspace provision). Of critical importance to the day-to-day experience of hubs is the social and organisational environment, their governance and representation, individual and collective spaces and services, as well as the opportunities to learn from, and interact with, others. Our collection of essays seeks to open up the scope of enquiry to embrace this position; in so doing, we have sought to create a platform for authors to start with what actually happens, rather than what should, or might, occur. We hope that this strategy will bring us to

---

[3]The St Katherine's Dock development ran between 1968 and 1970. However, SPACE as an organisation that is run by artists, for artists, is still going strong providing studio spaces in London: it celebrated 50 years in 2018.

a more satisfactory point of departure from which we may develop a richer understanding of the phenomenon of creative hubs, including what goes on inside them whether it is in spite of, or because of, their organisational form.

In summary, creative hubs have become a cornerstone of economic and cultural policy with only the barest amount of critical discussion or scrutiny. It is as if we have all unwittingly become caught up in the hyperbole about creative hubs as an unquestioned good. Yet, do hubs fulfil the promises that are claimed for them? Our contributors explore a range of questions, including, but not limited to:

- What makes a hub 'a hub': is it a co-working space, district or cluster by a different name?
- What kinds of different forms or models of hubs exist?
- What is it like to work in a creative hub?
- Do/can hubs address questions of austerity and inequality?
- How are creative hubs materialised differently in various parts of the world and in contrasting environments, e.g. urban versus rural?
- What does the notion of 'creative hub' achieve performatively or ideologically for its sponsors, users and communities?
- Do creative hubs contribute to a variety of social 'goods'—good working environments, successful businesses, more equal and socially just communities?

Contributors to this book use the tools of qualitative research and take an interdisciplinary perspective to engage with the phenomenon of creative hubs including Sociology, Geography, Economics, Media and Communications, Culture and Creative Industries, Critical Policy studies and Urban Studies. We also asked our contributors to provide a combination of empirical studies of actual hubs, as well as theoretical reflections on the concept of creative hubs; moreover, we have sought to provide a wide range of international examples so as to broaden and deepen the debate.

The remainder of this introduction is divided into two parts. The major part sketches out the overlapping discursive realms of creative hubs. Here, we discuss how two perspectives have, in different but generally complementary ways, framed the creative hubs debate: the economic and the political. We suggest a third approach that has been neglected, the social, which we offer as a routeway into addressing the concerns of our contributors to this collection. Our aim is not to offer a discrete mapping of various conceptions and related functionalities. Instead, we use this framework to illustrate what might be considered as three different lenses on the creative hub phenomenon; each lens frames a type of action and problem, sometimes covering the same issues from a different perspective. On the basis of this meta-framing of the debate in the second section, we pose the question of 'what are creative hubs the answer to?'. Our answer is conditional and related to the particular situated circumstances of the hub, its creatives and the communities in which it is embedded.

Creative Hubs View Through 3 Lenses

We have argued in the previous section that the common, and even specialist, usage of the term creative hub has become unclear: a cloud of meanings and interpretations wrapped around a signifier. The various perspectives that have been deployed to justify or support hubs create specific in/visibilities, invite/dissuade actions and open up or close off possibilities. Classically, political rhetoric and policy choice have such a character; less obvious is the power that economics, or that which social or cultural analyses provide. Normative economics is articulated from a number of assumptions which do not necessarily hold in empirical circumstances (such as 'perfect information'); moreover, they are founded upon the smooth operation of the free market where correct prices are always allocated to objects. In contrast, social accounts focus on people and the social structures that enable or constrain them, and they seek to account for non-economic (non-market) values as well as economic ones. All three discourses offer partial insights. It is the framing and discursive accounts of the world that suggest appropriate actions and the resources necessary to achieve them.

In this section, we review creative hub debates; our objective is to highlight the research gap concerning the social aspects of hubs.

We argue that it is not simply prioritising one perspective above another: that is simply the exercise of power and authority. Rather, we want to point to the different visibilities that each discourse provides, thereby demonstrating the 'silencing' of social/cultural discourses in the creative hubs debate up to this time.

Political Discourse

The political discourse of hubs concerns the object that is 'hubbed': the creative. Of course, the terms 'creative' and 'creative industries' have a particular history that has been mobilised to support political programmes. The usage of creative and creativity has relatively recent usage; Pope (2005: 19) points out that the abstract noun 'creativity' first appeared in the Oxford English Dictionary as late as 1933 and did not achieve common usage until the 1950s. Arguably, the turning point for creativity's specific recent usage came in 1997 in the UK with the naming of the 'Creative Industries'. Previously, those economic activities that had as their 'product' culture were referred to as the cultural industries, a term that itself emerged from an economic analysis and a novel taxonomy of the economy (Garnham 2005). The terminology of the 'cultural industries' was used discursively to challenge the pervious terminology—the Culture Industry (the ideologically damming term used by Adorno (Horkheimer and Adorno 2002 [1947])). The (new) term cultural industries sought to pluralise, to remove a determinate moral censure and to challenge the binary between culture and economics.

The contemporary choice of the term 'creative industries' had no roots (arguably every human activity could be described as 'creative'): its political value was that it was different to the 'cultural industries' which is a terminology that had been used in the Britain by 'Old Labour' municipal authorities; New Labour sought to distance itself from this (Old Labour) legacy, and coining a new term proved an effective way to do it (Hesmondhalgh and Pratt 2005). Additional political traction was gained via the abstract noun—creative—which freights youth, expectation and modernisation: precisely the themes that the New Labour government sought to promote post-1997. Not surprisingly the term was much copied internationally.

Previously in Britain, the cultural industries had seldom been discussed as a collective 'industry'. The norm had been to discuss the film industry differently from, say, theatre (and those that worked in these art forms reproduced this practice). It was only in the 1990s that a collective label (the cultural or creative industries) was been used in both academic and policy texts and gradually been adopted by practitioners to refer to a sector of the economy. What we now know as 'creative hubs' emerged at this time, when what we now know as hubs were commonly referred to as 'cultural clusters': referring to the co-location of (old industrial) buildings that local authorities sought to reuse to promote the 'new' industries. It was a relatively short step to rebranding them as 'creative' clusters and traducing what had often been happenstance co-location into a cause of the 'cluster'; and, then elevating it to a 'model' that might be copied. Despite the British national government's loud promotion of the creative industries, the policies were in fact those that had predated this national concern with creativity, previously put in place at a municipal level by cities who had sought to establish 'cultural clusters' (Pratt 2004b) or 'cultural quarters' (Bell and Jayne 2004) to sustain and to promote local 'cultural industries'.

The 'creative' label received a further fillip in 2004 when Richard Florida (2004) named insurgent urban entrepreneurs 'the creative class'. Definitions are not critical here, it is the rhetoric of a 'creative class' that conveys the notion of a future, and those will play a dominant in it. Florida's argument to policy makers was—to really simplify it—to create cities and neighbourhoods that the creative class want to live and work in, which, in turn, will generate economic growth: these were called 'creative cities'. Unusually for an academic, Florida's (2008) message hit the 'sweet spot' for City Mayors: who would not support making their city 'the most creative city in the nation/world'?

In the early 2000s, the attachment of the label 'creative' to anything suddenly made it attractive, innovative and successful: from Apple products to management textbooks, to baristas. The creative city message, although a little subtler, was a powerful add-on to existing practices of 'place marketing' or branding (see the critical debates by Mould

2018; Ross 2008). Whereas making cars or mining coal, or even producing biotech can become outdated, creativity (appears to) remain fresh and 'future proof'. Despite the fact that the creative industries per se had no part in Florida's argument, the buzzword of creativity and the eagerness to brand places made the notion of 'creative hub': a label that somewhat overdetermined the outcome and was thus politically very successful.[4] Simply, it was a term that signified much, without being specific about anything: potent political discourse.

The political discourse of the creative hub (and the flexibility of its terminology) demonstrates that politicians and policy makers sought to address contemporary concerns, and those of the future. Their policy aspirations (of more, of better) are represented by the building is illustrative of that concern. However, this framing leaves little space for, or recognition of, either the operation of, or work within, a particular hub; economic and social discourses provide a partial repair to this incomplete picture.

Economic Discourse

Perhaps the most surprising shift in the last 20 years has been the rise of an economic discourse about culture and the creative industries. This has involved a challenge to cultural policy which has generally viewed economics at least inimical to, if not undermining of, cultural values. For their part, mainstream economists have long discounted, or diminished, the role of culture in the economy: from their perspective, culture was consumption, and hence not productive; moreover, it had little direct economic value. It is only since the 1970s that economic discourse has sought to embrace culture.[5] Even then, sympathetic

---

[4]Before the obligatory, 'hub' label was applied creative hubs laboured under variants of the 'art factory' (with an obvious reference to Andy Warhol). The early trend was to name the cluster after the previous industrial use of a particular building, examples included: the cable factory, the chocolate factory and the custard factory.

[5]Baumol and Bowen (1966) are usually regarded as the founding text of modern cultural economics.

economists sought not to attribute an economic value to culture (as this would succumb to Adorno's objection) (Throsby 2001); accordingly, much effort was spent on the calculation of indirect 'economic multipliers' for culture (Myerscough 1988), which was a way of valuing culture without directly putting a price on it: so-called shadow pricing. The ascent of neoliberalism and its castigation of the legitimacy of the state seemed to be the death knell for culture as it was assumed that it generated no direct economic value. However, recuperation was achieved for the 'creative industries' by emphasising their economic value to national economies. The approach was to not seek to value cultural outputs themselves, but the economic effort spent on their production. The creation of measures of the employment, exports, and value added by the sector enabled it to be represented as a net contributor to national well-being (UNCTAD 2008). However, the side effect was that only the parts of the creative economy that 'looked like' economic actors (such as the film industry with a more commercial output) were valued. The efforts to measure and render culture 'visible to' economic analysis had two downsides. First, that by focusing on inputs and outputs, and not meanings it potentially missed the 'heart' of the cultural industries; second, it tended to play down what made the cultural industries different from other industries, their non-normative organisation, and affective labour conditions that once again render them invisible to (economic) analyses.

Normative economic discourse views a good location as a result of monopolistic behaviour, and one that firms will seek to gain, but only one can attain, thereby forcing competitors to be 'sub-optimal', and at a disadvantage. As such, it is a distortion of the market, and resultant 'natural' monopoly confers unfair advantage. Initially, such natural monopolies were measured in terms of proximity to consumers. Such a location is described as one that minimises 'transactions costs', that is all the costs of doing business, like transport, but also including local regulations and customs. From this shallow perspective of human action, the most efficient solution will be co-location, everybody will seek to be as close to the most efficient place as possible. This was the origin of discussion of 'industrial districts' by Marshall (1920), and it has a powerful 'common sense' associated with it. Whilst the co-location or clustering phenomenon was not visible to mainstream neo-classical economics, it did reappear in the 1980s when Italian scholars discussed the phenomenon of 'new industrial districts' that did not seem adequately explained by neo-classical economic assumptions (Becattini 2004; Santagata 2010); this research pointed to 'extra-economic' factors such as the co-dependences of politics, social forms and economic accounts. From business studies, Porter's (1996) influential ideas of the value chain (again something outwith the neo-classical economic mindset) gave a new twist to the benefits of co-location. It was Porter's notion of the 'concentration' of the value-added elements of a manufacturing system that came to dominate policy in no small part because many nation states employed Porter's consultancy to collect the evidence for, and establish their, 'cluster strategies' of which one such cluster type was the 'creative cluster' (DTI 2001).

Economic discourse is constrained by its adherence to neo-classical theories and assumptions. Generally, economic accounts of co-location or clustering are rational accounts of cost minimisation and the 'potential' of interaction. The actual interaction, the 'what goes on in a cluster', is not something that economic discourse can address beyond the assumption that interaction, and innovation, and creativity 'will happen'. In fact, most of what we might want to call the 'factors' of clustering are formally not factors at all, but 'externalities' (that is, out-with the formal model of economic action). Accordingly, economic ears are deaf to questions of organisation, as well as social, cultural and political factors. Importantly, major contributions to understanding the creative economy by those outside of economics have referenced its 'peculiar' (compared to the 'industrial' norm) organisational and market structures, as well as non-market roles (Caves 2000): hence, the need for more nuanced approaches to the creative economy generally, and to creative hubs in particular.

Social/Cultural Discourse

The main focus of this book relates to the lack of research, and the framing of that research, as it relates to creative hubs. Creative hubs can be considered as a 'solution' to the problem of outsourcing work and the workplace that has occurred in across all parts of the economy, but led by cultural work. Generally, the shift from large factories to smaller workshops has occurred; but, in the case of cultural work has involved the development of 'the studio' rather than a workshop: a self-organised creative workplace.

As the cultural industries have expanded and developed, the nature of cultural production has also changed, as has cultural work (Hesmondhalgh and Baker 2011a; Prenger and Deuze 2017). Cultural work has not always been characterised by the isolated creator or the creator working in quasi-factory conditions (Luckman 2012; Taylor and Luckman 2018). Cultural work has increasingly been organised around temporary project work, a process that brings together free-lancers who move from one project team to another. This process has created, for creative workers in particular, a precarious work pattern, in contrast to the idealised—if atypical—model of the workplace and job, and career. The uncertainty about future work brings risk, and often low pay and no social protection although, for some, it might be regarded as freedom from conventional work constraints; however, the costs can be high when the workflow is intermittent. Summarising an important new collection of studies of contemporary creative working, Stephanie Taylor and Susan Luckman (2018: 9) argue that the 'new normal' includes a strong sense of motivation for 'a shift in how people want to work and how they organize their lives'.

Extensive research now explores the experiences of 'creatives', documenting the social, psychological and affective realities of working in fields that are marked by precarity, informality, intense sociality and an 'always on' sensibility. Cultural workers commonly have to invest in their own training, both financially and in terms of time spent in learning new skills and 'keeping up'. These topics and concerns were seldom examined in the same detail in previous times when such social reproduction could be assumed to be taken care of by the state or a large organisation; now they are an additional burden for the precariat to bear.

Whilst cultural and creative workers are seldom governed by an algorithm whereby they have to complete tasks as quickly as possible (such as contemporary taxi services and fast food delivery services), they are subject to internalised discipline. For many, this leads to 'self-exploitation' of overwork or 'sacrificial' or 'hope labour' (Kuehn and Corrigan 2013) (where extra labour is carried on for low or no return in the hope, or expectation, of a future opportunity) (Ross 2009; McRobbie 2016). Frequently, the only opportunity that is available to many is simply to work from one temporary contract to another, and absorb the costs of 'down time'. Cultural workers are thus in a complex position of balancing autonomy and risk, fulfilment and self-exploitation. Clearly, these social conditions of work are maintained through the structure and organisation of the cultural industries more generally, where those in power and control are able to shift the risks to the most vulnerable workers.

These are the conditions that bring cultural workers to seek out (shared) workspace, some manage with using their homes (again taking on more risk and responsibility), many others seek a workspace that offers some 'value added'. What constitutes 'value added' varies, but commonly it involves a sense of community, an opportunity to share and learn from others, as well as having security of a dedicated space. Many workers bring with them a sense of the moral economies of work, seeking 'good' work, that is that aligns with a personal sense of politics (Banks 2007). Mobilising a moral politics of work in conditions of potential super-exploitation is problematic (Hesmondhalgh and Baker 2010). However, it is because cultural workers have a degree of autonomy (and many believe that it is critical to their practice) that they seek to mobilise around their work conditions and the organisation of workplaces and their communities. As Mark Banks (2017) has argued, a notion of 'creative justice' is central to this field and may be thought about through concepts such as 'objective respect', 'parity of participation' and 'reduction of harms'. Where questions of place and space fit into this is a central question for this book. Put simply: Are hubs making things better or worse? How do they sit in relation to questions of equality, inclusion and justice?

As our contributors demonstrate, cultural workers bring a wide range of expectations and aspirations to creative hubs. Accordingly, much more than other types of hubs, creative hubs are effectively a stage upon which the contradictions of creative work are played out. The traditional industrial era divisions between crafts and disciplines are broken down, as are those between profit-making activities and informal or experimental ones. The opportunity of working together can be a means of pushing back against individual isolation and competition. It is not surprising that cultural workers commonly value 'affective communities' and 'communities of practice'; at the same time, this lays them vulnerable to the compulsory sociality that may be necessary to maintain contacts, or stay 'in the loop' for jobs, or professional knowledge (Gregg 2011).

If Creative Hubs Are the Answer, What Was the Question?

As we have argued, it is useful to explore the 'problem' of creative hubs from what might conventionally be seen as 'back to front'. Rather than reducing the variety and diversity of hubs to the one best way, instead we should seek to understand the reasons for, and benefits of different forms. Rather than seeing creative hubs as framed by economic, political or social discourses, we should follow the internal logics to see where they lead beyond these discursive limitations. Simply, we should move from an assumption of what hubs should do to an understanding of what hubs actually do, and what roles they perform for their users (the creatives).

Historically, the development of hubs emerged from a context of economic change (manufacturing decline) and urban dereliction, and the under-appreciation of the creative economy. The assumption has been that what had been sufficient for manufacturing would be just as suitable for the creative industries, for example workspace provision. There has been a belated recognition that those activities which work without an institutional framework of a stable market or audience, as well as a complex network of diverse production and creative skills, require a different type of support as much social as physical: support that 'fills the gaps' previously supported by institutions. Research on innovation, technology and creativity has indicated the value of the social environment that supports experimentation and innovation (Pratt and Jeffcutt 2009a). In the past, 'institutional support structures' were provided by large corporations in the cultural sector (such as the BBC in broadcasting). This organisational form enabled a cross-subsidisation, and long lead time of product development to be buffered. After outsourcing and contracting out (a cost-saving initiative that many public sector organisations have had to submit to, e.g., 'producer choice' at the BBC), a plethora of small micro-sized organisations were produced but with little to 'connect' them aside from market contracts. Such organisations could seldom afford research and development, let alone training; many chose to concentrate on the risky strategy of getting their 'one big idea' to market or an audience: a high-risk strategy. It is not by chance that networks, clusters and hubs found favour in the period of economic organisation changes where many large companies were replaced (what has been referred to as being 'hollowed out') by a host of small and project enterprises (Pratt and Gornostaeva 2009). Effectively, the cost saving in large organisations such as the BBC had been at the expense of smaller companies who have had to shoulder significant risks. The everyday realities for cultural labour involve maintaining access to a large number of contacts and being within ideas networks: all 'non-'productive time which is a cost to their businesses.

The 'soft-skills' of management and governance that such a balancing act requires have been under-reported. The social and organisational setting of the creative economy has evolved in order to cope with ongoing risk and uncertainty, along with the rapid 'fashion'/'taste' cycle. However, such changes have seldom been recognised by researchers who have tended to focus on innovative outcomes rather than mundane process. The implicit assumption that co-location magically generates interaction and learning is a weak one; just as the existence of an innovation 'pipeline' is unhelpful (Simmie 1997). However, alternative views have pointed to more common 'cultural practices': based upon an understanding of 'flow' and 'interaction', and 'learning and reflection'. This has been the focus of recent work on learning and innovation, in particular the focus on (cultural) intermediaries to curate, facilitate and articulate knowledge (O'Connor 1998; Nixon and Gay 2002; Virani and Pratt 2016). The importance of intermediaries has been long recognised in the creative economy, just as the notion of a community of practice has been recognised as important in innovative situations. There is the potential that a creative hub can internalise these important social relations of work. However, for this to happen the processes of creative work in hubs need to be made visible.

For the creative economy, communication with other producers is important, as it is also with audiences and consumers. In this sense, we can see the value of a two-way flow across the boundaries of hubs where audiences' knowledge and understanding can be brought to bear on the understandings of producers. Contributors to this collection explore how those in creative hubs struggle to organise themselves so that creative hubs to provide such support, something that can buttress the inherent structural weakness of the creative economy (such as the lack of mediation and high-risk projects).

Introducing the Collection

The chapters within this collection cover a wide range of issues in the previously neglected 'social discourse': they tell us about the experience of working in a hub, and the dimensions of the identities of creative workers; they tell us about the histories and struggles for particular hubs; they highlight some of the significant differences between hubs and, conversely, some of the similarities with other modes of organising, e.g. workers cooperatives. This is a clear response to the body of work that is only concerned with physical arrangements of space; our contributors show how place (that is how social relations help to make up the particularity of a space and its social relations) and the desires and aspirations of creative workers are critical to understanding the operation of creative hubs. The mobilisation of these issues has a significant bearing on how successful (and on whose terms) a creative hub is and whom it benefits.

Our contributors start from the position that a focus on the experience of cultural labour matters; obviously, as it is constitutive of cultural and creative practices. We have already noted that the individual and collective identity of creative workers is forged in their creative practices, and the constitution of a cultural community of practice in and across spaces is significant in understanding their diverse experiences. It is the particularity of cultural work, and identity, and its distinctive moral economies, and cultural values that create a multifaceted value and decision system, one that cannot be represented by singular economic values.

The collection is divided into two major parts, and these should not be considered as a dualistic either/or, but rather as a way of looking: flowing inward or outward from the creative hub. The particular balance is unique to communities in specific places and times. Our contributors report on communities in one phase or another: bringing the two together offers a more holistic perspective. The first section highlights the internal constitution of communities of practice; the notion of internal is stretched by some from micro to macro; it is not limited to a building, but to a network, or commonly overlapping networks that are relevant to a particular cultural practice. Three strands amongst many can be highlighted: immaterial labour, knowledge exchange and affective relations.

Whilst art and cultural practice may be solitary activities in one moment of their production, they are social at others. One of the legacies of the Bauhaus movement was the 'foundation art course' which sought to break with the simple repetition and learning of skills, but rather to remake and reconceive artistic practice: as a social activity. Debates about immaterial labour have pointed to the interweaving of manual and mental labour; in this case, we see a parallel of artistic or creative values. The chapter by Vasilis Avdikos and Eirini Illiopolu articulates participants' desire for sociality, and how the 'economic' hub is individualistic in its operation, compared to the social 'creative hub'. In practice, the boundaries between individuals, projects and firms are a temporary outcome, not a starting point: organisation is strategic. Hence, the research evidence of the varieties of organisational form that people are prepared to assume; as well as the permeability and value of a commons, a shared space.

We can also see these concerns threaded through both George Morgan and James Woodruff's and David Lee's contributions in different ways; they view the creative hub itself as another 'temporary fix' for precarious conditions produced under contemporary neoliberal capitalism: likewise, the turn to collective working, or specifically the constitution of working relations along cooperative lines (Marisol Sandoval and Jo Littler). However, despite these notable attempts to challenge the position of precarious labour in hubs, as Rosalind Gill and Tarek Virani's chapter shows, inequalities mark the condition of labour in creative hubs.

A close partner of these diverse organisational strategies as a 'temporary fix' for capitalism is the investment in affective relations of work. Although not extensively discussed in the communities of practice literature, the affective dimension is clearly an integral component. Both George Morgan and James Woodruff, and David Lee, highlight the particular challenge of the vulnerability of youths working in the cultural economy at this time.

The contributions by Carolina Brandinelli and Alessandro Gandini, and Vasilis Avdikos and Eirini Illiopolou focus on a discussion of hubs and networks which might be seen as effectively two sides of the same coin. In this way, they share another common theme which is the resistance to a simple dualism of description or practice of: individual/collective, network/hub, inside/outside and youth/experience. The strategic responses that emerge in the case studies show them as a situated and strategic move, one that explores a potential 'third space' of pre-figurative practice and social relations (see the chapter by Ceren Mert). The challenge for those managing a creative hub is to acknowledge these desires, and to channel them. This is why the job is so difficult, and the reason is that normative management techniques, let alone reducing the job to building caretaker, do not work.

All of these contributions tell us about the (often hidden and silent) social life and aspirations that are not naïve, but are actually seeking to create and sustain alternative platforms that will be a stage for their creative practices. Janet Merkel's discussion of the varieties of models of workspaces identifies both social and affective dimensions, but also a strange (temporary and situated) alliance between the 'work space' providers, who purposefully use collective practices (albeit temporarily) to incubate small business. This explains the confusion that the casual observer may come across in the similarity of physical forms and arrangements and the constitutive organisation and affective roles played out.

The second part of the book concerns the perspective of the hubs where their users are seeking to look 'outside'. As with the 'internal' focus, this is also cut across with conflicting situations and practices. Oyvid Okland's discussion of the iHub in Nairobi highlights the tensions and challenges of resolving tensions between imposed top-down initiatives, and those which build from an indigenous foundation and the instabilities that are commonly experienced. By contrast, Paul Long and Annette Naudin explore what is possible where a strong alliance and shared vision can be formed, in this case to be part of, and to benefit, the hub's local community and to articulate this to practice, and vice versa.

Most studies of creative hubs are urban. The superficial assumption is that agglomeration economies, and co-location, must 'explain' them. However, our contributors roundly challenge such a notion; some proximity (real or virtual), and interaction, is necessary, but critically it is not sufficient. As noted in the previous section, the community building is where the real work is. So, it should come as no surprise that 'rural' hubs exist and that the 'rurality' (if that is assumed to mean dispersal, not concentration) has to be counterbalanced by community. Nicola Thomas's chapter shows how a community vision (and echo of Paul Long and Annette Naudin's chapter here) and an engagement outside of the 'hub' may not be simply desirable, but necessary as a resource.

Boukje Cnossen's contribution about the Volkskrant in Amsterdam examines its evolution from a publicly funded cultural space to a 'creative hotel'. Here, we learn of an internal consequence of gentrification, as rents rise, producers are priced out, and the 'superficial' hipster/consumerist simulacra of 'networking' and community remain. Again, echoing Janet Merkel's insights into how the 'form' of the hub and its practice can be quite different. Terek Virani's chapter on Hackney Wick, London casts another beam of light on how creative hubs can be eroded from the outside, where the community breaks its links with the hub, leaving it relatively isolated. This disconnect and cleaving of trajectories is illustrated clearly in Andy Pratt and Tom Gill's work on London's

Soho, where the divisions cut the same place, but at different times of the day. The tensions between the cultural economies of day and night time London and between production and consumption underlines that hubs are vulnerable.

Marianna D'Ovidio and Valentina Pacetti's chapter addresses the issue of scale, whilst implicitly addressed in the other chapters, here it becomes a challenge of harnessing a network that has resources and different scales, and how we might conceive of local communities of practice as well as those that may stretch to a regional, national or conceivably international scale; this chapter raises the question of the potential for networking hubs to one another. An old spatial division and organisational division are represented by the phrase 'town and gown': the division of university and city (or creative practices). Daniel Ashton and Roberta Comunian's paper shows what a struggle such linkages are to manage (see also both Tarek Virani's and Boukje Cnossen's chapters); despite the potential and the possibility of universities acting as a commons, the organisational isomorphism and corporate management styles adopted by universities used to dealing with 'Big Science' end up defeating, or threatening to bankrupt the cultural economy. Remaining at the lower end of the age spectrum, and this time, with no (formal) skills, Michael Seaman's chapter brings us full circle to youth. This is a salient example, of how much art and cultural practice is ignored by policy and other support; instead, it is: 'Do It Yourself'. This reminds us that a lively history and experience exists for those with enthusiasm and affective desire.

The overall aim of this collection is to concentrate on what goes on inside hubs; moreover, not simply at an organisational level (although that is important), but also in an affective register. We need to learn to take fuller account of the moral economies, desires and affective relations of hub users, and what they want to use the hub for, and where they want their art and cultural practice to go. This collection underlines that creative hubs are not some sterile 'warehouse' of creative activity but that they are living organisms that need respecting for what they are, and dealing with in their own terms. The economic and political dimensions will always be important; but, we should not use that as an excuse to say that the social dimension is unimportant, especially where the source of the creativity and the practice is social: affective, material and immaterial. We hope that this collection will provide a springboard for a more nuanced investigation of creative hubs, and one that is concerned with processes and meaning rather than only buildings and hyperbole about the creative economy.

Bibliography

Bagwell, S. (2008). Creative clusters and city growth. *Creative Industries Journal, 1*, 31–46.

Banks, M. (2007). *The politics of cultural work*. London: Palgrave Macmillan.

Banks, M. (2017). *Creative justice: Cultural industries, work and inequality.* Pickering & Chatto Publishers.

Banks, M., Gill, R., & Taylor, S. (2013). *Theorizing cultural work: Labour, continuity and change in the cultural and creative industries.* London: Routledge.

Baumol, W. J., & Bowen, W. G. (1966). *Performing arts—The economic dilemma: A study of problems common to theater, opera, music and dance.* New York: Twentieth Century Fund.

Becattini, G. (2004). *Industrial districts: A new approach to industrial change.* Cheltenham and Northampton, MA: Edward Elgar.

Bell, D., & Jayne, M. (2004). *City of quarters: Urban villages in the contemporary city.* Aldershot: Ashgate.

Cairncross, F. (1998). *The death of distance: How the communications revolution will change our lives.* Boston: Harvard Business School Press.

Caves, R. E. (2000). *Creative industries: Contracts between art and commerce.* Harvard: Harvard University Press.

Chapain, C., Cooke, P., De Propris, L., MacNeill, S., & Mateos-Garcia, J. (2010). *Creative clusters and innovation: Putting creativity on the map.* London: NESTA.

DTI. (2001). *Business clusters in the U.K.: A first assessment.* Report by Trends Business Research. London: Department of Trade and Industry.

Evans, G. (2001). *Cultural planning: An urban renaissance?* London: Routledge.

Evans, G. (2009). Creative cities, creative spaces and urban policy. *Urban Studies, 46*, 1003–1040.

Florida, R. L. (2004). *Cities and the creative class.* London: Routledge.

Florida, R. L. (2008). *Who's your city?: How the creative economy is making where to live the most important decision of your life.* New York: Basic Books.

Garnham, N. (2005). From cultural to creative industries: An analysis of the implications of the 'creative industries' approach to arts and media policy making in the United Kingdom. *International Journal of Cultural Policy, 11*, 15–30.

Gill, R. C., & Pratt, A. C. (2008). In the social factory? Immaterial labour, precariousness and cultural work. *Theory, Culture & Society, 25*, 1–30.

Gregg, M. (2011). *Work's intimacy.* Cambridge: Polity Press.

Harding, A. (Ed.). (2018). *Artists in the city: SPACE in '68 and beyond.* London: SPACE.

Hesmondhalgh, D., & Baker, S. (2010). 'A very complicated version of freedom': Conditions and experiences of creative labour in three cultural industries. *Poetics, 38*, 4–20.

Hesmondhalgh, D., & Baker, S. (2011a). *Creative labour: Media work in three cultural industries.* London: Routledge.

Hesmondhalgh, D., & Baker, S. (2011b). Toward a political economy of labor in the media industries. In *The handbook of political economy of communications* (pp. 381–400). Chichester: Wiley.

Hesmondhalgh, D., & Pratt, A. C. (2005). Cultural industries and cultural policy. *International Journal of Cultural Policy, 11*, 1–14.

Horkheimer, M., & Adorno, T. W. (2002 [1947]). The culture industry: Enlightenment as mass deception. In *Dialectic of enlightenment: Philosophical fragments.* Stanford, CA: Stanford University Press.

Kuehn, K., & Corrigan, T. F. (2013). Hope labor: The role of employment prospects in online social production. *The Political Economy of Communication, 1*(1). Retrieved from http://polecom.org/index.php/polecom/article/view/9.

Luckman, S. (2012). Introduction: Space for creativity. In *Locating cultural work* (pp. 1–13). London: Palgrave Macmillan.

Marshall, A. (1920). *Principles of economics: An introductory volume.* Macmillan: London.

McRobbie, A. (2016). *Be creative: Making a living in the new culture industries.* Cambridge: Polity Press.

Mould, O. (2018). *Against creativity.* London: Verso.

Myerscough, J. (1988). *The economic importance of the arts in Britain.* London: Policy Studies Institute.

Neilson, B., & Rossiter, N. (2008). Precarity as a political concept, or, fordism as exception. *Theory Culture Society, 25*, 51–72.

Nixon, S., & Gay, P. D. (2002). Who needs cultural intermediaries? *Cultural Studies, 16*, 495–500.

O'Connor, J. (1998). New cultural intermediaries and the entrepreneurial city. In T. Hall & P. Hubbard (Eds.), *The entrepreneurial city: Geographies of politics, regime and representation*. Chichester: Wiley.

Pope, R. (2005). *Creativity: Theory, history, practice*. London and New York: Psychology Press.

Porter, M. (1996). Competitive advantage, agglomeration economies and regional policy. *International Regional Science Review, 19*, 85–94.

Porter, M. E. (1998). *The competitive advantage of nations*. London: Collier Macmillan.

Pratt, A. C. (2000). New media, the new economy and new spaces. *Geoforum, 31*(4), 425–436.

Pratt, A. C. (2004a). The cultural economy: A call for spatialized 'production of culture' perspectives. *International Journal of Cultural Studies, 7*, 117–128.

Pratt, A. C. (2004b). Creative clusters: Towards the governance of the creative industries production system? *Media International Australia, 112*(1), 50–66.

Pratt, A. C., & Gornostaeva, G. (2009). The governance of innovation in the film and television industry: A case study of London, UK. In A. C. Pratt & P. Jeffcutt (Eds.), *Creativity, innovation and the cultural economy*. London: Routledge.

Pratt, A. C., & Jeffcutt, P. (Eds.). (2009a). *Creativity and innovation in the cultural economy*. London: Routledge.

Pratt, A. C., & Jeffcutt, P. (2009b). Creativity, innovation and the cultural economy: Snake oil for the 21st century? In A. C. Pratt and P. Jeffcutt (Eds.), *Creativity, innovation in the cultural economy*. London: Routledge.

Prenger, M., & Deuze, M. (2017). 12 A history of innovation and entrepreneurialism in journalism. *Remaking the news: Essays on the future of journalism scholarship in the digital age*, 235.

Ross, A. (2008). The new geography of work: Power to the precarious? *Theory, Culture & Society, 25*(7–8), 31–49.

Ross, A. (2009). *Nice work if you can get it: Life and labor in precarious times*. New York and London: New York University Press.

Santagata, W. (2010). *The culture factory: Creativity and the production of culture*. Heidelberg: Springer.

Simmie, J. M. (1997). *Innovation, networks and learning regions?* London: Jessica Kingsley Publishers and the Regional Studies Association.

Taylor, S., & Luckman, S. (2018). *New normal of working lives*. Cham, Switzerland: Springer.

Throsby, D. (2001). *Economics and culture.* Cambridge: Cambridge University Press.

UNCTAD. (2008). *The creative economy report. The challenge of assessing the creative economy: Towards informed policy-making.* Geneva and New York: UNCTAD/UNDP.

Virani, T., & Pratt, A. C. (2016). Intermediaries and the knowledge exchange process: The case of the creative industries and higher education. In R. Comunian & A. Gilmore (Eds.), *Beyond the campus: Higher education & the creative economy.* London: Routledge.

Wilson, A. (2018). May '68 in London and the emergence of AIR and SPACE. In A. Harding (Ed.), *Artists in the city: SPACE in '68 and beyond.* SPACE: London.

Part I
Looking Inside the Cluster

2

Herding Cats: Co-work, Creativity and Precarity in Inner Sydney

George Morgan and James Woodriff

The World Economic Forum's *Future of Jobs Report* (2016) observed that '[t]elecommuting, co-working spaces, virtual teams, freelancing and online talent platforms are all on the rise, transcending the physical boundaries of the office or factory floor and redefining the boundary between one's job and private life in the process' and that these developments are being accompanied by new forms of workers' representation and new industrial regulatory regimes. The principal challenge for governments, workers and employers is to ensure that the changing nature of work benefits everyone'. Economic restructuring in the West has led to the decline of the conventional employment relationship, as new capitalism seeks to outsource parts of the long production-chains that run from the boardrooms of global cities to the sweatshops of the

G. Morgan (✉)
Institute for Culture and Society and School of Humanities and Communication Arts, Western Sydney University, Penrith, NSW, Australia
e-mail: george.morgan@westernsydney.edu.au

J. Woodriff
Western Sydney University, Penrith, NSW, Australia

© The Author(s) 2019
R. Gill et al. (eds.), *Creative Hubs in Question*, Dynamics of Virtual Work,
https://doi.org/10.1007/978-3-030-10653-9_2

developing world (Tsing 2009; Pang 2009; Hardt and Negri 2001). The erosion of Fordist wage labour and the rise of unorthodox forms of employment—ranging from casual employment, often with no guaranteed minimum hours, to various forms of outsourcing—is functional to capitalism's quest for greater workforce flexibility. The role of digital platforms—e.g. Uber, Deliveroo—in facilitating these arrangements has been well documented. There is some ambiguity about what forms of work should be included in what has become known as the gig economy (McGuire 2018), and about the levels of satisfaction with such arrangements (Morgan et al. 2013), but there is evidence that the rise of micro-enterprises correlates with a decline in incomes. Recent data from the UK (Bounds 2015) suggest that while there was a spectacular growth in the number of small businesses established after the 2008 global financial crisis, and the average income across all such enterprises dropped quite sharply.

Many of the subcontracting arrangements amount simply to 'arms-length' exploitation of people who are de facto employees, in that they obtain most of their work from a single corporate or institutional source. In some cases, those who work exclusively for one company, Uber drivers in the UK, for example, have (successfully) argued for legal recognition as employees but such recognition has not been extended elsewhere. With the dwindling of job security in the West, the rate of unemployment has become less reliable as a marker of a society's economic health and inequality. Many of those who work as casual employees or freelancers are officially deemed employed, but are unable to procure sufficient work/income to keep poverty at bay. The Australian Bureau of Statistics (2018) has classified more than a million workers as underemployed, representing around 8.4% of the workforce. However, it is not just in low-paid fields that the freelancing ('permalancing') life is becoming increasingly common. Such arrangements are part of working life in established professions (Chan and Tweedie 2015) as employers seek to reduce fixed costs and minimise the risk associated with, and entitlements enjoyed by, full-time employees. This is particularly true in creative industries where workers are funnelled towards setting up as sole traders and often struggle to make a living. While such working arrangements have long been characteristic of performance fields (musicians moving from gig to gig), those engaged in different kinds of immaterial labour—the production of ideas, knowledge, symbols: design, architecture, media and public relations, film and video production etc.—are increasingly subject to gig economy arrangements. The proliferation of this arrangement is reflected in the growth in the number of businesses operating in creative fields that are 'sole traders' without employees (Arts Council of England 2015). New capitalism has sought to inculcate the idea that stable wage labour is a thing of the past and that the natural arrangement for working lives is that they should be episodic and project-based (Boltanski and Chiapello 2005; Lazzarato et al. 2017). This disposition towards work is better accommodated in freelancing rather than conventional employment.

As a consequence of the growth in subcontracting/freelancing, the traditional workplace—set up and maintained by employers—is on the decline. In outsourcing aspects of production to freelancers, employers effectively relinquish the responsibility and cost of running workplaces, along with the cost of equipment and training. The rise of co-work spaces in metropolitan areas in the Western world has been spectacular in recent years. An annual survey reveals that in 2018, there are 18,900 such spaces globally and that they accommodate 1.7 million workers (Foertsch 2018). This has risen from 8900 to 545,000 in 2015. Such places are increasingly important for those who perform immaterial labour as freelancers. In places of high residential rents, such freelancers can usually only afford only small living spaces, often in shared dwellings, and working at home is impractical.

This chapter will consider independent co-work spaces, in Sydney, Australia, a city where land values have increased spectacularly over the last twenty years. It draws on data from a small pilot study and argues that while such places emerge most commonly in gentrifying metropolitan districts, usually around, and as part of, larger clusters of creative economic activity, they can be vulnerable to rising rents and rapid urban renewal. This precarity afflicts both the spaces themselves, the tenants of those spaces and the networks that potentially form between them. Despite being guided by cooperative and idealistic philosophies—particularly around sustained collaboration—such co-working is inherently precarious, particularly for those early career freelancers whose labour is artistic and experimental and therefore unlikely to guarantee short-run commercial returns. We briefly brief observations of three Sydney co-work spaces—Kommonz, The Sandpit, and The Pyrmont premises of WeWork a transnational co-work company—and compare and contrast them: their differential location within the symbolic spectrum of co-work. We will also present data from a single interview with JoJo,[1] who works as the 'host' at Kommonz and is also the editor of an online magazine, *Obscura*, that is not yet commercially viable and she calls her 'passion project'. Her testimony demonstrates that the 'communities' that form in such independent spaces, far from being determined by the random processes of market demand, are consciously 'curated', thus mirroring the informal social processes that shape network relations in more widely in the new economy. We also draw on JoJo's biographical narrative testimony to demonstrate the appeal of co-work, as an ethics of working life for creative freelancers, but also to show that such arrangements can be as fragile as the creative incomes and careers of those who rent co-work spaces. New forms of public investment are required to sustain the spaces that accommodate much creative labour.

Although there is a much longer history of cooperative workspaces in the form of artists' studios, craft/makerspaces and, more recently, digital 'hackerspaces', commentators generally accept that the co-work movement began in 2005 with the opening of the first co-work space at Spiral Muse in San Francisco (Foertsch and Cagnol 2013; Moriset 2013). The centre aimed to provide freelancers with an alternative to the soulless and atomised work environments available at the time in business centres. While, as Brown (2017) has observed, it is doubtful whether co-working is a completely novel social arrangement, what distinguishes it from similar forms of shared workspaces are the guiding ethical tenets of 'collaboration, openness, community, accessibility and sustainability' (http://coworking.com/). Merkel (2015) advocates the view of co-working as part of the sharing economy, pointing to antecedent improvised social arrangements—gatherings of freelancers in

---

[1]Kommonz, The Sandpit, JoJo and Obscura are pseudonyms.

cafes, libraries and other public places, known as jellies. There has been an enthusiastic take-up of the idea of co-working in the management/ business studies literature (Bouncken and Reuschl 2016; Spinuzzi 2012; Schürmann 2013) and by those writing from a human resource management perspective (Sunsted et al. 2009). They see co-work spaces as filling the need to house an ever-present precarious workforce, the frontline troops of the post-Fordist economy. In the twenty-teens terms like collaborative, co-work and collective have become part of everyday corporate language. Co-work spaces have challenged the very foundation of what a workplace looks like and can provide freelancers— including craftspeople—with access to equipment that is particularly important for those with specialised skills: allowing architects to use prohibitively expensive drafting tables, 'culinary incubators' with gadgets usually only found in commercial kitchens.

The Co-work Spectrum

Co-work emerged through the establishment of small independent operations in a number of global cities, some run on a not-for-profit basis. However, the evident popularity of this new way of organising working life soon attracted large-scale commercial investment. Some companies (like WeWork, discussed below) were founded as providers of co-work spaces, while others, like Regus, diversified into co-work rentals from their established business of providing standard corporate office space. Additionally, a number of transnational companies now cater for 'global nomads': those whose work and communication with clients and colleagues are almost exclusively digitally mediated allowing them to travel and live in different places in the world. Such companies offer membership arrangements allowing access to workspaces in a number of global cities and in some cases providing residential accommodation alongside the co-work centres in 'live-work' arrangement. The itinerant creative freelancers who can enjoy this lifestyle, however, remain a small and privileged cohort, usually established in their professional fields and with a strong work/client base or with inherited resources to support their lifestyle. The great majority of aspirants in various fields of immaterial work/enterprise rely on emplaced networks in order to build their careers. For these people, face-to-face contacts that extend beyond the co-work space and into local creative hubs remain centrally important. We will explore three co-work spaces (1) Kommonz, a small independent operation where tenants are freelancers working on screens (2) The Sandpit, another independent space but one that houses a range of independent creative workers: craft-workers, artists and those performing digital immaterial labour or more conventional business operations (3) The Pyrmont premises of WeWork, a global co-work space provider, that charges high-rents to more prosperous clientele.

Kommonz is a small co-work space of around twenty-five tenants, a mixture of shorter and longer term, in Sydney's Inner West. In the early part of the 2010s, the local neighbourhood housed many students, recent graduates and young independent freelancers, but a rapid rise in rents has made the area much less affordable to those on low incomes. A digitally oriented, 'boutique' co-working space, Kommonz is located in a small exposed brick and steel-beamed warehouse. Several rows of desks, a kitchen area and a small meeting room instantly register the space as functional and chic but also homey. This space exemplifies the middle ground between the serviced office/business centre and more eclectic, multidisciplinary spaces like The Sandpit (discussed below). Like many such independent spaces, Kommonz offers a high level of collaboration, where the sharing of skills, services and monthly meals are a priority. It exemplifies what various commentators (Oldenburg 1989; Brown 2017) call a third place: the space that does not fit into the home and work/public and private binaries so central to modern societies. Importantly, a heightened level of community and professional collaboration still exists. This is consistent with that of the more actively communitarian co-working environments globally.

Co-work spaces grounded in this idealism—particularly independent operations—generally try to encourage tenants to network and share skills and information. JoJo saw the role of Kommonz host as partly to curate or 'build' the right form of community. It has a range of tenants from those who are casual hot-deskers, who rent by the week, or even by the day, to those who have committed to longer contracts and pay lower rents as a result. While there is no compulsion to become involved in communal activities (*There's a few people who have their headphones on all day... and heads down*), there is a general sense of encouraging tenants to recognise the benefits of social interactions and the serendipitous collaborations they may produce. JoJo says that *When you collaborate...that's when stuff happens ... And so many of the things that I have worked on since then have come out of connections I've made purely by working out of this space.*

JoJo feels the co-work space should not just be composed of a random assortment of tenants, but that it has the potential to provide a source of encouragement, mentorship, skill-sharing and even the formation of networks on which work opportunities are based and workgroups built. Therefore, she seeks to build the Kommonz profile so as to encourage, at the very least, harmonious relations between members:

> ... picking people and personalities that are good for this kind of co-working environment. Now if we have full time spaces, people can't just apply and get a space. They can apply for it and have a chat. We can suss out them as much as they can suss out the space. It's really important to have people who kind of gel well... it's quite an intimate space and you do have to see everyone who works here every day. We don't have these separate floors of separate or really private areas. It is more relaxed and intimate than a lot of co-work spaces so having the right mix of people is really important. There have been ... people who've come in and it is a shift in how things work. It hasn't quite worked.

In the dispersed networked environments of the new economy, the ability of aspirant workers/freelancers to access the networks and work groups that perform much of the project-based labour in the new economy—especially in fields like film and television—is often based on informal judgements (Morgan and Nelligan 2018). Are you the right fit for the work group? Will you work well together with others in the hothouse, deadline-driven and project based working lives? In this sense, we can see a co-work centre such as Kommonz as a constituting a surrogate (or perhaps proto-) work groups, where potential tenants are judged on their ability to 'gel' with existing tenants, whether or not they end up working with them. Co-work centres can operate in some senses as clearing houses or nodes where information is exchanged about projects and possible contracts. Kommonz has the feel of the third space, ambiguously located between public and private, by contrast with the impersonal feel of many commercial spaces. JoJo contrasts the clean, vapid interiors of commercial co-work centres, with their clean lines and minimalist 'Scandi' design and the improvised, cosier and hipster feel of Kommonz. This marks the divide between the arty and commercial ends of the co-work spectrum.

The Sandpit has a similar bohemian vibe but is a more broad-based co-working space than Kommonz, housing both craftwork and those engaged in various forms of immaterial labour. Located in semi-industrial suburb of Sydney's south that is undergoing rapid urban renewal and spectacular urban consolidation, this once unfashionable area has become trendy. The Sandpit hosts a variety of different sole traders, entrepreneurs and small businesses that are categorised under the umbrella 'creative'. Situated in an 850-sqm open-plan warehouse, the space offers hot-desks, and 3 × 5 m spaces that are rented on an hourly, daily, weekly or monthly basis. The Sandpit's large post-war, iron roofed, industrial structure has two floors and a small leafy atrium. On entry, the view of the expansive ground floor is interrupted by hanging decorations, plants, a plywood grand piano replica and the resident cat. The rented allotments of floor space are divided by makeshift walls made from old shipping pallets and timber boards. The individual stylings and furnishing of each 3 × 5 m space offer quick reference to the nature of the businesses they house. Some spaces simply have desks and shelving holding laptops, mandatory reusable coffee cups and various kitsch items of decoration. Other more production-oriented spaces are shrouded in paint-splattered drop sheets, stacked canvases-in-progress, finished ceramics and kilns.

As in Kommonz, The Sandpit's managers are curators and community leaders. They are balancing their desire to provide an accessible, supportive and sustainable co-working community with commercial success. They have sought to accommodate a diverse group with a variety of skill sets and to enhance the collaborative culture and the sharing of skills. The assistance-based forms of support—ranging from professional to emotional—exemplify the 'third place' in which tenants and their friends/associates from outside can 'convene and socialise in a free, informal manner' (Oldenburg 1989). The design of The Sandpit encourages these social exchanges. It has a communal dining and kitchen area decorated with chic bohemian additions including a large glass vessel, which houses the communal Kombucha supply. On the second 'mezzanine' level of the warehouse, a large polished wood floor room caters to yoga classes and band rehearsal and the other similarly sized space across the stairs is divided into wood and glass panelled cubicles for more office-bound activities such as film editing, graphic design and travel consultancy. Socialising events range from coffee breaks, meals and casual evenings to larger promoted events, including experiential dinner evenings with new music launches and molecular gastronomy offerings. Co-workers and their associates seek support, culture and social capital during and long after the conclusion of their tenures. The Sandpit also provides a hub for a wider network of associates both local and members of visiting international community. For the latter group, it is often a first stop after arriving in Sydney and a gathering place prior to local creative or arts events. There are examples of 'Sandpitters' continuing their collaboration elsewhere after ending their tenancy—two former members now work together in Berlin—and Sandpit now has a number of sister spaces worldwide.

WeWork is a transnational company with premises in twenty-one countries that has hitched the co-work ethic to its corporate image: *more than just the best place to work, though, this is a movement towards humanizing work.* It has five premises in Sydney including Pyrmont, a comprehensively gentrified area on Darling Harbour on the Western edge of the CBD. Local residential rents are well beyond most young freelancers who are starting out in fields like media, PR and design. WeWork is the largest of several organisations housed in a renovated nineteenth-century heritage-listed wool store warehouse, reflecting a pattern, observed globally (Foertsch and Cagnol 2013) for co-work spaces are housed in converted industrial buildings—new work in place of old. The organisation occupies more than two floors. The interior

aesthetics are familiar post-industrial chic—all exposed brick and timber beams, with designer furniture. In contrast with more conventional
office buildings, which have minimal foyers alongside security desks,
WeWork has designed its premises to blur public and private spaces giving with attractive common areas that form something of a buffer zone
before the swipe card access spaces with banks of desks: *[t]he heart-and-
soul of our locations, these lounges are living-room-style spaces designed for
creativity, comfort, and productivity.* The building makes claims for sustainability: there are bike lockers, access to car-sharing scheme vehicles
and environmentally friendly design features. The reception staff are
young, smiling, good-looking and groovy, and there are flyers advertising WeWork events and services. A hipster barber visits the building weekly, as does a massage therapist from 'Zen Now'. There is free
'micro-roasted coffee' and 'refreshing fruit water to keep you and your
guests hydrated throughout the day'. The lunchtime talks seem to
reflect the philosophy of New Age capitalism the organisation is trying
to cultivate (*"Lunch and Learn: Power of Our Minds"*). The tenants at
WeWork Pyrmont are more power-dressed than those at Kommonz and
the commons space buzzes with meetings.

If this buzz is anything to go by, then WeWork appears to accommodate more lively commercial/networking with outsiders than either
Kommonz or The Sandpit. There is much more foot traffic in and out
of the building, which houses the premises of a number of successful
start-ups, and is much closer to the city's commercial heart and reasonably close to the creative industries centre in the Inner South. The freelancers who work here pay for the chance to be located closer to those
with resources, power and connections who might be able to open
doors. Most of those who rent spaces—ranging from single person hot-
desks to private offices—do so on a monthly basis and rents per square
metre of space are more than double those charged by Kommonz and
The Sandpit. The words 'It Must be a Sign' are displayed in pink neon
on an interior wall that carries some of the fatalistic zeitgeist of the 'creative class'. Freelance careers are played out in diffuse and networked
social environments and images of magical happenstance can profoundly shape the way freelancers think about and narrate their careers
(Morgan and Nelligan 2018).

Passion Projects, Precarity and the Promise of Co-work

In this section, we will use a single life history case to examine the appeal of co-work and its communitarian ethical principles and explore the structural conditions that conspire to undermine the communities built on those principles. JoJo grew up on Sydney's peri-urban fringes, the daughter of a horticulturalist father and teacher mother. She describes how she was drawn to the idea of co-work while studying design at university, having become aware of how important collaboration was to creative work. Having taken longer to complete her degree than many of her contemporaries—because she worked while studying—she was able to chart the difficulties they encountered in finding work.[2]

> Seeing what they were doing when they graduated…Not a single one of the people who had graduated and who I was friends with is working in the design industry … And they were like posting about it all the time, looking for opportunities and hardly any of them were progressing into that next stage… So many that were really struggling to find work… ended up in hospitality and retail … The people that were successful were starting self-initiated projects. They were starting their own thing and that was leading to bigger opportunities.

For her final-year undergraduate research project, JoJo decided to focus on collaboration in creative industries, believing that freelancing was increasingly common in design and networking was the key to being successful as a small freelancing entrepreneur. In the mid-semester break, she went to visit her sister, a musician, in Berlin and went in search of co-work spaces in a city that had had for some years developed a reputation as something of a low-budget sanctuary for creative workers.

---

[2]The Design Industry of Australia president Oliver Kratzer stated that: *Everybody loves to study design and all the universities supply a multitude of design degree courses but with little correlation to actual demand* (Lacey 2013).

At this time, there were not many co-work spaces in Sydney. There were collaborative studios but nothing much for non-artists. The co-work space boom has happened since then ... Agora [the co-work space in Berlin] it blew my mind. They had like four levels. At the ground floor, they had this café that was like filled with gorgeous projects the creatives had worked on and implemented in the café. So, one of them had worked on the reusable water plant system and created these beautiful sculptures to recycle all the water. They won a residency to work [in the building]. Then to pay back their residency they implemented it into the café and then volunteered their time working there ... They had one floor of busy, loud group co-working with like big desks, then they had a quiet floor of solo individual works... and then they had a floor with a residency programme and then the top floor was for yoga, cinema nights, dance classes. It was magical. I thought we need this in Sydney. This is the future of creative work, the future of collaboration.

JoJo's epiphany occurred in post-Cold War unified Berlin, a city lacking a substantial industrial base and where the government was by far the largest employer. The abundance of floor space—both commercial and residential—produced a low-rent environment that drew creative workers from across Europe (Colomb 2012). In Berlin, such people were not compelled to produce the sort of commercial returns required to survive in high rent cities like London, San Francisco, New York and Amsterdam. The proliferation of temporary use spaces at this time—particularly in the former East Berlin—generated a sense among young people that Berlin was a creative utopia—a place where art was not completely subservient to commerce. As JoJo said:

Having my sister living there. She was a professional musician living on low money but having low rent and Berlin was basically the only place she could afford, to be creating in that sort of way.

However, as Colomb (2012) has demonstrated in her study of Berlin's transformation, city authorities traded on this creative utopian image to attract investment. The proliferation of creative spaces—galleries, performance spaces, independent bars, cafes and shops—many of which were 'temporary-use', and therefore precarious—helped to renovate the image of neighbourhoods like Kreuzberg and created the conditions for the demise of bohemian creativity. Ironically, as has happened elsewhere (Ihlein 2009), the presence of artists helped prime the pump of gentrification. While Berlin remains relatively low-rent, by comparison with many other global cities, the costs of housing and of the performance, studio and work spaces that might house independent co-work initiatives like Agora, are now much less affordable.

After going home, JoJo was keen to find a similar co-work environment (*I took that back with me to Sydney and thought 'how can we cultivate these kinds of places in Sydney?'*). She was aware that in a city much more subject to property speculation there were financial constraints that did not exist in Berlin (*I knew that you couldn't just pop-up a five-storey building [in Sydney]*). Additionally, the pubic regulations restrict the possibilities for performance spaces, work spaces, studios etc. There was more stringent regulatory oversight of fire and building standards, service of alcohol, for example. Zoning restrictions limit the possibilities, and add to the complications in setting up independent spaces—for performance, entertainment and work. By this time, JoJo had obtained steady work in the university in which she studied, firstly in the call centre but eventually in a web-design position. She completed her final-year research project and wanted to publish her own magazine—*Obscura*. In search of co-work spaces in Sydney, she heard that Kommonz, one of the few independent co-work spaces that operated in city was having an open day and she went along.

After attending the open day at Kommonz, JoJo chanced upon an opportunity to participate in a week-long residency there on crowdfunding, with the idea of raising money for her magazine: *Happenstance, and probably a number of Facebook algorithms popped up an ad*. It was during this week that she first met the people who ran Kommonz and most of those who worked there. The founder of Kommonz was:

a designer and photographer who worked in lots of agencies and worked those crazy hours and went 'I don't want to be in those industries anymore and I want to run my own thing'. He had a couple of other friends and they went … let's just create what we need out of a creative environment that will support us in being able to support our business but then like turning it around and opening it up to other people.

He recognised that JoJo was organised, personable and talented, and asked her to come to work part time in two roles: that of marketing manager and what they called community manager. She accepted and worked three days a week. The latter role involved being the organisation's front-of-house person, involved with organising events and functions, and liaising with tenants, both long-term and casual. She was also responsible for running the nearby Kommonz events space. The managing committee were very keen to support *Obscura* and in 2016, after she graduated, they offered JoJo the chance to work for the organisation full time, taking on the additional responsibility of managing the event space, in separate premises nearby. This would allow her to work on *Obscura*, to this point, in JoJo's words, a 'passion project', during the down times at Kommonz. She was happy to leave the steady-but-creatively inert position at the university for something that was both more precarious and fulfilling.

The communitarian economics that informs co-work holds that freelance workers are more productive and motivated when gathered under one roof, than they are working in isolation. Such settings have more prospect of generating communities of practice (Lave and Wenger 1991), and creative initiatives, than where freelancers work in isolation. JoJo spoke of the days, before she was employed full time, when she was working at Kommonz on her own projects:

> There were days when I thought, 'I just want to stay at home' and I didn't have that pressure of having paid for the space [because Kommonz was sponsoring Obscura] … I would come in and almost immediately go 'I am SO glad I came in because there would be one conversation that happened that inspired another idea; there would be a new hot desker who come in that I struck up a relationship with. There was always at the end of the day 'I am so much more inspired'…

Yet it is difficult to sustain the sorts of improvised arrangements that can spring up in co-work spaces where those spaces are threatened by the juggernaut of property development. This echoes throughout Kommonz's story, where their 'biggest frustration' has been 'never being able to plan more than a few months ahead'. JoJo spoke about this in relation to the launch of *Obscura* at the Kommonz event space.

> I got a call just before … saying 'you're going to have to find a new venue because we're demolishing the space on the weekend. I'm like 'Are you really going to knock it down on Sunday because I've got my launch on Monday'. That's the short version….

Although the event had been planned months earlier, it was clear that the development imperative superseded the claims of a local cultural event. Such experiences are common for early career creative workers for whom working life is configured around low-budget projects, the social and institutional environments in which those projects are conducted can often be inherently fragile. One of the tenants of The Sandpit, told us that the building has been earmarked for redevelopment for some years, that several times they have been told it would be demolished 'within the next six months', but that so far they have received several stays of execution. This uncertainty is particularly difficult for those, including craftspeople, whose creative work involves heavy and expensive equipment, and for whom relocation is costly and difficult. As JoJo observes in situations of insecure tenure, it is not possible to undertake long-term strategic work or creative projects that take a long time to mature. This threatens the enterprise of co-work:

> You can't plan for … anything outside that very small timeframe. That also puts an incredible amount of pressure on these community events and things because you have a very short lead-up time it's very stressful and pressured. Trying to get it done because it has to be done in that window.

It is not only freelancers who experience such pressures. Many of those employed in corporate/institutional settings must also endure intense deadline-driven work cultures. This is particularly true in adrenalin-fuelled work environments characteristic of the media industries, where youthful workforces can be called upon to long-hours to put projects to bed. However, such people are less vulnerable than freelancers. The fact of being employed means their professional status remain intact even if a project they are working on fails. For freelancers, such failure means that they have wasted their own labour and resources, and that their occupational identity claims are undermined.

The Right to the Metropolitan Workplace

Inner-urban gentrification often proceeds in two distinct phases (Zukin 1989). The first see the influx of students, artists, bohemians and members of the creative precariat, to low-rent post-industrial areas. Their presence encourages new commercial activity in the neighbourhood: restaurants, cafes, bars, artists' studios, galleries and performance spaces. These changes are both harbingers and catalysts of larger changes to the local demographic/class profile. An area becomes cool—a desirable place to live and work—both because of the presence of young creatives and of public and commercial activities with which they are associated. The rise of freelancing means that independent co-work spaces should be included among the changes to commercial land-use and the built environment that are symptomatic of proto-gentrification.

Policy-makers now recognise the importance of this creative presence to urban renewal. It is now common for city authorities to seek to persuade local landlords in depressed areas to provide retail/warehouse spaces to creative workers/artists for temporary use on a low-rent or even no-rent basis. Many of those charged with overseeing urban renewal have been influenced by the work of writers like Charles Landry (2012) and Richard Florida (2002), who write of the nexus between cultural and economic changes in cities. In particular, many civic leaders have read Florida's *The Rise of the Creative Class* as providing a 'paint-by-numbers' formula for kick-starting gentrification. In Australia, one of the best known civic experiments is 'Renew Newcastle' under which local authorities and a community groups sought to regenerate the central business district of a post-industrial city, by providing artists and creative workers with shops and other commercial spaces on temporary low-rent or even no-rent basis (Westbury, n.d.). However, such schemes can provide only short-term solutions for marginal freelancers, and fail to address long-term concerns about equity and access to key metropolitan districts. In a study of temporary use space in inner-London, Madanipour (2018), described such spaces as 'a moment in a complex process, offering some opportunities, but also revealing the precariousness and vulnerability of its users' (p. 1105). The artists and creative freelancers inadvertently serve to hasten their own local demise: *One displacement leads to another: while artists displace the image of decline, they are displaced by the image of prosperity, a process in which opportunity and precarity are entwined* (p. 1101, see also Colomb 2012; Peck 2005; Pratt 2011).

The second phase of gentrification sees the arrival of the professional middle class and rapid rises in rents and land values, undermining both the tenure of long-term poor/minority residential tenants, and also of the independent businesses and cooperative ventures that appeared in the first phase of gentrification. Many such endeavours are replaced by generic streetscapes of retail chains and global brands. Without secure tenure, independent co-work spaces like Kommonz and The Sandpit can form part of this transient commercial presence. They are vulnerable to rising commercial rents and development pressures. And spiralling residential rents mean that members of their marginal freelancer clientele are less likely to live nearby. Companies like WeWork move into fill the breach, catering for a more professionally established clientele who are more embedded in the mainstream business networks and who are increasing represented in the local population. Those low-income creative workers—many pursuing passion projects—must move to gentrification's next frontier, sowing the seeds of their own future displacement as they go (Ihlein 2009).

Metropolitan real estate markets have become key exemplars of the growing social and economic cleavages in contemporary society, especially those in global cities where transnational capital flows help to drive property speculation (Lees 2003). Social movements, like Occupy and Los Indignados, are symptomatic of the struggles over urban space, asserting what David Harvey (2003) calls the 'Right to the City'. While the demand for more affordable and secure housing is rightly the primary political priority of urban activists, the dramatic rise in freelancing, and in the demand for co-working space, indicates the need for secure tenure for workplaces as well as for living places.[3] Much of what has been written about creative hubs and innovation in cities, vaunts the importance of the serendipitous encounters that take place in areas of urban density, social complex and diversity (Lloyd 2002). The co-presence of artists, tech geeks, start-up schemers, cultural brokers and entrepreneurs, can promote innovation. Creative enterprises can often emerge at a tangent to original start-up ideas and random local social encounters both within co-work communities and in localities can open up those tangents. Even in the digital age, the 'bridging capital' that helps to generate such enterprise is often built through accidental encounters in lively neighbourhoods. This points to the importance of propinquity and the need to assist creative workers to survive the process of gentrification to allow projects to come to fruition. Every new phase of capital accumulation requires forms of public investment and one key policy strategy to prime the pump of the new/creative economy is to provide such workers with spaces in creative hubs beyond 'temporary-use' arrangements. Having been a key architect of the creative cities, Richard Florida himself has undertaken an auto-critique (2017), indicting the idea of creative cities as fuelling gentrification and exacerbating social cleavages in cities social cleavages in cities.

---

[3]There is, of course, a connection between the two. As dwellings become smaller and more crowded—a process that occurs more quickly in cities where there is little social and affordable housing—so it becomes more difficult to make space for working at home.

Conclusion

JoJo: I'm not one of those people who needs to know what I'll be doing in three-years' time.

The language of fate crops up frequently when young people speak about their working lives, probably as a way of accounting for the circumstances of churn and precarity they face. Some commentators have welcomed new capitalism's vocational adventure, arguing that improvised, project-based careers provide an antidote to Fordism's repetitive work and drab routine (Leadbeater 2000; Lazzarato et al. 2017). In the 'social factory', production has spilled over the factory wall, pervaded the city, blurring the lines between public and private, and work and play (Hardt and Negri 2001). Autonomist theorists see the potential for new cultural politics and solidarities as emerging among members of the multitude, a term recognising the break-up of the traditional working class, and the diverse contractual arrangements through which people make a living under Post-Fordism (Hardt and Negri 2005). Critics see the new economy as hyper-competitive and individualised, a neoliberal social laboratory of small entrepreneurs (Gill and Pratt 2008). Co-work is a collectivist response to the decline of the routines and solidarity old labour. It represents not just the flexible provision of workplaces for freelancers, but also an ethics of collaboration—the idea that art and enterprise flourish when people pool skills and ideas, and form communities of practice. This larger philosophy informs the ways spaces are designed and 'curated' and it shapes the decisions and practical ethics that people like JoJo bring to their careers. However, without significant public investment—such as has preceded every new phase of capital accumulation in modern history—co-work remains essentially utopian. Young freelancers working in precarious fields, oversupplied markets for immaterial labour, many paying debts from post-school education, require public support to become established, especially those without family money to keep them afloat. We have argued in this chapter that one form such support should take is the provision of subsidised co-work spaces to protect precarious creatives from the vicissitudes of property development and spiralling rents. The situation of both Kommonz and The Sandpit is homologous with the situation of their freelancer tenants. The local hubs and networks, where cooperative work practices thrive, are vulnerable to the developers' wrecking balls. Once disbanded, they can be recomposed elsewhere but this is difficult. It relies on tenants being prepared to carry over to new premises, to endure the disruption associated with the relocation usually to places more remote the centres of metropolitan economic life and professional networks.

References

Australian Bureau of Statistics. (2018). 6202.0 Labour Force, February. http://www.abs.gov.au/ausstats/abs@.nsf/mf/6291.0.55.003.

Arts Council of England. (2015). *Contribution of the arts and cultural industry to the UK economy*. https://www.artscouncil.org.uk/economic-contribution.

Boltanski, L., & Chiapello, E. (2005). *The new spirit of capitalism*. London: Verso.

Bouncken, R. B., & Reuschl, A. J. (2016). Coworking-spaces: How a phenomenon of the sharing economy builds a novel trend for the workplace and for entrepreneurship. *Review of Managerial Science, 12*(1), 1–18.

Bounds, A. (2015, June 15). Small business growth returns to pre-recession levels says study. *Financial Times*. Available at https://www.ft.com/content/c0bbf34c-1335-11e5-bd3c-00144feabdc0.

Brown, J. (2017). Curating the "third place"? Coworking and the mediation of creativity. *Geoforum, 82*, 112–126.

Chan, S., & Tweedie, D. (2015). Precarious work and reproductive insecurity. *Social Alternatives, 34*(4), 5–13.

Colomb, C. (2012). Pushing the urban frontier; temporary uses of space, city marketing and the creative city discourse in 2000s Berlin. *Journal of Urban Affairs, 34*(2), 131–152.

Florida, R. (2002). *The rise of the creative class: And how it's transforming work, leisure, community and everyday life*. New York: Basic Books.

Florida, R. (2017). *The new urban crisis: Gentrification, housing bubbles, growing inequality and what we can do about it*. New York: Oneworld.

Foertsch, C. (2018). 1.7 million members will work in cowork spaces by the end of 2018. *Deskmag*. Available at http://www.deskmag.com/en/1-7-million-members-will-work-in-coworking-spaces-by-the-end-of-2018-survey.

Foertsch, C., & Cagnol, R. (2013). *The history of coworking in a timeline.* Available at http://www.deskmag.com/en/the-history-of-coworking-spaces-in-atimeline. Accessed March 20, 2018.

Gill, R., & Pratt, A. (2008). In the social factory? Immaterial labour, precariousness and cultural work. *Theory, culture & society, 25*(7–8), 1–30.

Hardt, M., & Negri, A. (2001). *Empire.* Cambridge: Harvard University Press.

Hardt, M., & Negri, A. (2005). *Multitude: War and democracy in the age of empire.* New York: Penguin.

Harvey, D. (2003). The right to the city. *International Journal of Urban and Regional Research, 27*(4), 939–941.

Ihlein, L. (2009). Complexity, aesthetics and gentrification: Redfern-Waterloo/Waterloo tour of beauty. In K. De Souza & Z. Begg (Eds.), *There goes the neighborhood: Redfern-Waterloo and the politics of urban space* (pp. 45–49). Sydney: Creative Commons.

Lacey, S. (2013, March 23–24). You can go it alone and design yourself a future. *Sydney Morning Herald*, p. 14.

Landry, C. (2012). *The creative city: A toolkit for urban innovators.* London: Earthscan.

Lave, J., & Wenger, E. (1991). *Situated learning: Legitimate peripheral participation.* Cambridge: Cambridge University Press.

Lazzarato, M., Bove, A., Gilbert, J., & Goffey, A. (2017). *Experimental politics: Work, welfare, and creativity in the neoliberal age.* Cambridge, Mass: MIT Press.

Leadbeater, C. (2000). *Living on thin air: The new economy.* Harmondsworth: Penguin.

Lees, L. (2003). Super-gentrification: The case of Brooklyn heights, New York City. *Urban Studies, 40*(12), 2487–2509.

Lloyd, R. (2002). Neo–bohemia: Art and neighborhood redevelopment in Chicago. *Journal of Urban Affairs, 24*(5), 517–532.

Madanipour, A. (2018). Temporary use of space: Urban processes between flexibility, opportunity and precarity. *Urban Studies, 55*(5), 1093–1110.

McGuire, R. (2018). *Ultimate guide to gig economy data: A summary of every freelance survey we can find in Nation 1099.* Available at http://nation1099.com/gig-economy-data-freelancer-study/#history. Accessed 21 March, 2018.

Merkel, J. (2015). Coworking in the city. *Ephemera, 15*(1), 121.

Morgan, G., & Nelligan, P. (2018). *The creativity hoax: Precarious work in the gig economy*. London: Anthem Press.

Morgan, G., Wood, J., & Nelligan, P. (2013). Beyond the vocational fragments: Creative work, precarious labour and the idea of 'flexploitation'. *The Economic and Labour Relations Review, 24*(3), 397–415.

Moriset, B. (2013). *Building new places of the creative economy: The rise of coworking spaces*. Available at https://halshs.archives-ouvertes.fr/halshs-00914075.

Oldenburg, R. (1989). *The great good place*. New York: Paragon House.

Pang, L. (2009). The labor factor in the creative economy: A marxist reading. *Social Text, 27*(2 (99)), 55–76.

Peck, J. (2005). Struggling with the creative class. *International Journal of Urban and Regional Research, 29*(4), 740–770.

Pratt, A. (2011). The cultural contradictions of the creative city. *City, Culture and Society, 2*(1), 123–130.

Schürmann, M. (2013). The business model coworking space. In *Coworking Space*. Wiesbaden: Springer Gabler.

Spinuzzi, C. (2012). Working alone together: Coworking as emergent collaborative activity. *Journal of Business and Technical Communication, 26*(4), 399–441.

Sundsted, T., Jones, D., & Bacigalupo, T. (2009). *I'm outta here: How co-working is making the office obsolete*. Austin, TX: Not an MBA Press.

Tsing, A. (2009). Supply chains and the human condition. *Rethinking Marxism, 21*(2), 148–176.

Westbury, M. (n.d.). *Creating creative enterprise hubs: A guide* (Create New South Wales). Available at https://www.create.nsw.gov.au/wp-content/uploads/2010/11/19.0-Creating-Creative-Enterprise-Hubs-A-Guide.pdf.

World Economic Forum. (2016). *Future of jobs report*. Available at http://reports.weforum.org/future-of-jobs-2016/. Accessed 12 March 2018.

Zukin, S. (1989). *Loft living: Culture and capital in urban change*. New Brunswick, NJ: Rutgers University Press.

3

Curating Strangers

Janet Merkel

Introduction

After the global financial and economic crisis of 2007–2008, new collaboratively oriented shared flexible workspaces have emerged in cities. These co-working spaces and the associated social practice of co-working exemplify a new form of work organisation for mainly independent freelance workers but increasingly small businesses and remote working employees from companies. However, these workspaces are not just flexible shared office spaces for professionals "working alone together" (Spinuzzi 2012). Instead, they promote a community-based approach to the organisation of freelance work and creative sociability in cities (Garrett et al. 2017). One of the big challenges in these spaces is to facilitate interaction and collaboration among the independent freelance workers with quite diverse knowledge sets, work practices and professional experiences. Despite providing spatial proximity and a "plug and

J. Merkel (✉)
Institute of Urban and Regional Planning (ISR),
Technical University of Berlin, Berlin, Germany
e-mail: janet.merkel@tu-berlin.de

© The Author(s) 2019
R. Gill et al. (eds.), *Creative Hubs in Question*, Dynamics of Virtual Work,
https://doi.org/10.1007/978-3-030-10653-9_3

51

play" infrastructure for flexible workers, co-working spaces illustrate that spatial proximity does not necessarily lead to interaction, collaboration and cross-fertilisation (Spinuzzi 2012). The question then becomes: How to create an environment that is conducive to the emergence of new ideas and different forms of working together?

In the context of this volume, the chapter aims to highlight the crucial role of co-working hosts in establishing social relations and in facilitating a collaborative work atmosphere in which individual co-workers might engage in knowledge exchange and collaborative practices. This chapter will look into specific social and material strategies that hosts use to facilitate encounters, interaction, collaboration and mutual trust among co-workers. It draws on a qualitative research project involving desk research, a convenience sample of 25 semi-structured interviews as well as visits to spaces and their events, informal chats with hosts and participant observation through co-working in the past seven years in Berlin, London, New York and Paris. The chapter will first discuss the rise of flexible shared workspaces and critically engage with the notion of a "creative hub" in understanding co-working spaces and then introduce different empirically grounded social and material strategies that co-working hosts use to curate co-working spaces. It will conclude discussing broader implications of this research.

The Rise of Shared Workspaces

The past decades have seen tremendous shifts in the organisation of work and labour because of processes of flexibilisation, casualisation, globalisation and informalisation in employment relationships (Beck 2000; Castells 2009). Moreover, the advancement of communication and information technologies has transformed where people work, when and how. The most visible outcomes of these shifts are the growth of freelance work (see, e.g., Kitching and Smallbone 2008; Mould et al. 2014) and the mobilisation of work. Work is not connected to one specific place (formerly factories and offices) anymore, but stretches across multiple sites and has turned the whole city into an extended workplace (see, e.g., Felstead et al. 2005; Martins 2015). As a response to these changed labour market conditions, that have been aggravated by the financial and economic crisis beginning in 2007–2008, and technological advancements shared flexible workspaces spread throughout cities worldwide and became a critical lens to explore the changing nature of contemporary work and related social practices in cities. While these spaces emerged to challenge the professional isolation of freelance workers in their home offices, these workspaces can offer various social, cultural and economic resources to sustain a freelance or self-employed livelihood in a highly competitive and volatile job market. Research studies have found a variety of reasons why freelancer are motivated to work in a co-working space: from relative cheapness, social isolation, to search for creative sociality towards lowering transaction costs (see, e.g., Garrett et al. 2017; Waters-Lynch and Potts 2016). The practice of co-working is rooted in creating new collaborative and supportive relationships with other freelancers and aspires to cultivate cooperation than competition among them (Coworking Manifesto 2014). Furthermore, co-working takes now place in varied spatial settings that range from co-working in private homes, temporary meetings ("Jellys"), self-organised spaces with less than 20 members to high-end office architectures in prime real estate locations with up to 500 co-workers (e.g. WeWork or The Office Group).

Managed shared workspaces are not a new phenomenon and at least date back to the early 1970s. The first wave of managed workspaces began in 1972 when architects started subdividing older vacant buildings into "working communities" as workshops for artists (e.g. the shared workspaces at David Rock in Covent Garden or Alan Baxter Associates offices in Clerkenwell, London [NLA 2016, p. 41]). Artists' started to develop vacant buildings into managed workspaces too. ACME and Space are two London artist-led studio developers that started out in the 1970s (Moreton 2013). Today, both organisations are the biggest studio space provider in London with more than 500 studios each and supporting more than 1400 artists. The second wave of managed workspaces emerged as a response to the closing of industrial plants and structural changes in the economy in the late 1970s. The British Steel Corporation set up "community workshops" for former workers to help create new businesses and jobs. By 1984, the number of managed workspaces in the UK was estimated between 200 and 500 as more companies, and governmental agencies started to invest in them. From 1980 to 1985 existed the Small Workshop Scheme from the UK government, an industrial building allowance that gave incentives for companies to develop small workshops (Green and Strange 1999). The growth of workspaces for culture and creative industries business under New Labour's Creative Industries Initiatives can be considered a third wave. With public support, many old vacant factory buildings were redeveloped as studio spaces for creative professionals and businesses (Montgomery 2007), often as part of creative cluster or cultural quarter developments (see for London's Creative Hub initiative Evans [2009]). However, in the last ten years, a growing number of managed co-working spaces, industry-led incubators and accelerators, especially for tech businesses in the digital sector, have emerged (Bouncken and Reuschl 2016; Schmidt et al. 2014). This development can be considered a fourth wave. According to the 2017 Global Co-Working Survey, the number of co-working spaces rose worldwide from 600 in October 2010 to 13,800 in 2017 with over one million people working in shared workspaces by the end of 2017 (*Deskmag* 2017, p. 2). What distinguishes these co-working spaces from those older shared workspaces is the short-term rent of desks (per day, week, month), and thus their flexibility and continuously changing social composition, and their emphasis on community orientation.

With the rise of co-working two dominant trends can be observed. On the one side, there is an increased commercialisation of co-working through the mushrooming of commercial office and real estate developers (e.g. Regus, Workspace Group, WeWork, The Office Group). Moreover, public (often facilitated through universities) and private organisations set up incubators and accelerators for young entrepreneurs as part of open innovation strategies (Dovey et al. 2016; Ferm 2014; NLA 2016). On the other side, there is a continuous rise of bottom-up initiatives with mostly smaller co-working spaces for freelance workers. Those are driven by ideas of commoning resources to enable mutual support, encounters and exchange and to create commons-based alternatives, often embedded in notions of a post-growth economy (Avdikos and Kalogeresis 2017; GLA 2015; Schmidt et al. 2014). As the phenomenon of co-working continues to diversify with a variety of collaboratively organised workspaces now claiming to be "creativity and innovation labs" (Schmidt et al. 2014, p. 245), this growing diversity needs a thorough investigation of the differences and similarities between those different types of managed workspaces.

Co-working Spaces as Creative Hubs

With the global proliferation of co-working spaces, a growing body of empirical research interrogates co-working and situates it within different academic debates. For example, from a sociology of work perspective, scholars discuss co-working as a coping strategy with the precariousness of freelance work (Bouncken and Reuschl 2016; Garrett et al. 2017; Merkel 2015; Moriset 2014). In economic geography, co-working spaces are discussed as innovative microclusters or intermediaries (Capdevila 2013, 2015) and as creativity and innovation labs (Schmidt et al. 2014). Also, in economics co-working spaces are studied as a new business model for office provision (Salinger 2013) or their supportive role for entrepreneurship (Bouncken and Reuschl 2016). What has hardly been looked at systematically is how those workspaces get "activated" (Thrift 2006, p. 290) and "enacted" (Dale and Burrell 2008) as co-working spaces? How do they produce the social qualities freelance workers value and how can they become interactional settings in which unaffiliated, independent co-workers engage informally with each other in socially supportive interactions, knowledge exchange or innovative processes?

While Schmidt et al. (2014) propose to use "open creative labs" as an umbrella term for the new variety of shared workspaces, I will use the term creative hub and suggest a sociological understanding of them—see Virani and Malem (2015) for a detailed discussion of the term creative hub. Two theoretical perspectives that both highlight relational approaches in sociology and geography inform the understanding of hubs here. First, and more descriptively, in social network theory a hub is a nod in a network that has a disproportionately high number of links (connections) to other nods (see Barabasi 2002). Subsequently, hubs can be conceptualised as intersections of different social networks and therefore spaces of circulations, flows and movements that enable connectivity. Second, from assemblage theory (Deleuze and Guattari 1987). I take an understanding of hubs as an "ongoing process of forming and sustaining associations between diverse constituents" (Anderson et al. 2012, p. 174) to focus on the performative aspect of networking and how those socio-spatial relations in a co-working space emerge and form. Assemblage thinking "foreground[s] ongoing processes of composition across and through different human and non-human actants; rethink[s] social formations as complex wholes composed through a diversity of parts that do not necessarily cohere into seamless organic wholes; and attend to the expressive powers of entities" (Anderson et al. 2012, p. 172). Analytically, assemblage helps to understand creative hubs as a social formation constituted through dynamic processes of assembling (but also reassembling and dissembling) and as relations among heterogeneous elements (such as co-workers, but also ideas, objects and spaces). It highlights the distributed agency among those elements, the open-endedness of the process and the potentialities of these social formations such as new ideas, collective action or alternative organisational formations (see, e.g., Daskalaki 2017; Jakonen et al. 2017). In the following, I want to point out activities and practices that facilitate the emergence of a "co-working assemblage" and enact the co-working space as a creative hub.

Organising Distributed Creativity or How to Curate a Co-working Space

How to organise creativity, and subsequently innovation has become a crucial question for companies, organisations and even cities (Florida 2004). As Thrift (2006, p. 290) critically suggested, in current globalised capitalism's search for new sources of profit "new time-space arrangements have to be designed that can act as traps for innovation and invention". While the recent growth in co-working spaces can be explained by commercially organised incubators and shared workspaces (see, e.g., for London NLA 2016) to create those "traps", the following discussion derives from smaller, self-organised grassroots co-working spaces for free-lance workers which are the focus of my empirical work. As Liegl (2014) underlines, freelance nomadic creative workers are driven by a "care of place" (p. 168), an affective and aesthetic sensibility to where to work best to be productive and where inspiration might be encountered.

Co-working hosts have received little attention in the research lit-erature, despite several empirical studies pointing to their crucial role in the social formation and organisation of these spaces (Brown 2017; Capdevila 2014; Parrino 2013; Rus and Orel 2015). They are crucial for nurturing community in these spaces, as it is the community and the potential social relationships that make those spaces attractive and not just the available office space (see *Deskmag* 2017). Additionally, many spaces want to enable social interaction and collaborative working—but, how can collaboration be encouraged among different independent freelance workers if collaboration means working together with a shared goal (Spinuzzi 2015)?

Hosts are usually the founders of the space. However, more often they are hired community managers, especially in more commercially oriented co-working spaces. Sometimes, hosts can be actual members of these spaces who volunteer to assist the community building and to host a few hours a week for a reduced membership fee or for free as part of community-building initiatives. What co-working hosts emphasise is that interaction and collaborative activity does not develop between co-workers just from sitting next to each other (see Spinuzzi 2012 on the problem of "good neighbours" vs. "good partners" in co-working spaces). Most hosts claim that physical proximity and co-presence do not lead to interaction, collaboration or innovation. Instead, a form of animation is needed to engage co-workers in the social practice of work-ing together collaboratively. Subsequently, hosts describe their work as "conducting", "mothering", "community-building", and "social gar-dening" (see Merkel 2015, p. 128). For example, Tonya Surman (2013, p. 192) from Toronto's Center for Social Innovation explains:

> What begins as a group of people looking for a place to work becomes a community through conscious and careful animation. To this end, we

employ community animators who hold the shared workspace together and breathe vitality into the lives of all who move through it. The community animator role incorporates elements of operations, relationship-building, hosting, and knowledge/skill sharing. Often described as a cross between a triage nurse, a guidance counsellor, and a potluck organiser, each community animator builds social capital, makes connections, and looks for ways to support our members.

Hosts are skilled social actors (Fligstein 2001) that can provide identities and cultural frames to motivate others and, thus, might help to understand how new ideas or practices emerge or how cooperation is enabled in co-working spaces. The interview analysis pointed to two types of host, differentiated by how they understand and interpret their activity: the "service provider" and the "visionary" (for a similar typology, see Spinuzzi 2012). While the service providers concentrate on facilitating a good work infrastructure and attendant services, the visionary hosts are more interested in enabling communication, community and collaboration among co-workers and aspire to translate the co-working values into their space. Two intertwined strategies can be differentiated based on the recognition of the mutual constitution of the material and social (see Dale and Burrell 2008). While the material strategies focus on the physical and symbolic design of the spaces and how it can facilitate communication and encounters, the social strategies aim at connecting co-workers, creating a sociable atmosphere, a sense of belonging and to enable collective learning (see Merkel 2015).

Practices of Social Curation in Creative Hubs

To conceptualise hosts' practices in facilitating co-working, this chapter suggests understanding them as a form of social curation. Originating in the art world, "curatorship is a distinct practice of mediation" (O'Neill 2012, p. 1), and no longer limited to the person of the curator in a museum (Krzys Acord 2014; O'Neill 2012). As a practice, curation aims at establishing relations by assembling and gathering. For example, the Swedish curator Maria Lind (2010, p. 63) highlights:

Today I imagine curating as a way of thinking in terms of interconnections: linking objects, images, processes, people, locations, histories, and discourses in physical space like an active catalyst, generating twists, turns, and tensions.

In curating a co-working space, hosts take on the role of that "active catalyst"; creating new socio-material infrastructures where people can meet, exchange ideas and work. For example, Furnari (2014), discusses the role of "catalysts" as a necessary condition in the development of what he calls "interstitial spaces" where people from different institutional fields meet. The following six categories highlight the specific activities and practices of hosts. They are empirically derived from interviews with co-working hosts and discussed with literature from art theory and sociology.

Assembling and Arranging

Hosts bring together people, spaces, ideas and objects, they often create the space in the first place and continuously rearrange the co-working spaces to adapt it to the needs of the co-workers but also along the lines of certain assumptions about how the material can facilitate the social. For instances, O'Neill (2012, p. 104) claims the first task of a curator is "to produce 'spatial installations' in their own distinct styles, which provide the environmental setting for the staging of discussions, events and visitor participation". Also, von Bismarck (2012) emphasises that the crucial task of a curator today is to assemble instead of to care for a collection. All co-working spaces provide opportunities for social gatherings such as kitchen, lounges, meeting rooms, libraries, workshops and a café. The physical design of the co-working space with its open floor plan, the arrangement of tables (e.g. to enable eye contact between co-workers) or the location of social areas plays an important role in turning the space into a collaborative space (see Dorley and Witthoft 2012). The particular design influences movement flows and interaction patterns between people, shapes co-workers' perceptions of the particular space as a collaborative space and provides affordances for the formation of social relations (such as conference rooms for meet-ups, pin boards for searches, whiteboards to show activity and thought processes, round corners on tables or flexible furniture). Through assembling and gathering, hosts aim to create conducive affective work "atmospheres" (Gregg 2017) to different types of knowledge and cultural work, and hope to facilitate creative processes.

Selecting

While in many co-working spaces member selection works via the price mechanism and a convenient location from home, there is a growing number of spaces that apply specific selection criteria and where hosts act as gatekeepers (see Foster and Ocejo 2015) to the professional community within the space. The potential applicants are asked to specify their professional activity, interests and what kind of support they would like to receive to enable more synergies and a "cultural fit" among co-workers. Then, hosts compare those profiles with existing members and decide according to professional activities that are already in the space and what kind of networks might be accessible through other co-workers. Moreover, hosts organise talks by members, as well as seminars, courses or regular consultation hours (e.g. on legal or tax issues) with invited experts or bring in potential partners for collaborative projects. Most spaces have educational programmes, which are often accessible for the broader public without a membership card, and encourage peer-to-peer-learning networks for professional skill development. In organising those events, they want to enable shared interests among co-workers and connect them.

Caring

As co-working is associated with cultural values of collaboration and sustainability, hosts consider their responsibility to care for individual co-workers and the community within the space. In describing their work as "conducting", "mothering", "community-building", "social gardening", "triage nurse" or as to "breathe vitality into the lives of all who move through it", hosts indicate a considerable amount of affective and emotional investment in their hosting activities. They display a strong "pro-social motivation" (Obstfeld 2005) that is necessary to initiate and sustain social interactions among co-workers as well as "to induce cooperation in others" (Fligstein 2001, p. 105). A hospitable attitude (see Dikeç 2002; Lugosi 2017) is vital for hosts to create a welcoming and inclusive space for interactions among different co-workers and in establishing mutual support structures. Hosts attempt to create a hospitable atmosphere through talking to co-workers, asking for their specific interests, and connecting them with other co-workers. Hosts claim that eating together is the most effective socialisation mechanism and, therefore, organise informal events around food, such as the breakfast or lunch meetings, where new members will be introduced, specific projects discussed and co-workers can seek help from each other. Moreover, in their daily activities, they embody and practice the particular values every space wants to enact (which do not necessarily need to be the co-working values proposed by the co-working movement) and feel socially responsible for the co-workers in the space. In turn, co-workers' attitudes reflect this hospitality. Most studies highlight that for co-workers a sociable and enjoyable atmosphere is the most important reason to be in a particular space and many spaces show high retention rates (see *Deskmag* 2013, 2017; Garrett et al. 2017).

Mediating

Hosts have a privileged structural position within the space: they know all members but also connect with various partners outside the space. It is often the host who instigates contact between co-workers and build relations to the immediate surrounding and local contexts, whether to neighbourhood institutions, public or private agencies, other intermediaries, political actors or businesses. Hosts promote relationships but also their space and often, specific ideas or people from the space (see Welter and Olma 2011). Furthermore, different governance structures can be found (see Schmidt et al. 2014). Most spaces have participatory governance structures where members can decide on what happens in the space. For example, regular town hall meetings are organised to bring together the members and discuss the development of the space or to agree on rules within the space (e.g. if dogs shall be allowed or if an expansion shall support more workspace or a lab). Here, again, hosts enable sustained interaction and shared interests among co-workers (see, e.g., Furnari 2014), create a sense of belonging, mutuality and ownership to emphasise a community-driven approach.

Meaning Making and Translating

Hosts engage in meaning-making processes by creating new meanings around collaborative freelance work. For example, commonly used qualifiers for co-working in these stories are collaboration, community, sustainability, openness and accessibility—those values promoted by the global co-working movement (Coworking Manifesto 2014). For instances, Butcher (2016, p. 94) found that co-workers explain their work style as "posthuman, more humanistic, fluid and sustainable". As an extreme example, the global co-working provider WeWork promotes the narrative (or in this case more the brand) of an entrepreneurial "We Generation" to embed co-workers in a social project that goes beyond the individual freelance worker (WeWork 2015). With events and even annual summer camps, they aim to intensify the group feeling. Thus, hosts engage in the construction of meaning, through forms of translation and symbolic work (Foster and Ocejo 2015), whether in embedding freelance work in a narrative of a different, collaborative work style, in promoting co-working or in work with partners.

Exhibiting and Displaying

A crucial task of a curator is to exhibit and to help art "becoming public" (Smith 2012, p. 43). Similarly, hosts show the temporary co-working assemblage to potential new co-workers, partners or policy-makers to attract new associations. However foremost, they give visibility to the growing share of freelance and self-employed workers in contemporary labour markets.

Conclusion

This chapter aimed to critically engage with the notion of a creative hub through the lens of social curation. Scrutinising the role of co-working hosts demonstrates that they do more than to "manage" a space but engage in multiple ways of mediation to facilitate new socio-spatial relationships. Introducing the notion of social curation for hosts' practices sheds light on processes of assembling, gathering, caring, mediating and translating that help to enact the co-working space as a creative hub. Curation also emphasises the indeterminacy inherent in processes of assembling and gathering (see, e.g., Furnari 2014; Hutter and Farías 2017). Because of the transient nature of co-working spaces with an ever-changing social composition, with new co-workers joining and others leaving, the "co-working assemblage" is always moving in space and time, and thereby enables new ideas and practices to emerge. Subsequently, a creative hub cannot be conceived as just a particular place but rather as a dynamic, interactive process of the formation of associations.

This perspective has implications for further research. Firstly, following co-working hosts' practices provides a comprehensive micro-perspective into social dynamics of knowledge generation because these spaces bring together heterogeneous actors and different knowledge bases and could further illuminate the role of different types of proximity or distance and shared practice for knowledge generation and innovation. Secondly, while interrogating hosts' practices, it becomes apparent that just providing a material space, such as a building, for work is not enough to become a creative hub. A space is essential to enact and perform co-working but more crucial is a facilitator who instigates relationships and helps to sustain interactions over time. This conclusion has broader implications for initiatives around the support for co-working in many public and university-driven approaches. Thirdly, as new and distinct knowledge sites, co-working spaces might become meaningful actors within the urban creative economy mediating between freelancers, firms and organisations, providing an empirical lens into theoretical questions of relational and spatial proximity for creativity and innovation beyond the firm and within creative urban milieus. Moreover, they might also become meaningful actors in social transformation processes by providing a platform for dialogue and engagement that can give rise to new subjectivities, collective action or alternative organisations.

References

Anderson, B., Kearnes, M., McFarlane, C., & Swanton, D. (2012). On assemblages and geography. *Dialogues in Human Geography, 2*(2), 171–189.

Avdikos, V., & Kalogeresis, A. (2017). Socio-economic profile and working conditions of freelancers in co-working spaces and work collectives: Evidence from the design sector in Greece. *Area, 49*(1), 35–42. https://doi.org/10.1111/area.12279.

Barabasi, A.-L. (2002). *Linked: The new science of networks*. Cambridge, MA: Perseus.

Beck, U. (2000). *The brave new world of work*. Malden: Polity Press.

Bouncken, R. B., & Reuschl, A. J. (2016). Coworking-spaces: How a phenomenon of the sharing economy builds a novel trend for the workplace and for entrepreneurship. *Review of Management Science, OnlineFirst.* https://doi.org/10.1007/s11846-016-0215-y.

Brown, J. (2017). Curating the "third place"? Coworking and the mediation of creativity. *Geoforum, 82,* 112–126. https://doi.org/10.1016/j.geoforum.2017.04.006.

Butcher, T. (2016). Co-working communities: Sustainability citizenship at work. In R. Horne, J. Fien, B. B. Beza, & A. Nelson (Eds.), *Sustainability citizenship in cities: Theory and practice* (pp. 93–103). London and New York: Routledge.

Capdevila, I. (2013). *Knowledge dynamics in localized communities: Coworking spaces as microclusters*. SSRN. Available at http://ssrn.com/abstract=2414121. Accessed 20 August 2015.

Capdevila, I. (2014). *Different inter-organizational collaboration approaches in coworking spaces in Barcelona.* SSRN. Available at http://ssrn.com/abstract=2502816.

Capdevila, I. (2015). Co-working spaces and the localised dynamics of innovation in Barcelona. *International Journal of Innovation Management, 19*(3). https://doi.org/10.1142/s1363919615400046.

Castells, M. (2009). *The rise of the network society* (2nd ed.). Malden, MA, Oxford: Wiley.

Coworking Manifesto. (2014). Coworking Manifesto (Global—For the world). Retrieved from http://wiki.coworking.com/w/page/35382594/Coworking%20Manifesto%20(global%20-%20for%20the%20world. Accessed 25 May 2017.

Dale, K., & Burrell, G. (2008). *The spaces of organisation and the organisation of space: Power, identity and materiality at work.* Basingstoke: Palgrave Macmillan.

Daskalaki, M. (2017). Alternative organizing in times of crisis: Resistance assemblages and socio-spatial solidarity. *European Urban and Regional Studies*, 1–16. https://doi.org/10.1177/0969776416683001.

Deleuze, G., & Guattari, F. (1987). *A thousand plateaus.* Minneapolis: University of Minnesota Press.

Deskmag. (2013). The third global coworking survey 2012. Retrieved from http://de.slideshare.net/deskwanted/global-coworking-survey-2012?ref=http://blog.deskwanted.com/. Accessed 28 August 2014.

Deskmag. (2017). First results of the 2017 global coworking survey. Retrieved from https://www.dropbox.com/s/8kfdsrtel6hpabd/First%20Results%20Of%20The%202017%20Global%20Coworking%20Survey.pdf?dl=0. Accessed 25 July 2017.

Dikeç, M. (2002). Pera peras poros: Longings for spaces of hospitality. *Theory, Culture & Society, 19*(1–2), 227–247.

Dorley, S., & Witthoft, S. (2012). *Make space: How to set the stage for creative collaboration.* Hoboken: Wiley.

Dovey, J., Lansdowne, J., Moreton, S., Merkel, J. Pratt, A. C., & Virani, T. E. (2016). *Creative hubs: Understanding the new economy.* London. Retrieved from https://creativeconomy.britishcouncil.org/media/uploads/files/HubsReport.pdf. Accessed 20 February 2018.

Evans, G. (2009). Creative cities, creative spaces and urban policy. *Urban Studies, 46*(5–6), 1003–1040. https://doi.org/10.1177/0042098009103853.

Felstead, A., Jewson, N., & Walters, S. (2005). The shifting locations of work. *Work, Employment & Society, 19*(2), 415–431. https://doi. org/10.1177/0950017005053186.

Ferm, J. (2014). Delivering affordable workspace: Perspectives of developers and workspace providers in London. *Progress in Planning, 93,* 1–49.

Fligstein, N. (2001). Social skill and the theory of fields. *Sociological Theory, 19*(2), 105–125.

Florida, R. (2004). *The rise of the creative class.* New York: Basic Books.

Foster, P. C., & Ocejo, R. E. (2015). Brokerage, mediation, and social networks. In C. Jones, M. Lorenzen, & S. Jonathan (Eds.), *The oxford handbook of creative industries* (pp. 405–420). Oxford: Oxford University Press.

Furnari, S. (2014). Interstitial spaces: Microinteraction settings and the genesis of new practices between institutional fields. *Academy of Management Review, 39*(4), 439–462.

Garrett, L. E., Spreitzer, G. M., & Bacevice, P. A. (2017). Co-constructing a sense of community at work: The emergence of community in coworking spaces. *Organization Studies, 38*(6), 821–842.

GLA. (2015). *London open workspaces.* Retrieved from https://www.london. gov.uk/what-we-do/regeneration/places-work. Accessed 15 January 2018.

Green, H., & Strange, A. (1999). Managed workspace. Do tenants stay too long? *Local Economy, 14*(3), 245–256.

Gregg, M. (2017). *From careers to atmospheres. CAMEo Cuts #3.* Leicester: CAMEo Research Institute for Cultural and Media Economies, University of Leicester.

Hutter, M., & Farías, I. (2017). Sourcing newness: Ways of inducing indeterminacy. *Journal of Cultural Economy, 10*(5), 434–449.

Jakonen, M., Kivinen, N., Salovaara, P., & Hirkman, P. (2017). Towards an economy of encounters? A critical study of affectual assemblages in coworking. *Scandinavian Journal of Management, 33*(4), 235–242. https://doi. org/10.1016/j.scaman.2017.10.003.

Kitching, J., & Smallbone, D. (2008). *Defining and estimating the size of the UK freelance workforce.* A report for the professional contractors group. Retrieved from http://eprints.kingston.ac.uk/3880/1/Kitching-J-3880.pdf. Accessed 20 August 2015.

Krzys Acord, S. (2014). Art installation as knowledge assembly. In T. Zemblyas (Ed.), *Artistic Practices: Social Interaction and Cultural Dynamics.* (pp. 151–165). London, New York: Routledge.

Liegl, M. (2014). Nomadicity and the care of place—On the aesthetic and affective organization of space in freelance creative work. *Computer*

Supported Cooperative Work (CSCW), 23(2), 163–183. https://doi.org/10.1007/s10606-014-9198-x.

Lind, M. (2010). The curatorial (2009). In B. K. Wood (Ed.), Selected Maria Lind writing (pp. 63–67). Berlin: Sternberg.

Lugosi, P. (2017). Using abstract concepts in impact-focussed organisational research: An empirical example deploying "hospitality". Qualitative Research in Organizations and Management: An International Journal, 12(1), 18–34.

Martins, J. (2015). The extended workplace in a creative cluster: Exploring space(s) of digital work in silicon roundabout. Journal of Urban Design, 20(1), 125–145. https://doi.org/10.1080/13574809.2014.972349.

Merkel, J. (2015). Coworking in the city. Ephemera: Theory & Politics in Organization, 15(1), 121–139.

Montgomery, J. (2007). Creative industry business incubators and managed workspaces: A review of best practice. Planning, Practice & Research, 22(4), 601–617. https://doi.org/10.1080/02697450701770126.

Moreton, S. (2013). The promise of the affordable artist's studio: Governing creative spaces in London. Environment and Planning A, 45(2), 421–437.

Moriset, B. (2014). Building new places of the creative economy. The rise of coworking spaces. Paper presented at the 2nd Geography of Innovation International Conference 2014, Utrecht January 23–25. Available at https://halshs.archives-ouvertes.fr/halshs-00914075/document. Accessed 20 August 2015.

Mould, O., Vorley, T., & Liu, K. (2014). Invisible creativity? Highlighting the hidden impact of freelancing in London's creative industries. European Planning Studies, 22(12), 2436–2455. https://doi.org/10.1080/09654313.2013.790587.

NLA. (2016). WRK/LDN. Shaping London's future workplaces. London: New London Architecture.

O'Neill, P. (2012). The culture of curating and the curating of culture(s). Cambridge and London: MIT Press.

Obstfeld, D. (2005). Social networks, the tertius iungens orientation, and involvement in innovation. Administrative Science Quarterly, 50(1), 100–130.

Parrino, L. (2013). Coworking: Assessing the role of proximity in knowledge exchange. Knowledge Management Research & Practice, 13(3), 261–271.

Rus, A., & Orel, M. (2015). Coworking: A community of work. Teorija in Praksa, 52(6), 1017–1038.

Salinger, J. H. (2013). Economic development policies through business incubation and co-working: A study of San Francisco and New York city. Retrieved from http://hdl.handle.net/10022/AC:P:20748. Accessed 20 August 2015.

Schmidt, S., Brinks, V., & Brinkhoff, S. (2014). Innovation and creativity labs in Berlin organizing temporary spatial configurations for innovations. *Zeitschrift fuer Wirtschaftsgeographie, 58*(4), 232–247.

Smith, T. (2012). *Thinking contemporary curating*. New York: Independent Curators International.

Spinuzzi, C. (2012). Working alone together: Coworking as emergent collaborative activity. *Journal of Business and Technical Communication, 26*(4), 399–441.

Spinuzzi, C. (2015). *All edge: Inside the new workplace networks*. Chicago: University of Chicago.

Surman, T. (2013). Building social entrepreneurship through the power of coworking. *Innovations: Technology, Governance, Globalization, 8*(3/4), 189–195.

Thrift, N. (2006). Re-inventing invention: New tendencies in capitalist commodification. *Economy and Society, 35*(02), 279–306.

Virani, T. E., & Malem, W. (2015). *Re-articulating the creative hub concept as a model for business support in the local creative economy: The case of Mare Street in Hackney* (Creative Works London Working Paper No. 12). Retrieved from http://www.creativeworkslondon.org.uk/wp-content/uploads/2013/11/PWK-Working-Paper-12.pdf. Accessed 20 December 2016.

von Bismarck, B. (2012). Curating curators. *Texte zur Kunst, 22*(86), 42–61.

Waters-Lynch, J. M., & Potts, J. (2016, April 26). *The social economy of coworking spaces: A focal point model of coordination*. SSRN. Retrieved from https://ssrn.com/abstract=2712217. Accessed 25 July 2017.

Welter, T., & Olma, S. (2011). *Das Beta-Prinzip. Coworking und die Zukunft der Arbeit*. Berlin: Blumenbar Verlag.

WeWork. (2015). *WeWork. Create your life's work*. Retrieved from https://www.wework.com/. Accessed 20 August 2015.

4

Creative Hubs, Cultural Work and Affective Economies: Exploring 'Unspeakable' Experiences for Young Cultural Workers

David Lee

Introduction

Although both cultural work and creative hubs have been objects of intense policy valorisation over the last twenty years or more, relatively little research has been carried out into the psychosocial consequences of creative work, although this is an area of increasing attention. Writers within cultural studies such as McRobbie (2016), Gill (2002) and Ross (2004) have pointed to the 'dark side' or toxic conditions of cultural work for some creative workers—showing how the 'glamour' of individualised labour and the promise of self-realisation too often masks the reality of precarity, exploitation and the erosion of a semblance of work-life 'balance'. But following this formative work, detailed empirical investigations into the psychosocial affective nature of these experiences have been thin on the ground, particularly as such issues become

D. Lee (✉)
Media and Communication, University of Leeds, Leeds, UK
e-mail: d.j.lee@leeds.ac.uk

© The Author(s) 2019
R. Gill et al. (eds.), *Creative Hubs in Question*, Dynamics of Virtual Work,
https://doi.org/10.1007/978-3-030-10653-9_4

more pressing in the context of 'austerity' and the intensification of new modes of freelance creative labour in the 'gig' economy.

This chapter aims to address this gap through an interrogation of the lived reality of working in creative hubs for a group of young workers in who have recently entered the British cultural industries labour market from higher education (HE). The research investigates the psycho-social experiences and consequences of cultural work for young people who have recently entered the cultural and creative industries under the political economic context of austerity. It investigates the ways in which working in hubs offers certain forms of value, including social and economic capital; as well as the specific affective and emotional pressures that hub working may generate. In so doing, it explores the 'unspeakable' feelings of shame, failure and anxiety amongst 'cultural workers in the making' (Ashton 2013) and considers the significance of the prevalence of such feelings and experiences within the creative industries.

Hubs and Cultural Work

In a recent report, the British Council defines a creative hub as 'a place, either physical or virtual, which brings creative people together. It is a convenor, providing space and support for networking, business development and community engagement within the creative, cultural and tech sectors'. The authors stress the importance of understanding creative hubs as spaces for 'work, participation and consumption' (Dovey et al. 2016, p. 7) and argue that we need to see them as distinct from creative clusters or quarters, where the definition is largely based on agglomeration and co-location of similar businesses. Creative hubs are often localised but are part of an 'urban cultural system' that includes linked networks and non-physical space. They are diverse and are slippery to define, but include variants such as studio space, centres, networks, clusters and online platforms. Such places would include Fusebox in Brighton, Birmingham Open Media, Site in Sheffield and many others. They can be publicly funded and subsidised spaces, although increasingly they are commercially run (ibid.).

To understand the psychosocial consequences for (some) creative workers located in creative hubs, it is important to recognise the discursive environment within which they find themselves, at the feted nexus of the 'knowledge economy' (Conventz et al. 2016). This is a discursive space where negative affective experiences caused by creative work are often 'unspeakable' (Gill 2014) and tend to be seen by creative workers as individualised failings rather than located as structural features of precarious work. Creative hubs (along with associated spatial concepts such as creative clusters, quarters and districts), for example, have been actively encouraged through economic and cultural policy and are often described in language that posits hubs as not only being the recipe for dynamic economic growth, but also as spaces of tolerance, diversity, innovation and self-realisation.

For those interested in working in a creative hub, the marketing rhetoric is celebratory. For example, the co-working hub Mindspace in Shoreditch promotes itself in the following fashion:

> We believe business is not just about work, it's also about inspiration. We create a stimulating atmosphere for your team to release their imagination. We scour local flea markets for one-off artefacts, handpick vintage furniture, commission local artists, build towering bookcases, and paint the walls with thought-provoking messages. We create an environment that lets your clients think outside the box and reach new heights. When you get your Mindspace with us in London, you also get space with us in Munich, San Francisco, Berlin, Frankfurt, Tel Aviv, Warsaw and others. Free. Yes, Free. (HubbleHQ 2018)

Of note here is the appeal to authenticity ('local flea markets'), imagination and a rejection of the mundane discourse of business as just 'work', stressing the 'inspiration' that comes from being part of a local hub, but one with global connections. And such a boutique environment is not cheap—a hot desk space at Mindspace costs from £300 a month at the time of writing in June 2018, with similar provision at the global workspace provider WeWork costing £500. Higher up the value chain, a private office at Huckletree in Clerkenwell costs £20,000 a month (ibid.).

Meanwhile, creative work, as anyone who has researched the valorisation of the creative industries since the 1990s will know, is positioned as a space for self-realisation, diversity, autonomy and freedom, particularly amongst policy-makers, business consultants and a range of regional, national and international agencies. As such, it also has many advocates, such as the once ubiquitous Richard Florida (2002), with his off the shelf prescription for municipalities seeking to attract the 'creative class', alongside any number of national, regional and local economic development plans, often drafted by consultants operating internationally, who are key intermediaries in the transmission of 'fast' creative industries policy (Peck 2005; Prince 2012). Cultural policy has been central to such a discursive environment. New Labour's creative industries mapping studies of the late 1990s set the mood music for the contemporaneous celebration of creativity (DCMS 1998), and a raft of cultural policies aimed at developing the 'creative industries', the 'creative economy' and the 'digital economy' have also been closely linked to regional spatial policies seeking to develop flagging post-industrial urban economies into citadels of the 'new economy', predicated on knowledge, creativity and attracting footloose capital investment and the 'creative class' (Hesmondhalgh et al. 2015). Indeed, if much creative industries boosterism and hype has been fairly devoid of actual policy (Oakley 2004), the more 'concrete' economic spatial politics of urban regeneration and 'clustering' has meant that the development of, or investment in, creative hubs, clusters and quarters has operated as the clearest area of actual policy in this area. In the UK, for example, this took its form in the investment of significant funds from regional development agencies (RDAs) into 'creative clusters' and forms of agglomeration, alongside matched funding from EU structural funds (Lee et al. 2014; Evans 2009). While much of this money dried up following the financial crash of 2008, the desire for 'clusters' and hubs is still dominant in city regions across the UK.

In such a context, it is very difficult for creative workers to find expression and give voice to the negative experiences that research shows often ensue because of the precarious, individualised and affective dynamics of cultural work. Ros Gill has written about the 'unspeakable' nature of negative affective experiences of labour (2014), preventing workers from developing a language of reflective critique. In a context where one is required to invest one's affective being, time and emotional labour into creative work, experiences such as failure, rejection, anxiety and burnout are difficult to articulate (Lee 2017). Where such experiences are narrated by cultural workers, they tend to be located as *individual* failings, rather than systemic features of structural inequalities within neoliberal labour markets. This connects to neoliberalism's injunction for individuals to fashion the self to meet the demands of the contemporary workplace (Scharff 2016).

In the analysis that follows, I seek to unpack these affective experiences and reflect on the relationship between creative work, affect and creative hubs. What role do creative hubs play as locations where 'unspeakable' and toxic creative work might play out? Do creative hubs offer resources for resilience against the structural affects and effects of precarious labour? Or do they serve as spaces for entrenching modes of social inequality based around class, gender, race and age?

The Sample

The study is based on a sample of 12 young adults aged 24–30. All respondents are graduates from arts, humanities and social sciences undergraduate degree courses in England, who left university between 2010 and 2012. The interviews were conducted between July and September 2016, and a snowball sampling approach was used, making use of the business networking website LinkedIn. As a small-scale qualitative study, the sample is not statistically aligned with national demographics but includes a fairly even mix of men and women and two respondents from Black and Minority Ethnic backgrounds (BAME) (see Table 4.1). Social origin was also analysed as a variable.[1] Table 4.1 below sets out the sample (with names and key details anonymised) and

---

[1]Respondents' social origin was grouped into three groups based on the National Statistics Socio-economic Classification (NS-SEC) classes; NS-SEC group 1 refers to those with parents in NS-SEC 1 and NS-SEC 2 (higher and lower professional and managerial positions), NS-SEC Group 2 to those with parents in NS-SEC 3, 4, or 5 (intermediate occupations or self-employed), and NS-SEC group 3 to those from NS-SEC 6–8 family backgrounds (semi-routine, routine occupations, or unemployed).

Table 4.1 Respondents details

Name/Age	Occupation	Location	Hub type	NS-SEC three-class model group	Ethnicity
Jack (23)	Software developer	London	Cluster	NS-SEC group 3	White British
Amy (25)	PR account manager	Manchester	Cluster	NS-SEC group 1	White British
Declan (26)	Digital content producer	Bristol	Network	NS-SEC group 3	White British
Jay (25)	Web designer	London	Co-working space	NS-SEC group 1	White British
Tina (24)	Film location manager	London	Network	NS-SEC group 2	BME
Katy (24)	Advertising agency creative	London	Cluster	NS-SEC group 1	White British
Eleanor (27)	Freelance copywriter	London	Network	NS-SEC group 3	White British
Paul (25)	TV researcher	Manchester	Centre	NS-SEC group 1	White British
Jade (26)	Freelance journalist	Manchester	Network	NS-SEC group 3	Black
Tom (26)	Social media marketing	Brighton	Co-working hub	NS-SEC group 1	White British
Harry (25)	Copywriter	London	Cluster	NS-SEC group 2	White British
Richard (29)	Public relations	Leeds	Network and cluster	NS-SEC group 2	White British

provides detail on the geography of their labour activity at the time of interview. All respondents could be defined as working in various forms of 'creative hubs' across urban centres within the UK.[2] Given the slipperiness of the term, this ranges from work in gentrifying post-industrial urban spaces in cities including Leeds, Manchester and London, to co-working arrangements as freelancers working in the corporate hipsterism of WeWork and other similar workspace 'hubs' across the UK.

Taking a psychosocial approach to exploring their work experiences, semi-structured interviews were carried out, and the material was coded using NVivo. The analysis presented below is based on an exploration of narratives around failure, shame, anxiety and compulsory sociality that emerged from the data.

The (Psychosocial) Benefits of Working in Creative Hubs

Clearly for some interviewees, hub working had various positive attributes. While these were largely connected to the economic benefits of agglomeration for individuals, such as finding work, interviewees also discussed the social benefits which accrue from collaboration, co-working and connectivity inherent to creative labour, with hubs offering spaces for solidarity, community and support. As such creative hub working allows for the consideration of the often contradictory and complex nature of creative work—which is simultaneously highly individualised and highly socialised. In the right circumstances, it is possible that creative hubs might also the possibilities of alternatives to, and opposition to, the current dominant individualised precarious pathways for creative work.

---

[2]The typology used is based on The British Council's Hub Toolkit (2015).

The Economic Benefits of Hubs

As Dovey et al. show, 'creative hubs can produce a wide range of impacts including start-up ventures, jobs, new products and services, future investment (public and commercial), talent development, regional talent retention, informal education and engagement, training, urban regeneration, research and development, new networks, innovative models of organisation, quality of life enhancements and resilience' (2016, p. 5). For many of the interviewees, hubs offered economic advantages. Finding work and business opportunities was the key impact, with ten out of twelve interviewees mentioning this. For example, Richard talked about how the proximity of digital agencies in the hub he worked in (including a digital network which he was part of) provided numerous 'catching up' possibilities which led to an enhanced knowledge of what contract were coming up and what the contracting companies were looking for:

> Being based at [x] has totally transformed how I find jobs. As a freelance I rely on a fairly small group of people who employ me regularly to do social media marketing work. I can pick stuff up on the internet and on spec but it tends to be pretty low quality low paid. Working here has meant I've doubled the number of people I get work from in less than a year. I mean, I'm still quite new to the industry, but it's so much better than sitting at home waiting for something to fall into your lap.

Hubs were also spaces for attracting business investment funding for a smaller number of individuals. Declan described the highly organised series of business development events which were hosted where he worked, often funded by the city council and various regional agencies. Connections to the local universities were important, and investors from across the region would come to such events to investigate possible investment opportunities:

> I found that there were a lot of events put on where you could meet people looking to make money by investing in a new start-up. So, for me, I was just freelancing doing coding and stuff, and decided to go along to a networking thing. I met this guy who worked for Innovate UK, and

was encouraged to put in a bid for start-up funding, which amazingly was successful. It really gave me a big boost at that very early stage.

Social Benefits

Beyond the financial, creative hubs provided clear social benefits for some creative workers. Hub working, most significantly, offered the benefits of collaboration and sociality. For these young workers, the opportunities to meet friends and connect with people through work (and after work) were a key attraction of a creative hub. The development of new networks was critical to this, as hubs provide opportunities to network, make and embed relationships and develop regional opportunities which interviewees saw as offering an enhancement of their quality of life.

For some interviewees, being connected to a creative hub provided a bulwark against the isolating effects of precarious and nomadic freelance work, which is becoming increasingly dominant in the cultural industries, particularly for early career workers (Gandini 2015). In a platform economy, hubs can serve as a social glue, creating a 'stickiness' to a specific place, and also offering connections and modes of cultural and social capital. As Naudin has argued, this mode of networking serves an extremely important function, particularly outside of London where networks are smaller, more supportive and less instrumental (2015, pp. 134–137). For example, Tom (26) reflected on the atomised nature of freelance 'spec' work, and how being part of a co-working space, on a 'hot desk' arrangement, had provided him with much needed company, networks and social support:

> I've always struggled a bit with depression and that, I'm a bit prone to that. Yeah, so working alone all the time probably wasn't the best idea! My friend suggested that I try out a hot desk contract at [x], and it's been really good for me. There's stuff on at lunchtime, like walks, workouts etc., and free coffee is always good for chatting to people. I think it's helped a lot and I feel much less alone in what I do now. It's good to know that there are other people out there doing the same thing.

Creative Hubs and Affective Pressures

Despite the positive attributes of hub working identified above, the research pointed to the distinct and intense psychosocial pressures of hub working for some individuals. This section briefly investigates several key areas where hub working had a significant impact on their affective experiences of creative work. These include experiences and narratives of failure and shame; the impact of 'compulsory sociality' in hubs; the lack of space for dissent, critique or mental illbeing in a context where enthusiasm, 'confidence' and well-being are celebrated above all else.

Narratives of Failure and Shame

In a culture focused on performativity and 'resilience', finding a space to consider experiences and feelings of failure and shame through work is increasingly difficult.[3] However, failure is not only routine, but structurally embedded into the nature of creative work, functioning as it does on a 'hits' based reputation economy, where the majority of products entering the market will 'fail' at a purely financial level. Where discourses of failure are able to circulate, they are overwhelmingly presented in a positive light, as a necessary prerequisite on the 'heroic' route to success:

---

[3]The experiences of failure were defined by respondents in a qualitative fashion, as career-events which they experienced and understood as failure. In other words, no singular empirical 'definition' of failure is given here, although there are clearly shared defining characteristics. They are events which respondents reflected on as ones where a sought-after goal was not achieved, or where the reaction of others towards work carried out was critical. Often, in the highly competitive freelance economies of the cultural industries, failure was intimately connected to a non-renewal of a temporary contract, or for some it was the failure to earn enough money to survive. Failure was highly internalised and subjective, and often connected to the perception that others were succeeding in a field while they were not. In other words, often failure was relative to other's perceived success and the failure to 'make it'. Failure was also highly connected to recognition, and often framed as failing to get recognition for one's work. Indicators of success or failure were also critical, such as the number followers gained on social media, the number of 'likes' of postings and 'shares' of those posts on social media.

"Success is most often achieved by those who don't know that failure is inevitable."—Coco Chanel
"There is only one thing that makes a dream impossible to achieve: the fear of failure."—Paulo Coelho
"Failure should be our teacher, not our undertaker. Failure is delay, not defeat. It is a temporary detour, not a dead end. Failure is something we can avoid only by saying nothing, doing nothing, and being nothing."—Denis Waitley

In reality, failure within the competitive individualised context of cultural work is often experienced in a far more complex subjective fashion, and one's ability to withstand the pressures of failure (or to be 'resilient'), are dependent on structural factors such as class, gender and cultural capital.[4]

Failure was widely internalised, individualised and experienced as aberrant from what was perceived to be the norm. It often led to feelings of pain and depression, where one's self-identity was disrupted. For example, Jack, a 25-year-old software developer, described the humiliation and emotional pain of losing his job at a software agency in 2014:

> So far, I guess failure for me has meant not being asked to work on the really interesting projects. I also lost my job at a software agency a couple of years, and that was really tough. We were all on sort of rolling contracts – so they just didn't renew my contract at the end of the month. Didn't tell me why. So I found it humiliating and although I asked why, I was made to feel that I should have just slunk off with my tail between my legs. Not bother them about it. That was the culture. Tough. I think it's worse in London because there is such competition for these jobs they can treat you like shit.
>   Author: How did it affect you?
>   I guess… I sort of got down afterwards. I found it hard to sleep. I kept thinking about it, you know about losing my job, and felt really shitty about myself.

---

[4]There is not space here to discuss in detail the role of social class in relation to psychosocial experiences for creative workers, but I have explored this elsewhere (Lee 2017).

Despite being a source of psychic pain, depression and anxiety, for many of the respondents talk of failure was a taboo topic—either within their social circles, or as something that one would consider as a possibility. Jay, a graphic designer, noted 'It's [failure's] not something that people talk about out and about. My friends all work in creative jobs but don't really talk about failure. They'll talk about how tough the industry can be, how the pay is low, living in London hard. But not failure'. The 'unspeakability' of the hidden injuries of creative work is particularly evident in Jake's narrative, showing the difficulty of speaking of failure and other 'toxic' experiences within the 'cool' and celebratory environments of creative work (Gill 2014).

Katy (24), an advertising executive in London, also talked about a culture where she worked where 'failure' or fear of failure is not something that can be discussed:

> The company I work in, you just can't talk about failure. Everything has to be 'cool', and everyone is supposed to be 'up' all the time. It's pretty oppressive really. That culture is pretty much driven by the managing director, who loves to promote himself at any opportunity as the ultimate self-made entrepreneur.

Failure, in these narratives, can only be discussed as part of a heroic tale of successful transformation, rather than as something that can have more damaging psychic consequences.

Compulsory Sociality

For Jack, working in a co-working hub in London, the highly socialised environment was a significant factor in his experience of cultural work and his affective response to it. The expectation of 'compulsory sociality' (Gill and Pratt 2008) well documented in creative work impacted upon him negatively because of his personal circumstances which left him unable to 'fit in':

OK, so it was kind of expected that you'd go out for beers after work – sometimes two or three times a week. [The company] was pretty much all guys, and being based in East London there were loads of places that they liked to go. Also, it was expected that we'd hang out with clients and other business contacts too. The thing for me was that I suffer from anxiety and find that kind of thing really difficult. Also, I'm on meds for anxiety which means I can't really drink. So I found myself making excuses all the time. After a while they stopped asking me, and that's when working there became really uncomfortable. I was pretty much left out of stuff, and in a small company like that it's pretty impossible. I could see the writing was on the wall for a while…

This speaks to the negative side of the highly socialised cultures of creative work and shows that expectations of socialising are deeply embedded in the network cultures of creative hubs. While enjoyable, and of course a source of entrepreneurial networking and support for many creative workers (Naudin 2015) it also shows the difficulties experiences for those who do not fit in, either through choice, or for individual reasons such as health. In such cultures where 'presence' is an expectation, there is a deep lack of transparency involved for those who don't or can't make themselves available outside of contracted hours, creating new modes of performative inequality.

For example, Eleanor (27), who comes from a working-class background, suffered powerful feelings of shame in relation to her experiences of working as a copywriter for a London-based advertising agency based in a creative hub. She described the intense workload pressure, coupled with the need to be seen to socialise after work in the bars and clubs near to the agency where she worked:

I suppose I enjoyed it to start with – as soon as I started there I found myself going out nearly every night with people from work. A lot of drinking, clubbing, drugs too… haha a bit of an ad agency cliché I guess! But the work was so pressured, I was working on some big client briefs and pitches and sometimes you'd be working until 10pm, then going out til 3am, then back in the office early doors – it was crazy. I started to suffer from really bad anxiety and depression, panic attacks, you name it, and in the end I had to go to the doctor about it. He signed me off work there and then for a week and put me on antidepressants. I couldn't get out of bed, I had to move home to my parents' house. I lost the job after a few months – I was on a probation contract anyway, so they didn't have to keep me on while I got better.

She works as a freelance copywriter now, and finds it suits her much better. But her difficulties with anxiety still exist:

I think that [anxiety] was there just waiting to come out, I don't know – who knows. But I've definitely not been the same since, I still get really stressed and anxious. I've got social anxiety in certain situations. I am still taking medication. I feel really ashamed about it if I'm honest – I'm still in touch with people from the agency who have done really well and I think 'what's wrong with me, why didn't I make it like them?'. But then, well, life's too short to worry about that kind of stuff I guess.

Interrogating her 'breakdown' in more detail, it became clear that social class and field competition involving tastes and middle-class dispositions were important factors. Feeling the strong need to 'fit in', and internal shame for not finding this easy, Eleanor described how she coped by reliance on alcohol and drugs too when they were available:

'I was drinking a lot when going out – I think I wanted to fit in and I was nervous because they all seemed so confident. I was hanging out with a young crowd at the agency, they knew other friends from university working at other agencies, and it was all really cliquey. I wasn't posh like them, didn't' have their natural confidence in the bars and restaurants. They all seemed to have gone to better universities, and came from posh places. The girls were so bloody trendy! Always wearing the latest stuff, going to the coolest bars, clubs, members bars... I guess I didn't really fit in with them, so drink and drugs was my way of coping with it. For a while at least.'

As her problems worsened, so too did her anxiety and shame about failing to fit in—or least her perception that she was failing to fit, echoing Walkerdine's (2011) analysis of working-class girls' experiences of

HE, suffering from the intense pressure to 'make it' within middle-class milieus. This led Eleanor to make to multiple 'retreats' from the specific field of cultural production which she was in, which in combination ultimately led to her leaving it altogether for a time. One form of retreat was through alcohol and substance abuse, another was a retreat from what she perceived to be her authentic self (rooted in her working-class origins) in order to 'fit in'. Ultimately, her final retreat was from the job itself.

Enthusiasm and the Disavowal of Critique

The final area of analysis examines relates to the difficulties faced by cultural workers who deviate in some way from the enthusiastic, positive script which is expected within the psychosocial landscape of the creative hub. This reflects the way that work has been transformed by the creative economy imaginary 'into something closer to a life of enthusiasm and enjoyment' (McRobbie 2002, p. 521), and this research into hub working would suggest that little or no discursive space is available for young cultural workers who do not embrace such a discourse. Being awkward or vocalising affective experiences which do not fit with the dominant culture of enthusiasm, youth, health and well-being expected in creative hubs quickly left some individuals on the margins.

For example, several respondents talked about the difficulties of vocalising any kind of critique of the precarious work culture inherent to much labour undertaken in the creative hub context. Here, insecurity was to be embraced and the ability to 'surf' the flux of uncertainty was a marker of ability, confidence and success, further consolidating the 'cult of confidence' that permeates the hub labour market. For example, Declan noted how he had been castigated by his peer group for expressing his anxiety about the precarious nature of much of his employment: 'they basically told me 'don't be such a wuss, man up'… it wasn't something that was cool to talk about. It was weird actually, but I understand the logic of it you know it's not as if it's going to make any difference to moan about it and we all need to boost each other's confidence. Yeah, I was definitely the wet blanket that day'.

Also, several interviewees noted the personal consequences not only of experiencing psychological difficulties such as anxiety and depression in hubs, but of being perceived to be suffering. Hubs may offer supportive spaces for those fully immersed in the 'creative economy' script, but for those marginalised by anxiety or depression such as Jack or Eleanor, hubs were unamenable spaces which individuals quickly spiralled out of. Indeed, the creative hub emerges from the research as a fairly homogenous space, with a climate intolerant of perceived weakness, difference and opposition. Negative experiences were certainly not vocalised, or even entertained by some. For example, for Amy (25), from an upper-class background, the very notion of failure was alien, and to her seemed a strange thing to be talking about:

> It's so funny to like be asked about failure. I mean... I just don't think like that. Erm... I guess I'm just an optimistic person! Things seem to have gone pretty well for me so far... I'm getting promoted, really like the people I'm working with and we all have great fun you know.

However, those from less affluent social backgrounds on the other hand were certainly not oblivious to how class (and race) played a key role in how the cultural industries operated. For example, Tina (24) a black woman from a NS-SEC Group 2 background elaborated on her experiences:

> Failure – not something you want to talk about is it really? But yeah.... I've found this industry can be tough. I wouldn't see it as failure as such, but I don't think I've achieved what I set out to in the timeframe I wanted to. That's been tough for me personally – I often feel depressed about it. I work really hard, so not sure what I'm doing wrong really. Sometimes I think my face doesn't fit in this place [work], as most of my colleagues are white, and pretty much posh. Some are really up themselves too – y'know arrogant? I find that tough – they seem to be progressing much quickly than me up the greasy pole .. They all seem oblivious to rejection and 'failure' – must have some kind of confidence drummed into them at public school.

She felt that you had to be prepared to be rejected to find work in film as it is so competitive, but also that once you are in employment you must push yourself and be 'driven' as there are so many other people out there who want your job. This suggests a relational component to hub working, where 'success' is based on evaluating yourself reflexively against others' performances, and certainly not through vocalising criticisms or negative experiences.

Conclusion

This chapter has investigated some of the inherent psychosocial factors of cultural work in creative hubs, providing an exploration of the lived realities of such work. Hubs are to some extent unavoidable spaces for contemporary cultural workers, as they are increasingly dominant features of the workspace environment in urban environments. Even when they are not physical spaces, they often play a role in the virtual networks that creative workers inhabit and form (Dovey et al. 2016). Understanding the dynamics of work in creative hubs is therefore a pressing and significant research task.

Creative hubs offer several distinct advantages—both economic and social. The ability to find work, network are important economic benefits. At a psychosocial level, hubs are also spaces for socialising, providing connections and a bulwark against the isolation and atomisation which characterises freelance creative work (Long and Naudin, this volume; Gandini 2015). However, hub working comes with significant affective pressures, reflecting an intensification of previously noted dynamics of cultural work. Most notably they are spaces where negative psychological experiences are not allowed to be given voice easily. Therefore, commonplace experiences of failure, shame and anxiety are hidden from view, and when they are raised or observed impact negatively on those giving voice to them. Moreover, the competitive individualised culture of hub working means that there is a relational aspect to perceptions of success or failure, where 'success' is based on evaluating yourself reflexively against others' performances, and certainly not through vocalising criticisms or negative experiences. Therefore, although researchers have written about the possibilities for collective mobilisation through the specific types of socialities fostered by creative work (de Peuter and Cohen 2015; McRobbie 2002), this research indicates the difficulties for creative workers in vocalising dissent in such discursive environments, let alone organising more equitable conditions.

In the meritocratic reality of contemporary society, a new shift towards 'grit' and a moral focus on character precludes discussions of weakness, failure or mental health issues. In the UK, for example, there has been a noted increase in mental health illnesses over recent years, with an estimated 1 in 4 people suffering from a mental health problem and almost a quarter of a million children and young people receiving help from NHS mental health services for problems such as anxiety, depression and eating disorders (Mental Health Foundation 2016). Neoliberalism's competitive atomised culture, coupled to the relational pressures exerted by social media and other forms of communication, appears to be leading to what some have described as an 'epidemic' of loneliness, anxiety and depression in late modern societies around the world (Monbiot 2016). The lack of spaces to share routine experiences of affective distress through creative labour is highly problematic. In creative work, long a frontline for the promotional discourses of meritocracy (Allen 2013), such disavowals are evident in this research, and yet also belie the lived reality for these young cultural workers.

The chapter also explores how social origin appears to have an impact on psychosocial experiences of hub working. Although a small sample, a link can be made between social class, confidence and 'resilience' in the face of the performative competitiveness expected within creative work. In this sense, narratives such as Eleanor's provide an insight into the psychosocial dynamics which help determine the social inequalities increasingly observed within the creative industries. Yet, if creative hubs provide spaces for many of the negative features of individualised cultural work to intensify (precarity, affective damage, compulsory sociality, (self) exploitation and inequality) they also offer opportunities for a resocialisation of labour through a normative orientation towards collaboration, mutual exchange, diversity and community (Merkel 2015). This suggests how the ongoing transformation of labour as a result of social, economic and technological change not only accentuates the potentially toxic psychosocial impacts of cultural work, but also offers possibilities for alternative models based on ethical as well as market values.

References

Allen, K. (2013). 'What do you need to make it as a woman in this industry? Balls!': Work placements, gender and the cultural industries. In *Cultural work and higher education* (pp. 232–253). London, UK: Palgrave Macmillan.

Ashton, D. (2013). Cultural workers in-the-making. *European Journal of Cultural Studies, 16*(4), 468–488.

British Council. (2015). *Creative hub toolkit.* Available at http://creativeconomy.britishcouncil.org/blog/15/06/28/creative-hubkitmade-hubs-emerging-hubs/. Accessed 27 June 2018.

Conventz, S., Derudder, B. Thierstein, A., & Witlox, F. (2016). *Hub cities in the knowledge economy: Seaports, airports, brainports.* London: Routledge.

DCMS. (1998). *Creative industries mapping document.* London: DCMS.

de Peuter, G., & Cohen, N. (2015). Emerging labour politics in creative industries. In K. Oakley & J. O'Connor (Eds.), *The Routledge companion to the cultural industries.* Abingdon: Routledge.

Dovey, J., Pratt, A., Lansdowne, J., Moreton, S., & Merkel, J. Virani, T. (2016). *Creative Hubs: Understanding the new economy.* British Council.

Evans, G. (2009). Creative cities, creative spaces and urban policy. *Urban Studies, 46*(5–6), 1003–1040.

Florida, R. (2002). *The rise of the creative class.* New York: Basic Books.

Gandini, A. (2015). The rise of coworking spaces: A literature review. *Theory and Politics in Organization, 15*(1), 193–205.

Gill, R. (2002). Cool, creative and egalitarian? Exploring gender in project-based new media work in Euro. *Information, Communication & Society, 5*(1), 70–89.

Gill, R. (2014). Unspeakable inequalities: Post feminism, entrepreneurial subjectivity, and the reputation of sexism among cultural workers. *Social Politics: International Studies in Gender, State and Society, 21*(4), 509–528.

Gill, R., & Pratt, A. C. (2008). In the social factory? Immaterial labour, precariousness and cultural work. *Theory, Culture and Society, 25*(7–8), 1–30.

Hesmondhalgh, D., Oakley, K., Lee, D., & Nisbett, M. (2015). *Culture, economy and politics: The case of new labour.* London: Palgrave Macmillan.

HubbleHQ. (2018). *Mindspace.* Available at https://hubblehq.com/office-space/4818/mindspace-shoreditch-1?option=11010. Accessed 23 June 2018.

Lee, D. (2017). *Class, character and inequality: Towards a sociology of failure in creative work.* Paper presented at MeCCSA Annual Conference, January 10, University of Leeds.

Lee, D., Hesmondhalgh, D., Oakley, K., & Nisbett, M. (2014). Regional creative industries policy-making under new labour. *Cultural Trends, 23*(4), 217–231.

McRobbie, A. (2016). *Be creative: Making a living in the new culture industries.* Cambridge: Polity Press.

McRobbie, A. (2002). Clubs to companies: Notes on the decline of political culture in speeded up creative worlds. *Cultural Studies, 16*(4), 516–531.

Mental Health Foundation. (2016). *Fundamental facts about mental health 2016.* London: Mental Health Foundation.

Merkel, J. (2015). Coworking in the city. *Ephemera, 15*(2), 121–139.

Monbiot, G. (2016). Neoliberalism is creating loneliness. That's what's wrenching society apart. *The Guardian.* Available at https://www.theguardian.com/commentisfree/2016/oct/12/neoliberalism-creating-loneliness-wrenching-society-apart. Accessed 28 June 2018.

Naudin, A. (2015). *Cultural entrepreneurship: Identity and personal agency in the cultural worker's experience of entrepreneurship* (Doctoral dissertation). University of Warwick.

Oakley, K. (2004). Not so cool Britannia: The role of creative industries in economic development. *International Journal of Cultural Policy, 7*(1), 67–77.

Peck, J. (2005). Struggling with the creative class. *International Journal of Urban and Regional Research, 29*(4), 740–770.

Prince, R. (2012). Policy transfer, consultants and the geographies of governance. *Progress in Human Geography, 36*(2), 188–203.

Ross, A. (2004). *No-collar: The humane workplace and its hidden costs.* Philadelphia: Temple University Press.

Scharff, C. (2016). The psychic life of neoliberalism: Mapping the contours of entrepreneurial subjectivity. *Theory, Culture & Society, 33*(6), 107–122.

Walkerdine, V. (2011). Neoliberalism, working-class subjects and higher education. *Contemporary Social Science, 6*(2), 255–271.

5

Hubs vs Networks in the Creative Economy: Towards a 'Collaborative Individualism'

Carolina Bandinelli and Alessandro Gandini

Introduction

The function and significance of 'hubs' in the creative economy are still nebulous. As Dovey et al. aptly remark, 'creative hubs tend to mean all things to all people' (2016, p. 7). The British Council defines the creative hub as: 'a physical or virtual place that brings enterprising people together who work in the creative and cultural industries' (British Council 2018). Based on this statement, one may conclude that every space can potentially become a creative hub. Yet, the proliferation of creative hubs seems to be one of the emerging features of so-called creative cities in recent years. Creative hubs

C. Bandinelli (✉)
University of Lincoln, Lincoln, UK
e-mail: cbandinelli@lincoln.ac.uk

A. Gandini
University of Milan, Milan, Italy
e-mail: alessandro.gandini@unimi.it

© The Author(s) 2019
R. Gill et al. (eds.), *Creative Hubs in Question*, Dynamics of Virtual Work,
https://doi.org/10.1007/978-3-030-10653-9_5

are seen as 'playing a major role in the growth of the creative economy' (British Council 2018), and are singled out as being capable of 'regenerating urban and rural areas', 'acting as lighthouses for invisible communities', and providing freelancers and micro SMEs with a 'sense of community' (British Council 2018).

In this chapter, we analyse the role of creative hubs in relation to the practices of networking that are deemed as typical of creative economies. We focus on the specific ways in which creative hubs mobilise communitarian and collaborative values, functioning as 'nests for freelancers and micro SME's to gather, connect and collaborate' (Dovey et al. 2016, p. 2). To do so, we take coworking spaces as a typical example of urban creative hubs. While coworking spaces are not the only kind of urban hubs (see Dovey et al. 2016), they are arguably among the most common and formalised ones: according to the magazine *Deskmag*, by the end of 2017 around 14,000 coworking spaces were operating worldwide (*Deskmag* 2018). Moreover, coworking spaces play a significant role in the relationship between creative spaces and networking practices that we want to analyse. Their foundational claim revolves around the idea of providing independent workers with a space to meet and collaborate (Bandinelli 2017; de Peuter et al. 2017; Gandini 2015). However, this translates into quite different cultures. There are coworking spaces that incite the entrepreneurial nature of creative work, and others that promote solidarity and bottom-up values. Some are large franchise brands operating internationally as a global business, while others are small scale local and independently run endeavours. Yet, the element that is common to both these visions is the prominence of a 'communitarian' ethos, within which the relationship among members (and between members and hosts) is inscribed. This communitarian assumption is largely taken as an unchallenged claim in the literature on coworking spaces in the creative economy. Our analysis aims to unpack and to some extent demystify this assumption.

We contend that in order to criticise this 'communitarian' assumption we must look at the relationship that exists between coworking spaces as creative hubs and the networking practices that have dominated the creative economy for decades (Wittel 2001). We describe this relationship as an 'osmotic' one, meaning one whereby creative hubs cannot exist without creative networks, and vice versa. Within this relationship, we argue coworking spaces emerge as 'heterotopic' spaces that fulfil the need of an extended networking battlefield. As 'heterotopic' spaces, coworking spaces provide workers with a space for the practising, learning and performing of the 'network sociality' (de Peuter et al. 2017), and inscribe these activities into an inside/outside dimension, whereby social commitment and entrepreneurial attitude work together as catalysers for the promotion of social and professional collaboration within and beyond the shared space.

However, this is ultimately an 'idealised' space, as coworking spaces ultimately serve individual rather than common or shared goals. This means that, irrespective of their spatial features as creative hubs, the primary function of coworking spaces is to offer a symbolic milieu whereby the values of community and collaboration are translated into a productive ethos that aligns with the transactional form of interaction required in the creative economy. We observe this as a specific mode of action that we deem peculiar to creative workers, and that we call 'collaborative individualism'. This term identifies a defined professional disposition by creative workers that builds upon the practices of 'network sociality' (Wittel 2001) but with the addition of an imaginary communitarian element. This is an element that creative hubs promote in their ideological self-description and self-enclosed nature to foster a socialising experience that actually fulfils individual needs and ambitions.

The reflections offered here build upon ethnographic research conducted separately by the authors in the UK and Italy on the forms of sociality in the knowledge and creative economy over the period 2011–2014. A first research was concerned with social entrepreneurs, focusing on their understanding of sociality, ethics and politics. It draws on a year and half ethnographic fieldwork in Impact Hub Westminster (London) and Impact Hub Milan, in which a qualitative mixed methodology was deployed. This comprised of in-depth interviews, participant observation, and action research (see Bandinelli 2017). A second research questioned the role of reputation, trust and social capital across networks of freelance workers in

London and Milan and is constituted of 80 interviews to creative professionals such as illustrators, communication designers, audiovisual producers and other similar figures, at different stages in their career (see Gandini 2016a, b).

In both cases, the accounts here provided should be seen as *ex post* reflections on the researches rather than a presentation of primary research findings. The aim of this paper is to build a conceptual bridge between the notions of creative hubs and networks—currently implicit in the existing literature—to show their complementary and inextricably intertwined nature in the current creative economy. By juxtaposing our researches, we aim to illustrate that creative hubs provide creative networks with a heterotopic spatialisation that allows individuals to engage 'network sociality', working both as a physical and a symbolic space for the nurturing of social relations. In so doing, we set the foundations for the theorisation of the concept of 'collaborative individualism', which we believe is able to grasp the changing nature of the individual dispositions and ethos of knowledge and creative workers towards their work.

The chapter is structured as follows: firstly, we provide a brief genealogical overview of the forms of network sociality that characterised the professional life of independent creative workers in the last decades and we discuss the emergence of coworking spaces as creative hubs that provide space for professional networking. Secondly, we look more closely into Impact Hub London as a case study of a heterotopic hub and argue that the spatialisation offered by coworking spaces is not only material, but mostly symbolic: it is a heterotopic space that provides networks with a world vision that on its turn function as a common narrative framework. Subsequently, we question the broader significance of the proliferation of coworking spaces as heterotopic creative hubs and put forward the idea that their distinctive feature is ultimately the enactment of a form of 'collaborative individualism', which we discuss in the conclusive section of the chapter.

Not for the Shy: Networking in the Creative Industries

Encapsulated in the adage 'it's all about who you know', an extensive interdisciplinary literature across sociology, cultural geography, cultural studies, urban studies and critical media research has analysed the role of personal contacts and social networks in the knowledge and creative economy, highlighting the relevance of practices of networking for professional affirmation (e.g. Blair 2001; McKinlay and Smith 2009; Gregg 2011; Hesmondhalgh and Baker 2013; Gandini 2016a, b). This body of work, which is wide in nature and focus, evidences two interrelated elements: namely, the individualisation of workers and the commodification of social relationships, which led to the socialisation of production that was described as a 'social factory' (Gill and Pratt 2008).

The reification of networking in the creative economy is a central aspect in the discourse around the rise of a 'creative class' (Florida 2002) of knowledge workers, which became mainstream in the early 2000s by ideologically promoting the entrepreneurialisation of the white-collar workforce through a mode of production based on the cult(ure) of creativity. As the 'creative class' vision became mainstream, networking soon came to be advocated as the driving force of job seeking practices in this 'new' economy, its relevance intensified by the individualisation and precarisation of work (McRobbie 2016; Gandini 2016b; Ross 2008). Within this context, whereby an entrepreneurial mode of working is taken as a baseline for the construction of a creative career (McRobbie 2002), research has showed that the nurturing of social relations absolves key functions with regard to knowledge transfer, reputation building, the learning of behavioural codes and the consolidation of interpersonal trust in the urban creative 'scene'. A creative worker has thus to be embedded in this 'magma' of relations, and hence cultivate these relations as a central part of their work (D'Ovidio and Gandini, in press).

To be sure, a certain form of sociality has always constituted an aspect of workers' life: after all, the office space of white-collar workers in the 1950s had its own social structures and socialising practices (Wright Mills 1951). Yet, the neoliberal redefinition of work as a means of self-actualisation—of which the creative economy is a paradigmatic example—has implied that the way in which the self gets actualised in social interactions becomes a fundamental part of one's work. It is in this context that the nurturing of social relationships has become fundamental practice for professional affirmation, for these emerge as what enables individuals to advance in their careers by establishing partnerships, identifying potential clients, collaborators or investors. If individuals become their own microstructure, their relationships with each other are what makes up the structure, which at a macro-level takes the shape of a network.

This 'invisible' labouring of relations, whereby sociality is no longer just an externality, a 'desirable' part or an effect, rather a substantial aspect of one's work, is framed in the notion of a 'network sociality' (Wittel 2001). Andreas Wittel coined the term 'network sociality' (2001) to refer to the social practices that are instrumental to the advancement of one's career and has stressed their ephemeral, informational and commodified character. On a similar note, Melissa Gregg has noticed that the rise of social media has made this practice more diffused, widespread and mandatory, heavily reliant on the marketisation of intimacy for professional purposes (Gregg 2011). What is at stake, in other words, is not only engagement in polite informal interactions among workers in a same field, but the creation of what is supposed to involve, at least discursively, a form of friendship. For this reason, Gregg claims, '…in neoliberal societies "friendship" is labour in the sense that it involves constant attention and cultivation, the rewards of which include improved standing and greater opportunity' (Gregg 2007, p. 5).

This contributed to the sedimentation of an understanding of the self as a form of capital, and of financial autonomy as an existential as well as professional objective. This reinterpretation of the self in economic terms is reflected in the practices and discourses of self-branding, where one's brand serves as a device for the management and communication of one's identity and value in the job market. To brand oneself as an individual capable of producing certain economic and cultural outcome is a necessary, if not sufficient, condition to attract enough social as well as financial capital (Hearn 2008; Marwick 2013; Bandinelli and Arvidsson 2013; Gandini 2016a; Arvidsson et al. 2016). At the same time, the failure to own, promote and sell one's identity can cause one's marginalisation because to fall 'out of the loop' can be fatal. This has exposed certain categories of workers, for instance women with children, carers, disabled people, those living outside of so-called creative cities, or even just the shy, to the constant risk of being excluded from the job market (Conor et al. 2015; McRobbie 2002). The digital domain has further propelled this dynamic; Duffy (2016), for instance, has described the work of fashion bloggers, beauty bloggers and designers as a form of aspirational labour that involves the enactment of a gendered entrepreneurial personality. These dynamics have been more broadly described as a reputation-based economy (Gandini 2016b), a notion that identifies the managerial and transactional nature of the forms of socialisation that characterise networking in creative contexts.

This evolution marked the emergence of an increasingly casualised and placeless job market in which workers have to take full responsibility of their work and individually bear the risk of their independent careers (McRobbie 2002, 2016; Ross 2004, 2008; Neff 2012). This also ties to the affirmation of digital technologies and social media, which brought along the (at least technical) possibility of performing work anywhere, anytime, in presence of an Internet connection (Johns and Gratton 2013) and resulted in a displacement of creative workers from the physical workplace, thus intensifying the necessity of practising and performing such forms of 'network sociality' (Wittel 2001) across various contexts and occasions, so that workers could be able to develop the necessary social capital needed to survive in this scene (Marwick 2013; Arvidsson et al. 2016). In the next section, we look further into how the practices of networking that characterise this context blend with coworking practices.

From Networking to Coworking

A textbook example of networking is offered by freelance workers active in the blurred territory of creative and tech economies. Freelancers in fact often describe their socialisation practices as a peculiar form of business-driven interaction. Paul, for instance, a London-based freelance business writer in his 40s, recounts that:

> Working as a freelancer requires good relationship skills. You have to know how to start and manage business relationships with people who you may not know very well, if at all. In some cases you might not even meet them face to face, having contact over the phone, via email or online collaboration tools. Being a journalist was good preparation – I had a good range of contacts and loads of experience with just ringing people up and asking them questions!

Others, however, usually involved in more creative and artistic-oriented endeavours, describe this kind of collaboration in more idealistic terms, referring to the idea of establishing relationship with like-minded individuals as a form of communitarian exchange around friendship akin to the dynamics described by Gregg (2007, 2011). Maria, a London-based designer in her early 30s, explains:

> At school you learn a business language, which gives a certain confidence, but the reality of things is that to you have to develop a network, to create relationships that are personal, business but personal, so you need to start talking to people, you need to get along with people and to work with people you like, and to create these things is not easy. Let's take networking events for instance: how one can create this quickly meeting 20 people in a room in an afternoon? Yeah you could do it, but a meaningful outcome resulting of meeting those people is really low. You have to talk to them again, invite them for coffee… it's about creating relationships, so it takes time.

Within such context, over the years a growing number of workers have found themselves seeking a space to engage in this kind of relational work. Somewhat as a response to this sense of displacement, and in coincidence with the growth of 'cool' innovation scenes of tech and creative workers, often low paid or unpaid, described with enthusiasm as an emergent 'flat white economy' (McWiliams 2016), a movement around shared workspaces emerged. This was born with the aim of restoring the physical sense of working that nomad, Starbucks-based creatives in search of Wi-fi were increasingly missing (Gandini 2016a; O'Brien 2011). This movement came to be broadly known as 'coworking'.

> The concept is simple: professionals from different working areas, independent workers, nomad workers and entrepreneurs find themselves in the same physical space to work on their own projects. They don't only seek to break with their isolation and to find an alternative solution to their home office or to the company office they are used to work from; But also to belong to a community of individuals who are open to exchange ideas, and eventually, who are ready to collaborate. (Coworking Europe 2016)

Born out of the tech scene in the mid-2000s in the urban environments of creative cities, coworking is a self-described 'movement' rooted in the vision that the sharing of a workspace represents the new way of working and a model of communitarian work relations that can be replicated across cities and countries (Johns and Gratton 2013). Rapidly, coworking spaces popped up all over the world (Moriset 2014) to enable the gathering of knowledge workers, mostly freelancers, for a variety of professional scopes and purposes. These include the restoration of a physical separation between home and work but also the nurturing of networking: physical, due to the sharing of a space, as well as digital, since coworking spaces provide workers with a reliable and unlimited Wi-fi connection (O'Brien 2011). Early theorisations of coworking spaces have described these as 'third places' (Oldenburg 1989), intended as 'places out of the home and office where people socialise in a free, informal manner' (Moriset 2014, p. 6). However, despite the intuitive analogy between coworking and traditional third places, such as cafes or libraries (O'Brien 2011), more recent research shows that coworking spaces and hubs actually represent the main place of work for a growing number of workers, representing both a meaningful alternative to homeworking as well as a favourable setting for the acquisition of social capital and reputation by workers (Colleoni and Arvidsson 2014; Gandini 2016a, b; Gregg and Lodato 2018).

As described in the introduction to this chapter, there are different kinds of coworking spaces, from large-scale, worldwide franchises to small, independently run spaces, all variously promoting a set of cultural values at work and a professional ethos largely based around an overarching idea of community and collaboration. Mostly, however, coworking spaces respond to the need to avoid isolation and to engage in networking. Ursula, a brand consultant in her late 20s in London, tells how she and her business associate had '*been working from home for some time, but we hated it. It's boring, and you end up working from 8 am to 3 in the morning*'. Joining a space was a big improvement for them, she claims, since this has given them the chance to restore a more traditional work schedule and meet a lot of new people since the place they chose '*is full of startups of any kind*'. Yet, she complains that their participation in the space has not provided them with professional opportunities as expected, as these mostly originate from '*friends, in general… they may not be friends but they come from friends of friends… previous jobs and friends*'.

It may be argued that the appearance of coworking spaces in this scene has been able to partially fulfil the 'missing middle' that Grugulis and Stoyanova (2011) identified in the development of skills among workers in a freelance-based labour market. With this expression, they highlight the gap in soft skills and skills development between those workers who are novices to a creative scene and more experienced professionals in the same context. Coworking spaces reconcile this gap, at the very least in the form of a symbolic space that offers the promise of a 'community of practice', whose main feature is that of 'bringing the social back into the workplace' (Hillman, quoted in Clark 2007). This suggests that hubs and shared spaces do not merely provide a space for the unfolding of network sociality, but also a space for socialisation that complements network dynamics with symbolic ones. Coworking spaces and hubs offer disconnected workers a secluded haven for their coming together in a dedicated environment where the nurturing of a notion of 'community'—one that is 'idealised' as a symbolic entity as much as it is defined by practices of socialisation—is as important as the socialisation practices that take place within it. Drawing on Foucault (1986), we define this kind of space as 'heterotopic'.

Creative Hubs as Heterotopic Spaces

Based on the empirical data collected during our research, we propose to think of coworking spaces as 'heterotopic' spaces that provide the facilities for the performance of the network sociality of creative workers and to articulate this performance through an inside/outside symbolic dimension. This means to understand coworking spaces as spaces where a specific world vision is articulated, a vision that is different from the one 'outside' and that as such provides the space itself with a symbolic distinction. At a first level, a heterotopic space is an existing, physical space in which the relations between the elements of the 'outside' space and time are reversed, distorted, or even altered. Therefore, it functions as spatio-temporal systems of relationships that depict and enact a somewhat different picture of the world. Yet, at the same time, it is a space that may enable its participants to construct and display their alterity outside of it. Heterotopia can thus be defined only in relation to the other spaces and times it reframes, reverts, distorts, transforms (Foucault 1986). A heterotopic space is an ethically burdened environment that attempts to produce an improved version of the outside world and 'to create a space that is other, another real space, as perfect, as meticulous, as well arranged as ours is messy, ill constructed, and jumbled' (Foucault 1986, p. 27). Importantly, when we suggest thinking of coworking spaces as heterotopic we do not point at an ontological feature, something that is part of a supposedly 'essential' core of the space as such. Rather, we intend to indicate that the heterotopic character of the space is constantly managed, produced and reproduced, both by its hosts and its members.

To substantiate this claim, we focus on one specific example: Impact Hub. Impact Hub is a social franchise of coworking spaces addressed to a category of workers often branded as 'impact makers', or otherwise defined as 'social entrepreneurs' or 'social innovators'. This comprises mostly of upper-middle-class, well-educated knowledge workers from a variety of backgrounds, who are engaged in entrepreneurial and creative projects aimed at having a positive impact on society at large (see Bandinelli 2017). The first Impact Hub was opened in 2005 by

Jonathan Robinson, Etty Flanagan, and Mark Hodge, in a warehouse in the London borough of Islington, with the name 'Hub' (the current name 'Impact Hub' is the result of a major rebranding undertaken in 2013). At the moment of writing, there are 92 Impact Hubs across the world, and 8 in the making, for a totality of over 16,000 members (Impact Hub 2018). The business plan of Impact Hub was inspired by that of mobile phone subscription plans and is based on membership: people pay a monthly fee to get access to the space and its resources. The fees may vary: at the moment of writing the cost of memberships at Impact Hub Islington ranges from £59 to £420 (Impact Hub Islington 2019).

The production of Impact Hub as a heterotopic space in the terms here described is evident from the narrative about its foundation. According to Robinson (Impact Hub co-founder), Impact Hub was created to give people with 'ideas for making the world a better place' a space where to 'connect' (Robinson, quoted in Bachmann 2014). Robinson points out emphatically:

> Everyone has ideas for making the world a better place… but where does one go to make them happen? …. What if these people could come together in the same physical space and have a place to connect? (Robinson, quoted in Bachmann 2014, np)

Robinson's statement highlights the importance ascribed to the presence of a 'physical space', as a way to (re)connect individuals. This reasoning is founded on the belief that by connecting people they could be enabled to realise their 'ideas', turning them into impactful projects. Impact Hub emerges as a place that makes possible what would have been impossible otherwise: it is a place where one goes to make ideas happen. It is to this extent that it is narrated as heterotopic. Indeed, it can be noticed that in this narrative Impact Hub acquires an almost alchemical character, an entity which is able to transform eidetic isolated contents in concrete projects with a global impact.

Liene Perkone, who works as an accountant for London's Impact Hub, tells the same foundational story, which assumes the traits of a myth of origin:

The four founders of the Hub came together and started thinking they are these young change makers and want to change the world and make it better... and then they thought many of these people are actually working from their bedrooms, from their homes or Starbucks cafes ... so they decided they could maybe create a space where all this people could come together, they could encourage each other, collaborate, come up with new ideas, also exchange experiences and knowledge, and actually change the world. (Perkone 2012, min 00:09)

This foundational myth is instrumental to the constitution of Impact Hub as providing people a shared space that works as an enabler and a catalyser for world-changing entrepreneurial activities. The provision of a space that can re-territorialise and re-spatialise the sociality of networks, is conceived of as conducive to the formation of relationships that are 'meaningful' insofar as they can have an impact, or even 'change the world'. In this regard, Impact Hub does not only provide independent workers with a physical space; hence, it is not to be understood solely as a spatialisation and materialisation of the fragmented and diffused sociality of networks. Rather, it has to be thought of also as a space that offers a symbolic characterisation to the sociality of networks. To put it in Robinson's words, it is meant to offer a space where 'to be proactive, optimistic and pragmatic, rather than merely critics in respect of the current state of affairs'. As it can be noticed, Impact hub is discursively constructed as heterotopic in so far as it is described as what can enable a peculiar kind of disposition and conduct, i.e. being 'proactive, optimistic and pragmatic'. A disposition and conduct that is narrated as radically different from the ordinary one supposedly pertaining to the 'outside' of Impact Hub, i.e. being 'merely critic'.

Impact Hub is designed as a space that 'brings the social back to the workplace' not only because it strengthens and supports networking practices, but also because it provides it with a particular narrative, one that depicts a better and possible world. At stake, there is a symbolic endeavour that aims at providing a physical space with a strong ethical connotation. This emerges with clarity in the words of Vera, an economics graduate in her 30s who, at the time of fieldwork, held a managerial role at Impact Hub Milan. During an interview, she claimed proudly that Impact Hub's goal is 'to replicate the outside world with our value-filter'. This statement is indicative of the importance ascribed to the ethical connotation of Impact Hub. The 'space' it offers is not merely physical (or digital, for that matter), but mostly a heterotopic one. At stake, there is a reproduction of the outside world, but 'filtered' by some specific values. The 'outside' is thus transformed and resignified in the light of certain beliefs and ideals. It is this resignification that provides 'hubbers' with a shared narrative and sense of belonging; which is to say, it is this resignification that constitutes the main function of Impact Hub.

Put differently, Impact Hub emerges as a heterotopic space because it reproduces an improved and perfected version of the world, creating a physical approximation of a utopia: it makes what is supposedly 'impossible' in the outside world—that is, 'changing the world'—suddenly perceived as possible. To an outside society marked by isolation, precarity and individualism, Impact Hub claims to substitute a 'better word' which 'evolves through the combined accomplishments of creative, committed, and compassionate individuals focused on a common purpose' (Impact Hub 2018). In this respect, the heterotopic nature of Impact Hub points at a particular ethos that is allegedly needed to fulfil the utopian injunction of 'changing the world'. This brings us back to networking. In the heterotopic space, networking and socialisation represent a mode of (discursive) production that serves the construction of a shared narrative ('community') upon which to base an eminently individual, productive disposition that we call 'collaborative individualism'.

Exploring 'Collaborative Individualism'

Arguably, one of the main functions of creative hubs (and their main value proposition) has been to provide workers with a trustworthy environment that may give them that sense of shared purpose and social recognition which they were deprived of by decades of precarisation and entrepreneurial ideology (Gandini 2016a, b). Yet, the workers who populate Impact Hub, and other similar spaces, live this 'communitarian utopia' in a yet very much self-oriented productive disposition. At stake, there is an ambivalent ethos: on the one hand it points at collaboration, while on the other it retains a prominent concern over self-interest. We propose to understand this ethos through the notion of 'collaborative individualism'. What follows is not a final argumentation, but rather an exploratory reflection with which we wish to provoke further research. In other words, with the notion of 'collaborative individualism' we do not want to offer a ready-made definition to be applied to a set of definite phenomena, but rather a thinking tool for future analyses.

Collaborative individualism identifies the entanglement of collaborative discourses and practices with the pursuit of individual professional success. It aims at capturing the stark oxymoron between individualistic behaviour in the creative class and the ideology of collaboration and socialisation that pervades it. We deem this concept grasps well the innate ambivalence (Stark 2009) that characterises the ideology of entrepreneurialism in the creative economy: i.e. the blending of an emphasis on socialisation with a selfish business mentality, the necessity of intimacy with the ephemerality of social relations that, in such context, are so volatile precisely because of their instrumental role.

Collaboration is a keyword in the coworking scene insofar as it chiefly indicates an ethos for which cooperation is favoured over competition. To give an example, the 2016 'coworking manifesto' opens up with the following sentence: '*We have the talent. We just need to work together*'. All value propositions listed in the manifesto point at this sense of 'togetherness', a few examples are: '*collaboration over competition; community over agendas; participation over observation; doing over saying; friendship over formality; boldness over assurance; learning over expertise; people over personalities; value ecosystem over value chain*' (Coworking Manifesto 2016).

Consistently, Impact Hub's tagline reads: 'We are a network of collaborators focused on making a positive impact in our world' (Impact Hub 2018), thus pointing at how the collaborative element is what enables the 'network' to impact on society at large. Indeed, what takes place at Impact Hub is the production of discourses and practices on collaboration, which are reproduced in a series of formalised activities. These include business clinics, 'skills-sharing' sessions, and so-called Sexy Salads. 'Business clinics' are aimed at improving one's business via workshops sessions that are offered free of charges by Hubbers; 'skills-sharing sessions' take various forms but they all refer to a conceptual core that constructs knowledge as something to be shared in a peer-to-peer way—for instance, at Impact Hub Westminster there is a running project called 'Academy at the Hub' which involves weekly classes on topics related to entrepreneurship. 'Sexy Salads' are a weekly lunch event in which everyone is encouraged to bring an ingredient to collaborate to the realisation of a salad. Each of these activities, along with everyday mundane practices such as using the same kitchenette or sharing suggestions for where to buy responsibly produced food, can be thought of as a material and discursive dispositive that produce the shared symbolic value of collaboration as well as the cultural imaginary behind this notion (Bandinelli 2017).

Yet, what strikes in this context is that workers describe this collaborative disposition by emphasising the somewhat ideological overlap between socialisation and individual targets. Collaboration, in other words, appears to be pursued by workers insofar as it benefits individual aims. To this extent, it seems to be disjoined from any substantial idea of collectivity; it is rather seen as a symbolic and material device that serves career advancement. The motivations that lead people to join a coworking space such as Impact Hub are by and large related to the need to catch careers opportunities. See for instance how Anita, a 31-year-old designer from the North of Italy, accounts for her choice to join Impact Hub:

> Being a hubber is like building a career… you are in an informal environment so they can really see who you are and which skills you have… Basically, you become friends, and then you may find a job, you know? Like, there was this guy working on a project and they needed a graphic designer, so he asked me, as we were already friends, and we knew we were sharing the same values. This is how I got my first job!

This excerpt is indicative of the strategic nature of the social practices that characterise hubs, in which 'friendship' becomes instrumental. This is something that independent workers seem to be well aware of. Nikki, a 30-year-old freelance event manager in London, recounts this in a quite peculiar way:

If you are someone who sits at home, doesn't go to networking events, doesn't go to opening exhibitions, I mean…everybody has its own networks and there can either be good things, and encouraging, or negative, and people just want to keep you there for themselves, for whatever reason. (…) You have to sniff the bullshitters, that is how I built up my network.

Put differently, collaboration at Impact Hub has 'an identitary value, being a means to the end of branding oneself that reputational logics propel' (Bandinelli and Arvidsson 2013). It could be argued that collaboration is what enables individuals to feel part of an imaginary, affective community: 'Surely, once you get into the Hub, you feel like in a family' claims Giulio, Impact Hub Florence co-founder. Consistently, at Impact Hub Westminster, the signifier 'community' is distributed throughout the space: a sign giving instructions on how to use the kitchen facilities reads 'Welcome to the Community Kitchen!', and concludes by reminding hubbers that 'Together we Make Community'. A glass house used for meetings is decorated with big capital letters claiming 'This is Community'.

While the notion of community is by and large a fictional one in a coworking space (Gandini 2016a; Lange 2011), it arguably provides members with a sense of belonging: the recurrent motivation to join Impact Hub is that of finding 'like-minded people'. In turn, 'finding like-minded people' is part of the 'work' of independent workers. What we are confronted with is the close intertwining of two orders of worth: on the one hand, collaboration and sharing; on the other hand, self-actualisation, and individual career advancement. This is evident in the words of Impact Hub co-founder Robinson, who states that Impact Hub was born out of frustration at the lack of a middle ground between corporate and charity career paths (Bachmann 2014).

The symbolic articulation of such 'middle ground' is to be understood as the synthetic combination of signifiers that are normally contradictory, or at least distant. This is the conceptual core of Impact Hub's heterotopic character, which is to be identified in its capability of 'juxtaposing in a single real place several spaces, several sites that are in themselves incompatible' (Foucault 1986, p. 25).

Impact Hub defines itself as a space for solidarity and collective action, but also for individual excellence and profit; it combines social commitment and entrepreneurial attitude. It is through this combination of otherwise incompatible elements that Impact hub creates a 'perfect' space, wherein one can be individualist and yet collaborate, where individualism and collaboration are no more antithetical but rather complementary insofar as they articulate, symbolically, a perfect synthesis.

Conclusion

In this chapter, through an *ex-post* reflection on empirical research on freelancers and Impact Hub members in London and Italy, which we have used as case studies, we have evidenced the osmotic relationship that exists between creative hubs and networks. Their existence is reciprocally necessary in the context of the creative economy, insofar as these complement each other in the fulfilment of those practices of socialising that knowledge workers, and particularly creatives, need to undertake in order to carry on their professional life. Thus, we have proposed to interpret coworking spaces such as Impact Hub, taken as the main example of creative hub in this context, as heterotopic spaces that confer the sociality of networks not just a space, but a narrative framework—centred around an imaginary notion of 'community'—that allows its production and reproduction within and beyond the spatial boundaries of the shared hub.

In turn, the identification of this narrative framework has led us to observe how it serves to elicit a specific productive disposition or ethos, which can be learned and performed within and outside the space. We call this productive disposition 'collaborative individualism' and argue that it represents an ambivalence in this context, insofar as it aims to keep together the 'social' dispositions of collaboration and community (albeit often largely symbolic) that characterise sociality within these spaces, with the self-oriented activity many of the participants engage in. Considering 'network sociality' as the defining mode of production of the creative economy, it may be argued that shared environments such as coworking spaces become arenas for practising, learning and performing this disposition. The acknowledgement of this ambivalence, we contend, seems useful to further the critique to the evolving realm of creative work in the fast-changing scenario of the post-recession economy.

References

Arvidsson, A., Gandini, A., & Bandinelli, C. (2016). Self-branding among freelance knowledge workers. In M. Crain, W. Poster, & M. Cherry (Eds.), *Invisible labor* (pp. 239–256). Oakland: University of California Press.

Bachmann, M. (2014). How the hub found its centre [Online]. *Stanford Social Innovation Review*. http://ssir.org/articles/entry/how_the_hub_found_its_center. Accessed 27 August 2017.

Bandinelli, C. (2017). *Social entrepreneurship: Sociality, ethics and politics* (Unpublished Ph.D. dissertation). Goldsmiths College, University of London.

Bandinelli, C., & Arvidsson, A. (2013). Brand yourself a changemaker! *Journal of Macromarketing, 33*(1), 67–71.

Blair, H. (2001). "You're only as good as your last job": The labour process and labour market in the British film industry. *Work, Employment and Society, 15*(1), 149–169.

British Council. (2018). *Creative hubs.* Creative Economy. https://creativeconomy.britishcouncil.org/projects/hubs/. Accessed 20 February 2018.

Clark, J. (2007). Coworkers of the world unite. *The American Prospect.* http://prospect.org/article/coworkers-world-unite. Accessed 24 February 2018.

Colleoni, E., & Arvidsson, A. (2014). Knowledge sharing and social capital building. The role of co-working spaces in the knowledge economy in Milan. Office for Youth, Municipality of Milan.

Conor, B., Gill, R., & Taylor, S. (2015). Gender and creative labour. *The Sociological Review, 63*, 1–22.

Coworking Europe. (2016). *About coworking Europe.* http://coworkingeurope.net/about-coworking-europe-conference/. Accessed 7 September 2016.

Coworking Manifesto. (2016). Available at http://wiki.coworking.org/w/page/35382594/Coworking%20Manifesto%20%28global%20-%20for%20the%20world%29. Accessed 7 January 2019.

D'Ovidio, M., & Gandini, A. (in press). The functions of social interaction in the knowledge-creative economy: Between co-presence and ICT-mediated social relations. *Sociologica*, forthcoming.

de Peuter, G., Cohen, N. S., & Saraco, F. (2017). The ambivalence of coworking: On the politics of an emerging work practice. *European Journal of Cultural Studies, 20*(6), 687–706.

Deskmag. (2018). The 2018 Coworking Survey. Available at http://www.deskmag.com/en/background-of-the-2018-global-coworking-survey-market-research. Accessed 7 January 2019.

Dovey, J., Lansdowne, J., Moreton, S., Merkel, J. Pratt, A. C., & Virani, T. E. (2016). *Creative hubs: Understanding the new economy.* Retrieved from London. https://creativeconomy.britishcouncil.org/media/uploads/files/HubsReport.pdf.

Duffy, B. E. (2016). The romance of work: Gender and aspirational labour in the digital culture industries. *International Journal of Cultural Studies, 19*(4), 441–457.

Florida, R. (2002). *The rise of the creative class.* New York: Basic Books.

Foucault, M. (1986 [1967]). Of other spaces. *Diacritics, 16,* 22–27.

Gandini, A. (2015). The rise of coworking spaces: A literature review. *Ephemera, 15*(1), 193–205.

Gandini, A. (2016a). Digital work: Self-branding and social capital in the freelance knowledge economy. *Marketing Theory, 16*(1), 123–141.

Gandini, A. (2016b). *The reputation economy: Understanding knowledge work in digital society.* Basingstoke: Palgrave Macmillan.

Gill, R. C., & Pratt, A. C. (2008). In the social factory? Immaterial labour, precariousness and cultural work. *Theory, Culture and Society, 25*(1), 1–30.

Gregg, M. (2007). Thanks for the ad(d): Neoliberalism's compulsory friendship. *Online Opinion, 21.* Available at https://lucian.uchicago.edu/blogs/politicalfeeling/files/2007/09/thanks4adddraft.pdf. Accessed 7 January 2019.

Gregg, M. (2011). *Work's intimacy.* New York: Wiley.

Gregg, M., & Lodato, T. (2018). Managing community: Coworking, hospitality and the future of work. In B. Rottger Rossler & J. Slaby (Eds.), *Affect in Relation* (pp. 175–196). London: Routledge.

Grugulis, I., & Stoyanova, D. (2011). The missing middle: Communities of practice in a freelance labour market. *Work, Employment and Society, 25*(2), 342–351.

Hearn, A. (2008). Meat, Mask, Burden: Probing the contours of the branded-self. *Journal of Consumer Culture, 8*(2), 197–217.

Hesmondhalgh, D., & Baker, S. (2013). *Creative labour: Media work in three cultural industries*. London: Routledge.

Impact Hub. (2018). *Impact Hub Network*. Available at http://www. impacthub.net/. Accessed 7 January 2019.

Impact Hub Islington. (2019). *Impact Hub Islington*. Available at https://islington.impacthub.net/membership/. Accessed 8 January 2019.

Johns, T., & Gratton, L. (2013, January–February). The third wave of virtual work. *Harvard Business Review*, 1–9.

Lange, B. (2011). Re-scaling governance in Berlin's creative economy. *Culture Unbound, 3*, 187–208.

Marwick, A. E. (2013). *Status update: Celebrity, publicity, and branding in the social media age*. New Haven: Yale University Press.

McKinlay, A., & Smith, C. (Eds.). (2009). *Creative labour: Working in the creative industries*. Basingstoke: Palgrave Macmillan.

McRobbie, A. (2002). Clubs to companies: Notes on the decline of political culture in speeded up creative worlds. *Cultural Studies, 16*(4), 516–531.

McRobbie, A. (2016). *Be creative: Making a living in the new culture industries*. New York: Wiley.

McWilliams, D. (2016). *The flat white economy*. London: Duckworth.

Moriset, B. (2014). Building new places of the creative economy. The rise of coworking spaces. In *Proceedings of the 2nd Geography of Innovation, International Conference 2014*. Utrecht, The Netherlands: Utrecht University.

Neff, G. (2012). *Venture labor: Work and the burden of risk in innovative industries*. Cambridge: MIT Press.

O'Brien, M. (2011). *Finding a home for the "digital nomad"*. http://www. michelleobrien.net/wp-content/uploads/2011/10/OBRIEN_Home_digital_nomad.pdf. Accessed 7 September 2016.

Oldenburg, R. (1989). *The great good place: Café, coffee shops, community centers, beauty parlors, general stores, bars, hangouts, and how they get you through the day*. Saint Paul, MN: Paragon House Publishers.

Perkone, L. (2012). *The Hub: Success Stories* [Online]. Available at https:// www.youtube.com/watch?v=dZ0S2BtWocs. Accessed 25 September 2016.

Ross, A. (2004). *No-collar: The humane workplace and its hidden costs*. Philadelphia: Temple University Press.

Ross, A. (2008). The new geography of work: Power to the precarious? *Theory, Culture & Society, 25*(7–8), 31–49.

Stark, D. (2009). *The sense of dissonance: Accounts of worth in economic life*. Princeton: Princeton University Press.

Wittel, A. (2001). Toward a network sociality. *Theory, Culture & Society, 18*(6), 51–76.

Wright Mills, C. (1951). *White collar: The American middle classes.* Oxford University Press: Oxford.

6

Community-Led Coworking Spaces: From Co-location to Collaboration and Collectivization

Vasilis Avdikos and Eirini Iliopoulou

Introduction

Third places and creative hubs (Virani and Malem 2015; Dovey et al. 2016) such as coworking spaces, business incubators and fablabs represent new forms of collaborative working practices that have emerged along with the rise of the creative economy and the sharing economy paradigms. Workers in third places share office space, technology, information, and also they can socialize, form social bonds and professional relationships, as coworking spaces facilitate encounters and interaction through the spatial proximity of the co-workers.

V. Avdikos (✉)
Department of Economic and Regional Development,
Panteion University, Athens, Greece

E. Iliopoulou
Regional Development Institute, Panteion University, Athens, Greece

© The Author(s) 2019
R. Gill et al. (eds.), *Creative Hubs in Question*, Dynamics of Virtual Work,
https://doi.org/10.1007/978-3-030-10653-9_6

111

Although there is a growing literature on the characteristics of coworking spaces and their importance upon several social and economic matters (Sundsted et al. 2009; DeGuzman and Tang 2011; Merkel 2015; Capdevila 2015; Spinuzzi 2012; Gandini 2015; Kong 2009, 2011; Avdikos and Kalogeresis 2017), there are still many gaps in the literature that have not been covered yet. One of these gaps has to do with the parallel emergence of an informal and more community-driven type of coworking space that will be termed 'community-led coworking space' (hereafter CLCS) in this paper. Contra to the typical entrepreneurial-led coworking spaces (hereafter ELCS) that represent enterprises that let individualized workspaces in creative professionals, the community-led ones are usually not-for-profit ventures that accommodate (in semi-permanent terms) a small number of creatives with a kind of social and even political proximity between them. Most of the studies that analyse features of coworking spaces over the last few years seem to refer to the ELCS type and very few studies highlight the characteristics of the community-led coworking spaces. This paper provides a framework to demarcate CLCS from ELCS and analyses some basic features of this demarcation.

If the ELCS are more entrepreneurial-driven and firm-centred and, as Gandini (2015) and Moriset (2014) stress, they could eventually lead to the creation of a 'creative class bubble', reinforcing neoliberal mechanisms of individual survival, the community-led ones, which are more grass roots and less managerial could pave the way for a kind of mutual survival through practices of collaboration that could sometimes extend to the collectivization of the creative work.

Therefore, the paper asks some basic research questions in order to unpack and understand some basic features of the CLCS and form an initial conceptual framework in three parts. The first part discusses the phenomenon of third places, its basic characteristics and introduces in broad terms the concept of the CLCS. The second part analyses the reasons that drive workers, and especially young freelancers, to choose this type of coworking. The third section analyses the organization matters of the CLCS of our sample and the internal relationships between the co-workers, in order to unpack the range of these relationships.

The Third Places Phenomenon and the Rise of Atypical Coworking Spaces

During the last decade, thousands of coworking spaces have appeared mainly in the USA, Europe and Southeast Asia; said spaces support freelancers, new creators who are just starting their professional life or micro-enterprises and start-ups, especially in the field of creative economy.

Apart from the fact that third places seem to help freelancers and self-employed to lower their professional-personal risks and the precarious working conditions that creative labour entails (Kong 2011), the development of professional relationships among them can lead to 'serendipity production' (Moriset 2013). This means that the random acquaintance of two or more professionals in such a space can lead to the birth of an idea that can later become a new service or product. Consequently, third places and the geographical proximity they offer to co-workers can facilitate the exchange of knowledge and encourage interactive learning by boosting other forms of proximity, such as cognitive and social proximity (Boschma 2005; Parrino 2015). The result is the development of 'coworking spirit', which is crucial for 'serendipity production', as well as for trust to be built among third places' professionals. We could argue that coworking spirit consists of positive externalities that arise from encounters in coworking spaces through interaction and the share of information, skills, equipment, etc. between the co-workers. Paraphrasing Marshall (1920 [2009]) there is something in the air in these collaborative spaces that stems from the proximity of co-workers and the relations that are developed between them.

During the last decade, a variety of coworking spaces has emerged that we would like to view and categorize them in two broad categories: the typical ELCS and the atypical and more CLCS.

The ELCS is usually a top-down entrepreneurial venture, where creative professionals rent office space and equipment in an individualized way and usually in short-term basis and benefit from the collaborative environment of coworking spaces. On the other hand, the CLCS are bottom-up initiatives, where usually a group of freelance/self-employed professionals or artists of the same or related professions jointly rent and share a working space (office, studio) and benefit from the coworking environment that is created. In Greece, these latter coworking schemes have risen dramatically during the times of economic crisis and they can be viewed as a response to the crisis and as community-driven survival solutions for young creatives. However, the form of a community-led coworking initiative can be found in other European countries (e.g. Germany, the UK, France) as well. These CLCS can be coworking offices, office communities— „Bürogemeinschaft" in Germany (Bender 2013), work collectives in Greece (Avdikos and Kalogeresis 2017) and grass-roots/bottom-up coworking ventures in London (Merkel 2015; Butcher 2016).

For the article CLCS can be regarded as 'institutions of mutual aid' (de Peuter and Cohen 2015) as they are usually self-governed through direct-democratic procedures, where decisions are taken in a communal way through a procedure of common negotiation between the members of the coworking space, whereas in ELCS decisions are usually taken by the director/proprietor of the space, where co-workers can only make suggestions to them (Merkel 2015).

According to Avdikos and Kalogeresis (2017), 'usually the members who form a work collective are friends or operate through a common network of colleagues and have a degree of professional proximity'; they may share technical equipment, expertise, personal and professional networks, as well as part of their free time. Members of a work collective can also set common goals and have mutual engagement in projects, thus collectivizing most of the work being done. Moreover, members of work collectives seem to have an ideological proximity (ibid.), that stems from common political backgrounds and beliefs and this is another reason that fosters trust between them, and demarcates their collective ventures (practices of collectivism) from the ELCS (practices of collaboration).

Merkel (2015) discusses the political role that bottom-up coworking spaces can play through the example of the Supermarkt coworking space venture in Berlin, which is a grass-roots initiative. She stresses that '[Supermarkt] is providing a platform for new social and political activists' grassroots movements and a coworking space for meet-ups, international *conferences, and workshops (Supermarkt, 2014)...one recurring topic at Supermarkt, for example, involves critical reflection on freelance work situations and potential forms of self-organisation, such as supporting a newly created freelancers movement'* (Freelancers Europe 2014).

CLCS and the opportunities for the collectivization of work in such spaces have many similarities with the loft spaces created by artists in New York, analysed in depth by Zukin (1989), the occupied cultural spaces in Italy (Bailey and Marcucci 2013) and the artist-run centres. All these were attempts to collectivize creative work and they were counterexamples to postmodern individualism, to the individualization of risk (Gill 2002) and to the corporatization of cultural and creative production. Thus, CLCS have a long history behind them, whereas ELCS represent a newly developed concept that is based on the marketization of recent discourses that have emerged out of the 'creative economy' and the 'sharing economy' approaches. Furthermore and depending on their openness in the neighbourhood, coworking spaces can often play the role of the intermediary in their locality, negotiating the commons and often securing social cohesion (Merkel 2015).

Research questions, methodology and data

The aim of this article is to find out (i) the reasons why professionals group together in CLCS and (ii) the different forms of internal organization and the relations between the co-workers, all of which will help clarify the difference between practices of collaboration and practices of collectivization.

The sample of the research is seven CLCS, six of which are located in Athens and one in Thessaloniki. Ten anonymous interviews took place during seven meetings, between December 2015 and April 2017. Each interview lasted approximately one hour. The interviews were carried out using a semi-structured questionnaire in the interviewees' working spaces. The selected CLCS had been spotted among creative economy networks, the web and by the snowball method (especially among same professions).

Table 6.1 presents in brief the profiles of the seven coworking ventures.

Table 6.1 Profiles of coworking ventures

Code	Year of establishment	Professions	Number of interviewees
A	2008	Graphic designers/architects	2
B	2009	Graphic designers/photographers/ decorators/marketing professionals	2
C	2011	Architects	1
D	2013	Architects	1
E	2016	Graphic designers/illustrators/ animation designers	1
F	2011	Artists	1
G	2016	Artists	1

Analysis

The main reason that brings the professionals of our sample together in a coworking space is the reduced operating costs of the venture. Especially since the beginning of the economic crisis, it has become quite costly for several professionals to maintain a private working space compared to the space provided within a coworking venture, where operating costs are shared among all people using it, therefore reducing individual business risk. This argument was used by every interviewee; operating personal costs (including rent) for an office in a coworking space in our sample ranged from 50€ to 130€ per month, much less from renting space in an ELCS (that range from 170€ to 250€ per month).

However, reduced operating costs are not the only reason why free-lance professionals prefer coworking. Another reason is detaching one-self from work at home. Quoting two interviewees:

I had finished my studies in 2001 and had been working in an attic above my parents' home for five years… so I needed to enter a strictly professional space. (A1)

Due to my personality, I can't combine my home with my work…I was not looking for something permanent, as I only come to Athens for a few days each time; I was just looking for a space. (C1)

Teleworking may give the freelancer a sense of autonomy, but at the same time it causes the no-space work phenomenon—the kind of work that can be carried out in any space where there is Internet connection (at home, at a typical working space, in the subway or the train, in restaurants and bars, etc.). The flexibility provided by teleworking corrodes the spatial boundaries of the above-mentioned areas. As a result, the employee/freelancer may become lonelier, which deprives him of any advantage offered by spatial proximity to other colleagues, which is offered by common professional spaces. Moreover, according to one of the interviewees, detaching oneself from teleworking increases productivity, as:

> To arrive at a strictly professional space and work for 5, 6 or 7 hours is more productive than being at home, trying to do the exact same amount of work during the whole day. (D1)

In addition to the above, a coworking space sets the ground for new cooperation possibilities among freelance professionals, while chances for serendipity production are also possible. As it has been mentioned during the interviews:

> We interact and influence each other because our relationships are formed in the same space. (A2)

> People drop by our space, either in or out of schedule, they hear or ask what is currently going on and contribute in their own way... and this has played its role both creatively and innovatively... even people that have completely different skills than ours can happen to participate... someone may make apt observations and end up helping in some way. (B2)

Commitment is a significant notion for freelancers in a CLCS with respect to their connection to space and the rest of the people. For instance, regarding their spatial involvement, they usually rent office space in a more permanent (or semi-permanent) basis than in ELCS. Although this makes a CLCS less renewable and therefore less open to newcomers, it concomitantly contributes to stronger personal interaction and engagement. It is the personal relations together with the random everyday 'visits' of friends, colleagues, clients, etc. that advance coworking spaces in micro-hubs of creativity.

> What nourishes me is that if I get up to take a break, I might get a glimpse of someone else's screen. I do not consider this to be an invasion of privacy; anyone that comes in can take a look at my screen and tell me 'hey, what are you working on?'; they might be interested and we could end up having an interesting conversation. (C1)

Moreover, it is spatial proximity that provides the opportunity for cooperation or interesting dialogues, the fruit of which can be new ideas that can later lead to joint projects (serendipitous production). The issues of privacy and personal space are of crucial importance in this regard. According to interviewee C1, the coworking spirit that is developed in these places permeates the workers' personal space; one's computer screen is always in plain view, prompting interesting dialogue in a community atmosphere that adds to the coworking spirit of the place. In most of the cases studied, coworking spirit seems to be developed through different procedures, such as common lunchtime; another such procedure is the expansion of coworking to personal leisure time (having drinks at the bar next door), as well as joint events that could attract co-workers. Quoting interviewee B2:

> Space is the gatekeeper, there is always a social agenda, certain tasks, so our space and time are not unstructured.

Therefore, commonly structuring free and 'community' time within a coworking space seems to enhance coworking spirit among professionals and seems to work as an antidote to the loneliness of teleworkers or other isolated professionals. Something that is also observed in more entrepreneurial coworking spaces, where the facilitator of the space plays also the role of social curator and tries through different events and practices to bring together co-workers of different and heterogeneous backgrounds.

However, the cooperation that can be developed within a coworking environment is not a practice adopted by all of the professionals. Put simply, some professionals choose to distinguish co-location from cooperation. In this sense, other people in the CLCS are perceived as 'flatmates' rather than colleagues or co-workers. The produced common space is limited to sharing the 'flat', while keeping separate working projects is seen as a way to preserve balance and not to risk internal relations. Interviewee A1 was adamant:

> No, I would not cooperate with a flatmate because I do not want to get in a fight with them.

The use of the term 'flatmate' by this specific professional brings up, again, the debate on the boundaries between personal and common space, since, in this case, it looks like the use of coworking space is limited to simply coexisting with the rest of the freelancers, without expanding to any professional relationship. The distinction between personal versus collective and private versus public practices/spaces/spheres is common among the interviewees. While building a collective project, a need emerges to define the role of the person. At the same time, public aspects of their work seek for creative combinations with their privacy. Their main goal is to continuously balance extrovert practices of communication and openness and personal needs for creativity, expression and psychological well-being. As interviewees have noted:

> It is clear by now that each individual has to be well within the group in order to contribute to the collective effort. We count on the individual. For instance, our clients like the fact that they communicate with us separately, in person. And we always help each other with our personal projects, apart from the collective ones. In terms of our work's 'character', we can keep our own style but the collective style will always be a blend.

> Well, we have this set of studios balanced by our public exhibition space. This public interface makes us sustainable in financial terms.

Finally, we should also note a couple of characteristics these seven case studies seem to have in common, which are related to the reasons coworking spaces are so appealing to freelance professionals. The first one is that all of the interviewees said that the age range in all seven coworking spaces was between 30 and 40 years old. People working in these spaces usually enter them after a few years' experience in working from home or for a medium sized or large company. Secondly, they belong to what we could call the 'educated youth', with a middle-class background—either upper or lower. Thirdly, there is a remarkable gender balance, where both male and female professionals share the same CLCS. Even when the initial core team is composed by people of the same gender (i.e. case G), this is not done in purpose and the CLCS is absolutely open to the opposite gender. Finally, we could not claim that there is a specific mixture in terms of nationality; in particular, only case G is founded by people from four different countries, while keeping an international profile in terms of networking and hosting.

In this context of personal and collective characteristics, the professionals make the decision to enter a coworking space a few years after they have essentially tried post-graduation working life. However, such a decision may last longer or not, depending on different parameters. For example, if, during their time in a coworking space, they end up having their own enterprise with its own employees, they usually need more space, which leads them to become more autonomous, leaving the coworking space, according to one of the interviewees. Consequently, there seem to be two different stages of input and output in CLCS, related to each professional's degree of professional maturity-progress and their individual professional risk; hence there is the input stage, where the freelance professionals are young, with a few years' professional experience. Here, they are required to create their own clientele and portfolio and take over a bigger risk of a future professional failure and personal precarious employment than older professionals who have—also by working in a coworking environment—created a satisfactory clientele that has transformed into a more stable income. The latter have significantly decreased their personal professional risk, while their workload often causes them to hire more staff and thus look for more office space.

However, additional space is not the only reason why they decide to leave the coworking space:

The noise at the space annoys me, I do not find it convenient any more... the excessively relaxed environment (of the space) offends some of my clients; it would be better if I had my own, well-designed office... it is a matter of prestige for my clients; this way I would raise my pay by 10-15%. (A1)

For this particular interviewee, the ongoing projects at the coworking office as well as the communal relationships that are created are noisy and the space is considered to be too 'relaxed', which affects this professional's prestige in the eyes of his clients; on the contrary, a typical personal 'well-designed' office would boost his professional status and ensure a higher income.

On the other hand, collective spaces can also be perceived as something prestigious as another interviewee highlighted:

It can happen that I'll come to a higher stage that will lead in something separate. This doesn't necessarily mean that I'll abandon our collective studio. Because it is not only about money. Having a collective project is something prestigious, too.

Therefore, the stage during which freelance professionals choose to enter a coworking space is a stage of professional 'growing up'. This phase helps professionals stand on their own feet, by sharing individual risk and giving them the opportunity to cooperate and socialize with other professionals, by benefiting from the geographical proximity provided by coworking spaces. Once they have entered professional 'adulthood' and on, the above needs, that were being met by the coworking scheme, seize to exist or are minimized and replaced by new needs (e.g. status issues, need for more space). Professional adulthood refers to the stage where the freelancer has already a mature portfolio, a stable clientele and an expanded professional network and all these are associated with a lower professional risk. As a result, the professional moves on to a private space, which involves a new—this time private—autonomy, as well as the possibility of surplus value seizure from the work of waged labour. The latter will be examined in other dimensions in the next section of the paper.

However, it is not easy to leave these spaces for another area and more private space, since the co-workers seem to have developed a connection and an attachment to the places; that is because, when they first rented the spaces, they renovated them themselves. Quoting interviewee A1:

'When we first came here it was a total mess, the place must had previously been rented by a telephone provider company and there were cables everywhere, we had to take everything off.... And we shaped the office on our own, through personal effort', while interviewee B1 mentioned:

Everything you see around, we have made; then the rest of the people that came contributed as well.

Then, the sense of attachment to the coworking space can be regarded as another characteristic of CLCS that has been developed by a collective process of making of the space.

Organization of Coworking Schemes and Co-workers Relations: From Co-location to Collectivization

The second area of study is the way these ventures are internally organized, as well as the professional relationships developed within the co-workers.

In six out of seven schemes, the initial tenants of the space are the ones managing the collection of contributions for rent, operational costs, etc. from the rest of the co-workers. The main reason is that there is no fixed coworking team in the midterm, as 'people come and go usually every six to ten months' as an interviewee highlighted. Moreover, the original tenants are the ones who 'guard' the endeavour by—informally—subletting part of the office space to other professionals. Other decisions concerning the day-to-day management of the space are taken collectively.

The seventh scheme is quite different when it comes to the economic and the organizational management of the place, which extends (or is based) on the professional relationship of the people working there. In coworking scheme D, the space's administration, as well as its management and that of the commons, is carried out through the general assembly of co-workers, which takes place at least once every month and where each member has one vote. Apart from management topics, they may discuss issues related to the office's operation, such as:

> We work shifts at the office... someone is always here, so we are open almost every day from 9a.m. till late at night. (D1)

In addition to the above, the general assembly makes decisions on professional issues, such as the distribution of work, the members' shifts and annual leaves, as well as the issue of 'equal pay'. According to interviewee D1:

> the office aims to ensure work for everyone (a stable flow of work)... our personal pay is based on the total of hours worked... hence there are two types of relationships: personal projects, from the gains of which each one gives 5% to the common fund, and joint projects, from which 30% goes to the common fund... once a year we review what everyone has made and act accordingly...e.g. if X has not had any work, we put her on a project... we try to avoid members exclusively doing either personal or joint projects....

The above description differentiates this particular coworking venture from the rest, since the relationships developed within this endeavour are not just based on sharing an office space, closing contracts and assuring one's social status, as we saw before; here the relationship is extended to and has its basis on work collectivization. As a result, priority is given to the development of collegiality against the individual and its individuality, which are of primary, more or less, importance in the rest of the schemes under study. According to interviewee D1, this collectivization also has a political background, since the professionals of the office have all been members of the same leftist university students' political group. We observe that, in addition to the social proximity they had developed as students in the past, their political proximity is the one that determines their decisions on a professional level, making collectivization the axis of their professional relationship. Consequently, a new hybrid coworking venture is created (work collective), which has certain characteristics that go as far as refusing to employ third parties:

> We do not want any employees, we do not want to profit from the sur-plus value of others, so we say no to dependent work... if we need a new member we will check their profile and, if it fits with ours, they can enter our space and work.

Apart from sharing technologies, technical equipment and free time, the collective's members also share a portfolio, since they collectively partic-ipate in exhibitions and competitions, under a common brand name. There also seems to be a certain solidarity between them and other work collectives. They enter into contracts or subcontract work from other coworking groups; apparently there is a preference for to outsource and subcontract with other coworking schemes that work in equivalent col-lective terms.

Thus, it seems that the common political (leftist) background and the specific ideological mentality seem to determine the level of collectiviza-tion in that particular CLCS. Although other coworking schemas of our sample did not have the same characteristics of the above CLCS, such as the feature of 'equal pay' or the denial of seizing the surplus value of other's work, we have observed that some of the interviewees have men-tioned the role of common political references. However, during the interviews they insist to leave those references aside, while underlining that their main political statement is the CLCS itself. In other words, they perceive this professional choice as a political attitude towards cow-orking, collaborating, coexisting. This is the common political identity they like to share and develop.

Interviewee F1 noted:

> "We have all participated in the student's movement during 2006-2007. We have a theoretical political discourse. And we also have the intention to demand some things. However, the latter is not highly prioritised (*in the coworking space*). The way we act is already an important political statement." Another interviewee (E1) highlighted:

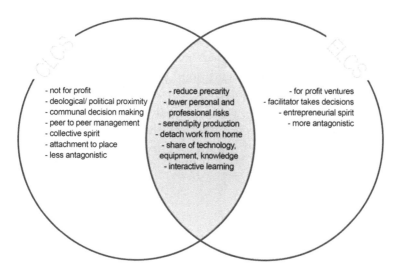

- not for profit
- deological/ political proximity
- communal decision making
- peer to peer management
- collective spirit
- attachment to place
- less antagonistic

- reduce precarity
- lower personal and
  professional risks
- serendipity production
- detach work from home
- share of technology,
  equipment, knowledge
- interactive learning

- for profit ventures
- facilitator takes decisions
- entrepreneurial spirit
- more antagonistic

Fig. 6.1 Characteristics of CLCS and ELCS

Working collectively is actually a stubbornness that involves something political in the debate. We have never 'announced' this identity by choosing certain clients, for example. We think that exchanging ideas, inspiration and motivation is a political act.

Figure 6.1 summarizes the above analysis through a concentric schema that contains all the possible relations between co-workers in CLCS. These relations could stay limited to co-location, where practical matters of the coworking space are commonly managed, while co-workers just share the costs of the place and have common facilities. It seems that the scope of these co-location practices is limited to the individual survival of the creative freelancer. In that case, the office space is individualized, with invisible spatial boundaries among co-workers. However, there are cases where co-workers, more than co-locating with other workers, they exchange professional information, share knowledge, subcontract parts of projects between them and seek to socialize with their colleagues. All these relational elements build collaborative practices that mark the nature of the coworking space and the spatial boundaries between co-workers start to erode. Moreover, in other ventures, co-workers form coworking environments that extend to the collectivization of the work, where apart from sharing knowledge and information, they also co-manage labour matters and share professional risks through practices of solidarity (e.g. equal pay) and non-hierarchical structures, they use coworking space as a common brand for their work and they deny the surplus value of waged labour. Through these practices of collectivization, space is collectively reproduced; and that reproduction is rooted in the co-workers' ideological and political proximity.

CLCS and ELCS

As discussed in brief in the first two sections, the paper attempts to demarcate CLCS from ELCS and form an analysis framework for the more community-driven coworking schemes. Here we try to provide the main characteristics of that demarcation (Fig. 6.2).

CLCS and ELCS have many similarities as seen from the analysis and the literature review sections of the paper. Namely, both forms of coworking spaces are chosen from freelancers in order to reduce precariousness, lower professional and personal risks, detach work from home and

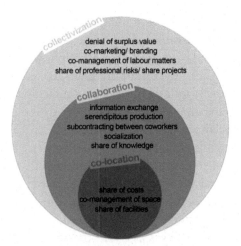

Fig. 6.2 Co-workers relations and types of CLCS

have more chances for serendipity production. Moreover, both forms of coworking spaces enable the sharing of technology and equipment and can be regarded as platforms for knowledge and information sharing, and interactive learning. However, ELCS are most of the times for-profit ventures, where the facilitator takes most of the decisions concerning the management of the place and where there is an entrepreneurial spirit 'on the air' that is usually backed by the presence of venture capitalists where they meet co-workers that pitch their ideas in regular events. On the other hand, CLCS seem to be more bottom-up not-for-profit initiatives that can also be regarded as collaborative survival platforms for young creative professionals, where costs are considerably less than in ELCS. Elements that demarcate CLCS from ELCS are the sense of attachment to place that some interviewees highlighted and also some other characteristics such as the communal decision-making procedures among the co-workers and the peer to peer management of the place, the ideological background and the political proximity that can form the basis for work collectivization, and in general the collective spirit that is 'in the air' that it also can be mirrored in a less antagonistic environment.

Conclusion

The paper attempted to conceptually demarcate CLCS that are more bottom-up and not-for-profit initiatives operating under common management, from ELCS that are usually top-down entrepreneurial ventures. As it has been shown through the case studies, the formation of CLCS is an alternative, especially for young freelance professionals who wish to minimize the operating costs of a typical office space, enjoy geographical and social proximity to other co-workers and, by extension, minimize any possible professional risks. However, the advantages of such a space seem to extend beyond the minimization of the peculiar costs of a freelancer; the cooperation and coworking spirit that is built as a result creates a less antagonistic collective environment.

CLCS can be considered as third places, while the degree of cooperation among their members can range from simple co-location to work collectivization. The main determining factor is professional relationships developed among co-workers, which are usually based on the political proximity of the co-workers. These relationships are also reflected in the way the space is used, in relational terms. Individual space and privacy start to erode when we move from co-location practices to collaborative ones, and it seems that coworking spaces that collectivize labour open up the possibility for the collectivization of space as well in broader terms that often include the locality that CLCS is based. That collectivization could also practically mean that CLCS such as work collectives can become a strategy of mutual survival for young freelancers working in precarious conditions in creative industries. CLCS can also be seen in the context of creative hubs as relational milieus and platforms that enable freelancers 'to enact distributed organizational practices made of continuously negotiated relationships' (Gandini 2015). An alternative to the individuality of creative work and the creative class' discourses of lifestyle and success, then, can be constructed, where the precarious creative freelancers could find communal alternatives that are materialized into mutual survival coworking strategies and a truly community-centred coworking lifestyle that can be extended beyond professional life.

References

Avdikos, V., & Kalogeresis, A. (2017). Socio-economic profile and working conditions of freelancers in co-working spaces and work collectives: Evidence from the design sector in Greece. *Area, 49*(1), 35–42.

Bailey, S., & Marcucci, M. E. (2013). Legalizing the occupation: The Teatro Valle as a cultural commons. *South Atlantic Quarterly, 112*(2), 396–405.

Boschma, R. A. (2005). *Proximity* and innovation: A critical assessment. *Regional Studies, 39*, 61–74.

Bender, D. (2013). *Mobile Arbeitsplätze als kreative Räume: Coworking Spaces, Cafés und andere urbane Arbeitsorte*. Bielefeld: Transcript Verlag.

Butcher, T. (2016). Co-working communities: Sustainability citizenship at work. In *Sustainability Citizenship in Cities* (pp. 113–123). Routledge.

Capdevila, I. (2015). Co-working spaces and the localised dynamics of innovation in Barcelona. *International Journal of Innovation Management, 19*(03), 1540004.

DeGuzman, G. V., & Tang, A. I. (2011). *Working in the unoffice: A guide to coworking for indie workers, small businesses, and nonprofits*. San Francisco: Night Owls Press LLC.

de Peuter, G., & Cohen, N. S. (2015). Emerging labour politics in creative industries. In K. Oakley & J. O' Connor (Eds.), *The Routledge companion to the cultural industries* (pp. 305–318). Abingdon: Routledge.

Dovey, J., Pratt, A. C., Moreton, S., Virani, T. E., Merkel, J., & Lansdowne, J. (2016). *The Creative Hubs Report: 2016.*

Freelancers Europe. (2014). *European freelancers movement 2014.* Available at http://freelancers-europe.org/.

Gandini, A. (2015). The rise of coworking spaces: A literature review. *Ephemera, 15*(1), 193–205.

Gill, R. (2002). Cool, creative and egalitarian? Exploring gender in project-based new media work in Euro. *Information, Communication & Society, 5*(1), 70–89.

Kong, L. (2009). Beyond networks and relations: Towards rethinking creative cluster theory. In *Creative Economies, Creative Cities* (pp. 61–75). Dordrecht: Springer.

Kong, L. (2011). From precarious labor to precarious economy? Planning for precarity in Singapore's creative economy. *City, Culture and Society, 2*(2), 55–64.

Marshall, A. (1920 [2009]). *Principles of economics* (Rev. ed.). London: Macmillan. Reprinted by Prometheus Books.

Merkel, J. (2015). Coworking in the city. *Ephemera: Theory & Politics in Organization, 15*(1), 121–139.

Moriset, B. (2013). *Building new places of the creative economy. The rise of coworking spaces.* Available at halshs-00914075.

Moriset, B. (2014, January). *Building new places of the creative economy. The rise of coworking spaces.* Paper presented at the 2nd Geography of Innovation International Conference 2014 (pp. 23–25), Utrecht, Netherlands.

Parrino, L. (2015). Coworking: Assessing the role of proximity in knowledge exchange. *Knowledge Management Research & Practice, 13*(3), 261–271.

Spinuzzi, C. (2012). Working alone together: Coworking as emergent collaborative activity. *Journal of Business and Technical Communication, 26*(4), 399–441. https://doi.org/10.1177/1050651912444070.

Sundsted, T., Jones, D., & Bacigalupo, T. (2009). *I'm Outta here: How co-working is making the office obsolete.* Brooklyn and Austin: Not an MBA Press.

Virani, T. E., & Malem, W. (2015). *Re-articulating the creative hub concept as a model for business support in the local creative economy: The case of Mare Street in Hackney* (Creativeworks London Working Paper Series).

Zukin, S. (1989). *Loft living: Culture and capital in urban change.* Baltimore: Johns Hopkins University Press.

7

Hip Hub? Class, Race and Gender in Creative Hubs

Tarek E. Virani and Rosalind Gill

Introduction

Where questions of equality and diversity are concerned, the cultural and creative industries (CCIs) have had a good press. Creative workplaces are often described as open, relaxed and bohemian, while the people who work in them are identified as members of a distinct 'creative class' characterised by lauded qualities and sensibilities such as inclusivity, tolerance and the assumption that rewards are based on a meritocratic system of hard work (Florida 2002). These assumed characteristics are often used as the basis for enacting creative industries policy

T. E. Virani (✉)
School of Business and Management, Queen Mary University of London, London, UK
e-mail: t.virani@qmul.ac.uk

R. Gill
Department of Sociology, School of Arts and Social Sciences, City, University of London, London, UK
e-mail: Rosalind.gill.2@city.ac.uk

© The Author(s) 2019
R. Gill et al. (eds.), *Creative Hubs in Question*, Dynamics of Virtual Work,
https://doi.org/10.1007/978-3-030-10653-9_7

on a national or city level, and work policy and educational institutions alike promote the idea that the cultural sector offers intrinsically satisfying 'good jobs' that are available to all those who possess the right talents and drive (Banks and Hesmondhalgh 2009; Morgan and Nelligan 2018).

In recent years, however, increasing numbers of scholars have pointed to an uncomfortable truth: that these qualities and sensibilities tied so habitually to the creative industries might in fact be inaccurate. Catungal et al. (2009, p. 116) argue that far from being sites of inclusivity, the spaces of CCIs are more often than not also sites of 'intense segmentation and hierarchy' along race and gender lines. Worse still, Gill (2014) argues, the myth of openness, egalitarianism and diversity, may in fact be part of the very mechanism that maintains significant exclusions and inequalities rendering them difficult to identify, let alone discuss or address. A growing body of research points to the CCIs, then, not as exemplary workplaces characterised by diverse workforces, but rather as occupations that are markedly striated by gender, class and racial inequalities—as well as by exclusions related to age and disability.

This chapter builds on this work and the nascent body of research about inequalities in the CCIs focussing specifically on how creative and cultural hubs are situated in relation to class, gender and race, thereby turning the lens of analysis and inquiry on the spaces and places of creative economic activity that are the subject of this book. Drawing on interviews, as well as secondary sources, previous work, and participant observation in three hubs in East London, we examine whether creative and cultural hubs contribute to greater diversity in the CCI workforce or whether they could be said to entrench privilege. It is apparent that work in this area is highly limited. Our analysis revolves around two interrelated questions: first, we ask what contextualises and constitutes inequality in creative and cultural hubs; and second, does an emphasis upon 'getting the community right' in these types of spaces contribute to a heightening rather than a diminishing of inequalities, particularly as decision-making gets concentrated in the opaque process of 'curation'?

The remainder of the chapter is divided into two broad sections. In the first part, we look at the literature about inequalities in the CCI in general. In the second, we draw on our research in three different hubs in East London to reflect on the processes that may contribute to persistent exclusions and inequalities. We conclude with a brief discussion.

Inequality and the Creative and Cultural Industries

Employment in the CCIs is characterised by stark inequalities relating to gender, race, class, age and disability. As Dave O'Brien (2018a) has argued 'the arts and cultural sector in the UK is currently not at all representative of the population as a whole'. Indeed, notwithstanding the myths of egalitarianism and bohemianism circulating within the cultural and artistic field, inequalities are often significantly *worse* than in other more traditional sectors. Numerous studies and reports exist documenting the lack of ethnic and racial diversity in the CCI (Arts Council 2018; Hunt and Ramon 2015). The class profile of the CCIs is also markedly skewed towards middle-class and upper-class workers, with certain occupational groups (e.g. in media and publishing) dominated by people who were privately educated (see Sutton Trust). In their report, 'Panic! Social Class, Taste and Inequalities in the creative industries' Orian Brook et al. (2018) used the Labour Force Survey to look at the class origins of people working in various arts and CCI fields. They found that only 18% of people working in the arts had a working-class background, and in publishing, film and TV this was even worse at only 13%. The same official statistics show that as a whole the working age population is comprised of 35% from groups categorised as working class.

Gender inequalities are also severe and characterised by multiple different forms. On the one hand, there are distinctive patterns of exclusion or underrepresentation—particularly in relation to tech-centred fields but also more generally in terms of whose art is exhibited or which playwrights get their work performed; on the other, there are marked patterns of horizontal and vertical segregation *within* fields or industries—such as within theatre or television or the music industry. In general, women are much less likely to be seen in the 'top' creative roles—for example, in Hollywood the most recent Celluloid Ceiling report reveals that women made up only 7% of directors, while in the category of writers, producers, executive producers, editors and cinematographers and directors they still only constituted 17%, a drop from the previous year. The gender pay gap is also worse in creative fields than it is in the rest of the economy (see ONS 2018)—a point highlighted in the UK by the recent scandals within the BBC, which showed shocking disparities in the amounts male and female talent earn, echoing earlier revelations about Hollywood. David Throsby and Katya Petetskaya's (2017) survey of Australian artists shows 'the income gap between women and men is wider in the arts than the average gap across all industries' at around 30%. In the USA, the gender pay gap is reported to be 32% for freelance creatives (HoneyBook 2017).

As Maura Edmond and Jasmine McGowan (2017) argue 'these reports make for grim reading, not just because of their conclusions' but also 'because of the dreadful sense of déjà vu they provoke'. Gender, race and class inequalities remain troublingly persistent, despite decades of attempts to document and challenge them. Indeed in some cases things seem to be getting worse. The austerity measures put in place to deal with the effects of the Global Financial Crisis in 2008 are widely understood as having exacerbated inequality, with women and BAME groups losing their jobs at disproportionate rates. In his speech at the 2014 BAFTA awards broadcaster, Lenny Henry argued that over a six-year period the number of BAMEs working in the UK TV industry 'declined by 30.9%... The total number of black and Asian people in the industry has fallen by 2000 while the industry as a whole has grown by over 4000. Or to put it another way—for every black and Asian person who lost their job, more than two white people were employed' (Lenny Henry quoted in Khaleeli 2014). Henry (2017) has recently criticised what he calls 'fake diversity' in which broadcasters and regulators collude in presenting figures which present an unrealistically rosy picture about the numbers or proportion of BAME staff. In his important investigation into race in the cultural industries, Anamik Saha (2018, p. 88) suggests that proliferating diversity initiatives may 'serve an ideological function that sustains the institutional whiteness of the cultural industries' while claiming to do something different.

Saha argues that such policies increasingly draw on neoliberal rationalities to make the case for diversity. This is similar, it would seem, to Elisabeth Kelan's (2009) critique of the 'business case' for gender equality. Kelan points to the 'gender fatigue' that may be produced by the repeated mobilisation of gender inequality as 'an issue' requiring attention. We would argue that a further dynamic also occurs where the mass coverage of an issue makes it appear that 'something has been done' or a problem has been resolved, even when little or nothing has changed. On this note, after 18 months of intense and unprecedented coverage of feminist protests, initiatives and actions about women's employment and representation in media, it was sobering read a report from Directors UK as this book was going to press (August 2018) which showed that the total numbers of TV programmes directed by women had actually *declined* over the period from 27 to 24% of programmes made.

Why so Unequal?

The reasons for these obdurate inequalities are multiple and complex. They must be understood as intersectional, recognising the way in which different locations and identities produce distinctive experiences, shaped by intersections of gender, race and class—as well as by age and disability and sexual orientation. They also vary across places and across different kinds of work—from architecture to web design. Although inequality characterises the entire artistic or creative labour market, it cannot be assumed that it has the same dynamics across all spheres—for example, there are major differences between large employers such as the BBC, the organisational forms of Hollywood, and the eco-system of small, temporary, precarious, reputation and network-based enterprises that mostly comprise the tenants or participants of the hubs we studied. All these complexities mean that there is a need to explore the specificities of what Joan Acker calls the 'inequality regimes' in the CCI: 'the inter-related practices, processes, action and meanings that result in and maintain class, gender and race inequalities' (2006, p. 443), and it is to this project that our examination of three East London hubs seeks to contribute.

Broadly speaking, a number of different explanations have been posited for the persistence of inequalities within the CCI. Firstly, barriers to entry into the CCI for those who come from ethnic minority or working-class backgrounds are high. The issues seem to revolve around affordability and the need for what Eikof and Warhurst (2013) describe as 'economic capital' or cultural capital that exists for those who come from more affluent backgrounds. This type of capital allows creative workers to weather the storms that come from work and income precarity—both of which are a characteristic part of life for workers in the CCI (Gill and Pratt 2008), especially at an early stage (Randle et al. 2007; Hope and Figiel 2015). Regarding the TV industry Lee (2011) underscores this by stating the fact 'that it is largely an imperative to work for nothing in order to enter the industry [which] means that individuals who come from poorer, working-class backgrounds often just cannot afford to get into the industry' (p. 557). As a knock-on effect, if these familial funds are not available to the creative worker than securing an income from outside the CCI becomes a necessity. This often takes the form of part-time work in the service sector which can 'constitute a double disadvantage, limiting the time available for creative work and curtailing opportunities for networking and sourcing work' (Eikhof and Warhurst 2013, p. 500).

Barriers to entry take other forms as well through what Christopherson calls 'hard-wired' social and economic networks (2008, p. 73). In her work on television and film production in the USA, she argues that these networks foster and reinforce labour segmentation among ethnic groups, as well as gender, thereby restricting access to job opportunities and careers. The case is not dissimilar in the UK where the TV industry is heavily segmented along racial lines but also along lines of class. Lee (2011) suggests that by focussing on 'cultural capital' uncomfortable questions about the social make-up of the labour market in the British TV industry are brought to the fore. He goes on to suggest that 'there is evidence of closed networks which are nepotistic and exclude outsiders' (p. 557), a point developed by Thanki and Jeffreys' (2007) account of 'institutional racism' in the audio-visual sector. Compared with other fields of endeavour, work in the CCI is much more likely to be allocated via personal networks and contacts and less likely to be based on formal qualifications or records of achievement. This informal contacts culture in which recruitment is routed via personal networks (Grugulis and Stoyanova 2009) produces decisions that are more likely to be based on (classed, gendered and racialised) judgements of worth and value such as 'he's a good bloke' or 'I don't know if she would be able to take tough decisions'. It is in such attributions—often warmly expressed—that discrimination is enacted, reproducing the predominantly white, male and middle-class order. Inequalities are generated through homophily—the preference for interaction with others who are similar to oneself—and what Suzanne Franks (in another context) called Hansard's Law—the notion that the clubbier the context the more likely people are to recruit in their own image. Deborah Jones and Judith K. Pringle (2015) talk about these areas of practice as 'unmanageable inequalities' because they exist outside of the legislation and management strategies designed to challenge such injustices, e.g. Equal Opportunities programmes, diversity policies and anti-discrimination law. Once within organisations, the lack of transparent mechanisms for allocating work or achieving promotion can further exacerbate these inequalities.

Another issue is the way that creative roles are understood and represented. For instance, working in 'the media' is often perceived as a middle-class, white pursuit, echoing other research in this area (Holgate and McKay 2007). This can often act as a hidden sign that others may not be welcome or 'need not apply'. Kelan (2007) found a 'male worker ideal'—but crucially one that was masked through gender-neutral language—in the tech companies she studied. Similarly, Nixon and Crewe (2004) describe how creative workers in advertising and magazine publishing are subject to, and feel pressure to, conform to the idea of the 'creative worker' through heterosexual and masculine lenses. This translates into 'particular forms of masculinity which shape the broader occupational culture of their jobs' (p. 145), thereby underlining a 'tightly regulated and circumscribed set of gender codes associated with these jobs' (p. 146). The authors also show that 'the flourishing of robustly masculine cultures within agency offices and publishing companies formed a considerable block to women's capacity to succeed in these occupations' (p. 146). Examples include the prevalence of creative workplaces in advertising in which table football, Sky Sports packages, social events on golf courses or in lap-dancing clubs work to exclude women. The 'youthfulness' of an industry where the average creative is 34 (Brodmerkel and Barker, forthcoming), and in which those over 40 can be made to feel like 'dead wood', highlights the way in which ageism intersects with gender, race, class and sexuality here.

In relation to gender inequality another particular challenge may be the nexus of issues associated with motherhood. Industry surveys have repeatedly highlighted the challenge of 'balancing' children and work in creative professions. A number of practical issues make this difficult. The long-hours cultures and bulimic patterns of working in many creative fields—in which intense round-the-clock work is required for a deadline—do not fit well with the social organisation of childcare. Schools and nurseries do not operate for someone who has to leave for a shoot at 4 a.m. or work until midnight. Mothers also report the intense workplace pressure they are under not to let their children— and sometimes even their pregnancies—'show' for fear of losing out. Discrimination against all women (including those who are not mothers) seems to be a major issue, as organisations decide that men are 'lower risk' (see Wing-Fai et al. 2015). Another significantly gendered issue is sexual harassment—which has come to the fore in recent cases across the entertainment industries and beyond.

Finally, it is worth noting the range of dynamic and changing practices of racism, classism and sexism that may operate within creative fields. Gill's (1993, 2014) research on 'new sexism' builds on discussions of 'new racism' to explore how discriminatory practices are becoming more subtle and agile particularly in the workplace. Her research shows that disclaimers are common, as are warm and positive endorsements of the under-represented group; this represents an evolution and mutation of forms of discrimination in order to take on board progressive ideas and to anticipate and rebut accusations of bias. In an interesting new study that develops this work, Dave O'Brien (2018b) looks at 'inequality talk' among senior men in UK CCIs, showing that recognition of structural barriers to marginalised groups is now much more common than denial of them. Nevertheless through the use of 'gentle-manly tropes' and the idea of their own career 'good luck' this seemingly enlightened or 'woke' approach serves to entrench rather than challenge inequalities.

Another related discursive move is what Sara Ahmed calls 'overing'—in which sexism and racism are safely consigned to the past—located in the 'bad old days' from which we are assumed to have moved on. 'Progress talk' (Wetherell and Edley 2001, p. 450) achieves a similar effect, disavowing the need for action to challenge inequalities, since this is assumed to happen inevitably without struggle. Optimistic assessments that things are 'getting better' may also be examples of what Ahmed terms 'happy talk' about diversity. Taken together, this work on the changing modes of (talk about) discrimination underscores the sheer flexibility and agility of sexism and racism in the current context—making it harder to recognise, and, arguably, harder to challenge. In the next section, we turn to the question of how this may play out in the context of cultural hubs.

Methods and Sites

To explore these questions of equality and diversity we conducted research in three different sites in 2017. The sites consisted of a co-working space in Shoreditch and one in South Hackney—and one live/work artists' hub in Hackney Wick. Open-ended interviews that lasted from 25 minutes to over an hour were conducted with a total of 30 interviewees all of whom have a vested interest in creative and cultural work space. Participant observation through hot-desking was also used at both of the co-working spaces once a week for six weeks in order to observe the role of the community manager as well as the community of tenants. Informal conversations with tenants and others were also used. All three locations can be understood as creative hubs because they have specific characteristics that identify them as such: 'first, they provide both hard and soft services to creative sector SMEs, including micro-businesses [and freelancers]; second, they are aimed specifically at early stage creative SMEs, [freelancers] and micro-businesses; third, they are facilitated by trusted managers who retain a number of important roles such as managers, curators and network builders; and fourth, they have become critical to the existence of the local creative economy because they provide the tools necessary to sustain a business' (Virani and Malem 2015, p. 22) (see Table 7.1 for research site information).

While they can all be understood as creative and cultural hubs they occupy different parts of the work space spectrum. The two co-working spaces are primarily concerned with innovative digital start-ups who occupy a number of digital-oriented sub-sectors including: financial technology (fintech), digital marketing, e-fund raising, health app development, e-learning, e-tourism, games development and app development more generally. Interestingly, the co-working space in Shoreditch was far more 'techy' than the one in South Hackney. Many of the start-ups in both spaces, oftentimes one or two person organisations, follow a specific type of growth trajectory much observed in the more creative digital industries. This includes seeking investment through angel investors, super angels and growth equity firms as well as perhaps being involved in accelerator or incubation programmes and/or spaces. Recent literature has argued that this can be understood as an 'innovation field' of creative economic activity (Shiach et al. 2017). Both spaces are located in the London Borough of Hackney which is at the forefront of this type of economic activity. It is home to Tech City, also known as Silicon Roundabout, embodying the urban economic processes associated with creative class theory and creative city policymaking (Florida 2002) which emphasises the importance for cities to become consumption sites for the creative class.

The artists' hub which is a live/work space is a different type of hub—more of an artist's space. Live/work spaces developed in this area of Hackney Wick (further east from Shoreditch) in around 2008 and are essentially old warehouses that have been converted into studios as well as places to live, hence the term live/work (Mayor of London 2014). It includes a number of artists who work in fine arts, arts and crafts, carpentry, sculpting, woodwork and paperwork such as origami. The area also includes a number of co-working spaces; however, these are again more oriented towards cultural production as opposed to innovation-type digital activities. This part of the east end is in the throes of

Table 7.1 Research sites

Hub type	Hub location	Sector orientation	Funding	Interviewees
Co-working space	Shoreditch	App developers, Fintech, Digital marketing, Health apps	Primarily private funding through growth equity firms, angel investment, super angels	Community manager, Tenants (10), Property developer
Co-working space	South Hackney	Digital fashion, e-tourism, e-marketing, e-learning, Games development	Mix of private fund-ing, product sales and public funding such as EU funding, Arts Council Funding and Government funding	Community manager, Tenants (10),
Live/work space	Hackney Wick	Arts and crafts, stu-dio-centric work, sculpt-ing, painting, carpentry, paperwork, woodwork	Arts Council funding, product sales, other public funding	Hub director, Artists (4), Creative intermediary (2)

gentrification processes associated with current urban area-based regeneration policy in London. It exemplifies well the 'creative tensions' associated with contemporary place-based renewal and megaproject legacy policy, in this case the London 2012 Olympic Games. These types of spaces belong to a different type of creative economy field, in this case the 'cultural' field (Shiach et al. 2017). This field is far more reliant on public-funding organisations like Arts Council England and is therefore more oriented towards public policy as opposed to the private sector. Thus, the infrastructure of investment that exists for the innovation field mentioned earlier is not as prevalent here.

All three hubs make up a spectrum of creative economic activity that spans everything from arts and crafts practitioners to software developers. Importantly, they facilitate and support creative economic work and cultural production. These hubs cater to early-stage creative workers and therefore are critical sites for the CCI and for questions of inequality and diversity.

Curating Inequality?

By spending time observing and hot-desking at both co-working sites, it was soon apparent that they were quite similar. The first co-working space, in Shoreditch, was more 'app-centric' whereas the second co-working space located in South Hackney had people working in a mix of sectors of the CCI such as fashion, tourism and e-marketing. Neither co-working space was explicitly corporate-facing; they were not run by Office Group, WeWork, or Regus—the three large office space companies in London. Through participant observation at the co-working space in Shoreditch, it became apparent that the occupiers of the space were not diverse. Most of the thirty or so tenants who occupied desks were white and male. Of the people interviewed one was from a mixed-race background, although interestingly it was soon discovered that the company she worked for did not get along with the community and was soon going to be asked to leave the co-working space—she was effectively being 'curated out'. The second co-working space was slightly more diverse with more women than the first one; however, most tenants were white. The community managers for both co-working sites were both white.

> Getting the community right is really important in these spaces and it's important to work with people that are like-minded. (Interview with Community Manager—Shoreditch)

Much work on co-working has discussed the importance of 'getting the community right' (Merkel 2015). Oftentimes this narrative is applauded and elevated as recognition of the importance of the nuanced ways in which the social engagement processes prevalent in creative work spaces occur. Also as many of these spaces espouse the importance of collaboration—where curating a community as an exercise in brokership between would-be collaborators—it becomes an important and attractive facet of these spaces—for many spaces it is their USP.

> I've worked in a lot of places that didn't do the curation and this space definitely did and you can tell, and that's a good thing. (Interview with Tenant—Shoreditch)

What is not often discussed is the notion of how easily 'curating a community' can falter and slip into the domain of subtle exclusion along lines of class, race and gender while in the pursuit of 'community'. This adds a further twist to the discussion of contacts culture and homophily above. When asked whether these spaces are diverse one tenant answered:

> Oh yes, this place is really diverse we have people from everywhere: Canada, America, other parts of England, Australia, France, all over. (Interview with Tenant—Shoreditch).

There are quite obvious 'versions of diversity' that occur in the curatorial process in many of these spaces and as one can clearly see from the statement above sometimes these versions can indirectly entrench privilege. The tenant quoted above clearly believes that the space where he works represents a diverse work space while some might argue that in actuality his version of diversity represents a rather lukewarm understanding of heterogeneity and hence quite a pronounced one of homogeneity, especially when it comes to Anglosphere countries from the 'developed' world such as many of the ones he listed. Getting the community and the peer-to-peer dynamics right is critically important for many co-working spaces, especially in the innovation field; however, they can run the risk of entrenching privilege through the process of curation.

Clearly, curation is not an open and unconstrained process. Sometimes the work space provider is in a position where they cannot afford to curate the community due to spiralling rent costs dictated partly by location but primarily by the landlords to whom they are beholden. In this instance, often what happens is community curation becomes a tokenistic part of the rhetoric of selling these spaces to would-be renters and in many cases large companies and corporates. In actuality what really matters according to one interviewee is 'bums on seats' (Interview with Workspace Provider). Here, the last thing on the work space provider's mind is building a community since they are preoccupied with the cost of running the space. This can lead to a cycle of exclusion as desk rental rate increases usually follow, especially in sites close to hotbeds of innovation activity like Tech City in Shoreditch. This then has an additional knock-on effect that reinforces barriers to entry by preserving the unaffordability of the work space. The rental increase essentially blocks access to the space allowing only large-sized companies and corporations who can afford to move in—either the workspace provider accepts this or the space is forced to close its doors. This occured in one of the research sites where the landlord increased rates by 400% forcing the space to choose to close its doors as opposed to hiking the rent. In this case, corporations usually end up occupying a large number of desks (sometimes over 20 desks in a single space), thereby placing it out of reach of smaller creative businesses and/or freelancers who do not have the economic capital to deal with the increase in rates. This also disrupts the 'community feel' that is supposed to be a hallmark of co-working. Thus a lack of curation, and a purely market-oriented approach to desk rental, results in exclusion as well—for everyone except those who can afford it who usually work for large firms that have dubious records on diversity as seen earlier.

Another issue that affects curation is when a space starts to 'scale'; in other words, when it starts to grow exponentially.

> When a collaborative space begins to scale curation gets thrown out of the window because it's too difficult. I mean curation can work with 30–60 desks, you can micromanage it; fill it with the right type of occupiers. When it starts to scale it's really difficult to do because you need to fill those seats. (Interview with Property Developer)

In this instance, the work space provider is again primarily concerned with filling the desk space in order to cater for increased demand. This demand usually happens as a result of medium and mostly large-sized companies moving into the space. When curation is dispensed with at this stage the community becomes dictated by the number of large corporate sponsors the space has signed an agreement with. This then has the knock-on effect of both reducing access to SMEs, micros and freelancers sometimes allowing businesses with problematic records on equality and diversity full access to these work spaces—as stated earlier. The notion of collaboration is then truly dispensed with as each large company moves to protect its intellectual property and reduce collaboration as much as possible.

The final crucial component that affects the curation of community is the role of the community manager in these co-working spaces. As discussed earlier in the chapter, there is a risk that community managers recruit 'in their own image', thus reproducing a tendency towards largely white, middle-class and often male spaces. Our research also foregrounds some of the challenges hub curators face, and thus, how low a priority a diverse tenant group may be:

> Being a community manager is mainly about practical things like watching noise levels, making sure the communal areas aren't being [turned into] places where people park themselves. But management is an issue;

it's hard to do the things you want to do and do it properly. (Interview with Community Manager—South Hackney)

The two community managers interviewed also stated that there were issues with how they themselves were being managed due to the costs associated with running these spaces. This usually manifests itself in a precarious existence for community managers, which in turn affects how these spaces are run and how communities within them evolve. While most interviewees view their community managers in a positive light, the managers themselves have to negotiate a position in-between curation and being economically viable. In other words, whatever community they end up managing is a community that they may not have had a hand in curating (if curated at all), and this can be problematic leading to tensions within the space. This is especially true when these spaces scale, as mentioned earlier, or when these spaces need to fill their desks in order to make ends meet.

In conclusion, it is important to note that there are many co-working spaces that do not curate their communities instead opting for the purely market-oriented option. This said they can curate in other ways, such as through the provision of speakers and workshops. For many co-working spaces, curation is an important piece of how to make these spaces work. The role of curating communities is intimately tied to issues of inequality in co-working spaces, and this is inextricably connected to how these work spaces attempt to negotiate the urban financial landscape that underpins them.

Gentrification and Artistic Cultures

Turning to the third site of our research—the artists live/work space—the issue of inequality is different at this end of the creative economy spectrum and manifests itself in two overarching ways; first, it is closely tied to gentrification processes; and second, it is more evident along lines of class.

The creative hub in Hackney Wick is an artists' hub nested within an artists' cluster on the border straddling the London Borough of

Tower Hamlets and the London Borough of Hackney. According to Pratt (2009) artists began to populate disregarded industrial buildings resulting in artistic/cultural clusters around Shoreditch and Brick Lane in the 1990s. There is also evidence of considerable artistic, and especially musical, activity happening in the Shoreditch area back in the mid-1970s. Through the all too familiar processes of land remediation and rising property values linked to gentrifying processes artists began to move further east resulting in the artist cluster that exists in Hackney Wick today. According to Rosner (2010, p. 15), 'the first colonizers [here] who broke out of its traditional strategic industrial land use were independent artists, designers and craftsmen looking for cheap and abundant studio space'. Since the first studios date to 1980 (Acme Studios 2011), it is not unlikely that the area had a healthy number of creative people there until around 2005 when plans for the area were consolidated with Olympic legacy plans. Where there is consensus it shows that the biggest influx of artists happened in and around 2008.

> Because it is so isolated it allows this community to exist, you don't come here by accident…All the people here are of the same mind-set and interest, a community is quite inevitable. (Live/Worker since 2009 from Rosner 2010, p. 25)

This part of Hackney Wick had a lot of attractive qualities for those wanting to move there in 2008. It afforded artists and would be new live/work residents ample space, attractive space, the 'feel good factor' and a guarantee of no complaints from neighbours. This revolved around the existence of abandoned warehouses. These warehouses quickly became creative and cultural hubs in their own right and in the early days had an important community role as well:

> In 2009, when we originally started, people walked by our space from a lot of different cultural and ethnic backgrounds and we would help them with a whole bunch of things. We were a small group then and we helped with all sorts … like knocking down walls or putting up shelves for some of the elderly who lived in the area. There was no hierarchy, all very equal. Then when other people started moving in and driving up the costs then

we saw a different type of face move into the area. I would say we were a very diverse area back then but not so much anymore. (Interview with Artist)

The question of inequality in artistic-oriented hubs is closely linked to the gentrification story in this area. According to the interviews, the area started out as quite diverse due to the resident population as well as the artists' hub itself but changed over time as a consequence of the changing demographics of Hackney Wick.

> We were very participatory with local schools and local community groups at the beginning. We need to reach all aspects of communities anyways because it extends our reach. It is unfortunate for everyone that because you do something, you make it better, and then sadly you drive up the costs and lose that grass roots diversity or genuine diversity. We are by the sheer fact of being here creating our own downfall. (Interview with Hub Director)

What is evident through speaking to those who occupy the live/work space is that the level of genuine neighbourhood-scale diversity was negatively affected by their moving into the area; they acknowledge this and also reiterate how this is part of the gentrification story that has engulfed the east end of London since the early 2000s. Another interesting aspect has to do with the hub itself. On the face of it the space is genuinely diverse with a number of different ethnicities working and living in the area and with a large number of women being part of the local ecology of arts and crafts practitioners:

> We have always tried to be as inclusive as possible, you know we're not elitist in any sense of the word and it was always important that we hold on to that from the beginning when we actually started. (Interview with Hub Director)

However, just as we noted above that diversity could be glossed as the participation of people from different countries (mainly Europe, the USA and Australia) rather than seen in terms of a deep-rooted power relation regarding race and ethnicity, so too there was often a loose understanding of diversity in terms of an everyday cosmopolitanism. The following interviewee offers a critical reflection on this:

> You know the whole thing about a counterculture moving in to cheap parts of town to do artistic things is a very western thing. So actually it's no surprise that artists clusters are more cosmopolitan then they are multi-ethnic. (Interview with Artist)

Cosmopolitanism in this respect is understood in terms of the history of artists moving into derelict parts of cities in order to take advantage of the rents and the spaces afforded to them. It is steeped in counter cultural history and enacts the story of one large community bound together not by ethnicity or gender but by a communal language and ethos. Paradoxically, rather than challenging classed and racialised inequalities, this can quickly turn into an exclusive lifestyle making the spaces themselves inaccessible to outsiders. It is a process that can be heavily influenced by gatekeepers primarily concerned with keeping the community together in order to preserve this ethos. This very much chimes with the example of co-working spaces and the notion of curating communities, although in this particular case it is about how a cosmopolitan identity evolves as a result of what these warehouses and neighbourhoods afford the artists and their practices. This is essentially what Lave and Wenger (1991) have identified as 'communities of practice' as well as 'communities of interest', thereby making them difficult to break in to. Interestingly, the division between the notions of cosmopolitanism and multi-ethnicity speaks to the strength of bonds within communities; multi-ethnic communities do not necessarily become sites of community cohesion (see Amin 2002).

> You know just down the road is Westfield Shopping Centre and you know there are people in there from all over the world, different ethnicities and the face of globalisation, but whether or not that equates to community is a different thing. (Interview with Artist)

This leads to another aspect which is that of class; many in this part of Hackney Wick expressed the view that the issue of inequality is more about class than it is about gender or ethnicity—especially at the level of the space itself:

> It is more about class then ethnic diversity in this area. I'm from quite a poor background, never any money and you know it's easier for people from lower classes to recognise traits of people from an upper class because you know they don't really get the value of things which as an extension would be value to communities. A lot of people in the early days came from a background with a harder life, now it's a little different. (Interview with Hub Director)

One problem is the lack of accessibility to these spaces for people from working-class or lower-class backgrounds due to the classed nature and practice of artistic culture.

> When I was younger going into an art gallery I had no idea what to say... but you know we wanted people to engage with the art. The language can exclude people....less well-off people may and do find these spaces intimidating. (Interview with Hub Director)

Thus in this specific area inequality seems to be a result of gentrifying processes that force out existent diverse working-class and creative communities and replaces them with an influx of largely white, middle-class inhabitants. In turn the perpetuation of inequality is exacerbated by class through what are perceived as intimidating art community spaces.

Conclusion

In this chapter, we have begun an analysis of some of the factors that contribute to inequalities in creative and cultural hubs. The analysis presented here is preliminary and by no means exhaustive; however, we suggest that it offers some indications of the complex issues that contribute to hubs becoming more exclusive spaces than their proponents believe and in some cases hope. Building on a growing literature on inequalities in the CCI more generally, we have flagged some additional issues relating to gentrification, increasing rents and market forces; the inaccessibility and exclusiveness of artistic culture; and questions of what it means to 'curate' a co-working or live/work space, particularly when curators or managers are often themselves precarious subjects. We have highlighted the way that 'curation' becomes a site of tacit and unaccountable decisions about who belongs in a hub, with the risk of heightening inequalities along lines of gender, race and class (and also age and disability). We have also highlighted the tendency for slippage between a loose notion of cosmopolitanism and questions of patterned social, economic and cultural power relations. Clearly, the case studies are specific, and they are focussed in a fast-changing area of a metropolitan city however our analysis highlights two areas where policy can contribute to reducing inequality in creative and cultural work spaces such as hubs. First, there is a need for hub managers and/or curators of hub communities to *actively promote diversity* if creative and cultural hubs are to avoid becoming predominantly white, middle-class spaces; and second, there is a need to stem the displacement processes tied to gentrification as it also contributes to a reduction in diversity and an increase in inequality.

References

Acker, J. (2006). Inequality regimes: Gender, class, and race in organizations. *Gender & Society, 20*(4), 441–464.

Acme Studios. (2011). *Unearthed, the creative history of a brownfield site.* Available at http://www.acme.org.uk/residencies/unearthed?admin=1.

Amin, A. (2002). Ethnicity and the multicultural city: Living with diversity. *Environment and Planning A, 34*(6), 959–980.

Arts Council. (2018). *Equality, diversity and the creative case.* Available at https://www.artscouncil.org.uk/publication/equality-diversity-and-creative-case-data-report-2016-17 (Report downloaded on 24 August).

Banks, M., & Hesmondhalgh, D. (2009). Looking for work in creative industries policy. *International Journal of Cultural Policy, 15*(4), 415–430.

Brodmerkel, S., & Barker, R. (forthcoming). Hitting the 'glass wall': Investigating everyday ageism in the advertising industry. *The Sociological Review*.

Brook, O., O'Brien, D., & Taylor, M. (2018). *Inequality talk: How discourses by senior men reinforce exclusions from creative occupations*. Available at https://osf.io/preprints/socarxiv/y6db7/.

Catungal, J. P., Leslie, D., & Hii, Y. (2009). Geographies of displacement in the creative city: The case of Liberty Village, Toronto. *Urban Studies, 46*(5–6), 1095–1114.

Christopherson, S. (2008). Beyond the self-expressive creative worker: An industry perspective on entertainment media. *Theory, Culture & Society, 25*(7–8), 73–95.

Directors UK. (2018). *Who's calling the shots? A report on gender inequality among directors working in UK TV*. Available at https://www.directors.uk.com/news/who-s-calling-the-shots.

Edley, N., & Wetherell, M. (2001). Jekyll and Hyde: Men's constructions of feminism and feminists. *Feminism & Psychology, 11*(4), 439–457.

Edmond, M., & McGowan, J. (2017). We need more mediocre women! *Overland, 229*, 81.

Florida, R. (2002). *The rise of the creative class: And how it's transforming work, leisure, community and everyday life*. New York: Basic Books.

Gill, R. (1993). Justifying injustice: Broadcasters' accounts of inequality in radio. In E. Burman & I. Parker (Eds.), *Discourse analytic research: Readings and repertoires of texts in action*. London: Routledge.

Gill, R. (2014). Unspeakable inequalities: Post feminism, entrepreneurial subjectivity, and the repudiation of sexism among cultural workers. *Social Politics: International Studies in Gender, State & Society, 21*(4), 509–528.

Gill, R., & Pratt, A. (2008). In the social factory? Immaterial labour, precariousness and cultural work. *Theory, Culture & Society, 25*(7–8), 1–30.

Grugulis, I., & Stoyanova, D. (2009). 'I don't know where you learn them': Skills in film and TV. In *Creative labour: Working in the creative industries* (pp. 135–155). Basingstoke: Palgrave Macmillan.

Henry, L. (2017). *Ofcom is practising 'fake diversity' with on-screen targets*. Available at https://www.theguardian.com/media/2017/jul/19/lenny-henry-ofcom-practising-fake-diversity-on-screen-tv-targets.

Holgate, J., & Mckay, S. (2007). Institutional barriers to recruitment and employment in the audio visual industries. *The effect on black and minority ethnic workers*. London: Working Lives Research Institute.

HoneyBook. (2017). *2017 gender pay gap*. Available at https://www.honeybook.com/gender-pay-gap.

Hope, S., & Figiel, J. (2015). Interning and investing: Rethinking unpaid work, social capital and the "Human Capital Regime". *Triple C: Journal for a Global Sustainable Information Society, 13*(2), 361–374.

Hunt, D., & Ramon, A. C. (2015). *Hollywood diversity report: Flipping the script.* Los Angeles, CA: Ralph J. Bunche Center for African American Studies at UCLA, University of California at Los Angeles. Retrieved 10 February 2017.

Jones, D., & Pringle, J. K. (2015). Unmanageable inequalities: Sexism in the film industry. *The Sociological Review, 63*(1 suppl.), 37–49.

Kelan, E. K. (2007, November). 'I don't know why'—Accounting for the scarcity of women in ICT work. *Women's Studies International Forum, 30*(6), 499–511. Pergamon.

Kelan, E. K. (2009). Gender fatigue: The ideological dilemma of gender neutrality and discrimination in organizations. *Canadian Journal of Administrative Sciences/Revue Canadienne des Sciences de l'Administration, 26*(3), 197–210.

Khaleeli, H. (2014, June 20). Lenny Henry: Diversity in the TV industry "is worth fighting for". *The Guardian.* Available at http://www.theguardian.com/culture/2014/jun/20/lenny-henry-interview-diversity-tv-industry.

Lave, J., & Wenger, E. (1991). *Situated learning: Legitimate peripheral participation.* Cambridge: Cambridge University Press.

Lee, D. (2011). Networks, cultural capital and creative labour in the British independent television industry. *Media, Culture & Society, 33*(4), 549–565.

Mayor of London. (2014). *Artist's workspace study: Reports and recommendations.* Greater London Authority. Available at https://www.london.gov.uk/sites/default/files/artists_workspace_study_september2014_reva_web.pdf.

Merkel, J. (2015). Coworking in the city. *Ephemera, 15*(2), 121–139.

Morgan, G., & Nelligan, P. (2018). *The creativity hoax: Precarious work in the gig economy.* London and New York: Anthem Press.

Nixon, S., & Crewe, B. (2004). Pleasure at work? Gender, consumption and work-based identities in the creative industries. *Consumption Markets & Culture, 7*(2), 129–147.

O'Brien, D. (2018a). Tackling class discrimination. *Arts Professional.* Available at https://www.artsprofessional.co.uk/magazine/article/tackling-class-discrimination (Downloaded on 24 August).

O'Brien, D. (2018b). *Inequality talk: How discourses by senior men reinforce exclusions from creative occupations* (draft paper under review).

ONS. (2018). *Understanding the gender pay gap in the UK.* Available at https://www.ons.gov.uk/employmentandlabourmarket/peopleinwork/

earningsandworkinghours/articles/understandingthegenderpaygap-intheuk/2018-01-17.

Pratt, A. C. (2009). Urban regeneration: From the arts 'feel good' factor to the cultural economy: A case study of Hoxton, London. *Urban Studies, 46*(5–6), 1041–1061.

Randle, K., Leung, W. F., & Kurian, J. (2007). *Creating difference, Creative industries research and consultancy unit.* Hatfield: University of Hertfordshire.

Rosner, N. (2010). *The temporality of practice space: Towards a theory of the live/work community on Fish Island* (MSc dissertation Cities Programme). London School of Economics and Political Science, East London.

Ruth Eikhof, D., & Warhurst, C. (2013). The promised land? Why social inequalities are systemic in the creative industries. *Employee Relations, 35*(5), 495–508.

Saha, A. (2018). *Race and the cultural industries.* Cambridge: Polity.

Shiach, M., Nakano, D., Virani, T., & Poli, K. (2017). *Report on creative hubs and urban development goals (UK/Brazil).* Creative hubs and urban development goals (UK/Brazil). Available at https://qmro.qmul.ac.uk/xmlui/handle/123456789/28705.

Thanki, A., & Jeffreys, S. (2007). Who are the fairest? Ethnic segmentation in London's media production. *Work Organisation, Labour and Globalisation, 1*(1), 108–118.

Throsby, D., & Petetskaya, K. (2017). Making art work: An economic study of professional artists in Australia. *The Australia Council for the Arts.*

Virani, T. E., & Malem, W. (2015). *Re-articulating the creative hub concept as a model for business support in the local creative economy: The case of Mare Street in Hackney* (Creativeworks London Working Paper Series).

Wing-Fai, L., Gill, R., & Randle, K. (2015). Getting in, getting on, getting out? Women as career scramblers in the UK film and television industries. *The Sociological Review, 63*(1 suppl.), 50–65.

8

Creative Hubs: A Co-operative Space?

Marisol Sandoval and Jo Littler

Creative Hubs, Cultural Work and Creative Industries Policy

Work in the cultural sector is increasingly precarious, persistently une-qual, structurally individualised and competitive (see, e.g., Banks and Milestone 2011; de Peuter 2011, 2014; Hope and Richards 2015; Gill 2010, 2014; Gill and Pratt 2008; McRobbie 2015; Oakley 2011; Oakley and O'Brian 2016; Ross 2010). These realities of work stand in stark contrast to the idealised depictions of cultural work that are often promoted in cultural policy documents (McRobbie 2001; Banks and Hesmondhalgh 2009; Oakley 2011). Banks and Hesmondhalgh for example have identified a "reluctance of policy-makers and governments

M. Sandoval (✉) · J. Littler
Centre of Culture and Creative Industries, Department of Sociology,
City, University of London, London, UK
e-mail: marisol.sandoval.1@city.ac.uk

J. Littler
e-mail: jo.littler.1@city.ac.uk

© The Author(s) 2019
R. Gill et al. (eds.), *Creative Hubs in Question*, Dynamics of Virtual Work,
https://doi.org/10.1007/978-3-030-10653-9_8

to address the specific conditions of creative work – even as they continue to vigorously promote the 'creative industries' that both contain and depend upon it" (Banks and Hesmondhalgh 2009, p. 415). Similarly, Kate Oakley argues that for many years "policy on creative industries concerned itself with supporting small businesses and expanding related training and education; little attention was paid to conditions of labour" (Oakley 2011, p. 285). Any policies targeting work in the cultural and creative industries have tended to focus on training, mentoring, internships and scholarships, but did not pay much attention to the cultural sectors potential to offer good work on a large scale (Oakley 2011, p. 286; Banks and Hesmondhalgh 2009, p. 425). Issues such as low pay, unreasonable working hours, insecurity and discrimination have often remained absent from "relentlessly upbeat" policy narratives (Banks and Hesmondhalgh 2009, p. 425).

Given the absence of work in cultural industries policy in general, it is hardly surprising that policy literature on creative hubs emphasises their potential contribution to business development, but pays little attention to working conditions. In its 2003 *Creative London* report, the London Development Agency for example stressed that hubs "provide a space for work, participation and consumption. This includes the help to nurture emerging talent and to link it to broader networks, a first-stop for businesses support and access to finance, and promotion of local talent and local businesses [...] they support communities of practice, not for profit and commercial, large and small, part-time and full-time activity – they are not just incubators for small businesses, but have a wider remit" (London Development Agency 2003, 34f). Here, creative hubs are seen as both beneficial for creative businesses and their surrounding communities. Similarly, a more recent report on creative hubs issued by the British Council identifies "a wide range of impacts including start-up ventures, jobs, new products and services, future investment (public and commercial), talent development, regional talent retention, informal education and engagement, training, urban regeneration, research and development, new networks, innovative models of organisation, quality of life enhancements and resilience" (Dovey et al. 2016, p. 5).

Existing literature on creative hubs tends to foreground business support services as key means for supporting the creative sector and local communities. Acknowledging the structural precarity of the cultural and creative industries, Virani and Malem (2015, p. 7) argue that an approach to creative hubs that focuses on the services they provide to small creative businesses can create opportunities for growth and sustainability. He describes hubs as "a putative model for providing mainly business support in a local context for specifically the creative sector" (Virani and Malem 2015, p. 3). According to Dovey et al., "Hubs represent a collective approach to coping with uncertain social, cultural and economic environments and processes of creativity and innovation" (Dovey et al. 2016, p. 4).

However, whilst focusing solely on job creation, education, talent and business development can contribute to an expansion of the creative industries, it does little to improve the quality of jobs that are being created. Realising any potentials hubs might have to encourage collectivity among cultural workers, reduce precarity and improve working conditions in the sector requires a shift in perspective that zooms in on the needs of workers, rather than industry and businesses.

Whilst the image of creative hubs is therefore often one of creative conviviality, as this book illustrates, their political economies are often fairly diverse: they include a range of forms of cultural industry from the corporate to the co-operative. We might, for example, envisage a spectrum or a taxonomy of "co-working"—often a key feature of hubs—ranging from corporate industries leasing communal space to cultural workers through to the worker's co-operative where responsibilities and profits are shared (see de Peuter et al. 2017). To accomplish a shift in perspective towards putting the needs of all producers in creative hubs first, we argue that policies, processes and practices connected to cultural hubs could take inspiration from the model of worker co-operation.

Co-operatives

Worker co-operatives are businesses that are collectively owned and democratically controlled by the people working in them. The World Declaration on Worker Co-operatives highlights that worker co-ops aim at "creating and maintaining sustainable jobs and generating wealth, in order to improve the quality of life of the worker-members, dignify human work, allow workers' democratic self-management and promote community and local development" (CICOPA 2004, p. 3).

The co-operative model is as old as the history of capitalism. And yet it has not lost its appeal to those looking for alternatives to unequal, exploited and precarious work. In recent years, the co-operative model has gained renewed popularity and been adjusted to suit contemporary working realities. Advocates of platform co-operativism for example suggest turning private Internet platforms such as Airbnb or Uber into co-operatives owned by all users (Scholz 2017). This movement envisions a true-sharing economy in which technology is employed to serve people's needs rather than being used as a tool to facilitate super-precarious work. Another adaptation of the co-operative model is the suggestion to create freelancers co-operatives as a response to the rise in precarious freelance employment over the past decade (Co-operatives UK 2016). The report *Not Alone* issued by Co-operatives UK argues that co-operatives can provide important services for the self-employed including advice and companionship, back office support, legal and financial advice, shared workspace, shared equipment, access to finance, collective insurance and marketing (Co-operatives UK 2016, p. 49). These services largely resemble those often provided by creative hubs. However, the report does not just focus on what services are beneficial for the self-employed but on how these services should be delivered and highlights the advantages co-operative models have over commercial providers.

A co-operative insurance model for example is the so-called Bread Fund. In a Bread Fund, 25–50 self-employed people come together as a group in order to collectively create sick pay insurance for all members. Each month the members pay a defined amount of money into the fund. If a member becomes unable to work due to health issues, the fund pays this member a monthly sick pay allowance.[1] Contrary to commercial insurance schemes, this co-operatively organised model

---

[1] http://breadfunds.uk.

ensures that all money paid into the fund is returned directly to members in need rather than contributing to the profits of a private insurance company. In addition, Bread Funds help to create a sense of community among otherwise isolated workers. Similarly, co-working can beneficially be organised in a co-operative manner. Workplace Co-operative 115 was set up in London in 2002 as secondary co-operative of self-employed workers and small businesses in the creative industries to create secure, affordable and communal workspace. In an interview, a member of 115 described the decision to set up the co-op as a response to the lack of good quality workspace that also offers a true sense of community: *"We wanted to set up something where sole practitioners, and companies of two, can work in a way that felt good. And co-ops seem to offer that [...] There are lots of places that are hubs, but have that sort of feeling of community that it feels slightly spurious sometimes, it feels a bit like it's a kind of add on and really it's a kind of money making proposition"* (Workspace Co-operative 115).[2]

Collaboration, community, mutual support and solidarity are among the core values of co-operatives. Co-ops therefore actively challenge individualised working cultures that often shape work in the creative industries and beyond (Sandoval 2017). While often remaining unmentioned in cultural policy documents, models of worker co-operation have in fact been successfully applied in the creative sector. The directory of Co-operatives UK currently lists 348 co-ops under the category "creative".[3] A series of interviews conducted with cultural sector co-operators across the UK[4] showed that co-op members often feel that the model offers a real alternative to dominant industry patterns. One interviewee for example stressed that co-ops are *"challenging the art system as it is now: highly exploitative, really bad relations between people"*

---

[2]This quote is taken from an interview Marisol Sandoval conducted together with Greig de Peuter at Workspace Co-operative 115 in April 2017.

[3]Co-operatives UK directory. https://www.uk.coop/directory?loc%5Bdistance%5D=20&loc%5Bunit%5D=3959&loc%5Borigin%5D=&keys=&cat=6. Accessed on 17 May 2016.

[4]The semi-structured interviews were conducted between August 2014 and June 2015. They were part of a larger project on cultural work and the politics of worker co-operatives (Sandoval 2016, 2017).

(Interviewee 4). Similarly, another interviewee described the decision to start a co-operative as "*a reaction against what we met in a previous job. We were determined not to have a hierarchy when we formed a co-op*" (Interviewee 17).

A key structural difference to most workplaces is that co-operatives offer equal say and often also equal pay to all members. In practice, this means that "*if you work here, you own the business, basically. And we are all on equal pay*" (Interviewee 12). As a result of collective ownership and decision making, co-operators tend to experience their day-to-day work routines as highly self-determined: "*in short, working conditions are lovely, we get to decide what we do every day*" (Interviewee 21). The absence of hierarchies between workers and bosses is experienced as particularly rewarding: "*I have no boss! It's like, you get that we are all bosses and we are all workers [...] Nobody has power over me and I don't have power over anyone and that is really important. So you get a sense of satisfaction, a sense of being listened to*" (Interviewee 15). Instead of competitiveness and individualisation, as they are commonly experienced in cultural sector work, co-operators report about practices of mutual support and solidarity: "*it's about solidarity and not competition and inside the organisation people support each other*" (Interviewee 1). Contrary to regular businesses in which workers are expected to serve the needs of the company, co-operatives are designed to serve the needs of the people working in them. One co-operator for example stressed: "*We are able to respond to people's needs, you know. Day to day or periods in their life, we can step up and be flexible for people. And it's not just like another employment where they see what they can get out of you*" (Interviewee 15). Similarly, a member of another long-running co-op emphasised the combination of security and flexibility as a main benefit of her workplace: "*Very very secure working conditions and very flexible working conditions. In the truer sense, not in some horrible kind of 'neo-liberaly co-optive flexy work'! It's flexible, if I need to go home at 2 o'clock, I go home at 2 o'clock, that's ok*" (Interviewee 12).

However, this is not the reality of all co-operatives. Like many alternative projects, co-ops often are confronted with conflicts between creative processes, economic necessity and political aspirations (Comedia 1984, p. 96; Hesmondhalgh 1997). For example, starting and running a co-operative, similar to any other business, requires investments of both time and money. To maintain their independence, co-ops do not accept venture capital or any investment that gives investors power over the operation of the co-op. This often means that a lack access of financial resources forces co-operators to invest considerable amounts of free labour, sometimes called "sweat-equity" (Whellens 2014): "[We work] *full time plus overtime. And we can't quite pay ourselves for this right now. Possibly later we can pay out something. We will see how it goes*" (Interviewee 4). Especially newly founded co-ops often struggle to combine the benefits of self-determination and freedom co-ops offer with equally important economic security. As one co-operator stressed: "*What I do experience at the moment in my co-op is a lot of freedom in the way we work and I absolutely love and enjoy that whole process. The difficult thing is because of finances is creating the security, and can we develop our business to the point that we can actually guarantee a regular income and not always be stressing about where is this going to come from*" (Interviewee 6). Co-operatives do not provide an automatic escape from precarious working lives.

While co-operatives might succeed in creating internal structures of support and solidarity, they continue to operate within competitive markets within an increasingly commercialised cultural sector. The difficulty in accessing funding and resources is exacerbated by the fact that co-ops seek to maintain their operative independence and therefore might reject external investment or refuse to accept contracts with a too powerful client. One co-operator for example argued: "*Also in terms of funding, it does boil down to that: We are operating on such a minimal budget. We need to find ways to fund ourselves without compromising our politics as well*" (Interviewee 22). He added that in addition to difficulties generating commercial income, funding from governmental or other funding bodies is often hard to obtain due to co-operatives' status as business rather than a charity: "*Yes, we find it actually quite tough for funding. For many reasons, but partially because we are not a charity and a lot of funders just fund charities*" (Interviewee 22).

Creating funding schemes to support co-operative organisations is an opportunity for cultural policy-making to specifically target working conditions in the cultural sector and overcome the primary focus on business support. However, the co-operators interviewed in this study expressed little confidence in current governments and policy-makers to provide effective support for co-operatives. One interviewee argued: "*I don't think from a government level there is particularly very much support... occasional good words, but not that much on the agenda*" (Interviewee 17). Another co-operator emphasised the underlying problem that the democratic structures of government at the moment are insufficient and lag behind the level of democracy practised in many co-operatives: "*the thing about the government is that they have a massive control over resources and to build this new economy we need them to direct loads of resources towards this. So of course they can help. But I don't believe in the government in its current structures. I would want a far more participatory, democratic structure of government to be making these decisions*" (Interviewee 6). Thus, while embedding financial support for co-operatives within policies on creative hubs would be an immediate and important step to encourage better quality work in the cultural sector, co-ops at the same time point towards the need for large-scale structural changes in order to create a truly co-operative economy and society.

Past and Present: Co-operatives and Creative Hubs

As the 2016 British Council *Creative Hubs* report points out, there are already creative hubs in existence which are run along a co-operative model (Dovey and Pratt 2016) although they are relatively thin on the ground. The Roco Creative Coop hub in Sheffield was launched in 2012 and opened in 2015 in to support the creative industries in the city and is registered as a community benefit society which is solely owned by its shareholder members.[5] £1.2 million was raised through community shares and social lending, which was used to convert seven listed Georgian townhouses in the city centre into a hub including 30 studios, co-working space, bookshop, design store, café, galleries,

---

[5]https://www.theroco.org/join-us/. Accessed 1 November 2017.

a bottle shop and maker space. Through the close proximity of these facilities, the Roco coop has aimed to facilitate and connect environmentally and socially conscious design, architecture, consumption and creative practice. The shop stocks primarily fair-trade and ethical products, there is a green roof, and the creative facilities are strongly oriented towards encouraging design with a positive social impact (Dovey and Pratt 2016, p. 38).

Such spatial, working and affective linkages have the potential to cross-pollinate not only "creativity", but a shared purpose of creating for the common good. As one of the initiators of the project, Chris Hill, points out, the political-economic logic of the co-operative model works to mitigate against commercial competition and paranoia about originality:

> The great thing about the co-operative model is that you're prepared to share things in the knowledge someone isn't ripping off your idea to turn it into their own profit.
>
> It's particularly true of creative workers where project groups can come together and dissolve when the project's finished. Roco will be a rallying point for these people; they'll know where to find each other. (Collier 2014)

As this last part of this quote illustrates, the spatial proximity of the hub model means that it has a particularly potent potential to link together and to be "a rallying point" for co-operative projects and practices.

The terminology of co-operative creative hubs may be new, but there are of course many historical examples of cultural policy and activity which has encouraged creative public co-operative space. The Greater London Council in the UK in the 1980s for example notoriously adopted a range of strategies to stimulate a more inclusive cultural sector and city, one which attempted to make cultural spaces more co-operative places run for citizens rather than commodified services oriented solely for paying consumers. These strategies included opening up the Royal Festival Hall at the Southbank Centre as a place where the public could go for free: before then, it had been locked up all day, and you could only enter as a visitor who had paid for a performance

(Kirsch 2017). It also included subsidising extremely popular free music festivals for Londoners, alongside community radio, women's theatre and a range of black arts projects (Bianchini 1987; Mulgan and Worpole 1986). Interestingly, however, whilst both encouraging co-operative *practices* and inclusive community arts were the much-discussed hallmark of GLC cultural policy, it is hard to find too many specific named institutions which are defined precisely as worker's co-operatives in the literature on GLC history—although they did exist, such as the co-operative book distributor Turnaround (McGuigan 1996; Lewis et al. 1986).

It is true that the historical research into the GLC is still not as expansive as it deserves to be.[6] It is also more than possible that there are many instances of worker's co-operatives in that context which are simply not discussed or labelled as such. Yet the very fact that it is underplayed in the critical literature on the subject is itself both deeply significant and a missed opportunity that we should learn from. Indeed, in many ways it is symptomatic of a wider tendency in the literature on alternative cultural sector organisations to lump together various different types of "progressive" groups—even when their progressiveness or quality is being questioned.

For example, in 1985 the searching and acerbic critique *What a way to run a railroad: an analysis of radical failure* took to task the organisational skills and assumptions of radical cultural groups that were born out of various strands of the libertarian movements of the 1960s and 1970s (the book opens with a list of recently deceased radical organisations). As the title indicates, the book devotes itself to questioning the organisational inadequacies and debilitating assumptions of radical political projects in the cultural sector, including participants mistaking their own self-righteousness and self-satisfaction for an effective project. The book functioned as a powerful rallying call for radical organisations to think hard about organisational structure. Yet interestingly, and

---

[6]The oral history project "The GLC Story" has been recently constructing a history and collating resources on the GLC for younger generations. See http://glcstory.co.uk/ and their *GLC Story Oral History Project* zine (2017).

despite discussion of different types of organisation including mutual aid, there is not a lot of intellectual traffic in the book with work on the structure of worker co-operatives or the wider co-operative movement. This is not so much a problem with this particular book as symptomatic of a wider *lacuna* in the existing literature on cultural policy and cultural organisations.

We would argue that cultural policy needs to pay far more attention to cultural co-operatives. This is particularly the case at a moment when there is a revival of interest in what has been termed "the new municipalism", or "re-municipalism"—in creating democratic, non-capitalist relationships, services and spaces which are also non-authoritarian and involve forms of co-production, for which Barcelona En Comú is often held up as the flagship example (Reyes and Russell 2017). Such projects often involve mayors alongside wider mobilisations which seek to reclaim civic institutions and infrastructure from private ownership, returning them to (or creating anew) public ownership and exist alongside innovative digital platforms in order to enable participatory forms of democracy, co-production and co-operation. The role of co-operatives is for example foregrounded very explicitly in Mississippi's largest city, Jackson, where the new mayor is working closely with Cooperation Jackson, which aims to find ways of building a solidarity economy "anchored by a network of co-operatives and worker-owned, democratically-managed enterprises".[7] Cooperation Jackson is inspired by both Black Lives Matter and the international co-operative movement; its 13 core principles "were crafted by adapting aspects from the basic principles of the Mondragon Cooperative Corporation" from the Basque region/country in Spain.[8]

Within this bubbling up of interest in the potential formation of new co-operative dynamics in civic spaces comes the possibility for expanding co-operatives in cultural hubs, in the cultural sector and in cultural policy. Indeed, cultural policy-making in general has much more to learn from co-operatives. A "policy from below" framework that

---

[7]http://www.cooperationjackson.org/. Accessed 10 November 2017.

[8]http://www.cooperationjackson.org/. Accessed 10 November 2017.

encourages "bottom-up solutions proposed by workers and their collective organizations" (de Peuter and Cohen 2015, p. 310) is a means of expanding the participation and democratic accountability of policymakers. More participatory forms of policy-making could take their inspiration from the wide range of existing and historical alternatives, practices and visions of how cultural work could be organised, co-operatively and for the common good.

References

Banks, M., & Hesmondhalgh, D. (2009). Looking for work in creative industries policy. *International Journal of Cultural Policy, 15*(4), 415–430.

Banks, M., & Milestone, K. (2011). Individualization, gender and cultural work. *Gender, Work and Organization, 18*(1), 73–89.

Bianchini, F. (1987). GLC RIP? Cultural policies in London 1981–1986. *New Formations, 1,* 103–117.

CICOPA. (2004). *International declaration on worker co-operatives.* Available at http://www.cicopa.coop/IMG/pdf/Declaration_approved_by_ICA_EN-2.pdf.

Collier, H. (2014, June 24). The Roco: A £1.1m arts coop in Sheffield. *The Guardian.* https://www.theguardian.com/uk-news/the-northerner/2014/jun/24/the-roco-a-11m-arts-co-op-in-sheffield.

Comedia. (1984). The alternative press: The development of underdevelopment. *Media, Culture & Society, 6,* 95–102.

Co-operatives UK. (2016). *Not alone. Trade union and co-operative solutions for self-employed workers.* Available at https://www.uk.coop/sites/default/files/uploads/attachments/not_alone_-_trade_union_and_co-operative_solutions_for_self-employed_workers_3.pdf.

de Peuter, G. (2011). Creative economy and labour precarity: A contested convergence. *Journal of Communication Inquiry, 35*(4), 417–425.

de Peuter, G. (2014). Beyond the model worker: Surveying a creative precariat. *Culture Unbound, 6,* 263–284.

de Peuter, G., & Cohen, N. S. (2015). Emerging labour politics in creative industries. In K. Oakley & J. O'Connor (Eds.), *The Routledge companion to the cultural industries* (pp. 305–318). London: Routledge.

de Peuter, G., Cohen, N. S., & Saraco, F. (2017). The ambivalence of coworking: On the politics of an emerging work practice. *European Journal of Cultural Studies, 20*(6), 687–706.

Dovey, J., Pratt, A., Moreton, S., Virani, T., Merkel, J., & Lansdowne, J. (2016). *Creative hubs: Understanding the creative economy.* British Council. Available at http://creativeconomy.britishcouncil.org/media/uploads/files/HubsReport.pdf.

Gill, R. (2010). "Life is a Pitch": Managing the self in new media work. In M. Deuze (Ed.), *Managing media work* (pp. 249–262). Los Angeles: Sage.

Gill, R. (2014). Unspeakable inequalities. Post feminism, entrepreneurialism, subjectivity, and the repudiation of sexism among cultural workers. *Social Politics, 21*(4), 509–528.

Gill, R., & Pratt, A. (2008). In the social factory? Immaterial labour, precariousness and cultural work. *Theory, Culture & Society, 25*(7–8), 1–30.

Grayson, D., Nkonde, N., et al. (2017). *GLC story: Oral history project.* http://glcstory.co.uk/.

Hesmondhalgh, D. (1997). Post punk's attempt to democratise the music industry: The success and failure of rough trade. *Popular Music, 16*(3), 255–274.

Hope, S., & Richards, J. (2015). Loving work. Drawing attention to pleasure and pain in the body of the cultural worker. *European Journal of Cultural Studies, 18*(2), 117–141.

Kirsch, Brenda interviewed in Grayson, D., & Nkonde, N. (Eds.). (2017). *GLC Story Oral History Project zine.* Available at http://glcstory.co.uk/.

Lewis, J., et al. (1986). *Art—Who needs it?* London: Comedia.

London Development Agency. (2003). *Creative London: Vision and plan.* London: London Development Agency. Available at https://creativeindustrieslondon.files.wordpress.com/2014/11/creative-london.pdf.

McGuigan, J. (1996). *Culture and the public sphere.* London and New York: Routledge.

McRobbie, A. (2001, August 30). *Everyone is creative: Artists as new economy pioneers?* Open Democracy. Available at https://www.opendemocracy.net/node/652.

McRobbie, A. (2015). *Be creative. Making a living in the new culture industries.* Cambridge: Polity Press.

Mulgan, G., & Worpole, K. (1986). *Saturday night or sunday morning? From arts to industry—New forms of cultural policy.* London: Comedia.

Oakley, K. (2011). In its own image: New labour and the cultural workforce. *Cultural Trends, 20*(3–4), 281–289.

Oakley, K., & O'Brien, D. (2016). Learning to labour unequally: Understanding the relationship between cultural production, cultural consumption and inequality. Social identities. *Journal for the Study of Race, Nation and Culture, 22*(5), 471–486.

Reyes, O., & Russell, B. (2017, August). Fearless cities: The new urban movements. *Red Pepper.* http://www.redpepper.org.uk/fearless-cities-the-new-urban-movements/.

Ross, A. (2010). The mental labour problem. *Social Text, 63, 18*(2), 1–31.

Sandoval, M. (2017). From passionate labour to compassionate work. Cultural co-ops, do what you love and social change. *European Journal of Cultural Studies, 18*(2), 117–141.

Sandoval, M. (2016). What would rosa do? Co-operatives and radical politics. *Soundings, 63*, 98–111.

Scholz, T. (2017). *Uberworked and underpaid.* Cambridge: Polity Press.

Virani, T. E., & Malem, W. (2015). *Re-articulating the creative hub concept as a model for business support in the local creative economy: The case of Mare Street in Hackney* (Creative Works London Working Paper No. 12).

Whellens, S. (2014). *The precarious generation of creative workers.* Available at http://bethnalbling.blogspot.co.uk/2014/03/creative-workers-precarious-generation.html. Accessed 5 February 2016.

Part II

Looking Outside the Cluster

9

Istanbul's Sounds and Its 'Creative' Hubs: Creative Actors Articulating the City into Transnational Networks Through Music

Ceren Mert

Introduction

Music has been integrated into interdisciplinary fields since the mid-1990s with a focus on its social, cultural and economic sides (Krims 2007; Watson et al. 2009). Authors have emphasized the role of agency and networks when discussing the complex interplay between music and place (Crossley 2015; Prior 2015a; Crossley and Bottero 2015). These networks can be disseminated through the production of creative work, where the latent relationships between actors can be reactivated by Internet and media technologies (Watson and Beaverstock 2016). Nevertheless, within *place*-based research around creative industries, face-to-face networks are as important as interactions performed through the Internet. For instance, creative workers within the field of advertisement in London's Soho district have put a substantial emphasis on the visual and creative character of places where networks of social relations are articulated (Clare 2013, pp. 52–53). Or as in another example, Hoxton

C. Mert (✉)
Faculty of Social Sciences, Özyeğin University, Istanbul, Turkey

© The Author(s) 2019
R. Gill et al. (eds.), *Creative Hubs in Question*, Dynamics of Virtual Work,
https://doi.org/10.1007/978-3-030-10653-9_9

attaining one of the 'coolest places' title due to the opening of art studios
and music clubs in the area (Pratt 2009, p. 1047), is indicative of how
social networks between creative actors/entrepreneurs drastically transform places; however not ignoring the constraining affects of neoliberal
urban policies. In other words, creative industries themselves are also
stimulating increasing attention as '*hubs* of managerial innovation and
experimentation' (Lampel and Germain 2016, p. 2327).

This chapter thus dwells on how various music worlds and tastes
emerge in relation to place being temporarily bounded, especially when
reconsidering creative hubs and networked cultures in *flux*. This allows
for rethinking creative hubs as being *beyond* static localities (see Tironi
2010; Virani and Malem 2015). Likewise, here I argue the significance of the actors/entrepreneurs in the actualization and performance
of these hubs. As it is through these music hubs and its actors that the
city of Istanbul continues to vibrate its diverse, contemporary identity
together with its peculiar ambience.

Scrutinizing *four* of the music spaces in various parts of Istanbul's
Beyoğlu district, this chapter discusses Babylon, Salon, Minimüzikhol and
Peyote, in relation to urban space(s), creative actors and entrepreneurs, as
well as cultural policies. These venues can be thought of as creative hubs
as they allow musicians and various other art performers to collaborate
and form networks nationally and internationally by giving stage to their
work. Nevertheless, this paper initially focuses on Babylon and Salon,
which are the venues of Pozitif and IKSV, respectively. It focuses on how
capitalism is *performed* through its actors, playing a significant role in the
formation of tastes and lifestyles around music, which forms a considerable part of its creative hubs. The creative actors of these venues and institutions have acted as incubators when thinking about the lack of financial
assistance and funding for the arts and culture initiatives from the government agencies. Besides, these music hubs, through their actors, have
contributed to the city's cultural and artistic imagery—which is starkly in
mismatch with the contemporary government's values and ideals.

The latter section elaborates on the other two venues, Minimüzikhol
and Peyote, which, in comparison with the aforementioned two, are
more *rhizomatic*, recalling Deleuze and Guattari. They do not entail
hierarchized and bureaucratic structuration, allowing for more amateur

musicians to take stage. Initially being more open to the emerging music genres and styles, Minimüzikhol and Peyote evidently allow for more hybrid artistic ideas and expressions to blossom outside of the mainstream creative industries. Accordingly, Istanbul as a city-space gets articulated into different geographies and cultures in respect to the performativity of its creative actors, by building networks through music and arts, hence enabling hubs to be in flux.

These neighbourhoods/areas have been transformed into places that can be reconsidered as creative clusters, which inhabit creative hubs such as the four music venues this paper focuses on. Consequently, such neighbourhoods/areas have articulated the city into global cultural flows of music, arts and culture, especially through these venues, that is, the creative hubs as this paper argues. The mentioned venues give stage to an eclectic array of sounds, including various forms of indie, house, experimental, dubstep, electro-acoustic and folk-acoustic, world music, jazz, techno, ambient and so on. As the production and consumption of music have changed enormously in our digital age, the circulation and mixing of different genres due to accelerated technological advancements have created more hybrid and avant-garde sounds, affecting the ways they have been performed. These hubs in Istanbul trigger new and innovative tastes in music and arts, enabling face-to-face interactions between its creative actors. As within the processes of creative projects, which involve emotional labour, face-to-face interactions are crucial as they form trust between its actors, necessitating travel, hence mobility (Watson and Beaverstock 2016).

The aim here is to present another image of Istanbul as a city-space that stands in contrast to its current political reflection. Such an image, being part of, and containing plurality, is analysed from the point of its creative hubs, which are particularly the music hubs as referred to above and its creative clusters such as the mentioned neighbourhoods of the Beyoğlu district; an identity deploying a beautiful 'cacophony' of a wide range of sounds through its creative actors.[1]

---

[1]Accordingly, nineteen in-depth, semi-structured and open-ended interviews were conducted with various creative actors related to the music venues discussed throughout this chapter. Each interview ranged approximately 35–90 minutes and they were carried out from February 2011 to November 2012. The interviewees who have been anonymously utilized in this chapter have been numbered in order of their initial appearance of the text.

Correspondingly, starting with the second half of this paper, I will be emphasizing Deleuze and Guattari's concept of *rhizome* when reconsidering these music spaces as creative hubs. The rhizomatic characteristics are attributed in this paper to Minimüzikhol and Peyote, the two music venues discussed in the latter section, when compared to Babylon and Salon. Nevertheless, considering the 'image' of the city imposed and represented by the government's retrogressive political implementations, even the actors/entrepreneurs in relation to Babylon and Salon at times stand out as rhizomes via the musicians and artists they give stage to. It is through the networks that these actors form which bring forth the creative hubs, that is, through these music venues. In this regard, I will be elaborating on these music venues as creative hubs, and how they have the potential to invigorate and transform the urban life of Istanbul.

'Creative Entrepreneurs' and Incubators of Contemporary Urban Sounds

Interviewee-1, who was part of the managerial staff at Babylon during the time of the interview, stressed that a decade prior to our meeting, Asmalımescit neighbourhood in Beyoğlu was rather an isolated area. People were once afraid to walk down from Asmalımescit to Tünel, which has become one of the areas where the 'creative' urban buzz is. Before Babylon opened in Asmalımescit in 1999, the building was a carpenter's shop and the surrounding streets were rather dangerous. For interviewee-1, after the opening of Babylon:

> Asmalımescit turned out to be a 'cool' place and everyone started to come here. When Asmalımescit became popular and new spaces [of entertainment] began to have [customers with] different profiles, naturally the profiles of those who came here [Babylon] also underwent a change.

Inhabited by the Levantines in the nineteenth century, Asmalımescit later became an area where artists, picture-framers, booksellers and old traditional pubs called 'meyhane' were clustered. In the beginning of the twentieth century, this neighbourhood turned out to be a place where

European artists resided, while working in restaurants and entertainment spaces initiated and managed by the White Russians. In the mid-1960s, it slowly started to lose its old image and popularity, becoming a neighbourhood with empty streets where people were afraid to pass by. By the end of the 1980s and early 1990s, artists started to move here again, paving the way for the organizing company Pozitif to open in 1989 and its venue Babylon ten years later, which inaugurated serious transformations in the area (Yener 2009; Ince 2006, 2008).

Gentrification of the once 'local' Asmalımescit in the late 1980s and 1990s was the result of the new elites' quest for new spaces in the city, reflecting neoliberal economy's limitless expansion. Institutionalized finance sectors and their upper strata brought forth a new Istanbul bourgeoisie including the professional-managerial class, together with industrial and self-employed business people. Such a neoliberal context generated a 'class' of young entrepreneurs in their thirties; enabling another transformation: these new entrepreneurs, who completed their (under)graduate degrees in the USA, knew one or more foreign languages, were nourished with a cosmopolitan culture, were discontent and critical of Turkey's situation, and were working mainly in the areas of advertising, public relations and the media. Showing a great interest in arts and culture, this new class started to reside in neighbourhoods like Asmalımescit, Cihangir and Galata, triggering the appearance of new lifestyles and tastes (Bali 2006, pp. 209–210).

Mehmet and Ahmet Uluğ brothers and Cem Yegül, founders of the company Pozitif and its venue Babylon, accelerated the pace and variety of music and entertainment in Istanbul; initially yearning to cultivate their music experiences gained in the USA after returning to this city in the late 1980s. They invested and contributed to the creative industries mainly in Istanbul and can be regarded as incubators of creative hubs, such as the case of Babylon in Asmalımescit and recently Bomontiada in the Şişli district. In the beginning, Pozitif was organizing live music concerts, particularly jazz; however in time they started to give stage to a vast number of (sub)genres including the diverse world of today's electronic and indie music scenes. Pozitif also arranged workshops and a considerable amount of music festivals over the years, alongside developing their own music label, online radio station and magazine.

They opened other venues such as Babylon Bomonti, Babylon Alaçatı and Babylon Kilyos in different regions. As mentioned, in 2015 Babylon relocated from Asmalımescit to *Bomontiada* which is in the Bomonti neighbourhood of Şişli district, and a hub that consists of various entertainment and leisure spaces including those of music, dining and drinking, art exhibitions and workshops and so forth. Hence, it has been transformed into a creative hub from Istanbul's historic Bomonti Beer Factory. Here, Bomontiada can be considered as a creative hub rather than a cluster because it stands out as a single 'enclosed' open area, a courtyard, with only one entrance to different spots of entertainment, including the venue Babylon. Thus, as Virani and Malem pinpoint, 'regarding what they look like, creative hubs can take on a number of manifestations, or combination of manifestations, such as co-working spaces, business incubators, etc.' (Virani and Malem 2015, pp. 7–8).

Interviewee-2, professionally an architect, a music enthusiast and a radio programmer, denoted that the more intensive transformation around Asmalımescit up to the Tünel area started with the opening of Babylon. As he highlighted, other music spaces also had an immense effect on the reshaping of the remaining quarters of Beyoğlu. Pozitif and its venue played an important role in the neighbourhood's transformation; nevertheless as interviewee-2 emphasized, there had been several other music and entertainment venues, such as Hayal Kahvesi, Jazz Stop and Sofyalı that had triggered the transformation in the adjacent neighbourhoods alongside Istiklal Street before Babylon.

Silvia Rief explains in her comparative analyses of Istanbul and London around the issue of cultural strategies of urban renewal and night-time economy that both cities' cultural policies have been interpreted in different ways. Despite the long tradition of nightlife in central Istanbul, especially those in Beyoğlu, music scenes and spaces have not been incorporated into the projects of the political elites and local governments (Rief 2009, p. 24). For instance, in the case study of Tarek E. Virani (2016) on a venue giving stage to experimental music in Dalston, received a grant for its contribution to the local neighbourhood as well as the experimental music scene. It formed a partnership with an organization that has collaborations with various institutions and funding agencies such as the Arts Council England. In Istanbul, however, there is no such funding from the government organizations, but rather from private institutions, such as Pozitif, and foundations like IKSV—which was established by Eczacıbaşı Inc. According to interviewee-2, as a foundation, IKSV is a non-profit organization, whereas Pozitif is a private company, organized around a private enterprise mentality.

Interviewee-3, a prominent figure at IKSV, stressed the significance of providing infrastructural improvements for arts and culture in Istanbul. For interviewee-3, the city does not have a sufficient amount of concert and performing arts halls, exhibition centres; hence these should be developed in line with a contemporary understanding. He underlined that if there were not enough funds and facilities, then the existing transformable spaces should be efficiently utilized for exhibitions and performances. For him, the main problem in Turkey was not the resources but the inefficiency of how these resources were put into use and how they were distributed. Interviewee-3 pointed out that the financial amount given to non-profit culture institutions by the state agencies should be at least 35–40% of the annual budget. According to him, this amount should also not exceed 50% because it would then start becoming a public enterprise and not a non-profit institution. Unfortunately, IKSV was given a 5–6% financial support from the state and even this was not a continuous one. 'If the Ministry of Culture and Tourism sees it appropriate that year, it supports us on the basis of projects, festivals' said interviewee-3, whereas for him the state should be legally organizing, economically providing and facilitating the infrastructures of the culture and creative industries. In order to achieve this, the Turkish Ministry of Culture and Tourism should not be receiving the lowest share within the general state budget. He added that the resources of the local authorities were also significant. As IKSV, they were not informed how and where the funds of these local authorities were spent. Interviewee-3 thus criticized the consumption of the funds by the local authorities for their own 'cultural events'. For him, these authorities were not event organizers, and should be instead fundraising and supporting the profit- and non-profit-oriented creative industries.

Interviewee-4, a managerial figure at Median Müzik Edisyon, a private organization in Istanbul that provides the communication between musicians and production companies that want to use certain music in films, TV serials and commercials, offering consultations on copyright and other legal issues, criticized the way the state intervened in arts and culture in Turkey. Although the Turkish government financially supported certain art and music events, it automatically claimed itself as the only decision-making actor—which for interviewee-4 hindered the cultural production and its publicity. Hence, despite being ironical, it is not surprising that various banks and corporations are among the main sponsors of music festivals and events in Turkey, including those organized by Pozitif and IKSV.

'Increasing pressure to innovate has led to a much greater emphasis on *creativity*' (Thrift 2000, p. 676). This overlaps with the emergence of new entrepreneurs in Turkey, as a consequence of neoliberal implications, and Pozitif being one of the early examples par excellence within the music and entertainment sector. As Thrift denotes, innovation has been crucial for the business practices and self-image. Nevertheless, in our contemporary era 'creativity' is acknowledged by the managerial staff to enable its own form of 'knowledge', thus generating value in itself, which in turn leads to innovation.

For Thrift, creativity is performed through capitalism via its actors through the production of new spaces, which means new spaces of visualization, of embodiment, and of circulation. These are enabled by the information technologies, which contribute to the new economy in countless ways, signifying youth, speed, excitement and 'buzz' (ibid., pp. 676–677). This coincides with the emergence of creative hubs in Beyoğlu as well as Bomonti neighbourhood in Şişli district where Babylon is now located. Events which Pozitif organizes at its venue or outdoor music festivals are shared and advertised efficiently through their social media and online radio, including reviews or interviews with local and international musicians and information about recent albums through their website and smartphone applications.

As mentioned previously, compared to Pozitif, a private enterprise, IKSV is a non-profit and non-governmental foundation dedicated to arts and culture, primarily sponsored by Eczacıbaşı Inc.—which is primarily a pharmaceutical company. IKSV collaborates with both private and public sectors for various art and music events held in Turkey and overseas.

According to interviewee-5, who performed numerous times at Babylon and Salon with his music group, emphasized that it is significant to form a relationship culturally with the geography one is in; nevertheless such a relationship not being necessarily traditional. For interviewee-5, forming cultural relationship can be constructed in a variety of levels; including the social, individual, technical, artistic and so forth. It is important for him that this relationship also involves contemporary technologies, ways of thinking and lifestyles. He underlined that it is noteworthy to fuse together various components of local cultures in his music that he witnesses in his own geography, without ignoring the advanced technologies and prevailing global cultures. His statement overlaps with the theoretical stance emphasized before, that is, space and networks reconsidered in this chapter as being fluid and temporarily bounded, rather than static, yet influenced by the social and political milieu, or *place*.

D.I.Y. Cultures and 'Rhizomatic' Music Formations

The other two venues, Minimüzikhol and Peyote, embody a more *rhizomatic* characteristic, to deploy Deleuze and Guattari. Briefly, a rhizome disrupts the hierarchical, organized and controlled *(arborescent)* spatial practice, allowing multiplicity. What are inside a rhizome are lines, in contrast to points and positions found in arborescent structures. Thus, what brings forth ruptures and cuts through such hierarchical structures are the *lines of flight* inside rhizomes. For Deleuze and Guattari, there is also a danger of coming across organizations that re-stratify such ruptures (see Deleuze and Guattari 2007; also Bonta and Protevi 2006).

Hence, Pozitif and IKSV, in spite of presenting music and tastes that may act as a rhizome against the conservative government's values and practices,[2] have also turned into arborescent structures.

Interviewee-6, musician/sound engineer and academic, criticized Babylon and Salon in terms of different level of conditions they provided for artists coming from abroad on the one hand, and to the less recognized local ones on the other. Interviewee-6 emphasized that these two venues contributed immensely to the foreign musicians and artists' interests towards Istanbul. Babylon in its early years was reluctant to give stage to local musicians who did not have an album. Interviewee-6 told that when the notion of the imprinted album died out following the flourishing of Internet technologies, this criterion of Babylon also disappeared. In fact, interviewee-6 drew attention to how he, with his band, in the initial years of Babylon had to work for almost a year to take stage there. Initially, this venue was mostly hosting jazz, blues and reggae sounds, which started to diversify enormously in its later years, due to the accelerated distribution of sounds through the Internet and the emergence of netlabels. For interviewee-6, such a process brought forth a lot of local musicians to take stage at Babylon and Salon, even if they only had tracks on the Internet.

Alongside Internet's expansion as a diverse technology, consumption practices diverged with it allowing music fans to promote music, generating new relationships between artists and fans (Prior 2015b, p. 499). Transformation of such relationships paved the way for the expansion of independent music labels, enabling musicians to record their music, as well as marketing and distributing them independently. Internet usage has given musicians the possibility to easily and cheaply set up websites, enabling them to engage with their fans/consumers through social media platforms (Hracs 2012, p. 455; 2016, p. 41). This coincides with

---

[2]For instance, in 2012 summer, Pozitif was organizing its 11th annual 'Efes One Love' music festival; however the municipality of the district was furious about the main sponsor being the Turkish beer company Efes. Pozitif, taking out the name from its poster in the following years arranged this particular festival under 'One Love' in a different location in Istanbul. This time, picture of a beer cap writing 'hayat bu kapağın altında' (meaning 'life is under this cap' in Turkish), obviously signifying Efes and beer, became part of its new logo.

interviewee-6's statement about Babylon's restrictions on local artists in its former years and how this situation changed, that is reflective of the technological convergences, which, as a 'rhizomatic' process impeded the music label monopolies. As interviewee-1 underlined, for example, Farfara, a new local band at the time of the interview, became known to them through Internet, took stage at Babylon—as well as Salon—which gave the band members the chance of an increased number of interviews where *Myspace* announced them as 'the talents of the year'. Or the local band Büyük Ev Ablukada was a rather interesting case according to interviewee-7—then a senior staff at Salon-IKSV. As she highlighted, although founded in 2006, Büyük Ev Ablukada was not actively performing live until much later on, after becoming known through the social media and other music media sites, their live performance ticket sales both at Salon and Babylon was sold out immediately.

In the 2000s, illegal downloading of MP3 tracks and albums brought a decrease in the value of recorded music due to consumers buying them less and their increasing participation in live music performances (Hracs 2016, p. 50; Hracs et al. 2016, p. 6). 'While recorded music became free and thus valueless, live music rose in value because it wasn't something you could copy or share. It was exclusive' (Reynolds 2011, p. 124). The emotive side to music production and performance also prevails between artists and audience. This has given a more profound emphasis on live performances where consumers want to *feel* and experience rather than solely listening to music online, and musicians wanting to connect with their listeners in a live setting. As was the case for interviewee-8, a musician from the UK, who highlighted during the interview that performing numerous times at Babylon with his band, he felt as if they were communicating with their audience and denoted that he enjoyed watching people dance to their tunes.

Minimüzikhol, located in the Cihangir neighbourhood of Beyoğlu, which opened in 2009, is a small, cosy venue, giving stage to mostly eclectic electronic sounds, hosting artists, DJs/producers both locally and globally. During the interview, interviewee-9 and interviewee-10 told that Minimüzikhol founded by six people who, apart from having shared managerial roles in regards to the venue, undertook various creative operations. For instance, apart from the managerial work, interviewee-9 was mainly responsible for communicating with the artists abroad and engaging them to take part in Minimüzikhol events— in addition to writing about and making music programmes. Whereas interviewee-10, alongside his shared executive duties, was concurrently involved in artistic and financial works of this music space. Interviewee-10 also had a small art gallery back then, which gave place to young contemporary artists who were yet unknown. He emphasized that they all enjoyed working project-based, and prior to Minimüzikhol they had been preparing proposals to come up with a more *institute-like* formation where they could carry out artistic and cultural events (see White 2017, pp. 9–10 and 53–60; Scott 2017, pp. 61–62); however finally agreeing to establish a music space after finding the venue in Cihangir. Comparing Minimüzikhol to Pozitif's Babylon and IKSV's Salon, they stated accordingly:

> *Ours is more collective, more amateur.* These institutions and venues that you've mentioned are more professional; hence more people work there, enabling them to come up with more comprehensive [music] programmes. We don't have that kind of labour force. We all are dealing with this venue both as something central to our lives, but also as a secondary occupation; that's why Minimüzikhol can be seen as a project in itself. Sometimes it becomes our primary work, sometimes our secondary work… Besides, we came from a more *underground scene…* We work in accordance with our own means… Becoming institutionalized is not our goal… We are more *network-based, peers coming together and doing something.* Maybe initially they had started out differently too, but in time they've turned out to be more bureaucratic. We don't have that; *we are formed through articulation:* someone new coming with a project, opening another door and proceeding to something else, etc…. Our work spreads out like a *rhizome*[3] as we don't have a top-down structure. When compared, this might be our major distinction.

---

[3]At this point, interviewee-9 in particular underlined this concept himself.

Minimüzikhol, although not entirely devoid of being a striated space, carry the characteristics of a smooth space. For Deleuze and Guattari, *striated space*, hierarchical, thus vertical in structure, and *smooth space* with its potential disruptive attribute proceeding horizontally, exist in mixture, constantly being transversed and reversed into one another (Deleuze and Guattari 2007, p. 474). By 'spreading out like a rhizome', Minimüzikhol is a space where different assemblages are formed. In other words, as interviewee-9 and interviewee-10 expressed, this music space, by the articulation of various projects brought forth by different actors, enable new (re-)territorializations to emerge. Such rhizomatic 'openings', or territorializations, could actually be thought of as being highly porous, which instigate transnational mobilities.

Lastly, when first opened in 1998, Peyote was hosting a lot of unknown music groups, requesting them to play their own songs; hence prohibiting covers. After this venue closed down for a short period, it re-opened in 2004 in the Nevizade area of Beyoğlu. Having another branch in the city of Eskişehir, Peyote in June 2017 also opened a new space as its summer venue in Burgazada, an island in the Marmara Sea. Since its start, Peyote has hosted musicians who can be considered avant-garde and experimental as well as indie in its broadest sense.

Interviewee-11, a senior staff at Peyote back then, highlighted that this venue was one of the initial places where the amateur bands first performed. Apart from live music, they were giving stage to local artists and establishing connections with these artists' friends/acquaintances abroad, thus hosting musicians from different geographies. This venue's independent music label Peyote Müzik was founded in 2008, giving importance to releasing the albums of musicians who had been part of Peyote's scene for some time. Interviewee-11 underlined the distinctive attributes of their financial structure, in relation to other labels', as follows: Peyote's economic infrastructure rests on the fact that it is primarily a bar and a concert venue. Having no sponsor made Peyote Müzik to take over all the responsibilities in relation to the technical, recording, post-production and distribution processes. Interviewee-11 highlighted that there were not many people who bought these albums, which for him was a situation applicable to other music productions that are part of popular culture—a case that can be said to go hand in hand with the aforementioned Internet technologies. For interviewee-11, a released album has no more meaning than the business card of a corporate personnel in our era. He stated that albums released from Peyote Müzik rather have a personal value for the musicians, acting as a significant reference on their behalf if they aim to take stage in music events abroad— recalling how Internet technologies' expansion has transformed certain relationships between the musicians, listeners/fans and the (creative) cultural products, alongside the platforms where they are performed. Thus, in terms of those artists outside the mainstream creative industries, it can be observed how the meaning attached to an album or tracks/songs has changed over time. This can also be considered as the consequence of *performativity* of the rhizomatic (music) spaces and processes.

Concluding Remarks

The four music spaces discussed here were in the Beyoğlu district, yet in different neighbourhoods: Minimüzikhol, slightly being further away from Istiklal Street, in Cihangir, however still a short walking distance to Taksim Square—where Istiklal Street starts. IKSV and its venue Salon, on the other hand, in Şişhane, is again a short walk to Tünel neighbourhood—the other end of Istiklal Street. These venues were chosen due to their contemporary eclectic sounds. They have been significant in engendering and diffusing tastes and styles peculiar to niche audiences as a result of their actors forming new ties and collaborations with musicians/artists abroad—although Babylon and Salon have become venues of highly hierarchized organizations, in comparison with Minimüzikhol and Peyote that could be considered more *rhizomatic*.

In 2011 summer, interventions by the government over the entertainment spaces took on a new form, triggering massive transformations in the district of Beyoğlu. The same year, due to Erdoğan's annoyance about the tables on the streets in front of the bars, pubs, restaurants and cafes—those that had kept the neighbourhoods in the district vibrant— were removed. This tremendously affected the operations of a considerable number of venues, shops, dine and wine spaces, resulting in their closure. After the 2013 Gezi events, shutting down of the traditional bookstores and movie theatres around Istiklal Street, pouring of concrete on Taksim Square, instigated the loss of the 'spirit' of Beyoğlu (Kalkandelen 2017).

In this respect, a common ground that can be developed here is that the actors/entrepreneurs discussed throughout this chapter can be thought of as curators of these aforementioned music hubs—both in terms of their physical and practical aspects. However, the liminality within which they have operated has been disrupted by the 'reforms' of Erdoğan administration. Consequently, the legal and regulatory 'fuzziness' of these regressive changes have become critical to the functioning of these hubs.

References

Bali, R. N. (2006). Sonuç (Conclusion). In D. Behar & T. Islam (Eds.), *İstanbul'da Soylulaştırma: Eski Kentin Yeni Sahipleri* (Gentrification in Istanbul: The new owners of the old city) (pp. 203–210). Istanbul: İstanbul Bilgi Üniversitesi Yayınları.

Bonta, M., & Protevi, J. (2006). *Deleuze and geophilosophy: A guide and glossary* (2nd ed.). Edinburgh: Edinburgh University Press.

Clare, K. (2013). The essential role of place within the creative industries: Boundaries, networks and play. *Cities, 34,* 52–57.

Crossley, N. (2015). *Networks of sound, style and subversion: The punk and post-punk worlds of Manchester, London, Liverpool and Sheffield, 1975–80.* Manchester: Manchester University Press.

Crossley, N., & Bottero, W. (2015). Social spaces of music: Introduction. *Cultural Sociology, 9*(1), 3–19.

Deleuze, G., & Guattari, F. (2007). *A thousand plateaus: Capitalism and schizophrenia* (12th ed.). Minneapolis: University of Minnesota Press.

Hracs, B. J. (2012). A creative industry in transition: The rise of digitally driven independent music production. *Growth and Change, 43*(3), 442–461.

Hracs, B. J. (2016). Working harder and working smarter: The survival strategies of contemporary independent musicians. In B. J. Hracs, M. Seman, & T. E. Virani (Eds.), *The production and consumption of music in the digital age* (pp. 41–55). New York: Routledge.

Hracs, B. J., Seman, M., & Virani, T. E. (2016). Introduction: The evolving economic geography of music. In B. J. Hracs, M. Seman, & T. E. Virani (Eds.), *The production and consumption of music in the digital age* (pp. 3–8). New York: Routledge.

Ince, A. (2006). Asmalımescit'te Kültür Endüstrisi Destekli Yer Değişim (Replacement in Asmalımescit by the support of culture industry). In D. Behar & T. Islam (Eds.), *İstanbul'da Soylulaştırma: Eski Kentin Yeni Sahipleri* (Gentrification in Istanbul: The new owners of the old city) (pp. 99–111). Istanbul: İstanbul Bilgi Üniversitesi Yayınları.

Ince, A. (2008). Yeniden Asmalımescit; Girişimciler ve Evrimleri (Asmalımescit again; entrepreneurs and their evolutions). *İstanbul –magazine, 62*, 52–54.

Kalkandelen, Z. (2017). Müzik Sektörüne Ağır Darbe: Yeni Türkiye Yeni Beyoğlu (A severe blow to the music industry: New Turkey New Beyoğlu). *Journo.* https://journo.com.tr/muzik-sektorune-agir-darbe. Accessed 24 February 2017.

Krims, A. (2007). *Music and urban geography*. New York: Routledge.

Lampel, J., & Germain, O. (2016). Creative industries as hubs of new organizational and business practices. *Journal of Business Research, 69*(7), 2327–2333.

Pratt, A. C. (2009). Urban regeneration: From the "arts feel good" factor to the cultural economy: A case study of Hoxton, London. *Urban Studies, 46*(5 & 6), 1041–1061.

Prior, N. (2015a). It's a social thing, not a nature thing: Popular music practices in Reykjavík, Iceland. *Cultural Sociology, 9*(1), 81–98.

Prior, N. (2015b). Beyond Napster: Popular music and the normal internet. In A. Bennett & S. Waksman (Eds.), *The Sage handbook of popular music* (pp. 493–507). London: Sage.

Rief, S. (2009). *Club cultures: Boundaries, identities, and otherness*. New York: Routledge.

Reynolds, S. (2011). *Retromania: Pop culture's addiction to its own past*. New York: Faber and Faber.

Scott, M. (2017). "Hipster capitalism" in the age of austerity? Polanyi meets Bourdieu's new petite bourgeoisie. *Cultural Sociology, 11*(1), 60–76.

Thrift, N. (2000). Performing cultures in the new economy. *Annals of the Association of American Geographers, 90*(4), 674–692.

Tironi, M. (2010). Gelleable spaces, eventful geographies: The case of Santiago's experimental music scene. In I. Farías & T. Bender (Eds.), *Urban assemblages: How actor-network theory changes urban studies* (pp. 27–52). Abingdon: Routledge.

Virani, T. E. (2016). The resilience of a local music scene in Dalston, London. In B. J. Hracs, M. Seman, & T. E. Virani (Eds.), *The production and consumption of music in the digital age* (pp. 101–113). New York: Routledge.

Virani, T. E., & Malem, W. (2015). *Re-articulating the creative hub concept as a model for business support in the local creative economy: The case of Mare Street in Hackney* (Creativeworks London Working Paper Series Number 12).

Watson, A., & Beaverstock, J. V. (2016). Transnational freelancing: Ephemeral creative projects and mobility in the music recording industry. *Environment and Planning A, 48*(7), 1428–1446.

Watson, A., Hoyler, M., & Mager, C. (2009). Spaces and networks of musical creativity in the city. *Geography Compass, 3*(2), 856–878.

White, J. (2017). *Urban music and entrepreneurship: Beats, rhymes and young people's enterprise.* London: Routledge.

Yener, Z. (2009). *Babylon on: Babylon Hakkında Bir Kitap* (A book about Babylon—For its initial ten years between 1999–2009). Istanbul: Stil Matbaa.

10

Nairobi's iHub: Technology for Society

Øyvind Økland

Introduction

In line with developments across the rest of the world, Kenya has experienced a digital revolution over the last few decades. Although Africa has lagged behind the Western world and Asia in this development, the continent has been increasingly catching up, and Kenya is now a leading force in the East African region and across Africa as a whole. One of the consequences of this digital revolution is the establishing of tech enterprises. Different kinds of innovation hubs are now popping up in Africa. According to the World Bank, in 2015 there were 117 tech hubs, and in 2016, there was suggested to be 314 active tech hubs in Africa, while the number was 287 in South and Southeast Asia (Sambuli and Witt 2017, p. 5). Thirty-seven of these hubs were found

Ø. Økland (✉)
NLA University College, Bergen, Norway
e-mail: oyvind.okland@nla.no

© The Author(s) 2019
R. Gill et al. (eds.), *Creative Hubs in Question*, Dynamics of Virtual Work,
https://doi.org/10.1007/978-3-030-10653-9_10

in Kenya[1] (Du Boucher 2016). In Kenya, 81% of all ICT companies were located in Nairobi (Mbataru and Wanjau 2013, p. 75).

These hubs may be categorized as creative hubs according to this definition:

> The concept of creative hubs …. As special places that nurture connections and exchange, and as such are important places to boost economic activity. They are urban agglomerations, which promote connection between entrepreneurs, small and medium sized businesses in the creative sector and where links and knowledge co-creation happen. (Shiach et al. 2017, p. 8)

iHub is such a creative hub. Founded in 2010, iHub is now a leading tech enterprise in East Africa, as well as in Africa as a whole (Wilbermuth 2014; Manyozo 2013; Ndemo and Weiss 2017). During his stay in Kenya, Mark Zuckerberg, the Facebook founder, posted the following on his Facebook profile in September 2016:

> Just landed in Nairobi! I'm here to meet with entrepreneurs and developers, and to learn about mobile money – where Kenya is the world leader. I'm starting at a place called iHub, where entrepreneurs can build and prototype their ideas… It's inspiring to see how engineers here are using mobile money to build businesses and help their community. (Zuckerberg 2016)

iHub exemplifies a creative hub as a place where it "support(s) activities across a variety of local institutions and networks" and "support(s) communities of practice, not for profit and commercial, large and small, part-time and full-time activity – they are not just incubators for small businesses, but have a wider remit. Creative Hubs will form a network that will drive the growth of creative industries at the local and regional level, providing more jobs, more education and more opportunities"

---

[1]The others were as follows: 12 in Uganda, 28 in Egypt, 15 in Tunisia, 21 in Morocco, 10 in Senegal, 16 in Ghana, 23 in Nigeria and 54 in South Africa (Du Boucher 2016).

(Dovey et al. 2016, p. 7). It is a centre, a network as well as a cluster, according to one categorization (Dovey et al. 2016, pp. 7, 9).

The world is closely watching this recent growth in the ICT sector. Head of Google in Kenya, Joe Mucheru, has pointed out that Nairobi has exported two major innovations in modern information technology, one is *M-Pesa*, the mobile money platform, and the other is *Ushahidi*, a non-commercial platform for exchanging information in emergencies or during elections. Most innovations are, however, in relation to local challenges (*Economist*, August 25, 2012).

iHub is analysed as a case of how a creative hub may, through vision, design and organizational culture, play a part in the general development of the digital revolution in Kenya, and thus also playing a part in the general development of Kenyan society, by for example boosting economic activity (Shiach et al. 2017, p. 8). In describing Kenya's general development within the ICT sector, and iHub especially, we will look at how these changes may have affected Kenyan society. The problem statement for this study is *how does Kenya's ICT development in general and iHub as a creative hub especially play a part in economic, social and cultural developments of the Kenyan society.*

Literature Review

iHub and sub-Saharan hubs are in general a rather recent innovation. Some research is appearing, but the amount is still limited. In 2013, the iHub research department presented a report on innovation hubs across Africa (Gathege and Moraa 2013a) and one report specifically on the iHub model (Gathege and Moraa 2013b). In 2016, a book called *Innovative Africa: Emerging Hubs of Excellence* highlighted different aspects of the emerging hubs across Africa (Adesida et al. 2016). There is obviously need for further research (Toivonen and Friederici 2015), especially when it comes to the impact of hubs on society (Friederici 2014; De Beer et al. 2016, p. 237). Chirchietti (2017) has looked at the relationship between start-ups and Hubs, and to what extent these Hubs are supporting the challenges faced by the start-ups, such as lack of skills, lack of experience and lack of information (Chirchietti 2017).

Other research shows that while developments in most sectors in Kenya are slow, the ICT sector is growing rapidly, due to a friendly policy framework and foreign assistance (Mwaniki 2017). Graham and Mann (2013) looked at different discourses of connectivity as a direct result of the placement of fibre-optic cabling in Mombasa in 2009, where iHub is an example of a strategy of aiding companies to put their ideas into practices, through technological innovation.

According to the British Council, creative hubs around the world are being mapped and surveyed in Indonesia, Vietnam, Malaysia, Europe and have now also started to map creative hubs in Southern Africa (British Council 2014). Much literature focuses on urban centres in the developed world (Virani and Malem 2015; Shiach et al. 2017; Dovey et al. 2016). This chapter seeks to bring forth a case study of one of the many resurging creative hubs in sub-Saharan Africa. This is important because the setting in Africa is dramatically different from the setting in the Western world, especially when it comes to resources available in establishing these hubs (Bramann 2017, p. 240).

Methodology

Methodologically, the data and insight for this chapter are gathered through short periods of fieldwork at iHub in 2014, 2015 and 2016 when they were located at Ngong Road, and in 2017 when they were relocated to Senteu Plaza near the Yaya centre. I interviewed representatives of the management, visitors and users of the place, as well as attending and interviewing participants at some of the events that are regularly held there. In addition, I have analysed relevant literature, specifically about iHub, from 2010 until 2018, with regard to topics related to the problem statement. Finally, I have analysed the web pages of iHub and Ushahidi, the predecessor of iHub.

To be able to put iHub into a greater perspective, I first need to give a brief summary of the last few decades of the technological development in Kenya. This is important at two levels, first, to understand the background for how and why iHub came into existence in 2010, and second, as iHub is to such a degree interwoven into the technology developments in Kenya. It is therefore not possible to separate the development of iHub from the technology development in Kenya.

Background

Digital Developments in Kenya

During the twentieth century, the world experienced the economic rise of Asia, called the "Asian tiger", whereas commentators today are talking about "The future is African" (Nash 2015). Currently, there is a rapid digital revolution in Africa. Kenya is now one of the leading countries in this process. This development started in Cape Town, South Africa, in 1995 and then continued to Ghana in 2001 with the start-up of BusyInternet, a multipower tech hub. Today five African countries are recognized to be leading the development in Africa. These are known as the "KINGS", namely Kenya, Ivory Coast, Nigeria, Ghana and South Africa (Osiakwan 2017, p. 56).

Seen in isolation, the growth in mobile phones has risen from less than four million in 1998 to more than 500 million in 2011 (Fox 2011). This has been possible because of local enterprises that have grown to be world-class companies, such as MTN in South Africa, Safaricom in Kenya, Airtel Africa, Orange and so on (Osiakwan 2017, p. 57). Kenya is currently the leading country among the "KINGS". This is due, according to Osiakwan, to "an aggressive and conscious government program to develop a broadband infrastructure, two critical innovations – mobile money and a crowdsourcing platform, and the development of a tech incubator and accelerator model for the continent, catalysing the innovation agenda that has swept through Africa like a wildfire" (2017, p. 66).

In order to see this in a historical perspective, we need to look at the early beginnings of the Internet of Kenya. This digital development is, naturally, closely linked to the general political situation in the country, maybe even more so than in most other countries. In the mid-1990s, the emerging Internet was a nuisance and problem to the government, regarded as a threat and a development that was not welcomed because their control of the information flow was threatened. The Internet was officially banned until 1999, regulated by the Kenya Information and Communication Act. This started a liberation process, from a state monopoly to increased competition between private companies (Mureithi 2017). The private sector saw many opportunities for profit in developing the infrastructure. The popping up of Internet cafés created a relatively low threshold for people to gain access to the new technology, due to low prices (van Rensburg 2012, p. 104).

The state telecommunications monopoly was broken up in 2004, but Telkom Kenya still kept some market advantages, such as being the backbone of Internet development. These benefits ended, however, in 2007, and competition in the market was introduced (Mureithi 2017, p. 39). Prices went down, and Kenya has today one of the most competitive Internet sectors in East Africa.

Kenya has ambitious goals for its investment in IT. In 2006, they launched a program that would bring Internet access to all villages. Moreover, the development of computer skills aimed at providing a computer for every student in primary school is in process (Kenya ICT Board 2012). However, challenges remain in relation to the relatively low access to the Internet in the general population, compounded by a lack of skill and motivation to use it (van Rensburg 2012, p. 97).

A milestone in Kenya and Africa's technological innovation was Safaricom's development of *M-Pesa*. *M-Pesa* is a system of mobile monetary transactions, via cellular connection. It is estimated that nearly 70% of the adult population in Kenya use this. Most of these developments have occurred since 2005, when Bitange Ndemo was minister for Information and Communication Ministry. Kenya was at that time in the backwater, technologically speaking, and the Internet was only possible through a satellite connection and very expensive.

Currently, Safaricom is the leading company for Internet services. Through the government's policy of involving the private sector as well as civil society organizations, Safaricom has gained a more prominent role in the society (Gagliardone 2013, p. 78).

The 2007 Election and Its Aftermath

The election in 2007 had great consequences for Kenya in many ways, also for the technological environment and policies. However, the election results were much disputed. Violence erupted when the incumbent president Mwai Kibaki was surprisingly declared the winner over the opposition leader Raila Odinga (Kagwanja and Southall 2009, p. 262; Lafargue 2009). Rioting in the following weeks resulted in about 1200 deaths and 500,000 displaced people (Dupas and Robinson 2012, p. 7). It was difficult to trust any media about what was going on, not even the national media. Local radio stations and text messages from mobile phones sent hate messages that ignited the violence and the killings. The years that followed saw a revolution in the development of digital communication. Smart phones and social media, such as Facebook, Twitter and YouTube, were now commonplace (Mäkinen and Kuira 2009).

Ushahidi

Because of the 2007 atrocities and the lack of trust in traditional media, citizens started to spread news themselves through text messages and e-mail in order to rectify false reporting. Out of this civic and grass-root journalism, a digital platform, called *Ushahidi* (meaning testimony or witness in Swahili), was developed (Ushahidi 2010). Software developers and bloggers joined forces because they saw the ineffectiveness of mainstream media to report accurately. This was an information centre where eyewitnesses could send their information and report irregular incidents. These reports were then triangulated with partners such as international media, government sources, NGOs and Kenyan journalists and bloggers (Ushahidi 2016a, b). The Ushahidi software became more reliable than the traditional media and is now exported to other many other developing countries. The platform is now used in more than 150 countries, translated into 35 languages and has been deployed 50,000 times (Ashforth 2009; Dundas 2014, p. 504; Crandall and Omenya 2015, p. 73).

Fiber-Optic Cables

A milestone in the Internet connectivity development of Kenya and East Africa was the placement of the first of four fiber-optic cables in Mombasa in July 2009, made possible due to private–public funding.

Kenya, in particular Nairobi, is among the leading countries in Africa in terms of investment in technology. Already in 2008, the government decided to build a completely new infrastructure and a "Silicon Savannah", south of Nairobi, called Konza city. This is a part of the fulfilment of the ambitions outlined in *Kenya Vision 2030*. According to the plans, it will be finished in 2020 and create, directly or indirectly, more then 100,000 jobs (Konza Technopolis 2018).

The Present Situation

Today Kenya, with its 48 million inhabitants, has 43 million Internet users, a penetration of nearly 90%, as of June 2017. Six millions of those are on Facebook, a penetration of 13%. Africa as a whole has a penetration rate of 31%, compared to 51.7% in the world. The growth has been more than 8000% since year 2000, as compared to 527% in Europe (Internet World Stats 2018).

Kenya's economy is the largest economy in East Africa, on average growing annually 5.46% (RoK 2007). The ICT sector contributes about 11.8% of the GDP growth, due to the increasing use of ICT in sectors such as health, finance, education, agriculture and government. Although Africa is far behind the rest of the world when it comes to how ICT contributes to the GDP, in Africa, Kenya leads at 2.9%, even more than South Africa. M-Pesa, a mobile payment platform, is today recognized as "the most significant factor in the development of the Kenyan technology and mobile ecosystem" (Jung and Feferman 2014), and a big contributor because this platform contributes to financial inclusion of huge portions of the population (Muchai and Kimuyu 2017, p. 1). Safaricom is the largest player with 69% of the market in 2012 (Gagliardone 2013, p. 76).

Establishing of IHub

The idea to start up iHub came during a meeting of young tech enthusiasts, called *BarCamp Nairobi* in August 2008. The post-election violence was still fresh in their memories, and some of them, such as Eric Hersman, had been involved in the establishing of Ushahidi. They decided that they should not only meet annually, but rather wanted to have a place of their own and meet on a regular basis (Hersmen 2013b).

It was difficult to raise money for it though. However, due to contacts and funding that were already in place for Ushahidi; iHub was founded and launched in March 2010. Eric Hersman, a Kenyan American, was a driving force both in the forming of Ushahidi and iHub (Marchant 2017, p. 314; Hersman 2010, 2012, 2013a, 2017).

In 2011, *mlab East Africa* was founded as a part of iHub. It was the first mobile incubation lab of this type. The objective was to "foster the innovation and scale-up of mobile application technologies in East Africa".

In the coming years, Hersman took on both leading and advisory roles in other start-ups as well, such as Savannah Fund, Gearbox, Afrilabs Association, AhiraChix and BRCK (Hersman 2017). BRCK is building a more robust Internet connection for people with poor Internet conditions (Ushahidi 2018), by producing gadgets literary looking like bricks. The links between Ushahidi, iHub and BRCK are strong.

iHub "catalyses the growth of the Kenyan tech community by connecting people, supporting start-ups, and surfacing information" (iHub 2015). iHub has launched a research arm because they saw a need to focus on how technology is used and facilitated within East Africa, so that decisions could become more informed. Some of iHub's customers include the World Bank, Google, Refugees United, Internews, Hivos, International Development Research Centre (IDRC), USAID, Indigo Trust and Squad Digital (Daniel et al. 2015, p. 4).

Currently, there are four levels of the iHub membership. In the first one, "Floating Desk", you are charged 200 Kenyan shillings (KES) by the hour. The next level, "Community Desk", starts at 7000 KES per month. This level provides a permanent desk to work. The "Dedicated

Desk" is your permanent desk, 24/7 and you can use it as your personal office. The fourth and highest level is the "Serviced offices", providing a fully furnished and serviced office for 4, 8 or 12 persons (iHub 2017).

iHub has today 23,000 square feet of space, including private offices, co-working space, meeting rooms and an outdoor terrace (Design Indaba 2014). The location attracts local people as well as foreigners. It is common to meet students, journalists, researchers or just young tech-interested people there. Some are there for shorter visits or curiosity, and others are hanging out there for longer periods. iHub had 14,000 members and had incubated more than 150 new start-ups in 2014. These start-ups have again created more than 1000 jobs. There are more than 10,000 people on the mailing list through social media and more than 200,000 followers are reached globally.

Findings

According to our problem statement, we asked *how does Kenya's ICT development in general and iHub as a creative hub especially play a part in the economic, social and cultural developments of the Kenyan society*. In the following, we will therefore look at them one by one, stating some of the main findings of each point.

Economic Development

Before the digital development in Africa, "innovation" and "creativity" were terms rarely used. In 1982, the Kenyan government banned the use of computers because they were afraid of losing secretarial jobs (Ndemo 2017, p. 5). The development that has taken place since then is often, and rightly so, called a digital revolution. From the early upstart of the Internet in the 1990s, the evolution has been fast and marked by disruption that has brought the development forward.

This was made possible by an opening up of the media and technological sector, with increasing involvement of private enterprises combined with innovative individuals that challenged the regulatory authorities.

M-Pesa is an example of this, the mobile movement that enabled huge portions of the population to participate in the national and global economy.

iHub is a meeting place for regular events, being open to non-members as well. The researcher observed one meeting for women who had or intended to start their own business. Presenters from the authorities, private enterprises, legal specialists and other relevant speakers were invited. Companies were invited to have booths to present their enterprises, where one example of this is was a company called "Bee happy". They had developed a concept of selling honey and jam in delicate jars, birthday cards and so on. Through support from iHub workshops, they had learnt how to advertise using social media with great success.

The creation of iHub, with its non-profit vision of helping young entrepreneurs to materialize their business ideas, has resulted in more than 170 start-ups and created more than 1000 new jobs (Egra Kemunto, personal information, 2016). One such successful story is mFarm. mFarm is a website, or an app you can download on your mobile phone to give you daily prices of different commodities, know when to plan, give power to negotiate and comparison among markets. It has become very popular all over Kenya and made it more popular to be a farmer (FarmD 2014).

AkiraChix is a non-profit organization with the objective to "inspire and develop a successful force of women in technology" (AkiraChix 2017). iHub, Ushahidi, the Swedish development organization (SIDA) and Microsoft, among others, sponsor it. This enables women to attend conferences, learning technology and putting their business ideas into practice, where the aim is to "provide opportunities for women in tech to connect and collaborate with each other" (AkiraChix 2017). In this way, both AkiraChix and mFarm are bringing technology out to groups of people not normally into technology (Gbedomon 2016). The intention is to integrate more people into the new and pending digital economy.

The success of the tech sector in Kenya has given the government a vision of the possibilities for economic growth and development (Kenya Vision 2030 2007). Seventy per cent of the population is below 35 years and the unemployment rate is 70%. Combined with digital divides, a gender gap, a poverty gap and a rural-urban gap, the challenges are many (Mureithi 2017, p. 42).

Social Developments

The very foundation of Ushahidi was a result of a recognized need for true and correct reporting of elections and related incidents across the country. The Ushahidi platform allowed users to express their opinions and allowed more people to have access to the digital sphere and to become digitally included (Soerensen and Petuchaite 2013, p. 125). iHub was created as a continuation of Ushahidi, and the two organizations are in the same building.

Several other social engagements are in some ways related to iHub or other hubs in the technological ecosphere. One of these is "ICT-for-social-change" (ICT4SC) (Wildermuth 2014). Another one is "ICT4democracy", where iHub is one of several partners. Here, iHub "is exploring the interaction between governments and citizens using ICT tools in Kenya, Uganda and Tanzania through a serious of field studies, focus group discussions, surveys and literature reviews. This is towards a better understanding of how innovative ICTs are being used to help reduce the cost of delivering services, stemming corruption and increasing transparency" (ICT4Democracy 2017). Research shows that ICT involvement has greatly benefited women and youth (Mitullah 2014; Mbure 2014).

As a continuation of the Ushahidi concept, Uchaguzi Kenya 2013 was launched to contribute to a free, fair and most of all, peaceful election process. Uchaguzi is a tool to monitor the elections through a facilitation of what local Kenyans report from the different election sites, election observers, humanitarian agencies, civil society, community-based organizations and law enforcement agencies (Crandall and Omenya 2015, p. 75; Daniel et al. 2015, p. 8).

Cultural Developments

Kraidy uses the term "hybridity" in relation to intercultural communication, meaning "a fusion of two hitherto relatively distinct styles, or identities, cross-cultural contact, which often occurs across national borders as well as cultural boundaries, is a requisite for hybridity" (Kraidy 2005, p. 5). Marchant (2017, p. 304) argues that the Kenyan tech sector undergoes hybridization as it develops over time and is a multicultural place. Another feature of iHub and the tech sector as a hybrid place is the mixture of being a non-profit organization, with a social development purpose and having a vision of financial stability. According to Marchant, iHub is an example of a hybrid organization as it has adopted a mindset belonging to both non-profit and for-profit organizations (Marchant 2017, p. 309). It is a philanthropic and a free market organization at the same time. The American Kenyan co-founder, Eric Hersman, with his blog, White African, adds to this picture, as does the multicultural and multilingual environment of the place, where both Swahili and English are frequently used.

The physical environment at the iHub premises is urban and modern. It could have been an office building anywhere in the world. In presenting themselves, iHub emphasizes the importance of an open space with room for relaxing, mingling and facilities to buy trendy coffee. iHub has engaged the best barista in Nairobi and thereby stressing this image of urban and global atmosphere (YouTube 2012).

Furthermore, Ushahidi and iHub were established in the aftermath of the post-election violence in 2007–2008. This violence was ethnically motivated. Throughout Kenya's history, tribal tensions have been latent and sometimes overt, and in 2007–2008, it erupted with full force. Ushahidi is an attempt to "witness" and document what was actually taking place across the country (Rotich 2017). The objective was to prevent similar riots occurring in the future. iHub's Umati project became a key project in order to map the actual occurrence of dangerous speech or "hate speech". Nanjira Sambuli, the Research Manager of iHub, emphasized the importance of the Umati Project for the Kenyan society, as the tension was still there and could erupt again (Sambuli, personal communication, 8 July 2014).

It is not easy to measure in what way, or to what extent iHub is contributing to more cultural integration and inclusion and less boundaries between the tribes, but in many respects it might be called a glocal organization, in Robertson's (1992) understanding of a dynamic relation between the local and the global.

Discussion

Many factors have led to Kenya's relative success in building a techno-logical infrastructure, where iHub is definitely playing a part. Several commentators emphasize the interplay between individual innovators, the flexibility from the government and efforts from private enter-prises. A valid topic for discussion is whether a bottom-up or a top-down process is to be preferred. If we consider the iHub model being a bottom-up model, we might consider the government project of a new Silicon Savannah in Konza city as a top-down model. It is not an accurate description, but iHub grew out of a felt need from individual entrepreneurs. They saw the need for a new software after the 2007 elec-tion riots and created Ushahidi. iHub was then created out of this as a closer-knit network of young tech enthusiasts. Private companies and the state were then facilitating it with funds, regulations and subsidies. This approach has proved itself viable to other parts of the world in many cases through export of the software. According to the UNESCO Science Report of 2015, it is important that these hubs are creating pos-sibilities for growth within the countries, and not imported from out-side (UNESCO Report 2015 2016).

The Konza city project, however, is not local in the same way. It is a state owned, huge state-planned project, with private investors, build-ing a new city, based on a strategic governmental plan for developing the technological ecosystem of the country further. It has great ambi-tions of creating 100,000 new jobs, directly or indirectly, when it is fin-ished in 2020, although some have doubts about the realism of this goal (Anderson 2015, 5 January).

Graham and Mann (2013) claim that this optimism, also seen in connection with the placement of the fiber-optic cable, has resulted in at least two different strategies. One of them was the official state pol-icy to build a "technocity" near the international airport in Nairobi with these large companies, and thus creating an "international hub", so that the distance between the markets and the technology was min-imized as much as possible. The other strategy is to see smaller compa-nies engaged in "social media work, software development, web design, mobile application development, IT consulting, Web mapping, and

various other information processing, design and development tasks",
exemplified by Nailab, Fablab, iLab and the biggest, iHub (Graham and
Mann 2013, p. 8).

Whether the models are called bottom-up or top-down, it is clear
that when modern technology is being implemented, it encounters
local worldviews, where, as we have seen, different hubs are products of
hybridity. What matters is how these different worldviews are matched.
According to Weiss (2017, p. 391), the best results are achieved when
the Kenyan struggle for a better life, is successfully combined with an
international worldview of innovation and self-realization.

The bottom-up model emphasizes the societal mission. Technology
is not only for profit, but also for empowerment of underprivileged
groups, such as women, minorities and in this way minimizing the digital divide. The strategy is to facilitate digital empowerment, rather than
just digital inclusion (Wildermuth 2010). It is in this new globalized
environment that Africa needs to find a balance between individualism and collectivism, between traditional values and new values (Weiss
2017, p. 467).

Conclusion

Hubs are playing a central role in the rapid growth in the technological sector in Kenya. iHub was not the first, but is now playing a leading part. Within a rather brief period, it has managed to win the trust
of huge transnational companies and in this way built a capacity to
become an economic, social and cultural factor in the society. There are
many challenges, such as different digital divides, but Kenya is strongly
investing in the technological sector and in this way has become a leading country within Africa.

To measure concrete effects of iHub and the technological developments in Kenya is rather difficult, and this has not been our attempt
to do here. Through a presentation of some of the activities and results
of the work that has been done, we might be able to see some signs
of the coming developments within the tech sector. A huge proportion of the Kenyan population is younger than 35 years of age and the

unemployment rate is high. The tech sector often attracts young people, and they can participate even with small means. Young tech enthusiasts are starting up hubs in different places, and hubs and the government may facilitate a lot, through funding and expertise, so that young people can be able to enter the labour market. However, to what degree a state policy and efforts from hubs may play, is hard to foresee. It is yet to be discovered what the actual effects of empowering people through such creative hubs are, and only more research can provide insight to this. Although Africa is still facing huge challenges, creative hubs such as iHub might give new possibilities to young people and give them a brighter future than it would otherwise have been.

References

Adesida, O., Karuri-Sebina, G., & Resende-Santos, J. (2016). *Innovation Africa: Emerging hubs of excellence*. Bingley, UK: Emerald.

AkiraChix. (2017). *About us*. Consulted 2 February. akirachix.com.

Anderson, M. (2015, January 5). Kenya's tech entrepreneurs shun Konza 'silicon savannah'. *The Guardian*. https://www.theguardian.com/global-development/2015/jan/05/kenya-technology-entrepreneurs-konza-silicon-savannah. Accessed 23 January 2018.

Ashforth, A. (2009). Ethnic violence and the prospects for democracy in the aftermath of the 2007 Kenyan elections. *Public Culture, 21*(3), 9–19.

Bramann, J. U. (2017). Building ICT entrepreneurship ecosystems. In B. Ndemo & T. Weiss (Eds.), *Digital Kenya. An entrepreneurial revolution in the making* (pp. 227–258). London: Palgrave.

British Council. (2014). *Creative hubs*. https://creativeconomy.britishcouncil.org/projects/hubs/. Accessed 16 May 2018.

Chirchetti, N. (2017). *The role of innovation Hubs taking start-ups from idea to business. The case of Nairobi, Kenya* (IZNE Working Paper Series, Vol. 7, No. 17). Hochschule Bonn-Rhein-Sieg, University of Applied Sciences.

Crandall, A., & Omenya, R. (2015). Uchaguzi Kenya. In R. Daniel, I. Soria-Donlan & J. Thompson (Eds.), *Humanitarianism 2.0*. London: UK Arts and Humanities Research Council.

Daniel, R., Soria-Donlan, I., & Thompson, J. (Eds.). (2015). *Humanitarianism 2.0*. London: UK Arts and Humanites Research Council.

De Beer, J., Millar, P., Mwangi, J., Nzomo, V., & Rutenberg, I. (2016). A framework for assessing technology hubs in Africa. *New York University Journal of Intellectual Property & Entertainment Law, 6*, 237.

Design Indaba. (2014). Inside Kenya's iHub. *Youtube.* https://www.youtube.com/watch?v=iVESsquYn64. Accessed 24 January 2018.

Dovey, J., Pratt, A. C., Moreton, S., Virani, T. E., Merkel, J., & Lansdowne, J. (2016). *The creative Hubs report.* London: British Council.

Du Boucher, V. (2016). A few things we learned about tech Hubs in Africa and Asia, GSMA. http://bit.ly/2iEOYRo. Accessed 24 January 2018.

Dundas, C. W. (2014). *Electoral essays and discourses.* Bloominton: Author House.

Dupas, P., & Robinson, J. (2012). The (hidden) costs of political instability: Evidence from Kenya's 2007 election crisis. *Journal of Development Economics, 99*(2), 314–329.

Economist. (2012, August 25). Innovation in Africa, upwardly mobile. http://www.economist.com/node/21560912. Accessed 25 November 2017.

FarmD. (2014). MFarm price information: Next generation agriculture in Kenya. Forum for Agricultural Risk Management in Development. http://www.agriskmanagementforum.org/content/mfarm-price-information-next-generation-agriculture. Accessed 5 February 2018.

Fox, K. (2011). Africa's mobile economic revolution. *The Guardian.* https://www.theguardian.com/technology/2011/jul/24/mobile-phones-africa-microfinance-farming. Accessed 12 March 2018.

Friederici, N. (2014). What is a tech innovation hub anyway? http://cii.oii.ox.ac.uk/2014/09/16/what-is-a-tech-innovation-hub-anyway/. Accessed 24 January 2018.

Gagliardone, I. (2013). China and the African internet: Perspectives from Kenya and Ethiopia. *Index Comunicación, 3*(2), 67–82.

Gathege, D., & Moraa, H. (2013a). Draft report on comparative study on innovation Hubs across Africa. *iHub Research.* http://research.ihub.co.ke/uploads/2013/may/1367840837__923.Pdf. Accessed 14 November 2017.

Gathege, D., & Moraa, H. (2013b). How ICT hubs models have impacted on the technology entrepreneurship development. In *Proceedings of the Sixth International Conference on Information and Communications Technologies and Development: Notes (2)* (pp. 100–103), ACM.

Gbedomon, R. C. (2016). *Empowering women in technology: Lessons from a successful woman entrepreneur in Kenya.* Case Study No. 10.

Graham, M., & Mann, L. (2013). Imagining a silicon Savannah? Technological and conceptual connectivity in Kenya's BPO and software development sectors. *The European Journal of Informations Systems in Developing Countries, 56*(2), 1–19.

Hersman, E. (2010). iHub: Nairobi's tech innovation hub is here. *Blog Posted on WhiteAfrican.*

Hersman, E. (2012). Mobilizing tech entrepreneurs in Africa (innovations case narrative: iHub). *Innovations: Technology, Governance, Globalization, 7*(4), 59–67.

Hersman, E. (2013a). The mobile continent. *Stanford Social Innovation Review, 11*(2), 30–31.

Hersman, E. (2013b). Mobilizing tech entrepreneurs in Africa. *Innovations, 7*(4).

Hersman, E. (2017). Exploring the ideal rold of government, NGOs, Angel investors, and universities for technology entrepreneurs. In B. Ndemo & T. Weiss (Eds.), *Digital Kenya. An entrepreneurial revolution in the making* (pp. 45–54). London: Palgrave.

ICT4Democracy. (2017). *Promoting human rights and democracy through ICT.* www.ICT4Democracy.org. Accessed 17 November 2017.

iHub. (2015). *Technology, innovation, community.* https://www.ihub.co.ke. Accessed 12 November 2017.

iHub. (2017). *Hello, we are iHub.* https://ww.ihub.co.ke. Accessed 18 November 2017.

Internet World Stats. (2018). *Kenya.* http://www.internetworldstats.com/africa.htm#ke. Accessed 2 February 2018.

Jung, R., & Feferman, F. (2014). *The development of the mobile Kenyan ecosystem.* Haas School of Business, University of California Berkeley. https://scholar.google.no/scholar?hl=no&as_sdt=0%2C5&q=%22jung+and+feferman%22&btnG=. Accessed 30 January 2018.

Kagwanja, P., and Southall, R. (2009). Introduction: Kenya—A democracy in retreat? *Journal of Contemporary African Studies, 27*(3), 259–277. https://doi.org/10.1080/02589000903216930. http://www.vision2030.go.ke/496/progress-2016-march-science-technology-innovation-sti/. Accessed 1 February 2018.

Kenya ICT Board. (2012). *Connected Kenya 2017. Inclusion. Innovation. Beyond broadband.* Nairobi: Kenya ICT Board.

Kenya Vision 2030. (2007). Kenya vision 2030. http://www.vision2030.go.ke/. Accessed 18 November 2017.

Konza Technopolis. (2018). Konza bulletin. http://www.konzacity.go.ke/news-updates/project-updates/. Accessed 2 February 2018.

Kraidy, M. (2005). *Hybridity, or the cultural logic of globalization*. Philadelphia: Temple University Press.

Lafargue, J. (Ed.). (2009). *The general elections in Kenya 2007*. Nairobi: IFRA, French Institute for research in Africa.

Mäkinen, M., & Kuira, M. (2009). Social media and postelection crisis in Kenya. *The International Journal of Press Politics, 13*(3), 328–335. https://doi.org/10.1177/1940161208319409.

Manyozo, L. (2013). Communication for development in Sub-Saharan Africa: From orientalism to NGOification. In T. Tufte, N. Wildermuth, A. S. Hansen-Skovmoes, & W. V. Mitullah, *Speaking up and talking back?: Media, empowerment and civic engagement among East and Southern African Youth* (pp. 37–52). Gothenburg: Nordicom.

Marchant, E. R. (2017). Organizational cultural hybrids: Non-profit and for-profit cultural influences in the Kenyan technology sector. In B. Ndemo & T. Weiss (Eds.), *Digital Kenya. An entrepreneurial revolution in the making* (pp. 303–330). London: Palgrave.

Mbataru, R., & Wanjau, K. (2013). Role of information system security in the growth of small and medium enterprises in Kenya: A survey of information communication technology firms in Nairobi. *European Journal of Business and Innovation Research, 1*(3), 74–83.

Mbure, W. (2014). Social media and digital democracy. An exploration of online forums for civic engagement and the involvement of Kenyan youth in participatory development. In T. Tufte, N. Wildermuth, A. S. Hansen-Skovmoes, & W. V. Mitullah (Eds.), (2013) *Speaking up and talking back?: Media, empowerment and civic engagement among East and Southern African Youth* (pp. 97–112). Gothenburg: Nordicom.

Mitullah, W. (2014). Institutional context of ICT and women's participation. In Kenyain T. Tufte, N. Wildermuth, A. S. Hansen-Skovmoes, & W. V. Mitullah (Eds.) (2013), *Speaking up and talking back?: Media, empowerment and civic engagement among East and Southern African Youth* (pp. 81–96). Gothenburg: Nordicom.

Muchai, D. N., & P. Kimuyu. (2017). *Prospects for information and communications technology-enabled services in Kenya. The case of the mobile money transfer industry* (WIDER Working Paper 2017/86). Helsinki: United Nations University World Institute for Development Economics Research.

Mureithi, M. (2017). The Internet journey for Kenya: The interplay of disruptive innovation and entrepreneurship in fueling rapid growth. In B. Ndemo & T. Weiss (Eds.), *Digital Kenya. An entrepreneurial revolution in the making* (pp. 27–44). London: Palgrave.

Mwaniki, D. (2017). Infrastructure developments in Nairobi: Widening the path towards a smart city and smart economic development. In T. Vinod Kumar (Ed.), *Smart economy in smart cities. Advances in 21st century human settlements*. Singapore: Springer.

Nash, B. (2015). The future is African. *Tech Crunch*. http://techcrunch.com/2015/09/05/the-future-is-african/. Accessed 12 January 2017.

Ndemo, B. (2017). Inside a policymaker's mind: An entrepreneurial approach to policy development and implementation. In B. Ndemo & T. Weiss (Eds.), *Digital Kenya an entrepreneurial revolution in the making* (pp. 339–362). London: Palgrave Macmillan.

Osiakwan, E. M. (2017). The KINGS of Africa's digital economy. In B. Ndemo & T. Weiss (Eds.), *Digital Kenya. An entrepreneurial revolution in the making* (pp. 55–92). London: Palgrave Macmillan.

Republic of Kenya (RoK). (2007). *Kenya vision 2030*. Nairobi: Government of the Republic of Kenya. www.vision2030.go.ke/lib.php?f=vision-2030-popular-version. Accessed 16 January 2018.

Robertson, R. (1992). *Globalization: Social theory and global culture* (Vol. 16). London: Sage.

Rotich, J. (2017). *Ushahidi: Empowering citizens through crowdsourcing and digital data collection* (Field Actions Science Reports, 16). http://journals.openedition.org/factsreports/4316. Accessed 6 January 2018.

Sambuli, N., & Witt, J. P. (2017). *Technology innovation hubs and policy engagement* (Making all voices Count Research Report). Brighton: IDS.

Shiach, M. E., Nakano, D., Virani, T., & Poli, K. (2017). *Report on creative Hubs and Urban Development Goals (UK/Brazil)*. UK and Brazil: Creative Hubs and Urban Development Goals.

Soerensen, K. K., & Petuchaite, V. (2013). Prospects for civil society empowerment through the use of the new media. In *Speaking up and talking back?: Media, empowerment and civic engagement among East and Southern African Youth* (pp. 113–128). Gøteborg, Sweden: Nordicom.

Toivonen, T., & Friederici, N. (2015). Time to define what a "hub" really is. *Stanford Social Innovation Review*.

UNESCO. (2016). *Unesco Report 2015*. Paris: UNESCO. http://unesdoc.unesco.org/images/0024/002448/244834e.pdf. Accessed 23 November 2017.

Ushahidi. (2010). *Uchaguzi. A case study. Successes, challenges, and new ways forward.* Nairobi: Harvard Humanitarian Found and Knight Foundation.

Ushahidi. (2016a). Ushahidi. www.ushahidi.com. Accessed 13 November 2017.

Ushahidi. (2016b). Ushahidi. https://en.wikipedia.org/w/index.php?title=Ushahidi& oldid=736920760. Accessed 13 November 2016.

Ushahidi. (2018). *Our blog. Product updates, user stories, and thoughts about our work.* https://www.ushahidi.com/blog. Accessed 6 January 2018.

van Rensburg, A. H. J. (2012). Using the internet for democracy: A study of South Africa, Kenya and Zambia. *Global Media Journal African Edition, 6*(1), 93–117.

Virani, T. E., & Malem, W. (2015). *Re-articulating the creative hub concept as a model for business support in the local creative economy: The case of Mare Street in Hackney* (Creativeworks London Working Papers Series). London.

Weiss, T. (2017). Entrepreneuring for society: What is next for Africa? In B. Ndemo & T. Weiss (Eds.), *Digital Kenya. An entrepreneurial revolution in the making* (pp. 461–482). London: Palgrave Macmillan.

Wildermuth, N. (2010). Empowerment: The real challenge of digital inclusion. In K. Drotner & K. C. Schrøder (Eds.), *Digital content creation: Perceptions, practices, and perspectives* (pp. 267–286). New York: Peter Lang.

Wildermuth, N. (2014). Communication for transparency and social accountability. In *The handbook of development communication and social change* (pp. 370–392). Oxford: Wiley.

YouTube. (2012). #INSIDE-AFRICA, THE KENYA EDITION:: [CNN's ERROL BARNETT at the ihub], from https://www.youtube.com/watch?v=005AbXWizog. Accessed 27 December 2017.

Zuckerberg, M. (2016). *Facebook.* https://mg-mg.facebook.com/zuck/posts/10103073829862111. Accessed 18 April 2018.

11

Producing Values: Impact Hub Birmingham as Co-working and Social Innovation Space

Paul Long and Annette Naudin

Introduction

Impact Hub describes a network providing co-working spaces with a global reach that stretches 'From Amsterdam to Johannesburg, Singapore to San Francisco' (impacthub.net). Online, it advertises an expanding provision servicing 'over 11,000+ members in 72+ locations' (ibid.). These locations are diverse, including sites across Africa and the Middle East in cities like Harare and Kigali, through South America in Bogota, Oaxaca and Recife or more northerly in Seattle or Honolulu. A recently established 'franchise' site is based in Birmingham UK, the object of investigation for this chapter.

To label a co-working space an *Impact* Hub might be considered something of a hostage to fortune, especially in the light of the avowed mission of the network to create spaces that are equally 'An innovation lab.

P. Long (✉) · A. Naudin
Birmingham Centre for Media and Cultural Research,
Birmingham City University, Birmingham, UK
e-mail: paul.long@bcu.ac.uk

© The Author(s) 2019
R. Gill et al. (eds.), *Creative Hubs in Question*, Dynamics of Virtual Work,
https://doi.org/10.1007/978-3-030-10653-9_11

A business Incubator. A social enterprise community center' (ibid.; for a history and character see: Shiach et al. 2017, pp. 11ff). As this collection attests, the concept of a hub itself merits some reflection as to its meaning, practices and associations (see also Virani and Malem 2015; Dovey et al. 2016). That the variety of sites in this network set out consciously and pro-actively to produce impact is particularly interesting as a means of understanding the hub idea and the importance of empirical specificity. In this regard, Impact Hub Birmingham (hereafter, IHB) is a suggestive site for scrutiny. It evinces a refreshing social commitment when considered in the context of concerns over the implications of co-working and the spaces devoted to them and indeed alongside the banal offer of other providers, commercial or otherwise. The transformative ambition of the global network (Shiach et al. 2017, p. 17) is echoed in IHB's sense of mission: 'to empower a collective movement to bring about change in our city, embracing a diverse range of people and organisations with a whole host of experiences and skills' (birmingham.impacthub.net). As we detail below, this mission inflects the distinctiveness of IHB and the kinds of activities that its managers organise, as manifest in the titles of events such as *People + Passion = Politics: A Guide to Making Change; Social Value on Your Organisation* and *Radical Childcare.*

In this chapter, we follow Dovey et al. (2016, p. 25) who note the necessity of a case study approach in apprehending the variety of hub forms. The individuality of sites—even across the Impact Hub network—presents a vista of 'messy relationships between generic description and day to day function' (Dovey et al. 2016, p. 25). We explore the character and specificity of IHB through the lens of its online presentation, assessing its objectives, organisation and activities. Our analysis frames IHB in terms of its status as social enterprise, detailing how this manifestation of 'the hub' idea engages individuals in debate and supports a particular idea of entrepreneurship that connects a wider set of issues and urban disjunctures. The chapter first considers the City of Birmingham as a setting for this enterprise, proceeding with a discussion of the hub and co-working idea illustrated with insights from IHB's operations. We then outline how IHB's avowed mission is defined by a commitment to this place. The penultimate section places projects cultivated within IHB in the context of critical perspectives on

social enterprise initiatives. As we conclude, the ambition of this itera-
tion of the Impact Hub network, as well as the commitment and verve
of its participants offers a progressive space for social innovation whatever its limits in addressing the city's considerable social and economic
problems.

Birmingham: A Tale of Two Cities

Once the 'workshop of the world', the 'City of a Thousand Trades',
Birmingham is a signal post-industrial site whose agents have sought
to reinvent and rebrand it. This has been pursued through a new economic rationale and entrepreneurial approach to governance (Cattacin
and Zimmer 2016), nurturing the service sector, seeking to develop and
attract banking, insurance, and conference hosting businesses (Kennedy
2004/2013). Indeed, much has been invested in re-development, manifest
in the building of flagship projects such as the International Convention
Centre, National Indoor Arena, Bull Ring and most recently the Library
of Birmingham, together illustrating an investment in assets that market this site as one offering cultural experience and consumption (Henry
et al. 2002). In addition to *trompe l'oeil* projects and the attraction of high
cultural organisations such as the Birmingham Royal Ballet and City of
Birmingham Symphony Orchestra, there has been an encouragement of
creative enterprise, the development of cultural industry clusters and areas
such as Digbeth and Jewellery Quarter (Chapain and Comunian 2010).

Creative England suggests that the city 'is at the heart of the West
Midlands creative and digital development industry and is home to
some of the UK's top creative and technology hubs', numbering Impact
Hub amongst a wider list of sites: Digital Birmingham; The Custard
Factory; Innovation Birmingham and iCentrum (creativeengland.
co.uk). While there are significant differences between these initiatives,
typological similarity lies in the provision of support to start-up companies and SMEs. In so doing, and alongside consultation services, some
on this list operate as incubators; others, as IHB does, offer co-working
space to individual freelancers and small companies. Here, these enterprises confirm Virani and Malem's (2015) description of differences

between the hub concept and other common descriptors of contemporary industrial organisation such as clusters or districts. As they write, 'Where clusters are usually understood due to their spatial organisation, hubs are framed here in regards to what they provide and how they provide it' (Virani and Malem 2015, p. 22).

Such activity is evidence of how Birmingham's narrative of remaking is coterminous with the extended validation of 'creativity' and cultural advantage in policy discourse. This is manifest in the idea of the 'creative city' (Landry 2000; Bianchini 2017), the ubiquity of Richard Florida's concept of the creative class (2002/2014) and the prodigious expansion of policy and practice in the cultural economy under New Labour (Hewison 2014). To some degree, these developments can be claimed to have informed aspects of the city's revitalisation and success stories certainly abound. The Local Economic Partnership (LEP) (GBSLEP 2016, p. 5) in its latest plan claims that 'Greater Birmingham' has the highest growth rate of any city region, is the key driver of the nation's economy outside London and the leading area for foreign direct investment (FDI) in the UK. Developments, such as the building of high-speed rail connection to London, mean that 'We are experiencing an economic renaissance' (ibid.).

From other perspectives however, the city's prospects do not appear so aglow. As Brookes et al. (2016, p. 88) observe, in spite of local government initiatives in pursuit of social inclusion goals and regeneration of the city centre 'it was acknowledged by all political parties that inequality still existed and lasting change for people living in Birmingham's most deprived neighbourhoods had not been achieved'. They identify how deindustrialisation's challenges endure alongside the impact of the financial crash of 2008 and austerity economics. While the city has the youngest population of any of the major cities in Europe: 'Over half of Birmingham is within the most deprived 20% of England and nearly 40% is in the most deprived 10%' (2016, p. 83). Unemployment rates are double the national average, with the city registering the highest figures in the UK amongst young people (those between the ages of 18 and 24). In some areas, figures reach 50% of those eligible for work and are in fact unemployment has become a generational issues.

Cattacin and Zimmer (2016) identify how Birmingham's relationship with 'a unitary state' limits the development of visionary social policies that are independent from those of the central government. Solutions to social problems in the city are thus viewed predominantly in economic terms, promoting growth with less attention to social services. The assumption is that benefits for the latter follow the former. Brookes et al. (2016, p. 95) note that while social innovation does occur, it is 'very much at the margins, through opportunistic and short- term support for small-scale projects'.

This might describe the particular remit of IHB as social enterprise, not just in terms of distinctiveness in relation to other types of co-working space in the city but in its address to these issues and the nature of its commitment to locale.

Inside Impact Hub Birmingham: The Consolations of Co-working

As with the idea of the hub, and as Butcher (2016, p. 94) notes, co-working is a fluid concept. Co-working practices take place in a variety of informal and formalised spaces, from the ad hoc appropriation of sites and meetings in cafes, to achieving fixity in specially designed and sometimes spectacular bespoke buildings. The variety of this sector can be appreciated by comparison between enterprises providing co-working space. The Regus Group, for instance, offers several sites across the globe including Birmingham, so presenting competition for IHB's offer. While Regus' spaces are advertised as providing proximity to established business zones and access to the attractions of the city, the appeal is generically business-like and the offer functional: 'Drop in whenever you need, with desk space in a professional, shared environment on a first come first served basis' (regus.co.uk). Such organisations manifest the profit-driven, corporate end of this plural sphere of provision. By way of comparison, the offer of not-for-profit IHB is described by member Christopher Jones as distinct from the 'unremarkable' mode of hot-desking one is likely to encounter at places like Regus. At IHB, he identifies a quality that is more than functional, describing 'a certain texture to the environment, a particular grain to the fabric … cultivating networks of both social and professional value, the two often undivided, whilst generating a collaborative and sharing environment with a distinctly non-competitive dimension' (Jones 2016).

Of course, users of Regus' provision may perhaps have similar things to say, as they might of other spaces in the city that are identified by online locator Coworker.com such as Moseley Exchange, The Engine, The Transfer or The Loft. Distinctive here are Jones' lyrical reflections—he is a professional writer—which are offered in an extended blog post at the online site of IHB. His piece forms part of a rich texture of such accounts, official statements and ideas that convey a sense of the dynamism of this space and its community. This is where a narrative can be garnered that conveys the commitment and personal investment in IHB of its founders. As we discover, some had 'a stint of chasing the bright lights in London', returning to Birmingham and finding like minds in the informal space of contemporary co-work, i.e., 'the coffee shop to which we owe so many of our founding ideas and brainwaves' (Anon 2014). In making the IHB, its 'young, naive, and independent' founders placed themselves at great risk, having: 'left our jobs, invested everything we had financially, emotionally and physically in bringing this dream to life' (ibid.). Such statements attest to a creative investment in IHB's presentation by its founders and managers but also by its members (Butcher 2016, p. 101). This suggests how such contributions are a form of 'sweat equity' on the part of the latter group that has mutual benefit in underwriting their location at IHB and faith in its distinctive offer.

As described by Merkel (2015, p. 130), the work of managers or 'hosts' oversees the social relationships of workers and use of environment 'thus turning co-working spaces into highly symbolically structured or curated spaces'. IHB's promotion builds from its physical manifestation in terms of the character of its building and the arrangement and population of its space: 'exposed, cleaned-up brickwork … as many clean lines and panes of glass as possible, creating a modern, naked environment which is both animated and permeable … underlying any particular arrangement of tables, desks, chair and screens is a sense of the spontaneous' (Jones 2016). Online testimonies from members about IHB's features and activity articulate the use of this space, its ethos and potential. Alongside the IHB's own website this takes place across those of its members and advocates (no adversaries are apparent) and rich also in the interactions of social media accounts operated by those connected to the space or those participating in its many events. Co-Founder Immy Kaur, for instance, has a substantive Twitter status, having nurtured nearly 14,000 followers. That she follows an even greater number of accounts indicates her investment in this avenue of communication.

As Gandini (2015) and others have noted, the development of co-working spaces has accentuated individualised sensibilities amongst workers as well as their concomitant isolation. Here, reflections by IHB members offer insights into the realities of co-working, its necessity, challenges and indeed the consolations of this space. Birmingham member Verity M. (2014) ponders the contemporary work sphere that what is missing for the freelancer is a sense of community which jeopardises one's potential, as 'Being a photographer can be lonely existence, and I don't believe a creative spirit can be fostered in isolation. We need our peers, we need our contemporaries to be part of the process'. Tara Buckley (2016), a Creative Producer of performance experiences, events and projects, records an impact of IHB on her practice where 'Having this space has allowed me to dedicate productive time towards projects, which can be difficult as a freelancer, it has shifted the way I think about the work that I do, and as a result I am producing more meaningful projects'. Such instances illustrate how co-working allows individuals to garner appreciation, recognition and ideas from peers (Olma 2012; Merkel 2015). This serves to counteract the precarious nature of freelance work where co-working is conducted in a spirit of mutual exchange and generosity. Thus, events such as *Coffee and Change* playfully foreground of the importance and availability of quality coffees, teas and cake in IHB discourse, accentuating conviviality but also issues of taste and tastefulness that distinguishes the discerning company and advantage one keeps there. In this way also, IHB invokes the feeling of the coffee shop, the place where so many established (and potential) members have co-worked informally.

At IHB, the creative investments of managers and users contribute to the production of a site that is much more than a functional vessel for the hosting of disparate workers and small businesses, redefining the idea of the entrepreneurial cultural worker. IHB is a layered space of signification reminding one of Doreen Massey's useful formulation that describes places as 'articulated moments in networks of social relations and understandings' (Massey 1994, p. 154). The global, cosmopolitan nature of the Impact Hub network offers one layering of these articulations, informed by a version of working together reified in San Francisco, of coffee shops and the cultural formations associated with 'boundaryless workers' (Brown 2017). While the boundaries usually considered in this label are those between home and work and which have become diluted, they might be extended to the apparent lack of situatedness of workers. What does location mean in a globalised economy and co-working culture, mapped by the digital where everything is potentially connected and where boundaries of time, space and culture are permeable? For a network like Impact Hub, what are the similarities but also distinctions in what its mission and activities mean to Khartoum, Kigali or Kings Cross? Certainly, experiences of co-working and the nature of co-working space are not entirely boundaryless. Each is defined too by location, by local culture and its demands. Here then, we can turn to consider the specificity of Birmingham as a location for IHB, its founders, members and the expression of its mission.

The Social Mission of Impact Hub Birmingham

Fidelity to place is an important feature of Impact Hub as network, something that appealed to the founders of the Birmingham franchise that placed 'global connectivity' alongside the fact that 'all Impact Hub's [sic] were locally owned and true to their respective local context' (Anon 2014). In establishing its truth to context, IHB's self-representation evinces a 'habitus of place' (Allen and Hollingworth 2013), at times calling on a form of local chauvinism, if not essentialism. An account of the IHB's origination identifies its inspiration in a TEDx event in the city, although the 'hunger for innovation' addressed there was already 'in our Birmingham blood', infused with the city's reputation: 'Steeped in pioneering history and responsible for patents and moments that have shaped the modern world as we know it' (Anon 2014). The Hub itself is based at The Walker Building in Digbeth, an area still bearing the marks of traditional industry but home too to sites synonymous with the ambitions of cultural regeneration and the creative city such as the Custard Factory, The Bond and 'Eastside' (Porter and Barber 2007). The IHB's home is referred to self-reflexively as a post-industrial site, once home to a company renowned for its owners' philanthropy, progressive approaches to labour (shorter working weeks and good industrial relations) and contribution to building the municipal reputation of Birmingham. Thus, while newly minted and a product of contemporary economic and sociocultural realities, IHB's rhetoric affirms a sense of continuity, that 'it's the Walker ethos and commitment to their community at large that has struck a particularly warm and fuzzy chord with us here at the Hub' (Modgil 2015). Likewise, across the kinds of companies and individuals it attracts, and in much of the activities it endorses, IHB connects to the overlooked civic history of Birmingham, a place that once drew international visitors to examine 'The best governed city in the world' (Hunt 2005, pp. xxxix). Here, we are mindful of the work of Virani and Malem (2015) and Dovey et al. (2016) which suggest that what matters here is the symbolism of IHB's rhetoric about its space and this lineage rather than any of its physical properties. As Dovey et al. (2016, p. 11) emphasise, it is not location which characterises these enterprises 'but the nature and quality of the productive relationships that occur inside the hub itself'.

Thus, IHB manifests the more social and political commitments associated with co-working (Gandini 2015). On this point, and as Merkel argues (2015, p. 124), co-working is 'not just about working "alone together" or "alongside each other" in a flexible and mostly affordable office space. It is also underpinned by a normative cultural model that promotes five values: community, collaboration, openness, diversity, and sustainability'. IHB makes such values paramount in its civic mission of 'Prototyping the Twenty-First Century Town Hall' (Impact Hub Birmingham 2015). In this idea, IHB positions its mission as a direct response to social challenges such as in-work poverty and structural inequality, addressing Birmingham's levels of economic disadvantage, inequalities in health and material deprivation. The possibility of 'transformational change' for this situation is offered in the form of 'disruptive innovation' and 'change technologies' such as open source and crowdsourcing. Thus, what is called for is 'a revolution that reimagines what the "us" is: dissolving the public, civic and private sector divide, disrupting democratic legitimacy and focussing on shared wealth, interdependence, interoperability and a fairer city for all' (ibid., p. 4).

These are high minding ambitions, and they have affective power for those attracted to locating at IHB and for their expectations of the serendipitous encounters likely to take place therein. Verity M. (2014) attests to the personal and communal response to this ambition and the perception of its freshness in the context of the city: 'to disrupt the old ways of doing things, and starting to work together from the grassroots to build a greater city, a more collaborative city'. Such instances indicate how 'impact' can be understood here initially, as something concerned with attracting and nurturing the human capital assembled in IHB, of generating mutual endorsement and a collective will towards achieving a civic mission (de Peuter and Cohen 2015). While members are of course independently constituted and not compelled by the IHB's managers, likewise, the sharing of values informs the kinds of work that each does—or for which is likely to find a welcome. Alongside creative workers like Verity M. and the aforementioned Christopher Jones, many residents are engaged in various other forms of 'immaterial labour': 'From design skills and public speaking to coaching and screen-printing' (birmingham.impacthub.net/become-member). Many are occupied by forms of consultation work, seeking to produce affective outcomes in what they do across the civic sphere. Iris Bertz Ltd for instance comprises 'a group of dedicated and experienced artists, designers, organisers, teachers and trainers who are all current practitioners in the creative and educational sector'. They offer 'European Project planning', 'Apprentice Placement programmes', 'Funding Bid development', Workshops and Training', 'Project Management' and 'Arts Projects' (irisbertz.co.uk). The Access Project aids entry to university for disadvantaged if gifted children by pairing them with volunteer tutors (theaccessproject.org.uk). Beatfreeks, now expanded and moved on from the IHB, is 'a creative youth engagement agency. We help young people and brands reach their potential by unleashing their creativity' (www.beatfreeks.com).

The hosting of such enterprises is framed at IHB by the curation of a prodigious range of events that speak directly to its mission and which aim to galvanise engagement with current issues for members and a wider constituency. Inspired by an initiative in Detroit, *Birmingham Soup,* is a group of volunteers with experience in outreach, arts, project management and training who run a regular 'microgranting' dinner in support of the city's creative projects in need of funding. IHB residents are presented with information about the projects, voting on that which fulfils best the brief, that it 'must benefit the Birmingham community ... to be democratic, creative, sustainable and inclusive'. Typical projects cover the arts, land use and urban agriculture schemes, enterprise, social justice initiatives, education, technology, housing and city services. Regular and one-off events are indicative of the wider engagement; these include: *Beyond Unemployment*; *United in Hope: 'How To Deal with Hate Crime Toolkit'* and *Trade School Digbeth*: 'a non-traditional learning community that runs on barter and not on a monetary exchange' (birmingham.impacthub.net/whats-on/trade-school-digbeth/).

Assessing Social Enterprise in Impact Hub Birmingham

Of course, these kinds of events, debates and ideas are produced and take place elsewhere in Birmingham too, but IHB ambitiously places its purpose in contradistinction to 'traditional institutions' such as universities, corporations and local authorities, which 'are struggling to create the rich, safe legitimate trusted and sandboxed environments for shared innovation, with a business model and civic legitimacy essential for the advancement of a collaborative economy and shared wealth' (Impact Hub Birmingham 2015, p. 19).

Nonetheless, there is a critical view of such approaches by co-working spaces to consider here. On a general note for instance, Gandini complains (2015, p. 194) that much of the literature on co-working sees it as a positive innovation, 'with few dwelling upon empirical findings and rarely offering a critical understanding'. He appears suspicious of the 'culturepreneurs', i.e. skilled knowledge workers with multi-portfolio careers, 'operating as self-entrepreneurs within scarcely-institutionalised economies'. Butcher (2016, p. 101), offers a similarly critical view, arguing that whatever the communal sensibility, 'the dominant dispositions within co-working spaces are entrepreneurial. The symbols of community are thus adapted for entrepreneurial identity work, and commodified for ambitions towards the capitalist idea of "progress"'.

Such perspectives are prematurely and too generally dismissive: we would argue for a more nuanced understanding of the possibilities of co-working social enterprise as a means of conceptualising a space beyond its compromise by the dictates of the profit motive. Some of this understanding lies in looking beyond the connotations of normative labels. By way of explanation, the term 'social enterprise' does not define a specific model or the legal status of a business; rather, it is used to refer to those that have social objectives as part of their mission, which are addressed in entrepreneurial manner. In the UK, most social enterprises opt to set up as a Community Interest Company (CIC) or co-operatives and operate as a not-for-profit organisation—as is the case with IHB. However, as they need to generate revenue to fulfil their social objectives, they often face a tension between sustainability and the fulfilment of their mission.

Critiques of social enterprise are particularly concentrated on and yet confused over the figure of 'the entrepreneur'. Being entrepreneurial has become synonymous with Schumpeter's ideas of the entrepreneur as 'creative destructor', of being a 'responsible' and 'good citizen' measured in economic terms. The idea celebrates particular modes of the individual, 'driven, determined, ambitious and charismatic' (Leadbeater 1997, p. 11), whose potential is realised in self-employment and self-interest. Associations of 'social enterprise' also came about in the mid-1990s and in European countries at least, coincidental with the dilution of the welfare state (Anderson et al. 2006; Chell 2008). Overall, this discourse and normative ideas of the entrepreneur seeps into the language, tone and descriptions of the socially driven agendas of social enterprises.

On the other hand, within entrepreneurship studies, scholars question limited definitions of the entrepreneur and suggest that rather than studying the figure of the lone hero, we should focus our attention on variant narratives and the nature of entrepreneurship in unusual spaces (Naudin 2018). Thus, Campbell's (2009, p. 165) exploration of social entrepreneurship considers 'the merits of localized, small-scale, non-heroic enterprise' with an emphasis on women and ethical conduct. This reflects a pro-active approach to intervention in social, ecological and economic development, crafting a 'new entrepreneurial belief system' (Campbell 2009, p. 186). These ideas connect with initiatives such as IHB and environments in which alternative forms of entrepreneurship are pursued and tested. Such forms are consciously distinguished from the male-dominated, individualistic and commercially driven capitalist narrative that dominates popular media and indeed, much academic literature. Such instances merit closer and more detailed attention for their meanings, achievement and indeed impact.

Conclusions: *Impact* Hub?

Cattacin and Zimmer (2016) consider that in Birmingham, while the shift to the entrepreneurial approach to nurturing the service and creative industries offers some means of addressing problems of governance, social innovations emerging in this context are unlikely to solve the 'wicked problems' of the city, of its social and cultural fractures. Taking this into account, what then might be the impact of IHB otherwise and how might we assess it?

As Dovey et al. suggest (2016, p. 17), while hub ventures might produce reports and records that might aid such an assessment, 'the overall picture is of a milieu that concentrates its limited resource on getting its process right rather than evaluating its product'. Certainly, the impact of

IHB is hard to quantify, but might be manifest in the profile of individuals such as Kaur, identified as one of region's top 250 most influential people (Brown 2016). Perhaps IHB's impact can be measured through the numbers who engage with it as members and attendees at its workshops, events and socials. Its first anniversary in 2016 was recorded in a blog post, presenting data that captured events and activities from that year: 140 members—organisations and individual freelancers—were recruited; 382 events were hosted (152 kg of coffee was consumed!). Beyond these locally situated and referenced activities, its individual identity and innovations connect too with the global network.

IHB's activities have reach but is this the way in which to assess its impact? A site that hosts co-workers might not need to have more than a functional quality, promoting conviviality to give it commercial advantage and to aid sustainability. However, with its mission of civic engagement, IHB explores issues such as unemployment, diversity and childcare with the aim of engaging with and sometimes initiating local debates. This activity seeks to begin a process of social transformation, but it is too early to demonstrate whether this is manifest in general consciousness raising and policy developments, or if any change in social inequality is likely to be attributed to such a small player in the city's infrastructure. That said, the impact of such enterprises might gain traction by way of connection with hubs with a sympathetic mission—directly or indirectly—by way of their collective contribution to the texture of the city's culture. One local referent for IHB for instance is Birmingham Open Media, described by Dovey et al. (2016, p. 42) as 'driven by socially engaged practice at the intersection of art, technology and science'. Nonetheless, between themselves, the collective and individual profiles of IHB staff and its members provides models of alternative entrepreneurial identities, revealing diverse narratives, far removed from the rhetoric associated with the celebrated creative economy worker of contemporary policy (Naudin 2018). Our study suggests that IHB provides an environment in which the tension between sustaining small enterprises, connecting to the locale and negotiating social objectives is reimagined as part of the fabric of a hub. Ultimately, the model IHB presents is not likely to be measured in economic value but in terms of the social values it generates and promotes. In the end, the potential impact is for social entrepreneurs and those involved in IHB itself and for the city, in raising awareness of its problems, offering experimental and alternative positions as part of its fabric of activity. In the anodyne and relatively toothless landscape of the creative city and cultural industries, this is a positive development.

References

Allen, K., & Hollingworth, S. (2013). "Sticky subjects" or "cosmopolitan creative"? Social class, place and urban young people's aspirations for work in the knowledge economy. *Urban Studies, 50*(3), 499–517.

Anderson, R. B., Honig, B., & Peredo, A. M. (2006). Communities in the global economy: Where social and indigenous entrepreneurship meet. In C. Steyaert & D. Hjorth (Eds.), *Entrepreneurship as social change*. Cheltenham and Northampton: Edward Elgar.

Anon. (2014). *Journey so far*. Available at https://birmingham.impacthub. net/2014/11/28/journey-so-far/. Accessed 1 October 2017.

Bianchini, F. (2017). Reflections on the origins, interpretations and development of the creative city idea. In I. Van Damme, B. De Munck, & A. Miles (Eds.), *Cities and creativity from the renaissance to the present*. London: Routledge.

Brookes, N., Kendall, J., & Mitton, L. (2016). Birmingham, priority to economics, social innovation at the margins. In T. Bransden, et al. (Eds.), *Social innovations in the urban context*. Cham: Springer.

Brown, G. (2016, April 2). The Birmingham post power 250. *Birmingham Post*. Available at http://www.birminghampost.co.uk/business/business-news/birmingham-post-power-250-west-11126796. Accessed 1 October 2017.

Brown, J. (2017). Curating the "third place"? Coworking and the mediation of creativity. *Geoforum, 82,* 112–126.

Buckley, T. (2016, February 10). *What's Impact Hub Birmingham?* Available at https://birmingham.impacthub.net/2016/02/10/whats-impact-hub-birmingham/. Accessed 1 October 2017.

Butcher, T. (2016). Co-working communities. In R. Horne, J. Fien, B. B. Beza, & A. Nelson (Eds.), *Sustainability citizenship in cities: Theory and practice*. London: Routledge.

Campbell, K. (2009). Rekindling the entrepreneurial potential of family business—A radical (old-fashioned) feminist proposal. In D. Hjorth & C. Steyaert (Eds.), *The politics and aesthetics of entrepreneurship*. Cheltnenham: Edward Elgar.

Cattacin, S., & Zimmer, A. (2016). Urban governance and social innovations. In T. Brandsen, S. Cattacin, A. Evers, & A. Zimmer (Eds.), *Social innovations in the urban context*. Cham: Springer.

Chapain, C., & Comunian, R. (2010). Enabling and inhibiting the creative economy: The role of the local and regional dimensions in England. *Regional Studies, 44*(6), 717–734.

Chell, E. (2008). *The entrepreneurial personality: A social construct*. Sussex: Routledge.

de Peuter, G., & Cohen, N. (2015). Emerging labour politics in creative industries. In K. Oakley & J. O'Connor (Eds.), *The Routledge companion to the cultural industries*. Abingdon: Routledge.

Dovey, J., Pratt, A. C., Moreton, S., Virani, T. E., Merkel, J., & Lansdowne, J. (2016). *The creative hubs report: 2016*. UK: British Council.

Florida, R. (2014). *The rise of the creative class–Revisited: Revised and expanded*. New York: Basic Books.

Gandini, A. (2015). The rise of coworking spaces: A literature review. *Theory and Politics in Organization, 15*(1), 193–205.

GBSLEP (Greater Birmingham and Solihull). (2016). *Greater Birmingham for a greater Britain Gbslep strategic economic plan 2016–2030*. Available at http://centreofenterprise.com/sep2016/.

Henry, N., McEwan, C., & Pollard, J. (2002). Globalization from below: Birmingham—Postcolonial workshop of the world? *Area, 34*(2), 117–127.

Hewison, R. (2014). *Cultural capital: The rise and fall of creative Britain*. London and New York: Verso Books.

Hunt, T. (2005). *Building Jerusalem: The rise and fall of the Victorian city*. London: MacMillan.

Impact Hub Birmingham. (2015). *Mission roadmap: Prototyping the 21st century Town Hall*. Available at https://issuu.com/impacthubbirmingham/docs/impact_hub_birmingham_mission_roadm. Accessed 1 October 2017.

Jones, C. (2016). *Co-working at Birmingham's hub: Feeling the impact*. Available at https://birmingham.impacthub.net/2016/07/18/co-working-at-birminghams-hub-feeling-the-impact/. Accessed 1 October 2017.

Kennedy, L. (Ed.). (2004/2013). *Remaking Birmingham: The visual culture of urban regeneration*. London: Routledge.

Landry, C. (2000). *The creative city: A toolkit for urban innovators*. London, UK: Earthscan.

Leadbeater, C. (1997). *The rise of the social entrepreneur*. London: Demos.

Massey, D. (1994). *Space, place and gender*. Minneapolis: University of Minnesota Press.

Merkel, J. (2015). Coworking in the city. *Ephemera, 15*(2), 121–139.

Modgil, K. (2015). *A history of Thomas Walker and Son*. Available at http://birmingham.impacthub.net/2015/05/05/a-history-of-thomas-walker-and-son/. Accessed 1 October 2017.

Naudin, A. (2018). *Cultural entrepreneurship: The cultural worker's experience of entrepreneurship*. London: Routledge.

Olma, S. (2012). *The serendipity machine: A disruptive business model for society 3.0*. Utrecht: Society 3.0 Foundation.

Porter, L., & Barber, A. (2007). Planning the cultural quarter in Birmingham's Eastside. *European Planning Studies, 15*(10), 1327–1348.

Shiach, M. E., Nakano, D., Virani, T., & Poli, K. (2017). *Report on creative Hubs and Urban Development Goals (UK/Brazil)*. UK and Brazil: Creative Hubs and Urban Development Goals.

Verity, M. (2014, December 13). *Creativity, collaboration and community: Falling in love with Birmingham*. Available at https://medium.com/hub-birmingham/creativity-collaboration-and-community-falling-in-love-with-birmingham-4a2b889139f9. Accessed 1 October 2017.

Virani, T. E., & Malem, W. (2015). *Re-articulating the creative hub concept as a model for business support in the local creative economy: The case of Mare Street in Hackney* (Creativeworks London Working Paper Series).

12

Punk Rock Entrepreneurship: All-Ages DIY Music Venues and the Urban Economic Landscape

Michael Seman

Introduction

It is increasingly common for music scenes to catalyze economic development on the urban landscape. There is a growing body of research examining this phenomenon and as it expands, the analysis more closely focuses on the nuances, details, and dynamics of the scenes (Currid 2007; Lloyd 2006; Seman 2015). One detail of successful music scenes that has yet to be closely examined is all-ages Do-it-Yourself (DIY) music venues. These venues are often critical developmental ingredients in successful music scenes yet their dynamics and value to these scenes and their host cities remain generally absent from discussion (Marzorati 2001; McMurray 2009; Seman 2010). This chapter briefly examines three all-ages DIY music venues to help define their value to music scenes and the broader urban economies they inhabit and argues they function as both "creative hubs" and "artists' centers," facilitating

M. Seman (✉)
College of Arts & Media, University of Colorado Denver,
Denver, CO, USA
e-mail: michael.seman@ucdenver.edu

© The Author(s) 2019
R. Gill et al. (eds.), *Creative Hubs in Question*, Dynamics of Virtual Work,
https://doi.org/10.1007/978-3-030-10653-9_12

arts incubation and entrepreneurship. Given this insight, urban planners, economic development professionals, and other city representatives may better understand the value of an all-ages DIY music venue to the cultural fabric and economic landscape of their cities, hopefully incorporating them more formally in their policymaking efforts targeting the arts.

The next section of this chapter is a brief literature review offering background concerning the emergence of the DIY movement in the music industry, comparative analysis of all-ages DIY music venues and community arts spaces, and related dynamics of arts entrepreneurship. Following that section is a discussion of the qualitative methods used in this research. The third section presents the case studies of the Cog Factory in Omaha, Nebraska, the Metropolis in Seattle, Washington, and Flint Local 432 in Flint, Michigan. The final section offers a discussion of the results and concluding thoughts.

Punk Rock, Artists' Centers, Creative Hubs, and Entrepreneurship

The "Do-it-Yourself" or "DIY" movement in music is a result of opposition to the corporatization of the music industry. By the 1970s, vertically integrated major recording labels created a monopolized industry that marginalized many musicians due to influencing the cost of entry into the marketplace (Thompson 2001). The punk rock movement of the late 1970s was partially spawned as a response to this transformation in the industry. Although many "punk" bands such as the Sex Pistols and The Clash were actually on major labels, other UK bands such as Manchester's Buzzcocks and London's The Desperate Bicycles made a conscious effort to operate outside of the increasingly corporately operated music industry, at least initially, and control all aspects of their career from pressing records to booking shows (Spencer 2008; Thompson 2001).

Bands and record labels independent of the major label machinery gained traction in the UK and their influence spread to music scenes in the USA where an "independent" or DIY ethos took hold and blossomed into established touring, distribution, promotion, and communication networks (Azerrad 2001; Botta 2009; Thompson 2001). The independent record label SST and the band who founded it, Black Flag were forerunners in developing these networks during the early 1980s. Black Flag expanded on the groundwork laid by pioneering Canadian band, D.O.A. and helped establish a flexible network of non-traditional venues across the USA. One outcome of this new DIY touring network was the emergence of all-ages DIY music venues (Azerrad 2001; Berg 2005; Oakes 2009).

All-ages DIY music venues can take various forms and have moved on from their punk roots to embrace a multitude of music genres. They can be temporary spaces in a band member's home operating completely off-the-radar of local policymakers. Some are located in commercial or industrial spaces that are still off-the-radar but are sophisticated in their operations resembling a traditional venue. Others are established non-profit or not-for-profit entities proactively engaging with local policymakers and offering resources beyond performance space like recording studios, rehearsal space, and after-school programs (Culton and Holtzman 2010; Stewart 2010). There are two common themes that cut across the venue types. The first is the majority of operations such as booking, promotions, sound, box office, security, and maintenance are handled by volunteers who are either participants in or have strong ties to the local music scene. The second is that these volunteers and the bands playing on stage are often under the age of 21 which can exclude them from attending shows at traditional venues where alcohol is served, hence the "all-ages" designation and the fact that many all-ages DIY music venues employ a strict policy against the use of drugs or alcohol (Stewart 2010).

The dynamics of all-ages DIY music venues and their impact on volunteers and music scene participants fit within the frameworks of both creative hubs and artists' centers. For example, like all-ages DIY music venues, creative hubs can take many forms including an individual building or "studio" operating as a co-working space or a larger building or "centre" incorporating items such as café, bar, or makerspace among other options (British Council 2015). While the physical place may differ (or sometimes not be present at all), creative hubs are spaces where "work, participation, and consumption" all happen facilitating incubation, networking, and business development (Dovey et al. 2016). The all-ages DIY music venues examined in this chapter all exhibit these characteristics.

Markusen et al. (2006) detail how artists' centers are community spaces focusing on the fine arts, offering artists at different career levels a place to develop in an environment that is supportive with opportunities for feedback, mentoring, and network building. The authors state artists' centers "act as forums for synergy and interaction that encourage artists to pursue their art form, plan their careers, and share their work in multiple venues" adding that "successful centers deftly bridge between artists just beginning their work and those who have launched careers and may even have attained fame and a comfortable living" (Markusen et al. 2006, p. 28). These observations are very similar in nature to how all-ages DIY music venues foster both emerging and established talent in the same evening (onstage, in the crowd, and sometimes in rehearsal spaces) while on occasion hosting financially successful national touring bands that specifically choose to play these spaces out of loyalty to the independent music scenes that launched them (Culton and Holtzman 2010; Stewart 2010). Grodach (2011, p. 75) suggests artists' centers help develop not only artists but the communities where they are located as they can be "a conduit for building the social networks and social capital that contribute to both community revitalization and artistic development."

Formal inclusion of artists' centers into a region's economic development policy is suggested by Markusen et al. (2006, p. 29) who urges that "policymakers responsible for economic development, urban planning, and cultural policy should acknowledge and support artists service centers as good investments, paying cultural and economic dividends." Grodach (2011) encourages planners to assist artists' centers by engaging with the centers to understand their individual dynamics and how best they might fit into localized opportunities for community and economic development, suggesting that planners and policymakers should encourage and help the spaces to engage in collaboration with each other as well as with local employers.

The dynamics of both creative hubs and artists centers position them as incubation spaces facilitating arts entrepreneurship. Thom (2015, p. 33) notes that although there is "still no consensus of what skills are really crucial for fine artists' commercial success," successful incubation spaces for the fine arts develop the "crucial" entrepreneurial skills of creativity, strategic and innovative thinking, opportunity recognition, networking, leadership, obtaining and managing financing, and marketing (Thom 2015). Patten (2016, p. 23) mines similar territory suggesting entrepreneurs in the creative industries "do not align themselves with traditional entrepreneurship discourses." Patten (2016, p. 26) does offer that arts entrepreneurs who build "corridors of knowledge," in part "socially constructed" are able to develop entrepreneurial skills in addition to the ability to identify opportunities, available or created. This echoes Grodach's (2011) insight into the value of social networks and capital for artist development as well as the networking focus inherent in creative hubs (British Council 2015). Boles (2009) suggests all-ages DIY music venues serve as incubators for not only musicians, but the "next generation of promoters and bookers" in a music scene adding one "might be surprised at how many of Toronto's behind the scenes movers and shakers got their start throwing all-ages punk gigs" (Boles 2009, p. 1).

Methodology

The venues examined in this chapter were selected due to their historical significance in the development of music scenes which helped drive economic development in their respective cities. These venues are by no means the only venues to foster this type of activity, but their popularity in the historical record (The Cog Factory and the Metropolis) and continued operation (Flint Local 432) offered an unparalleled ease of access to the phenomenon in question. A case study methodology was employed in order to use multiple avenues for data gathering including previously published accounts as source material (Yin 2003). The first step was gathering all available background information, e.g., magazine and newspaper articles, books, films, Web sites, etc., concerning the venues and corresponding music scenes. The next step was examining relevant literature across disciplines to create a framework for analysis. Questions both subjective and factual were then developed to help address the overarching research question—do all-ages DIY music venues operate in similar fashion to more traditional spaces for arts incubation and entrepreneurship?

Questions concerning venues in Omaha and Seattle were predominantly answered through interviews in previously published materials. For the Seattle case study location, the author was granted access to the Museum of Pop Culture's extensive archive of oral histories concerning the city's music scene. In the case of Flint, a convenience sample for interviews was developed with the help of a key informant. The sample included nine individuals representing the venue founder, scene members, and city stakeholders. Again, a set of questions both subjective and factual were developed, this time used in a series of "structured" and "semistructured" in-person interviews lasting from 30 to 90 minutes conducted on-site over five days (Bernard 1988). After transcription, analysis included coding responses and placing the results into the framework created by the literature analysis, secondary source materials, and results from the Omaha and Seattle case studies.

From the Cog Factory to Slowdown

The Cog Factory in Omaha, Nebraska was an all-ages DIY music venue located in a mixed-use section of downtown Omaha experiencing urban decay. The venue was the result of Omaha music scene participant Robb Rathe looking for an affordable space where he could live, host punk rock shows, and house his furniture workshop. Rathe moved into the space in 1991, began hosting shows shortly after performing needed, yet sparse renovations, and eventually left the space and the venue to new management in 1998. The venue continued for four more years until closing in 2002 (McMahan 1998; R. Rathe, personal communication, May 19, 2011).

The Cog Factory included many of the traits of a typical all-ages DIY music venue. It had a strict no drugs or alcohol policy and in initial years was largely overlooked by local and state authorities in terms of the building code regulations, occupancy restrictions, and taxes related to spaces hosting live music. The venue ran on an all-volunteer basis with a core handful of people (which grew to approximately 10–15) responsible for everything from booking bands and promoting shows to running the coffee bar and performing routine building maintenance. Shows at the Cog Factory were frequent with an average of just over three shows a week and two-thirds of the bands booked coming from Omaha and surrounding areas. As the venue increased in popularity, the sizes of the nightly audiences grew, the number of volunteers increased, and local and state authorities began to pay attention. Eventually, the venue had to pay a substantial amount of back taxes and become a non-profit corporation in order to remain open. Cog Factory founder, Rathe states, "we couldn't stay under the radar when 300 kids were hanging out on the sidewalk every Saturday night" (R. Rathe, personal communication, May 19, 2011).

The Cog Factory was a successful all-ages DIY music venue, but it was also a successful incubator for the city's internationally recognized music scene and the independent rock record label associated with it, Saddle Creek Records. Founded in 1993, Saddle Creek Records was the collaborative result of an extended group of friends and music scene participants who frequented the Cog Factory and wanted to release music by the bands the venue helped develop such as Bright Eyes and The Faint among many others. Those bands and the label eventually achieved international acclaim and financial success. One result of this success was developers working in conjunction with the label to open a $10.2 million-dollar mixed-use urban redevelopment project, "Slowdown" in downtown Omaha in 2007. In addition to Slowdown housing the label's offices and warehouse space, the project includes two venues booking local and national acts, an art-house theater, residential lofts, and retail space targeted for local businesses (Coffey 2015b; Seman 2010). Referring to the Cog Factory, one Omaha musician in a band signed to Saddle Creek Records states it was "probably one of the more important clubs that's ever existed in Omaha," adding, "a lot of bands played here, a lot of bands learned how to play live music here" (Jeffers 2008; Walters 2005).

Placed in the framework of Markusen and Johnson's (2006, p. 28) conceptualization of artists' spaces, the Cog Factory was a forum "for synergy and interaction" encouraging "artists to pursue their art form" by being a space where scene members could meet, form bands, rehearse (volunteers had 24/7 access to the venue as a rehearsal space), and serve as a training ground where they could hone their craft in front of audiences (Markusen and Johnson 2006, p. 28; R. Rathe, personal communication, May 19, 2011). Chris Esterbrooks who currently owns a screen-printing business and formerly played the Cog Factory as a member of the Carsinogents echoes this sentiment, offering that at the venue, "you hung around and met people. It was a community. All your best friends from school were in one spot. I remember going to shows not caring about who played, but you saw 10, 15, 20 of your friends." Omaha musician Matt Whipkey offers, "In retrospect, it is easy to see this era as a gelling point, but at the time it was your two favorite bands packing them in at the Cog and playing their guts out" (Coffey 2015a, b).

Grunge Incubation

Seattle was considered a "Mecca" of popular music in the early 1990s due to the international success of the "grunge" genre. The scene responsible gave the city an "audio identity," created an industrial sector with bands registering album sales revenues in the hundreds of millions of dollars, and positioned scene members for successful careers as graphic designers, photographers, managers, promoters, record label executives, entrepreneurs, and more (Bell 1998, p. 35; Florida 2002, p. 228; Pray 1996; Sillman 2011). The incubation of Seattle's music scene took place in a handful of small performance spaces including the all-ages DIY music venue, the Metropolis. Located in the then transitioning neighborhood of Pioneer Square in downtown Seattle, the Metropolis operated from approximately 1982 to 1984. The venue was owned by Hugo Piottin who ran it with a core group of volunteers handling daily tasks and a larger flexible volunteer crew made up of scene members helping to facilitate shows. A mixture of local and national touring bands played the venue; and, although it was not uncommon for national bands to draw several hundred people, local authorities never threatened the venue with closure until the very end of its lifespan when it was forced to close its doors due to the neighborhood gentrifying (Piottin 2009).

Like the Cog Factory, the Metropolis was more than just a venue, it functioned as an incubator giving scene members a place to congregate and develop as musicians, artists, and entrepreneurs in a city decidedly oppositional to youth culture at the time due to the Teen Dance Ordinance which severely hampered promoters organizing shows for audiences under-21 and a legitimate club scene not open to emerging, experimental or punk bands (Cameron 2009; McMurray 2009; Piottin 2009). Musician and scene member Alex Shumway states "If it wasn't for the Metropolis, I don't think 90%... of the 'Seattle Scene' bands would have been around." He adds, "It was the place... it kind of stirred the pot... One person from one band would move to another band and form... another band... if there was no underage club... there would have been no mixing" (Shumway 2009).

When addressing the topic of the Metropolis and its role as music scene incubator, the venue's occasional house DJ, Bruce Pavitt, founder and former co-owner of Sub Pop Records—the independent record label responsible for many Seattle scene bands achieving initial, international recognition—notes that the venue allowed "a lot of these grunge musicians and so forth... to play in front... of an audience for the first time. It's key to have all-ages venues in any city to allow... those opportunities" (Pavitt 1999). Pavitt states later "...a lot of younger people, who later went on to really help blow up the Seattle scene got their start at the Metropolis." (Pavitt 2009). Future members of multi-platinum selling bands such as Pearl Jam, Soundgarden, and Nirvana were either members of bands that routinely played the Metropolis or were frequent attendees of shows at the venue. Metropolis volunteers who became successful entrepreneurs include Pavitt and Susan Silver, the venue's juice bar operator and booking agent that went on to own her own management firm and handle the careers of multi-platinum selling bands Soundgarden and Alice in Chains. Additionally, photographer Charles Peterson and illustrator Ed Fotheringham spent time as scene members participating in shows at the Metropolis (Pavitt 2009; Piottin 2009; Shumway 2009).

DIY Downtown Redevelopment

The story of Flint, Michigan's economic decline is well documented. Since 1968, the city has lost an estimated 70,000 jobs and 100,000 residents due to economic restructuring and plant closures at the city's flagship employer, General Motors. The resulting changes to the urban economic landscape of the city are so extreme they inspired one researcher to compare Flint to the "subaltern urbanism" of large-scale slums in the global South (Schindler 2014; Young 2013). Against this backdrop, Joel Rash and his friends began to book predominantly punk all-ages shows at numerous spaces in Flint's mostly vacant downtown core in 1985; by 1994 they purchased their first physical location to host shows downtown with a $500 down payment. This location was entitled Flint Local 432 (a play on how local branches of labor unions self-identify and the building's location on 432 South Saginaw Street) and the name has come to include all of the booking activities in the numerous spaces the venue has occupied since that first physical location (J. Rash, personal communication, March 12, 2016). In addition to Flint Local 432 being an entrepreneurial endeavor in its own right, members of the music scene it fostered launched successful entrepreneurial pursuits in Flint's downtown as a result of the venue's influence. These pursuits include a barber shop, tattoo parlor, screen-printing and design studio, restaurants, and the internationally successful bands, Chiodos and The Swellers (J. Rash, personal communication, March 12, 2016; Seman 2013).

Flint Local 432 facilitated many of the skills Thom (2015) notes are crucial for success in entrepreneurship. Jonathan Diener, drummer of The Swellers looks to the venue as a space that helped him develop creatively, form a supportive network, identify opportunities outside of Flint, leverage the local press for marketing, and gain leadership qualities—all of which contributed to the band's decade of success nationally and internationally. Marcus Bieth, co-owner of Flint City T-Shirts and owner of Mark 3 Graphic Design also notes that the venue is the nexus of a supportive social network which helped position him as a business owner, identify business opportunities, and obtain financing for his design studio (M. Bieth, personal communication, March 9, 2016; J. Diener, personal communication, March 10, 2016).

Despite the success of Flint Local 432 as music venue and unofficial business incubator, it went on hiatus between 2006 and 2010. During this time, Rash leveraged his entrepreneurial acumen into a position at a local university to help launch an incubator for entrepreneurship. Rash eventually left the university and, at the urging of the Charles Stewart Mott Foundation, relaunched Flint Local 432 in 2012 as a component of a 501c3 umbrella organization, Red Ink Flint, which he directs.[1] The value of having an estimated 15,000 young adults annually visit the downtown core of the city for shows at Flint Local 432 was not lost on the leadership of the Charles Stewart Mott Foundation whose offices are also downtown. With the help of a $200,000 grant from the Charles Stewart Mott Foundation to the Flint-based Uptown Reinvestment Corporation, a vacant building in downtown Flint was brought up to code and minimally renovated to be the new home of Flint Local 432. By this time, the urban economic landscape of the city's downtown looked much different with many new businesses opening alongside those pioneered years prior by participants in the city's music scene. The programming goals of the venue changed as well to capitalize on its new abilities and resources as part of a 501c3 organization and past history of success incubating arts entrepreneurship (J. Rash, personal communication, March 12, 2016; R. White, personal communication, March 10, 2016).

The new space and organizational framework allowed Flint Local 432 to resume booking shows for local and touring bands in addition to expanding programming to include art, dance, theater, fashion, the culinary arts, music industry education, and makerspace activities as well as offering entrepreneurship programming such as Flint City Pop-up, a program created in conjunction with Michigan State University to develop the entrepreneurial skills of Flint's youth. Perhaps the biggest step taken to more formally foster entrepreneurship by Rash and Red Ink Flint was the opening of a 15,000 square foot community makerspace entitled Factory Two in 2017. This new venture addressed the

---

[1] A non-profit corporation in the USA is granted a number of tax breaks from the federal government and the state government where the corporation resides if it applies for and earns "501c3" status from the Internal Revenue Service. In addition to the benefits the non-profit corporation enjoys, those who donate to it are able to deduct from their taxes the value of their gifts.

popularity of the entrepreneurial makerspace activity which quickly overflowed its dedicated space at the new Flint Local 432 location (Ketchum 2015; J. Rash, personal communication, March 12, 2016; M. Wright, personal communication, March 11, 2016).

Discussion and Conclusion

All of the venues examined in this article exhibit dynamics and outcomes associated with more traditional spaces for artistic production and entrepreneurship. All-ages DIY music venues help develop scene participants as musicians and artists as well as equip them with the skills needed to navigate the industry side of their creative activities as Markusen et al. (2006) and Grodach (2011) suggest is the case with spaces dedicated to the fine arts. This training extends to the entrepreneurs driving the venues and those that are scene participants but are entrepreneurial outside of the arts. Like creative hubs, the venues examined in this chapter offered hybrid spaces for music scene participants to work on developing as artists, participate in the scene by creating record labels, managing bands, or volunteering for various administrative duties at the venues, and consume live music at various shows. In varying ways, the three venues examined in this article impacted their surrounding urban economic landscapes much as Markusen et al. (2006, p. 12) offer artists' centers do through influencing their "regional economies" as well as "neighborhood development." It is also important to note that like many creative hubs throughout the UK, a "defining" characteristic of all three venues is their locations in buildings that could be described as "old" and "disused" during their tenure (British Council 2016).

Examining how all-ages DIY music venues emerge and influence those who frequent them offers an opportunity to further define the emerging field of arts entrepreneurship. Preliminary results point to the entrepreneurial skills developed by music scene participants at Flint Local 432 largely match those noted by Thom (2015) as "crucial" for fine artists to cultivate while active in arts incubators. Although more research is needed, the activities music scene participants engage in while frequenting the all-ages DIY music venues detailed in this chapter suggests the validity of Patten's (2016) observations that social networks, in this case established via the venues, help develop bodies of knowledge benefitting scene participants in terms of refining their skills and building careers. Similarly, all three of the all-ages DIY music venues considered in this chapter resemble artists' centers and creative hubs due to functioning as incubation spaces fostering the social networks and capital Grodach (2010) suggests help develop artists and their communities. Again, more research is needed to more fully explore these initial observations.

All-ages DIY music venues should be formally addressed by policy-makers as multifunctional spaces for not only experiencing music, but for arts incubation and entrepreneurial activity. By identifying the all-ages DIY music venues in their communities and seeking ways to help them as they would other spaces for cultural production, urban planners, economic development professionals, and other city representatives may tap another resource capable of fostering neighborhood revitalization and economic development while at the same time benefitting their local music scene.

References

Azerrad, M. (2001). *Our band could be your life: Scenes from the American indie underground 1981–1991.* Boston: Little, Brown and Company.

Berg, N. (Director). (2005). *Floradora* (Motion Picture). USA: The Thumbscrew Agency, Inc. Retrieved March 30, 2016 from http://www.indievue.com/#!/app/theatre/Floradora/0_vbfhabpv.

Bernard, H. R. (1988). *Research methods in cultural anthropology.* Newbury Park: Sage.

Boles, B. (2009, December 10). Big Bop closes shop. *Now Toronto.* Retrieved July 8, 2013 from http://www.nowtoronto.com/music/story.cfm?content=172848.

Botta, G. (2009). The city that was creative and did not know: Manchester and popular music, 1976–97. *European Journal of Cultural Studies, 12*(3), 349–365.

British Council. (2015). *Creative HubKit.* London: British Council.

Cameron, M. (2009, August 20). *Interview with Malcolm Sangster, Museum of Pop Culture.* Retrieved May 24, 2011 from the Museum of Pop Culture archives.

Coffey, K. (2015a, April 12). Memories of The Cog Factory from its workers, performers and fans. *Omaha World-Herald*. Retrieved March 15, 2016 from http://www.omaha.com/go/memories-of-the-cog-factory-from-its-workers-performers-and/article_86fe8b4b-3ee4-5ad3-8b8b-1111089161b2.html.

Coffey, K. (2015b, April 12). The story of the rock club that shaped Omaha's music scene. *Omaha World-Herald*. Retrieved March 15, 2016 from http://www.omaha.com/go/the-story-of-the-rock-club-that-shaped-omaha-s/article_83c5ee86-0994-5629-89f7-41f21dec6094.html#comments.

Culton, K. R., & Holtzman, B. (2010). The growth and disruption of a "Free Space": Examining a suburban Do It Yourself (DIY) punk scene. *Space and Culture, 13*(3), 270–284.

Currid, E. (2007). *The Warhol economy: How fashion, art, and music drive New York City*. Princeton, NJ: Princeton University Press.

Davidson, A. (2011). *The indie-rock club behind Omaha's $100 million creative boom* [Radio Broadcast]. Washington, DC, USA: National Public Radio. Retrieved June 3, 2011 from http://www.npr.org/blogs/money/2011/06/03/136896920/the-indie-rock-club-behind-omahas-100-million-creative-boom.

Dovey, J., Pratt, A., Lansdowne, J., Moreton, S., Merkel, J., & Virani, T. E. (2016). *Creative hubs: Understanding the new economy*. London: British Council.

Florida, R. (2002). *The rise of the creative class: And how it's transforming work, leisure, community, and everyday life*. New York: Basic Books.

Grodach, C. (2011). Art spaces in community and economic development: Connections to neighborhoods, artists, and the cultural economy. *Journal of Planning Education and Research, 31*(1), 74–85.

Jeffers, T. (2008, July). Omaha rock city. *Spin*, 118–119.

Ketchum, W. E. (2015, October 1). Flint local 432 to celebrate 30th anniversary with gala weekend. *M Live*. Retrieved March 30, 2016 from http://www.mlive.com/entertainment/flint/index.ssf/2015/10/flint_local_432_to_celebrate_3.html.

Kulbel, J., & Walters, R. (Directors). (2005). *Spend an evening with saddle creek* [Motion Picture]. Manhattan: Plexifilm.

Lloyd, R. (2006). *Neo-bohemia: Art and commerce in the postindustrial city*. New York: Routledge.

Markusen, A., Johnson, A., Connelly, C., Martinez, A., Singh, P., & Treuer, G. (2006). *Artists' centers: Evolution and impact on careers, neighborhoods and economies*. Minneapolis, MN: University of Minnesota, Humphrey Institute of Public Affairs Project on Regional and Industrial Economics.

Marzorati, G. (2001, April 22). Nordic tracks: How did Reykjavik become a global pop laboratory? *New York Times*, p. 56, Section 6.

McMahan, T. (1998, October 29). The ultimate DIY guy says goodbye. *The Reader*. Retrieved March 15, 2016 from http://www.timmcmahan.com/rob_rathe.htm.

McMurray, J. (2009). The metropolis: Birthplace of grunge? *Seattle Post-Intelligencer*. Retrieved March 27, 2016 from http://blog.seattlepi.com/emp/2009/11/19/the-metropolis-birthplace-of-grunge/.

Oakes, K. (2009). *Slanted and enchanted: The evolution of indie culture*. New York: Henry Holt and Company.

Patten, T. (2016). "Creative?"... "Entrepreneur?"—Understanding the creative industries entrepreneur. *Artivate: A Journal of Entrepreneurship in the Arts*, 5(2), 23–42.

Pavitt, B. (1999, December 14). *Interview with Jacob McMurray, senior curator at the Museum of Pop Culture*. Retrieved May 24, 2011 from the Museum of Pop Culture archives.

Pavitt, B. (2009, March 3). *Interview with Jacob McMurray, senior curator at the Museum of Pop Culture*. Retrieved May 24, 2011 from the Museum of Pop Culture archives.

Piottin, H. (2009, December 30). *Interview with Jacob McMurray, senior curator at the Museum of Pop Culture*. Retrieved May 24, 2011 from the Museum of Pop Culture archives.

Pray, D. (Director). (1996). *Hype!* [Motion Picture] Santa Monica, CA: Lionsgate.

Seman, M. (2010). How a music scene functioned as a tool for urban redevelopment: A case study of Omaha's Slowdown project. *City, Culture and Society*, 1(4), 207–215.

Seman, M. (2013, January 4). Flint Local 432 and the remarkable power of a great music venue. *CityLab*. Retrieved February 12, 2016 from http://www.citylab.com/design/2013/01/flint-local-432-and-remarkable-power-great-music-venue/4310/.

Seman, M. (2015). What if Hewlett and Packard had started a band instead? An examination of a music scene as economic cluster. *Artivate: A Journal of Entrepreneurship in the Arts*, 4(2), 33–49.

Shumway, A. (2009, November 14). *Interview with Jacob McMurray, senior curator at the Museum of Pop Culture*. Retrieved May 24, 2011 from the Museum of Pop Culture archives.

Sillman, M. (2011). *20 Years later, Seattle music scene still channels spirit of Nirvana* [Radio Broadcast]. Washington, DC: National Public Radio.

Retrieved May 16, 2011 from http://www.npr.org/blogs/therecord/2011/04/21/135445333/20-years-later-seattle-music-scene-still-channels-spirit-of-nirvana.

Spencer, A. (2008). *DIY: The rise of lo-fi culture*. New York: Marion Boyars.

Stewart, S. (2010). *In every town: An all-ages music manualfesto*. San Francisco: Tides Center/All-ages Movement Project.

Thom, M. (2015). The entrepreneurial value of arts incubators: Why fine artists should make use of professional arts incubators. *Artivate: A Journal of Entrepreneurship in the Arts, 4*(2), 33–56.

Thompson, S. (2001). Market failure: Punk economics, early and late. *College Literature, 28*(2), 48–64.

Walters, R. (Director). (2005). *Sing! Write! Dance!* [Motion Picture] USA: White Light Media. Retrieved May 20, 2011 from http://www.whitelight-media.com/.

Yin, R. K. (2003). *Case study research: Design and methods* (3rd ed.). Thousand Oaks, CA: Sage.

13

Thinking Through the Creative Hub in Peripheral Places: A Long-View of the Dartington Hall Experiment in Rural Reconstruction Through Creativity

Nicola J. Thomas

Introduction

This chapter considers the creative infrastructure and social relationships that can be witnessed in peripheral locations, through the lens of a creative hub. The chapter historicises the apparent recent rise of hubs by locating the argument around the creative infrastructure of Dartington Hall, located on a rural estate in Devon, UK, founded in 1926, and still in existence. Dartington Hall enables an exploration of the ways in which a creative rural hub can become a focal point for the broader rural creative community, which in turn reaches out through sets of national and international connections. As a nexus it is also a place which generates a network spinning out into the surrounding regional countryside, creating new spatial social formations that serve the regional creative infrastructure.

N. J. Thomas (✉)
Department of Geography, University of Exeter, Exeter, UK
e-mail: Nicola.j.thomas@exeter.ac.uk

© The Author(s) 2019   **245**
R. Gill et al. (eds.), *Creative Hubs in Question*, Dynamics of Virtual Work,
https://doi.org/10.1007/978-3-030-10653-9_13

The history of Dartington Hall and the rise and fall of activities within the estate raises the question of how the 'spin-out' promise of hubs can be sustained. Dartington offers a way of understanding the importance of key infrastructure in peripheral areas as a generative device; however, this chapter offers a cautionary tale in this respect. Throughout its history as a creative arts hub Dartington Hall has been something of an experiment which has often struggled to achieve financial sustainability, creating risk for the surrounding community facing the loss of key infrastructure. The chapter will highlight the long-lasting effect on the broader regional community when rural centres like Dartington are successful, and what happens when change occurs that runs counter to the expectations of the stakeholder audience.

Dartington Hall Trust which manages the estate will celebrate its centenary in 2026; however, it is currently in the process of working through what the contemporary incarnation of the estate should be. Indeed, the finances of the Trust are such that developing a sustainable model is critical for its survival to 2026. In the light of financial pressures, the Trustees of Dartington Hall have had to dramatically reposition the work of the Trust over the last 20 years, with significant criticism from the creative community it evolved to support and work with. After the period of highly negative feeling, the current management team of Dartington Hall have returned to the roots of the ethos of the estate that it was founded on and have started a process of long-term change. To appreciate the current day activity, a long view of Dartington Hall is presented in this chapter, aiming to introduce readers to some of the key threads, recognising that the enormity of the history of creativity at Dartington Hall is a much larger story (see, e.g., Bonham-Carter and Curry 1970; Young 1982).

Situating Rural Creative Hubs

Creative hubs are commonly associated with city locations (Virani and Malem 2015), and one of the key aims of this chapter is to locate this key creative form within a rural context. This contributes to the growing body of work that locates rural creativity and seeks to explore the more marginal spaces of creativity beyond the creative cities agenda (Gibson et al. 2010). In the same way as creativity has been seen as a key constituent of urban growth in recent decades, rural development policy has seen the creativity consistently represented, hoping that it will transform derelict buildings and rural market towns, offering opportunities for creative production and consumption (see Luckman et al. 2009; Bell and Jayne 2010; Harvey et al. 2012). Of course, there is a long history to the presence of creativity within the countryside; however, the current desire for creativity to underpin economic growth has placed rural creativity in a new policy agenda (Harvey et al. 2011).

For people living and trying to make a living through creativity in rural spaces, the availability of creative infrastructure and its sustainability is a key question (see Luckman 2012). Where will one access creative business advice? Sell one's work? Gain access to inspiring content? Find like-minded people? Locate a mentor? Find people to share materials or expertise? Although creative practitioners may have purposefully chosen a rural location, access to professional services and kindred spirits is often still a necessity (Thomas and Jakob 2018). In these contexts, the different spatial forms of creative infrastructure are key whether a network, hub or cluster. Accessing such places requires the right combination of transport, affordability, format of space and location (Thomas et al. 2013). In marginal places, getting this combination right for the population it is intended to serve is a challenge. In addition, the finances of maintaining capital investment mean that rural hubs are difficult maintain, requiring a careful balance of a portfolio that raises income, while providing services to stakeholders. Often underpinned by public or philanthropic investment, these hubs often need to balance their commercial trading arm with their charitable or social purposes. There is not always the same dynamism within rural areas as found in city areas, in terms of the density of provision for creative infrastructure or the ready access to these creative spaces. The loss of these spaces presents a rupture to those it has served, perhaps not to be filled again. As such, the importance of rural creative infrastructure can be magnified in rural settings, and the desire to hold onto hard-won investment or sustain organisations that serve their stakeholders can be keenly felt.

This chapter places these debates in the context of a longer history of rural creativity that emanated from the work of Dartington Hall through the twentieth century to present. This is a creative hub that has faced a local, regional, national and international community, a respected space of avant-guard creative production, and a site where many of the most famous creative practitioners of the twentieth century have visited. The research on which this chapter is drawn stems from an interest in the development of rural creative networks and their place in the contemporary creative economy and an analysis of regional craft ecologies. The chapter draws on original archive research within the Dartington Hall archives around the creative policy context linked to Dartington Hall, interviews with contemporary practitioners working within Dartington and interviews with key stakeholders currently directing Dartington's next strategic plan. Part of the broader research of which this is part examines the regional craft ecology of South West Britain, and as such the work of Dartington Hall has been followed through ethnographic participant observation.

Establishing a Centre for a 'Many Sided Life'

Dartington Hall is situated within a large agricultural estate on the outskirts of the market town of Totnes, on the banks of the River Dart, in the Devonshire rural countryside of South West Britain. The estate dates to the medieval period complete with Great Hall and dwellings located around substantial courtyard. This forms the heart of Dartington Hall today, surrounded by landscapes gardens leading to the estate farm, deer park and woodland. The story of Dartington as creative hub starts in 1926, when Leonard and Dorothy Elmhirst, purchased the dilapidated estate. The devastation of the First World War on rural landed estates was well entrenched by this stage, with the loss of male labourers in the conflicts, and then the effects of the depression on the production capacity on outmoded forms of agricultural production. Dorothy and Leonard Elmhirst, bought the property, funded through Dorothy's wealth, and established their 'experiment in rural reconstruction' (Rural Industries Bureau,

Summer 1935, p. 22), establishing the Dartington Hall Trust to oversee the management of the enterprise in 1932.

Dorothy gave a Founders Day speech in 1967 and reflected on the underlying philosophy that guided their activities:

> there was an absolutely clear concept in Leonard's mind from the very start. He wanted to create here, in the countryside, a centre, where a many sided life, could find expression. Where living and learning could flourish together. Where there could be a balance, between all the practical things that were being done on the land, and the activities of the mind and the spirit which should be carried out together. (Elmhirst 1967)

Another fundamental element of this ethos was the desire 'that we must live with beauty' and that Dartington Hall should be 'a centre were human values would be respected' (ibid.). Although Dorothy talks of this being Leonard's idea, this was certainly a shared project, which saw the combining of practical work on the land, creative expression in all activities, education and learning throughout one's life, and a deep responsibility for others.

The establishment of this centre on the Dartington Hall estate, which could support this 'many sided life', started with pace in the mid-1920s. Leonard drew on his contacts from Cornell University and started farming the estate drawing on modern farming theory, aiming to move the estate from their cycle of decline to productivity. At the same time, Dorothy drew together her contacts from teacher training colleges in New York and established what would become the signature of Dartington, progressive creative education (Elmhirst 1967). Invitations to artists from America to join them in these early days resulted in the establishment of artists' studios, and the daily round of arts recreation in the evenings after the practical work of the day was completed. This placed music, performance and visual arts at the heart of the Dartington experiment. The creative life of Dartington was taken out into rural villages around the estate through performances and classes, and the local community brought into the estate, through work, opportunities for learning, amateur activity in theatre, orchestras and a choir, and as members of the audience in performances. Dorothy reminded her audience of these early years:

> We had a school right over there in the east wing for our children. We had in the evening recreation in the form of the arts right from the first year. … We all sang twice a week, we had play readings in our dining room. We had this delightful double life, the practical work every day and the arts. That is the pattern of Dartington that has continued all these years. (Elmhirst 1967)

The scale of ambition of Leonard and Dorothy's vision has to be recognised. Within a decade of setting up the estate the 'practical' work of the estate was far reaching: the rebuilding of the medieval courtyard dwellings, including a great hall which could be used as a concert venue; the commissioning of modern architect designed houses; the development of a working sawmill, textile mill, wood workshops, a pottery; an expanding school, arts classes and workshops being given by practitioners who flowed through the estate (see Bonham-Carter and Curry 1970). The rather extraordinary history of Dartington is one which sees the estate becoming a home to a density of creative practitioners, working within the estate, and a continuous arrival and departure of practitioners coming to stay at the Hall for varying lengths of time, contributing in rich ways to the creative spirit of the centre. Indeed, the humanity of the Elmhirst's experiment resulted in Dartington becoming a place of retreat for refugee artists from Europe in the 1930s and a home for those displaced through the Second World War: 'We had Michael Chekhov founding the Chekhov theatre studio, we had Hans Oppenheim who was going to found the School of Opera here, and he did put on one opera towards the end of the 30's' (Elmhirst 1967).

The financial resources of the Elmhirst's meant that they sought out well-qualified people to set up the experiments and resourced them well, particularly in the first decade of the experiment. One such person was Angus Litster, a weaver from Scotland, who worked for a number of years at the Dartington Textile Mill sharing his knowledge and expertise (Bovey Handloom Weavers, n.d.). More widely known is the celebrated potter Bernard Leach, who was encouraged to set up a studio at Dartington at Leonard and Dorothy's behest. Attracting these eminent practitioners to Dartington established its quality, but also created an atmosphere that attracted others to visit, and settle in the area. It is also here were the regional spillovers are to be found. Angus Lister later set up his own workshop in a nearby town of Bovey Tracy which exists to this day. When Bernard Leach departed, Marianne de Trey arrived who would work the pottery until her death over 60 years later (Whiting 2016). This pottery enabled other potteries to thrive in the area, such as the Lotus Pottery which gained from the availability of potters attracted by the employment opportunities at Dartington (personal correspondence with Elizabeth Skipwith, co-founder of Lotus Pottery with her husband Michael in 1957).

The focus of this experiment in rural reconstruction led to Dartington Hall becoming associated with rural policy innovation, around architecture and housing design, farming and cultural policy. By the mid-1930s Dartington Hall had offered a member of staff to support the work of the Rural Industries Bureau's activities in support of rural craft workers (see Dartington Hall archives, Rex Gardner Reports, C/RIB/1/C, Devon Heritage Centre). Later in the wartime period, Darlington would play an active role in the development of art policy which predated the establishment of the Arts Council (Upchurch 2013). Some of the creative policy work undertaken by Dartington focused on the wider creative infrastructure of the region specifically in relation to supporting rural craft practitioners. Activities undertaken in the 1930s including mapping and understanding the experiences of rural craft practitioners, and strategising the best way to support the development of their livelihoods (Gardner 1934). The seeds of this activity led to the development of the Devon Guild of Craftsmen in the post-war period. This is a rural networking membership organisation for designer makers which continues to thrive to this day (Thomas 2018). Many of the founder members of the Guild were living and working in Dartington (including Marianne De Trey, and Bernard Forrester, see below), and Dartington continued to be critical to the success of the network in the future decades as one member recalled:

we used to have an AGM and seminar at Dartington, it was a weekend and you could book a room and stay and they had really top class speakers, so that was always sort of April, that was lovely, I loved that, you

could stay there and have a nice meal and talk to all these people, interesting talks. (Janet Wingate, Interviewed, 11 December 2013)

The spirit of Dartington Hall was founded on the development of a
centre which would support the production and consumption of creative life worlds, in an atmosphere where people were cared for and
inspired. This should not be taken with rosy coloured spectacles, as of
course, this was a form of benevolent paternalism with the will of two
people channelling the passion and commitment of many people, supported with considerable financial resources, which became stretched
very thin over time, resulting in financial insecurity for some (see
Thomas 2018).

Nurturing the Creative Life of Devon

A feature of contemporary creative hubs are relationships with educational providers, often higher education, to provide access to a creative
talent pipeline, and also the infrastructure and opportunities of innovation and incubation that emerge from industry/higher education
interactions (see, e.g., Dovey et al. 2016). The antecedents of this can
be witnessed at Dartington, education was woven through the operation of the estate, but formalised through the establishment of primary,
secondary and higher education schools on the estate, as well as a Sumer
School of Music, an adult education centre and through courses and
training in studios and workshops.

The ethos of the schools of the Dartington estate followed the principles set out by Dorothy and Leonard Elmhirst: a progressive, art-led
education which was co-education, with a non-violent, humanistic
ethos that placed each child at the centre of their learning (see Kidel
1990). The Dartington Hall schools became noted for the creative education they offered and the nurturing of free, independent children. The
schools were built within the estate, with leading architects employed
to create a unique school environment at the time, well equipped with
workshops and studio spaces to support the broad creative curriculum
(Cox 1950).

Devon-based potter and member of the Devon Guild of Craftsmen, Phil Deburlet recalls her childhood education at Dartington and the environment that enabled the students to explore creative practices:

> I was sent to boarding school when I was 9 because my parents had been to the sort of boarding schools where they were beaten and starved, they chose what they thought was a humane boarding school, which was Dartington. Dartington had workshops, it had woodwork shop, art rooms and a pottery... and we could use them in the evenings and we were encouraged to just make things ... I just quickly found it was a strangely comforting place to be in the pottery workshop, so I began really quite young.... the pottery teacher was Bernie Forrester who was just delightful. I think I probably went into the pottery there because he was quiet and calm, and one day I watched him throw a jug, he just sat at the wheel with a lump of clay and he made, in about two minutes, he made this jug, and it was like watching a conjuring trick really. I must have been maybe 13 then and I just remember thinking 'I want to do that'. Which is an odd thing to want to do, you know, it was quite messy... the seed must have been sown then and I did do quite a lot at school. It wasn't until I was about 24, 23, that I took it up again. (Phil Deburlet, Interviewed, 4 December 2013)

This moment was transformative for Phil, her own professional work now includes her own practice as a professional potter, and the development of creative educational programming and outreach for the Devon Guild of Craftsmen. Bernard Forrester left his creative mark on generations of students at Dartington, and his own route into teaching was a product of the Dartington Hall experiment. He had come to Dartington with Bernard Leach when they set up the pottery, but over time he preferred spending time teaching as the schools developed on the estate (Dartington Hall, n.d.a)

The Dartington Hall education programmes and the interactions were part of the creative infrastructure that contributed to the reputation and creative vibrancy of Dartington Hall. The annual Summer School of Music brought the world's creative talent to the region, year after year from 1947 (Dartington Hall, n.d.b). As a field configuring event, this placed Dartington on an international stage as a site of creative innovation in music, and the place where aspiring and professional musician and established composers and conductors would spend time and work together. This pulse of energy was underpinned by the regular educational activity on the estate. The commitment to further and higher education was cemented through the development of the 1934 Dartington Hall Arts Department which launched the Dartington College of Arts in 1962. The College was noted for its 'radical and inventive approaches to arts pedagogy, embracing practice-based research praxis, and early innovation around interdisciplinary and prioritising context as a core factor and 'material' in art-making processes' (Dartington Hall, n.d.c). In its heyday, these educational institutions generated activities that fed the regional, national and international creative worlds.

Walking in the Valley

Speaking on Foundation Day, 1967, Dorothy Elmhirst addressed the friends and companions who had shared in the development of Dartington since the early days. She reminded them: 'You have walked with us in the valley, and you have stood with us on the hill. You have seen both the shadowy darker times that you have shared with us, and the moments of inspiration and joy on the hills' (Elmhirst 1967). Although Dorothy reflected at that stage that the journey of Dartington had not been easy, the challenges that the Hall would face in the closing decades of the twentieth century and start of the twenty-first century would have been identified by Dorothy as a period of time when they walked in the valley.

Leonard and Dorothy's vision of connecting arts and education started to unfold in the mid-1980s as the tragic death of a pupil and poor publicity around hedonistic and unruly student behaviour contributed to the closure of Dartington Hall School. The Dartington College of Art continued to exist, maintaining the presence of education on the estate; however, the college faced significant financial difficulties. During these this time, however, the practice and research led environment continued to serve the regional creative networks. The regional cultural agency 'Culture South West' regularly reported the research activities happening at the College in its newsletter 'Finding the Dots'. Projects included 'Fieldwork: community-based arts practice in rural areas' funded by the AHRC and commissioned research exploring 'Higher Education Continued Professional Development provision for arts and design practitioners' funded by Higher Education Funding Council for England, Arts Council England and Design Council Joint Working Group (Culture South West 2004a). Such projects emerged from the Centre for Creative Enterprise and Participation at Dartington College of Arts reflecting the ongoing interests within Dartington around the development of Arts policy (Culture South West 2004b).

The eventual demise of the College of Art within the Dartington estate can be tracked in the pages of 'Finding the Dots', this time through the publication announcement in 2007 of a piece of consultancy research undertaken by the Burns Owen Partnership Ltd, titled 'Initial Assessment of the Economic Impact of the Proposed Relocation of Dartington College of Arts' (Culture South West 2007). In summary, the report looked at the economic impact of the colleges relocation to three different sites, to the nearby town of Torbay, University College Falmouth or University of Plymouth. The assessment also addressed the wider review of Dartington's sphere of operations including 'the potential for other economically significant replacement activity on the site [Dartington College of Art]'. This report, including the scoping of future partners and models to find a sustainable future for the College, was released following the press annoucement on 13 July 2007 that 'Dartington College of Arts and University College Falmouth agree to merger' with the students and staff of Dartington being relocated from 2010 to a new proposed built site, with the aim of creating, in the words of the Principal of Dartington College of Arts: 'a unique University for the Arts in the South West and safeguarding Dartington's sustainable future in the region, while respecting its ethos and values' (University College Falmouth 2007).

Although the departure of Dartington College of Arts from Dartington reflected broader shifts in higher education provision in the UK, the depth of feeling within the arts community of the closure of Dartington within the estate is still keenly felt. In discussion with the current Executive Director (Arts) the upsetting legacy of this period of change for current stakeholders was acknowledged (interviewed, 1 February 2018). From this time, community stakeholders felt that the Dartington Hall Trust had abandoned its principles sold out to commercial interests. These feelings intensified as people noted the increasing importance of the estate income arising from the hire through weddings, conferences and other forms of venue hire. For local people, and those associated with the College, witnessing this change was deeply felt. The current management team recognise this: 'to feel like that has gone, is incredibly painful to people, and the fact they weren't consulted and that they felt it was just a done deal, that things happened behind closed doors, and then they became, quite rightly so, suspicious of motive' (ibid.).

Climbing the Hill: Managing Change

Dorothy Elmhirst was keenly aware of the challenge of change. When she looked back at the development of Dartington and reflected on the way in which organisations change over time and the challenge that faced Dartington in the future, Dorothy reflected on the difficulties of maintaining the ethos of a place, within a growth agenda:

> The thing that always strikes me as a kind of miracle as I look back, is the way in which Dartington has met the challenge of the moment, how Dartington has adjusted to change, a very difficult to thing to do. It has done that, it has met the challenges of change, and yet at the same time, has retained its central identity. That seems to me very remarkable.... Well now this present period... I think a very promising time, it is a time of challenge too, and I think we can beat it, but we must be careful and thoughtful, and see that nothing of the essential Dartington is sacrificed. You see the challenge today, is the challenge of expansion, go on growing bigger, and bigger, and bigger, as you grow bigger you grow more complex, and there is always the danger of losing the contact with the individual which is one of the human values that I mentioned at the start. And it is absolutely essential for the inner life, the real life. (Elmhirst 1967)

The current management team (at time of writing) recognise that the Trusts decisions in the years running up to the relocation of the Arts College and the commercialisation of the estate ran counter to the ethos of Dartington that Dorothy evoked. Indeed, the Executive Director (Arts), acknowledged that the decisions made were painful for the community. It is recognised that management strategies were linked to the 'corporatisation of Dartington as a money maker' and the speed of the change was 'quick and brutal', excluding people from the estate who had been used to integrating access to the property within their daily practices'. The sudden change of direction towards a corporate identity and a change in spirit where local people felt 'outpaced and not valued... made them feel furious', and their effect had a lasting legacy with staff acknowledging 'there are still people now locally who won't come here'. For the creative and local community, the loss was also felt around the absence of the 'kind of artistic identity and creative risk-taking, playful identity of the college, and also having young people here, people who are at the start of experiment and adventure' (Executive Director (Arts) interviewed, 1 February 2018).

Dorothy Elmhirst's reflections on how to nurture change within a growth agenda appear prophetic in the light of the fast way in which the local community became alienated from this creative space. She also recognised the challenge of developing and managing a complex portfolio organisation while keeping human values at the centre. The idea of an 'essential Dartington' which is in 'contact with the individual' is one which the current senior executive staff management team have returned to. Led by CEO Rhodri Samuel (appointed in 2015) the team have returned to the ethos of the founders of Dartington and are starting a long process of reshaping the management of the Trust. This has involved listening and understanding the ethos of Dartington, as the Executive Director (Arts) explains: 'and being inspired by its history and its heritage but the biggest thing that we've been doing ever since we came here... is really trying to listen to people about their feelings about Dartington and about their stories about Dartington, and very sensitively hold those and shape Dartington to move forward' (Executive Director (Arts) interviewed, 1 February 2018).

Listening involved the management team utilising an Open Space participatory approach to create participant-led discussion events to address the questions 'What can Dartington Be?' and 'How can Dartington Be?'. Four Open Space events were organised by an independent arts organisation, Kaleider, with Seth Honnor, a skilled Open Space facilitator holding the space (see Dartington Hall, n.d.d). It might not usually be important to note who facilitated these events, but in this instance, this was a critical decision which signalled the understanding of the new management about the importance of the community to Dartington. Seth Honnor's father, printmaker Michael Honnor has worked and led the print making studio at Darlington for over 40 years. Michael's own father lived locally to Dartington and was another founder member of the Devon Guild of Craftsmen. The sensitivities the Dartington management team wanted to open up were known to Seth, and part of the skill of facilitating this space, was allowing the potential for pain, anger, frustration, alongside optimism, excitement to be accepted and valued in the open space meetings.

At each Open Space event, Seth, supported by the team at Kaleider, enabled the participants to set the agenda at the start of the day by crowdsourcing discussion topics. Each was programmed and then allowed to happen. Each conversation recorded by the person who suggested the topic and shared through an online news board which was made public (ethnography, 26 November 2016). The topics brought forward by participants included 'How to revive the crafts on the estate', 'Dartington is our's! Lets reclaim it', and 'How can Dartington fund all of these ideas?' (Dartington Hall, n.d.d). Given the recent history of alienation and rapid change experienced by members of the community, the decision to create an Open Space was a brave one on behalf of the management team. It signalled a clear step change and a promise of active listening. The experience of these events has stayed with members of the management team: 'it humbled me actually… raw feedback comes at you…. People were crying and shouting, and wanted answers as to what they saw as the last decade being a fairly negative part of the grand history of Dartington, and for us not to have answers. But just listen, and let people be heard, and I think it stripped away any sense of ego one potentially had' (Executive Director (Arts) interviewed,

1 February 2018). This was not an easy process for those staff members, but one overriding feeling that emerged through this process was a feeling of being 'Bolstered by people's love and support for the place and the desire to see it work' (ibid.).

Conclusion

The challenge remains for the management team and Trustees of Dartington Hall to 'make the place sustainable for the future' (ibid.). It is noticeable that the current management team has invested time and energy thinking about the way in which the original intention of the founders is pertinent to the twenty-first century. Talking with the Executive Director (Arts), their awareness of the guiding principles of the Elmhirst in clear: 'When Dorothy Elmhirst talks at the end of her life about the purpose [of Dartington].. She talks about a space where you could live in beauty everyday… were the arts whether central to all human completeness and this kid of right that everybody has for this many sided concept, which is what we've picked upon as a contemporary group of people' (ibid.).

This ethos has led to discussions around the rebalancing of the Dartington Hall Trust which manages the trading company and charity: 'I think that really the fundamental change has been for the trustees to be reminded about what the charitable purpose of the trust is… to plough that money into good works and that means spending it. There's a really clear business case to value your charitable activity, and help tell your story' (ibid.). The dark days of the last decade of the Trust are identified by the dominance of the commercial side of Dartington (shops, accommodation, food and drink, wedding and conference venue hire). Rather than see the trading arm as the 'hungry, greedy capitalist side' of the organisation, the team want to tell a more compelling story, that focuses on the connection between the trading arm and the work that the income then does: 'buying a pot here funds the creation of new work, funds our sustainability and ecology, funds our projects around social justice and inclusion and our learning objectives, we really want to aim to be this mixed, self-sustaining economy'. It is hoped that the refocusing, and investment in the activities of the charity, will make 'the trading side a little but more palatable to local people' (ibid.).

This chapter has focused in large part on the social relations and ethos of practice that flow through the physical infrastructure of the estate. The people who gravitated towards Dartington have cemented this place as a creative centre, first invited by the Elmhirst's, and then those who came to study, work, or attend who were inspired by the creative programming and spirit that evolved as the decades progressed. Although creative production has always happened on the estate, the dark days saw this decline and Dartington moved more towards being venue for consumption. The next phase of the new management teams plan is to rebalance the production side and to 'think about how we support some of those artists to create work here, and how we combine a hub for creative to happen. Not just the final product, but the process' (ibid.).

The refocusing on the local community in recent years is a significant recognition by the management team that 'your local community are your biggest ally, there's nothing more powerful in a venue is under threat, than having the people who are around you gather round you and say "We won't let it happen"' (ibid.). These people are also part of the broader Dartington community who have been inspired by and learnt on the estate through generations. This legacy creates an audience which the management team know is ready for the programming that is inspired by the ethos of Dartington, fuelled by a spirit that aims to 'respond to big issues of the day and help us feel less helpless, internationally driven, and [brings] a sense of unusual, extraordinary experiences that you won't otherwise experience in Devon' (ibid.). The legacy of almost 100 years of Dartington programming is that 'the audiences for contemporary work are strong here, and that is a legacy of the college, and I think people in Totes and the surrounding areas are incredibly culturally aware' (ibid.). For those who are programming, this type of audience means that they 'can take some risk' and continue the experimental creative energy that has defined Dartington (ibid.).

Dartington Hall is an unusual example of what a creative hub looks like in a rural community, but also a familiar one for those looking to creative hubs as a force for regeneration. Approaching 100 years of activity, Dartington Hall started its life as a dilapidated estate at a time of global financial crisis. Capital investment combined with an ethos that sought to generate a 'many sided life' created a mixed portfolio of activity of the estate that brought internationally renowned creative recognition to this peripheral outpost. This 'experiment in rural reconstruction' had a strong ethos behind it looking for balance and beauty, inspired by learning, valuing practical work and fuelled by the care for one's fellow human, wherever they might be in the world. The history and experience of Dartington remind us of the promise of creative hubs, the way that bringing people together around a common purpose generates energy and change. It is also however full of reminders of the challenges of growth and sustaining a vision over the years. Without the substantial underlying capital that Dorothy Elmhirst brought and the subsequent management of the investments by the Dartington Hall Trustees, Dartington would certainly not be present to see in its centenary. However, the future of this centre still hangs in the balance with the new management team working out how to 'become this kind of cauldron of activity which may have far-reaching national and global influence' and a place where 'alchemy happens' (Executive Director (Arts) interviewed, 1 February 2018).

Acknowledgements I would like to acknowledge and thank the Arts and Humanities Research Council for funding the projects that have underpinned this research (AH/E/008887/1 and AH/I001778/1) and Doreen Jakob who was the Research Fellow associated with the original research linked to the Devon Guild of Craftsmen and Gloucestershire Guild of Craftsmen. I would also like to thank the staff and membership of the Devon Guild of Craftsmen, Gloucestershire Guild of Craftsmen, Kaleider, and Dartington Hall Trust for their support of the research.

References

Bell, D., & Jayne, M. (2010). The creative countryside? Policy and practice in the UK rural cultural economy. *Journal of Rural Studies, 26*(3), 209–218.
Bonham-Carter, V., & Curry, W. B. (1970). *Dartington Hall: The formative years, 1925–57*. Dulverton: Exmoor Press.

Bovey Handloom Weavers. (n.d.). *Our history*. Available at http://www.bovey-weavers.co.uk/history.html. Accessed 2 August 2018.

Cox, P. (1950, July 28). The arts at Dartington Hall: A rural experiment. *The Times*, Educational Supplement, Friday, p. 594.

Culture South West. (2004a, April). *Finding the dots 1—South West cultural sector research news*. Authors Own Copy.

Culture South West. (2004b, October). *Finding the dots 1—South West cultural sector research news*. Authors Own Copy.

Culture South West. (2007, May). *Finding the dots 11—South West cultural sector research news*. Authors Own Copy.

Dartington Hall. (n.d.a). *Bernard Forrester*. Available at https://www.dartington.org/about/our-history/people/bernard-forrester/. Accessed 2 August 2018.

Dartington Hall. (n.d.b). *History of the summer school*. Available at https://www.dartington.org/about/our-history/summer-school/. Accessed 2 August 2018.

Dartington Hall. (n.d.c). *Dartington College of Arts*. Available at https://www.dartington.org/about/our-history/dartington-college-of-arts/. Accessed 2 August 2018.

Dartington Hall. (n.d.d). *Open space events—What can Dartington be?* Available at https://www.dartington.org/whats-on/archive/open-space-events/. Accessed 2 August 2018.

Dovey, J., Moreton, S., & Hargreves, I. (2016). *REACT report 2012–2016*. Bristol: REACT, UWE Bristol, Pervasive Media Studio, Watershed.

Elmhirst, D. (1967). *Speech given on Foundation Day, 10 June 1967 at Dartington Hall*. Audio recording available at https://audioboom.com/posts/486188-dorothy-elmhirst-foundation-day-10-june-1967. Accessed 2 August 2018.

Gardner, R. (1934). Memo to Dr Slater 2/7/1934, *Survey of Devon craftsmen*. Available from Dartington Hall Archives, Rex Gardner Reports, C/RIB/1/C, Devon Heritage Centre.

Gibson, C., Luckman, S., & Willoughby-Smith, J. (2010). Creativity without borders? Rethinking remoteness and proximity. *Australian Geographer, 41*(1), 25–38.

Harvey, D. C., Hawkins, H., & Thomas, N. J. (2011). Regional imaginaries of governance agencies: Practising the region of South West Britain. *Environment and Planning A, 43*(2), 470–486.

Harvey, D. C., Hawkins, H., & Thomas, N. J. (2012). Thinking creative clusters beyond the city: People, places and networks. *Geoforum, 43*(3), 529–539.

Kidel, M. (1990). *Beyond the classroom: Dartington's experiments in education*. Bideford: Tree Books.

Luckman, S. (2012). *Locating cultural work: The politics and poetics of rural, regional and remote creativity*. Basingstoke: Palgrave Macmillan.

Luckman, S. H., Gibson, C., & Lea, T. (2009). Mosquitoes in the mix: How transferable is creative city thinking? *Singapore Journal of Tropical Geography, 30*(1), 70–85.

Rural Industries Bureau. (1935, Summer). *Advert for Dartington Hall published in the rural industries: The quarterly magazine for country trade and handicrafts*. Available from the Museum of English Rural Life, Museum of English Rural Life. Library Periodical Open Access—PER.

Thomas, N. (2018). Modernity, crafts and guilded practices: Locating the historical geographies of 20th century craft organisations. In L. Price & H. Hawkins (Eds.), *Geographies of making, craft and creativity* (pp. 60–77). Abingdon: Routledge.

Thomas, N., & Jakob, D. (2018). Making livelihoods within communities of practice: The place of guild organisations in the craft sector. In E. Bell, G. Mangia, S. Taylor, & M. L. Toraldo (Eds.), *The organisation of craft work: Identities, meanings and materiality*. New York: Routledge.

Thomas, N. J., Harvey, D. C., & Hawkins, H. (2013). Crafting the region: Creative industries and practices of regional space. *Regional Studies, 47*(1), 75–88.

University College Falmouth. (2007). *Dartington College of Arts and University College Falmouth agree to merger*. Available at https://www.falmouth.ac.uk/content/dartington-college-arts-and-university-college-falmouth-agree-merger. Accessed 2 August 2018.

Upchurch, A. R. (2013). 'Missing' from policy history: The Dartington Hall arts enquiry, 1941–1947. *International Journal of Cultural Policy, 19*(5), 610–622. Available at https://doi.org/10.1080/10286632.2012.724065. Accessed 10 September 2017.

Virani, T. E., & Malem, W. (2015). *Re-articulating the creative hub concept as a model for business support in the local creative economy: The case of Mare Street in Hackney* (Creativeworks London Working Paper Series).

Whiting, D. (2016). Marianne de trey obituary. *The Guardian*. Available at https://www.theguardian.com/artanddesign/2016/oct/19/marianne-de-trey-obituary. Accessed 2 August 2018.

Young, M. (1982). *Elmhirsts of Dartington: The creation of a Utopian community*. London: Routledge & Kegan Paul Books.

14

From Making to Displaying: The Role of Organizational Space in Showing Creative Coolness at the Volkshotel

Boukje Cnossen

Introduction

Although the Volkshotel in Amsterdam was never a squat, the roots of this infamous and inspiring place are in fact located in the squatting heyday of the 1980s. Originally built as the office for a major Dutch daily newspaper, the place gained its prominence as a so-called breeding place (*broedplaats*), an idiosyncrasy of Amsterdam's creative city policy which I shall explore below. Set up by a collective of former squatters called Urban Resort, it became a nexus of much artistic and underground production. Urban Resort saw the opportunity that empty property and a financial crisis offered and asked the owner if they could turn the empty building into a temporary creative hub, offering work space to artists, musicians, and other creative workers against a low rent. From 2007 until 2013, it was run in this way. After that, it became a hotel, while retaining much of its creative flavour by means of keeping

B. Cnossen (✉)
Institute for Sociology and Cultural Organisation,
Leuphana Universität Lüneburg, Lüneburg, Germany
e-mail: boukje.cnossen@leuphana.de

© The Author(s) 2019
R. Gill et al. (eds.), *Creative Hubs in Question*, Dynamics of Virtual Work,
https://doi.org/10.1007/978-3-030-10653-9_14

a third of the building reserved for artist studios, and curating a cultural programme in the hotel's open areas.

Between June 2012 and spring 2013, I conducted fieldwork on an almost daily basis in the building as it was then (Cnossen and Olma 2014; Sihvonen and Cnossen 2015). I was embedded in two organizations that resided in the building: the non-profit creative hub developer Urban Resort, which acted as a landlord and held office on the ground floor, and the creative agency Flight 1337, allowing me to be an 'observant participant' (Moeran 2009) rather than a classic ethnographer, and adopt the position of an 'at-home ethnographer' (Alvesson 2009; Cnossen 2018). Later, in the autumn of 2015 and again in the summer and autumn of 2017, I returned to the Volkshotel for interviews with the community manager, the users of the new co-working space that had been created in the hotel lobby, and had informal follow-up chats with the remaining tenants. I have also had an ongoing involvement with Urban Resort,[1] because of the fieldwork I conducted in one of the other creative hubs they run in Amsterdam. Finally, I conducted advisory work for them after termination of that fieldwork, which allowed me to remain informed about the Volkshotel. As such, this chapter is both a reflection on the ethnographic material which was mainly collected in 2012 and 2013, as it is a presentation of the development of the creative hub since.

The aim of this chapter is to demonstrate how the building's transformation from a subsidised creative hub to a 'creative' hotel, went hand in hand with a reconfiguration of the relationship between space and creativity, i.e. a different *spacing* of creativity. I will discuss this question from the perspective of the literature on organizational space. Hence, I will leave aside the many contributions to spatial theory made in sociology, geography, and other disciplines for the sake of conciseness, but also because a perspective on how space is organized and organizational, is particularly needed in order to understand how creative hubs (re)shape work practices (Kingma 2016; Gerdenitsch et al. 2016). A myriad of closely related yet distinct phenomena such as co-working (Gandini 2015),

---

[1]See www.urbanresort.nl for more background information.

teleworking (Leonardi et al. 2010), and third workspaces (Kingma 2016), all rely on the increased mobility and autonomy of workers, afforded by the availability of mobile technologies. However, the possibility to work anywhere does not mean that physical space no longer plays a role in facilitating work. On the contrary, the unexpected impact of these new types of work environments on the nature of the work conducted there, needs further inquiry (see also Beyes and Steyaert 2011). Creative hubs provide a useful empirical environment in which to look at this changing relationship between work and space.

In what comes next, I will first give a short overview of the main approaches to organizational space and how these have influenced the literature on creative hubs. Second, I will offer a descriptive account of the different stages the creative hub Volkshotel has gone through, relying on field notes and interview data, with a specific focus on how space features in all stages. I will develop an analysis of the intertwining of organizational practice and space throughout these different stages, and will argue that the underlying goal of the creative hub Volkshotel moved from facilitating creative production, to the display of an image of creativity. I will suggest this shift needs to be contemplated in studying the spacing of creative work in general.

Organizational Space in the Creative Industries

There has been a rapid growth of studies on the role of space in organizations (e.g. Dale and Burrell 2008; Kornberger and Clegg 2004), yet definitions of space and approaches to the study of space in organizations vary widely. Taylor and Spicer (2007) distinguish three views of space: (1) space as distance and proximity, (2) space as a materialization of power relations, and (3) space as lived experience. Research on the organizational spaces of the creative industries—in and just outside of the boundaries of organization studies—can be categorized according to the same typology. An example of the view that sees space in terms of proximity and distance is Ebbers' work (2014) on the effect of different degrees of co-location on collaboration between individual entrepreneurs. Using a survey methodology, Ebbers studied the same creative hub that is the focus of this chapter. He found a positive relation between physical proximity and collaboration only between those creative workers who were located in the same area and on the same floor (2014), thus conceptualizing space as the distance between two predefined points, in this case the residents.

Research on how office design helps manage productivity (McElroy and Morrow 2010), creativity (Haner 2005) and social interaction (Fayard and Weeks 2007) is based on the premise that space guides behaviour. Creativity is an important skill in employees (Amabile 1997; Christensen et al. 2014; Chua et al. 2015), and creating the ideal environment for creativity, whether in or outside traditional organizational structures, can be seen as a managerial objective (Lazzarato 2006). This also means that space is not neutral, and can be seen as the expression of power relations.

Space as lived experience is very much present in the literature on creative hubs. Studies focus on how workers perceive of the co-working spaces they chose (Garrett et al. 2017; Kingma 2016), how craftspeople in small creative clusters feel about the space they use (Drake 2003), and how people in creative companies perceive the space in which their social relationships are embedded (Clare 2013). This research conceptualizes space as what informants think and feel. Space is essentially what people think it is (see also De Vaujany and Vaast 2014, 2016; Musson and Tietze 2004), and the question becomes how that perception impacts a certain organizational phenomenon, such as identity (Drake 2003), or collaboration (Garrett et al. 2017). Perhaps the reason that much research on organizational space in the creative industries focuses on lived experience, is that feelings of belonging are important to creative workers, who seemingly effortlessly mix personal lifestyle choices with professional endeavours (McRobbie 2015; Eikhof and Haunschild 2006; Stahl 2008).

The goal here is to keep these different perspectives in mind as we look at the trajectory of the creative hub Volkshotel, while focusing specifically on the shift from creative production, to displaying creativity within the building.

From Volkskrant Building to Volkshotel

The Volkshotel owes its name to the very first occupant of the building: Dutch daily newspaper *De Volkskrant*. A literal translation of 'volkskrant' would be 'newspaper of the people'. In 2007, Urban Resort, a non-profit initiative run by former squatters (Cnossen and Olma 2014), had set their mind on the large building when the journalists were about to move out. They got the support from the city council to turn the place into a temporary creative hub, as was in line with the city's policy to fund temporary self-run places for artists and underground initiatives (Peck 2012). Just as the main squats of the 1980s, no effort went into renaming the building, which was now simply referred to as Volkskrant building. Keeping this name would prove consequential later on, but initially it was simply a result of the lack of time and resources to engage with such frivolous things as branding, given that so much had to be done.

Over the course of 2007, each floor was rented out to a collective of artists, creatives, craftspeople, entrepreneurs, and activists, who were supposed to take care of maintenance, pay rent as a group, and foster a climate of collaboration and sociality among themselves. This meant getting their hands dirty. The second floor had been an open space where journalists could shout the status of their copy across the floor to one another. When the artists moved in, they wanted to keep parts of it open, to set up machines for common use, but also started to build plaster walls in order to create separate studios. The artists on the fourth floor decided to build a kitchen for communal use in one corner of their floor. As for the musicians and music producers taking residence in the basement, they each had to build and soundproof their own studio.

Converting the building lasted months and went hand in hand with processes of group formation, conflicts, and financial surprises. Drawing from their activist network, Urban Resort had sought out the help of several anarchistic consultants, who guided these group processes in rather unorthodox ways. If too many people wanted the same space, they would tell them that the building's walls were elastic. Several months into the starting phase, it turned out that a certain illustrious individual had been living in the building all that time, roller skating through the hallways at night, adorned with bright-coloured Christmas lights. 'We also found out someone was occasionally using the oven to roast chicken in the old canteen on the top floor during the night, when everyone else was gone. To this day, we still are not sure who it was, but we suspect it was the same person', said one of the first community organizers.

In 2012, when I started my research on the Volkskrant building, the types of people I found in the 10,000-square metre-large building ranged from film-makers to privacy activists, from independent coders to stage designers, and from sculptors to dance teachers, and one hairdresser who specialized in dreadlocks. The basement was home to various music studios and would come to life at night, pumping with hip-hop beats and infused with the smell of marihuana. The ground floor and first floor hosted well-organized offices and spacious offices of digital creative agencies, while the second floor was half chaotic artist studios, and half start-ups, who took the lean management strategy so seriously that their offices would only contain a desk and a chair.

The building was now run based on individual rental contracts, meaning the idea that each floor would self-organize and pay rent as a collective, had largely failed. Substantial maintenance was taken care of by Urban Resort, and some floors even hired a cleaning worker. Nevertheless, there was a distinct freedom in the way people interacted with the space they rented. Many people took out ceilings for a more spacious feeling, or decorated the walls with spray paint. The tenants would also easily use different parts of the building. The software developers on the second floor would use the dance studio in the basement for a weekly yoga session. The artists from the fifth and sixth floor would go for food and drinks together at the club on the top floor, especially when someone from their crowd was DJ-ing. And although it was strictly forbidden by this time, some people were temporarily, or intermittently, living in their studios (see also Sihvonen and Cnossen 2015).

It was by no means an exaggeration to say that Amsterdam's cultural and underground infrastructure owes much to the Volkskrant building as it was known then. The Burning Man-inspired Magneet festival, hip-hop festival Appelsap, and travelling theatre festival De Parade all held office in the Volkskrant building. International superstar DJ Tom Trago had a studio on the fifth floor, which he kept even when his success allowed him to intermittently rent a studio in The Hague with much higher quality equipment, 'because the atmosphere here is so good'. The film-makers who shared studios on the sixth floors created documentaries for the renowned film festival IDFA. The building also hosted several visual artists who exhibited internationally, such as Wayne Horse, and who benefitted from having an inexpensive place to work. The best way to get in was through people who already had a studio there. A young architect returning from a few years abroad describes how he did this. 'I hung up ads everywhere on the fifth floor, which I knew had the best atmosphere, and spoke to everyone I could find in order to convince them to let me share a studio'. As such, the importance of a place where beginning creative professionals could work for several years without, cannot be underestimated. Add to this the increasing popularity of rooftop bar and club Canvas, and the neighbouring nightclub Trouw, for which several Volkskrant building residents would cross the street to DJ a set, and the creative hub was firmly planted on the mental map of many people.

It was only a matter of time before commercial investors would start to take interest. Given that Urban Resort had a temporary lease with the owner of the building, they themselves were open to new partnerships that could potentially sustain the building's creative and cultural functions. A former tech-entrepreneur looking for a new project took interest, and he had a specific plan in mind. Inspired by a hotel he visited in Berlin, he wanted to turn the Volkskrant building into the kind of hotel that would exude a creative and artistic flavour and an informal atmosphere.

The process that followed entailed convincing half of the tenants to move out of their studio before their lease expired, greasing the wheels with a financial compensation, and converting most of the building into a hotel while renovating the rest. Whereas the start of the creative hub was marked by a haphazard, improvised, and self-led remodelling of all floors, this was a relatively smooth operation, precisely orchestrated and prepared throughout. A well-known designer was assigned the interior design of the shared areas, and for more than a year, a creative team had worked on the overall look and feel of the new hotel. There was a tender for the building's creative tenants to design certain theme rooms, and the new hotel management hired someone specifically to monitor this process.

The most important change, however, was that from 2014 onwards, the creative hub became independent from public funding, and is now covered by the revenue generated by the hotel. Urban Resort was hired by the hotel owner to manage the remaining community of artists. Interestingly, instead of deciding that the studios would generate a lower rent than the hotel rooms, the hotel owner treated the lower income stream from the studio part of the building as a loss. As a result, the hotel's role in supporting the creative community of the building is best understood as one of continued sponsorship. This creates an interesting power dynamic. Instead of recognizing that the market for artist workspaces is different from the market for hotel rooms, the former is kept to the standards of the latter. A failure to live up to these standards then results in the hotel continuously 'saving' the creative hub from this lack of business performance.

On the one hand, the remaining tenants are very much aware of the value they create for the hotel and have emphasized their role in the successful transition to creative hotel at various occasion. This has, for instance, resulted in one of the tenants, a documentary maker, taking up a formal role in the governance of the creative hub. On the other hand, the renovated creative hub and increased opportunity to showcase their work in a trendy and respectable environment have made the working spaces in the creative hub very much in demand. A current model has been adopted where tenants are asked every few years to prove again why they make a good contribution to the creative hub and the Volkshotel at large. As a result of the increased popularity, even those tenants who question that they should be grateful to be able to work there, and rather espouse the view that affordable workspace for artists keep the city vibrant, comply nevertheless.

On a material-semiotic level, something else of interest happened. The new management could convince former resident *De Volkskrant* to lend them the original five letters that once lit up the façade of the building when it was still a newspaper office. 'Volkshotel', meaning 'hotel for the people', is meant to welcome everybody, from cosmopolitan travellers to local residents. The blurb on the website reads:

> Volkshotel is a place for single moms. For Stockbrokers and punk rockers. For dandies and poets. Dishwashers and Underwater Welders. For biologists, night bloomers and artists. A place for everyone. Volkshotel creates meetings and the meetings create Volkshotel. This is a hotel of the people. This is Volkshotel.[2]

Leaving aside the unconventional use of capital letters, let's consider the following sentence: 'Volkshotel creates meetings and the meetings create Volkshotel'. This statement suggests that the relationship between this place and its (organizational) activity, works through a particular manner, namely meetings. This is something the current community manager, who works for Urban Resort, confirmed: 'everything is about meeting, that is the keyword'. Keeping in mind the creative hub's beginnings, we see that the role of the place has shifted from facilitating creative production, to facilitating encounters. What does this mean for the type of creativity that is fostered here?

Using the Different Space-Perspectives to Make Sense of the Volkshotel

I will now demonstrate how the three perspectives of space set out in the beginning of this chapter, each help to make sense of the trajectory of this creative hub, and how it relates to the organization of the space within the hub, while also falling short in an important way. Studying space as distance and proximity (e.g. Ebbers 2014) revealed that independent workers are more likely to collaborate with close neighbours and showed the substantial impact of immediate co-location, which was reinforced even further by the fact that tenants, at the time of the study, did not have access to any other floors but their own. Indeed,

---

[2]www.volkshotel.nl/en.

some of the groups that were given a floor at the very beginning of the hub in 2007 have stayed. Individuals have come and gone, but the fact that these semi-permanent workgroups, of which the network identity has not changed (Daskalaki 2010), are still there, supports the view that immediate co-location matters for what goes on in creative hubs.

When looking at space as an expression of power relations, the paradox of access that is present in the current Volkshotel stands out. Within the area that contains artist studios, one space has recently been redecorated as a common lunch and meeting area. The Volkshotel now employs a team that curates the cultural events in the hotel, from band performances in the basement nightclub Doka, DJ's in the improved and expanded restaurant on the top floor, to street art exhibitions in the lounge area on the ground floor. Sometimes the content for these cultural events is provided by the artists residing in the building, but this is not always the case. The community manager noticed that despite the fact that the hotel had been open for almost three years, there was still very little integration between the artists and the team working for the hotel. Some of the artists, especially those remaining from the period when the place was still the Volkskrant building, were irritated that their key cards no longer gave them access to certain areas of the top floor. In an attempt to instigate more integration and fix any lingering animosity, a common area was created. Furthermore, a budget was reserved for events that would bring together hotel guests, locals, employees of the hotel, and resident artists. Thus, by creating spaces (temporary events, a common lunch area) accessible to different groups, the distinction that is spatially maintained in other parts of the building, is compensated.

The power relation between the hotel owner and the original artist residents is also noticeable in the following anecdote. Two years into the hotel's existence, the founder of the top floor bar decided to stop his partnership with the new hotel owner. He had named his venue Canvas, reflecting the idea that each person could make it into their own work of art (see also Sihvonen and Cnossen 2015). Concretely, this meant a changing interior, painted tables, and a chaotic feel. Part of the building's metamorphosis into a hotel, was a doubling in size, and an upgrade in terms of soundproofing and overall professionalism. Canvas' founder, an artist by training, was happy with this, until the hotel owner decided that the logo had to fit into the overall house style developed by the hotel's creative team. While this may seem a trivial matter, for someone who wanted a place that was as open for creative input as a canvas, this went too far, and he decided to hand over his business to the hotel management. This happened without much ado, as the running of restaurant and bar that was done by the original Canvas founder, could be absorbed into the overall management of the hotel.

Maintaining a certain freedom in the look of Canvas' logo would remind people of the legitimacy of the creative hub in terms of creativity because it foregrounds the fact that the most well-visited spot of the building was always a result of an ongoing creative process in which many residents of the building participated. While this observation fits with the third and final perspective of space, i.e. the view that space reflects and shapes lived experience, it also leads us to a more important point.

What all three perspectives on space do not illuminate, is how organized space favours *a specific kind of production*. The literature on organizational space seems to take for granted that the type of work, or production, is given, and that the study of the space in which that production happens merely adds a layer, whether of collaboration and interaction, or of power, or of (individual or collective) experience. However, in the case of creative hubs, the type of creativity that happens here can vary wildly. Looking at the trajectory of the Volkshotel, we indeed see that the type of creativity fostered in every phase, shifted significantly over time. In the early days of the creative hub, including the period of 2012 and 2013, creativity was understood not just in terms of what the artist residents do on their laptops, in their music studios, or indeed on their canvases, but was connected to the surrounding material space too. Building walls, taking out ceilings, creating secret rooms for sleepovers, and making the many mural paintings that decorated the walls of most floors, were all part of the creative hub. Whenever I visited the studios of the people during my fieldwork, they would, without exception, start by showing what they had done to the space, explaining how it was before.

Now, however, the artists who have remained in the building share slightly smaller studios. More importantly, the use of common areas is much more monitored than before. Alterations to shared spaces cannot be made without permission, reflecting the change from a space that was used for joint creative and social experimentation, to a space that carefully displays some of the results of that creative experimentation. The possibility of working quietly in relative isolation, one of the things the illustrators and designers previously residing on the fourth floor cited as indispensable, has become more difficult due to the fact that more people use the same surface. While the different perspectives on organizational space each reveal interesting elements about the creative hub, a simple focus on the decrease in space available per person, triggers the question what the 'creative' in 'creative hubs' stands for, and why are certain types of creativity fostered, and not others.

Conclusion: From Making to Displaying

The Volkshotel is characterized by an interesting paradox. On the one hand, it is more accessible and visible than ever, thanks to its thought-through interior design, many cultural events, and a free co-working space on the ground floor. On the other hand, its users are less able to use their creativity to modify the space, as was the case before. The reasons for this are simple: there are now resources to take care of interior design, and it is in the business' interest to have a hotel that looks presentable and stylish. Furthermore, people have less space for themselves, and will think twice before experimenting with mural paintings, or temporary installations.

This demonstrates that, as argued before about Amsterdam's creativity policy (Peck 2012), creativity is a term easily used for all sorts of branding purposes. In line with trends in other cities, setting up places for creative work is increasingly about 'curating' interaction and exchange (Merkel 2015). Furthermore, the presence of creative workers is equated with a certain image and lifestyle (see also Eikhof and Haunschild 2006) and spills over to the locales they choose to frequent. Indeed, in its move from improvised semi-squat to swanky hotel, the overall emphasis has shifted from affording creative experiment, to fostering meetings and displaying a creative image. This is evident not just from the emphasis on 'the people' (rather than the work), but even more so from the way space is used now. You can work for a bit on your laptop in the co-working space, visit a concert, or have a meeting about a creative project in the café, all in the scope of a few hours, and in the same building. This is not to say that creative production does not happen in the Volkshotel. About 3000 square metres remain dedicated to creative workspaces, which are used by creative workers who tend to work on laptops, sat at desks. While the presence of ninety workspaces means that the Volkshotel remains a place for creative work, the production facilities that were previously found in the building—of which a wood workshop, a cabinet for musical instrument repair, and several dance studios are only of few examples (Cnossen and Olma 2014)—are no longer there, making the possibilities for actual creative production in its various material and space-intensive forms, more limited compared to before. In the current incarnation of this creative hub, creativity is carefully curated, hosted on a temporary basis, and meant to be put on display. This creates a stimulating environment for the culturally curious city dweller, the intermittent co-worker, and the clubbing enthusiast. But the kind of creative worker who needs of a lot of space, and some freedom to tinker with it, will have to look elsewhere.

References

Alvesson, M. (2009). At-home ethnography: Struggling with closeness and closure. In S. Ybema, S. D. Yanow, H. Wels, & F. Kamsteeg (Eds.), *Organizational ethnography: Studying the complexity of everyday life.* London and Newcastle: Sage.

Amabile, T. M. (1997). Motivating creativity in organizations. *California Management Review, 40*(I), 39–59.

Beyes, T., & Steyaert, C. (2011). Spacing organization: Non-representational theory and performing organizational space. *Organization, 19*(1), 45–61.

Christensen, B. T., Drewsen, L. K., & Maaløe, J. (2014). Implicit theories of the personality of the ideal creative employee. *Psychology of Aesthetics, Creativity and the Arts, 8*(2), 189–197.

Chua, R. Y. J., Roth, Y., & Lemoine, J.-F. (2015). The impact of culture on creativity: How cultural tightness and cultural distance affect global innovation crowdsourcing work. *Administrative Science Quarterly, 60*(2), 189–227.

Clare, K. (2013). The essential role of place within the creative industries: Boundaries, networks and play. *Cities, 34,* 52–57.

Cnossen, B. (2018). Whose home is it anyway? Performing multiple selves while doing organizational ethnography? *Journal of Organizational Ethnography, 7*(2), 176–185.

Cnossen, B., & Olma, S. (2014). *The Volkskrant building: Manufacturing difference in Amsterdam's creative city.* Amsterdam: Creative Industries Publishing.

Dale, K., & Burrell, G. (2008). *The spaces of organization and the organization of space: Power, identity and materiality at work.* Basingstoke: Palgrave Macmillan.

Daskalaki, M. (2010). Building bonds and bridges: Linking tie evolution and network identity in the creative industries. *Organization Studies, 31*(12), 1649–1999.

De Vaujany, F.-X., & Vaast, E. (2014). If these walls could talk: The mutual construction of organizational space and legitimacy. *Organization Science, 25*(3), 713–731.

De Vaujany, F.-X., & Vaast, E. (2016). Matters of visuality in legitimation practices: Dual iconographies in a meeting room. *Organization, 23*(5), 763–790.

Drake, G. (2003). "This place gives me space": Place and creativity in the creative industries. *Geoforum, 34*(4), 511–524.

Ebbers, J. J. (2014). Networking behavior and contracting relationships among entrepreneurs in business incubators. *Entrepreneurship: Theory and Practice, 38*(5), 1159–1181.

Eikhof, D. R., & Haunschild, A. (2006). Lifestyle meets market: Bohemian entrepreneurs in creative industries. *Creativity and Innovation Management, 15*(3), 234–241.

Fayard, A.-L., & Weeks, J. (2007). Photocopiers and water-coolers: The affordances of informal interaction. *Organization Studies, 28*(5), 605–634.

Gandini, A. (2015). The rise of coworking spaces: A literature review. *Ephemera: Theory & Politics in Organization, 15*(1), 193.

Garrett, L. E., Spreitzer, G. M., & Bacevice, P. A. (2017). Co-constructing a sense of community at work: The emergence of community in coworking spaces. *Organization Studies, 38*(6), 821–842.

Gerdenitsch, C., Scheel, T. E., Andorfer, J., & Korunka, C. (2016, April). Coworking spaces: A source of social support for independent professionals. *Frontiers in Psychology, 7,* 581.

Haner, U. H. (2005). Spaces for creativity and innovation in two established organizations. *Creativity and Innovation Management, 14*(3), 288–298.

Kingma, S. F. (2016). The constitution of "third workspaces" in between the home and the corporate office. *New Technology, Work and Employment, 31*(2), 176–193.

Kornberger, M., & Clegg, S. R. (2004). Bringing space back in: Organizing the generative building. *Organization Studies, 25*(7), 1095–1114.

Lazzarato, M. (2006). Immaterial labor. In P. Virno & M. Hardy (Eds.), *Radical thought in Italy: A potential politics*. Minneapolis: University of Minnesota Press.

Leonardi, P. M., Treem, J. W., & Jackson, M. H. (2010). The connectivity paradox: Using technology to both decrease and increase perceptions of distance in distributed work arrangements. *Journal of Applied Communication Research, 38*(1), 85–105.

McElroy, J. C., & Morrow, P. C. (2010). Employee reactions to office redesign: A naturally occurring quasi-field experiment in a multi-generational setting. *Human Relations, 63*(5), 609–636.

McRobbie, A. (2015). *Be creative: Making a living in the new culture industries*. London: Polity.

Merkel, J. (2015). Coworking in the city. *Ephemera: Theory & Politics in Organization, 15*(1), 121–139.

Moeran, B. (2009). From participant observation to observant participation. In S. Ybema, D. Yanow, H. Wels, & F. Kamsteeg (Eds.), *Organizational ethnography: Studying the complexity of everyday life*. London and Newcastle: Sage.

Musson, G., & Tietze, S. (2004). Places and spaces: The role of metonymy in organizational talk. *Journal of Management Studies, 41*(8), 1301–1323.

Peck, J. (2012). Recreative city: Amsterdam, vehicular ideas and the adaptive spaces of creativity policy. *International Journal of Urban and Regional Research, 36*(3), 462–485.

Sihvonen, T., & Cnossen, B. (2015). Not only a workplace: Reshaping creative work and urban space. *Observatorio, 47–69*. Available at http://obs.obercom.pt/index.php/obs/article/view/973.

Stahl, G. (2008). Cowboy capitalism: The art of ping pong country in the new Berlin. *Space and Culture, 11*(4), 300–324.

Taylor, S., & Spicer, A. (2007). Time for space: A narrative review of research on organizational spaces. *International Journal of Management Reviews, 9*(4), 325–346.

15

The City as a Creative Hub: The Case of the Fashion Industry in Milan, Italy

Marianna d'Ovidio and Valentina Pacetti

Introduction

The chapter explores the extents to which the concept of "hub" is suitable to represent the role performed by the city of Milan in the spatial, social and economic organisation of the fashion industry. The system is territorially organised according to two main, complementary, forces: a strong local embeddedness and an equally strong internationalisation process. Through these analyses, the authors draw some reflections on the importance of the notion of hub for the urban and development policies. The resulting socio-economic space is to be conceived as re-territorialised in a multiple scales system in which the city of Milan can be better understood as a hub, since the traditional

M. d'Ovidio (✉)
University of Bari, Bari, Italy
e-mail: marianna.dovidio@uniba.it

V. Pacetti
University of Milano-Bicocca, Milan, Italy
e-mail: valentina.pacetti@unimib.it

© The Author(s) 2019
R. Gill et al. (eds.), *Creative Hubs in Question*, Dynamics of Virtual Work,
https://doi.org/10.1007/978-3-030-10653-9_15

concepts of industrial district and pipeline are not completely able to grasp the complexity of the two overlapping territorial processes.

In empirical terms, we will show such dynamics through examination of the spatialisation of innovation and creative processes in the fashion industry. The empirical material used for the chapter derives from various direct and indirect sources: in-depth interviews and life histories with fashion designers and fashion entrepreneurs; interviews with key informants (officials from the Department of Fashion, Design and Innovation of the Municipality of Milan, delegates from the Chamber of Commerce of Milan, fashion producers' associations; directors of R&D centres and of fashion schools); press reviews, policy and economic reports.

The theoretical focus of the chapter is the extent to which the concept of hub makes it possible to go beyond both agglomeration economy and globalisation in representing the spatialisation of the fashion industry, and, specifically, the role of the city of Milan. The notion of "hub", therefore, will be discussed in regard to local development policies.

Hub, Industrial Districts, Pipelines

The theoretical debate has been observing the spatialisation of the economy for many decades, and a large number of models have been developed to depict the different configurations that it may assume. In this section, three main concepts will be briefly outlined and then used to discuss the case of the fashion industry in the Metropolitan Area of Milan: the notions of "hub", "industrial district", and "pipeline".

The Emergence of the Hub

The concept of the hub was first developed in the literature dealing with social networks. It was then transferred to territorial entities (cities, metropolitan areas, regions), to represent transportation flows[1] (Neal 2014).

---

[1] Early in 1996, Markusen introduced the concept of hub-and-spoke in order to describe a possible local production system where one big firm, the hub (not necessarily locally embedded) is connected with other smaller firms through a series of spokes. Also in this case the term "hub" is a reference to transport hub.

The notion envisages a hub as a centre suited to managing flows, be they flows of people, freight, ideas, knowledge or other commodities. Recently, a growing literature has considered "creative" hubs, conceived, in general terms, as catalysts for the growth and innovation of the local creative economy (Virani and Malem 2015). They exhibit extremely variable features because they are shaped by the local conditions of the economy and society (British Council 2016).

Notwithstanding the high empirical variety of creative hubs, on exploring both the scientific and the policy-related literature, it is possible to find a number of services and functions that the hub provides. Regardless of the specific services that it may provide and the specific forms that it may take (be they buildings, neighbourhoods, even cities) the hub's main functions can be organised into three general areas. The first two areas are common to all hubs, also the transport ones; the third area is specific to the creative hub.

Firstly, its coordinating function: just as a transport hub manages flows of physical elements, so a hub in general coordinates the flows of information, knowledge, but also ideas, meanings and so on. Very importantly, this coordination happens at multiple scales and directions (Evers et al. 2010; Sedini et al. 2013).

Secondly, different networks are connected by and through the hub: networks of various kinds (formal, informal, locally based, international) are tied together as they pass through the hub (Oakley 2004; Sedini et al. 2013).

Thirdly, the creative hub performs the specific function of supporting diverse cultural forms (Currid 2007; Virani and Malem 2015), and, more importantly, of hybridising them.

The usefulness of the notion of hub to explore the role of the city of Milan within the wider fashion system is demonstrated by the city's performance on these functions.

Industrial Districts

In the 1970s, Becattini, on studying the Italian system of small and medium-sized enterprises, propounded the concept of *industrial districts* to describe and explain the rise and success of local productive systems specialised in the manufacture of different kinds of products. He used the traditional Marshallian concept, updated with new trends in economic development. He defined an industrial district as *a socio-territorial entity which is characterised by the active presence of both a community of people and a population of firms in one naturally and historically bounded area. In the district, unlike in other environments, such as manufacturing towns, community and firms tend to merge* (Becattini 1990, p. 39). Both the concept of industrial district and other ideas on agglomeration economy have evolved and been extensively debated (Piore and Sabel 1984; Markusen 1996; Martin and Sunley 2003). Notwithstanding the profound empirical and theoretical evolutions that the concept has undergone, the persistent feature of industrial districts is that they are socially integrated systems whose competitiveness is linked to the strong embeddedness of the economy in the social, political and cultural environment: all the resources for the economic competitiveness of firms are locally available (Brusco 1982).

Local and Non-Local Relations: Pipelines

One of the arguments that have most challenged the concept of local embeddedness is that of "pipeline", as developed, among many scholars, by Bathelt and colleagues.

On discussing how local actors acquire knowledge (any kind of knowledge), Bathelt et al. distinguish between a kind of knowledge that people acquire by just "being there" and a knowledge that is not place-based and that can be achieved through *selected providers* localised outside the local context. In order to acquire such kind of knowledge, actors use "pipelines", such as external linkages with other specialised actors willing to share knowledge (Bathelt et al. 2004; Bathelt and Turi 2011).

Without denying the importance of local embeddedness, these scholars show how local firms are connected through knowledge flows with extra-local actors. Indeed, firms establish trans-local or global relationships especially for the purpose of obtaining knowledge about external markets and different technologies developed elsewhere (Henn and Bathelt 2018, p. 451).

The notion of pipeline emphasises that the competitive success of a cluster can only be understood in relation to both its internal and external linkages (Bathelt et al. 2004), and it is extremely important for understanding the non-local dimension of knowledge transfer and innovation within clusters. Yet many local actors are connected to international networks which are part of global value and production chains (Gereffi and Korzeniewicz 1994; Coe and Yeung 2015).

Consistently with this concept, the notion of hub focuses on the place where these local and global networks are connected, not on the flows (or their content) themselves.

The Milanese Fashion Production System: Manufacturing and Designing

Italian competitiveness has always been linked to production systems based on crafts skills that have been able to renew their role in small and medium-sized enterprises as well as in large ones (Becattini 2004; Dunford 2006). The Milanese fashion industry is no exception. Its success is connected to the co-location of a production chain with many different steps, and it is characterised by very high quality, historical tradition and the capacity to connect local culture with innovation and creativity, which form an important local production system (White 2000; Segre-Reinach 2010; d'Ovidio 2015; Gilbert and Casadei 2018).

The Milanese Fashion Production System (MFPS) is thus characterised by a mix of design and production, creation and manufacture, innovation and crafts tradition. It comprises more than 6000 enterprises active in the field of design, clothing manufacturing, textiles production and leather processing.[2] Together with the overall commercial chain and the connected catering and accommodation businesses, around

---

[2]Data Source is the Milan Chamber of Commerce, 2013.

one-fifth of Milan's entire wealth is produced (directly and indirectly) by the fashion industry.[3]

The MFPS is concentrated in an area of between 4000 and 5000 sq. km comprising the city of Milan and its surroundings, and which extends between the Lombardy and Piedmont regions, including the towns of Como, Varese, Novara and Vigevano. It includes not only the famous Milanese *maisons* together with smaller design studios, but also, and especially, a complex agglomeration of small and medium-sized manufacturers and craftspersons engaged in the production of clothing, textiles and leather goods exhibiting a deep social, political and cultural embeddedness typical of the industrial district.

One observes a territorial specialisation of firms in that most of the design and symbolic production of fashion is concentrated in the city of Milan, while the material production is clustered in the rest of the region.

The relation between the two territorial levels is multifaceted and complex, particularly in the sphere of innovation and creativity. The relation is shaped as a deeply embedded local system which, at the same time, is strongly coordinated and internationalised at the global level by the city itself.

The Embeddedness of Creative Process and Innovation

In order to discuss the extent to which the notion of hub can be useful in explaining the role of the city of Milan within the overall MFPS, we will focus on creativity and innovation, arguing that they are both the result of a strong social, cultural and political embeddedness and, at the same time, fed by continuous relations and feedbacks operating between and across different scales (Bunnell and Coe 2001; Pratt and Jeffcutt 2011).

Three areas are taken into account here. The first area centres on innovations in the strategic positioning of firms in the market in order

---

[3]As stated at the opening of the Milan Fashion Week in September 2013 by Boselli, President of the Italian Fashion Council.

to react to global dynamics. Although changes at the global scale always affect the local economy, in the MFPS, global dynamics have been affecting the material and the symbolic producers very differently. Since the 1970s, the geography of textiles and clothing production has dramatically changed due to the relocation of most of the Western production to low-cost countries (notably India, China, Morocco, Turkey, South America and East Europe) (Gilbert and Casadei 2018).

The crisis has massively affected the Italian production of clothing and textiles, with no exceptions. China's entry into the WTO in 2005 exacerbated the ongoing crisis and especially hit those firms specialised in low-quality standardised production (Segre-Reinach 2010). One of the outcomes of the sharpening of international competition was that many of the firms located in the surroundings of Milan shifted their production to high-quality segments (items or processes), strengthening their local ties with the Milanese fashion houses. This strategic reorientation was made possible by many different kinds of relations developed locally: both formal institutions (local agencies, schools, research centres) and informal ones (personal networks, a culture of cooperation, long historical traditions) were involved in the process. Moreover, the (physical and social) proximity to the Milanese fashion *maisons* provided a strong competitive advantage for those firms, facilitating the innovation processes and enabling the early internationalisation of the local production.

The second example concerns process innovation, and it refers to how the co-location of many different elements of the production chain helps in responding to market demands. Recently, a request for more socially and environmentally sustainable fashion has emerged from the market; however, this is very difficult to achieve because of the complexity of the production chain, which may involve many different countries in the world (Mora et al. 2014). Nonetheless, precisely because most of the productive chain is co-located in the same place, the MFPS has been developing a labelling system guaranteeing that the entire process respects both workers and the environment. The labelling system has been implemented by a number of textiles and clothing producers, led by big names of Milanese fashion and thanks to the presence of local and collective research centres, aiming mainly at developing technologies within the textile industry. Such centres, serving as collective service centres for research and development within the textiles and clothing industries, originate from partnerships among local administrations, chambers of commerce, unions and private companies.[4] In terms of scale and multi-scalar relations, research centres develop relations mainly in two directions: they are strongly embedded in the local society, working with local small and medium-sized enterprises, collaborating with the local universities and so on; they are also connected, at a higher geographical scale, with similar centres in Europe, being involved in many European projects.[5]

The embeddedness and co-location of interconnected firms, which characterise the MFPS, thus show their importance for the growth of creativity and innovation, as envisaged by the classic interpretation of industrial districts (Brusco 1982; Ramella 2017). In this regard, during a research visit to a silk firm, an interviewee claimed, "it's impossible for a firm to keep an innovation secret: everyone will find out about it!", to express the fact that innovation spreads throughout the interconnected firms. The geographical concentration of the productive chain is undoubtedly a strong asset for innovation, but co-location is not enough: the complex multi-scalar relations and the embeddedness of the economic activity in social life are equally crucial for innovation to circulate and hybridise the local production.

The third area in which to explore the embeddedness of the creative process is the fostering of the creativity of fashion designers. This is strongly linked to immaterial urban factors such as the creative atmosphere, tailoring traditions, fashion schools and so on, as discussed by a large body of literature on local creative atmosphere (see, e.g., Van Heur 2009; Leslie and Rantisi 2011).

---

[4]Such centres are very common in the Italian industrial districts, an example being, for instance, ERVET in Emilia Romagna (Best 1990).

[5]For instance, in the Organza project, financed under Interreg IVC EU Framework, the Centro Tessile Cotoniero in the textile industrial district of Gallarate was connected, at the European level, with three universities, three municipalities and six other research centres, with the aim of sharing knowledge on how to stimulate the creative economy locally (www.organzanetwork.eu).

The Milanese fashion designers value urban stimuli as important sources of inspiration, but they tend to perceive Milan as lacking such elements. Therefore, they cite their frequent travels abroad, mainly to other fashion capitals, as the means whereby they fulfil the need to nourish their creativity (d'Ovidio 2010).

Locally, interaction with manufacturers is a very important source of a specific kind of creativity and know-how: local producers and craftspersons have a role in the education and skills of designers, and workshops become important sites for knowledge sharing and learning, for creativity and innovation. Thus, innovation and knowledge circulate not only among manual workers and among firms in the districts: they also circulate among designers and creative workers outside the borders of the material production, reaching the centre of Milan, where designers learn how to transform their ideas into objects, often drawing new inspiration exactly from the factories and craft workshops. In this relationship, also manufacturers acquire new skills and come in contact with novelties in fashion, as regards both product shapes and production techniques.

This is another case where the geographical proximity between manufacturing and design segments on the one hand, and the embeddedness of the entire production chain on the other, is one of the most distinctive competitive advantages of the Milanese fashion industry; this concerns both the traditional dimension of product and process innovation, and the creativity and inspiration of the design elements. Multi-scalar relations are crucial: on one level, the lack of creative stimuli and creative atmosphere in the city of Milan is resolved through bridging ties, networking and external resources enabling fashion designers to gain their inspiration and feed their creativity. On another level, the strong cultural and social embeddedness of the designed fashion in the local industrial environment nurtures the exchange between symbolic and material productions.

The competitiveness of the fashion industry in Milan is thus rooted on the one hand in the local embeddedness and co-location of material and symbolic productions, and, on the other, in the global ties that are cultivated by fashion operators.

Milan as a Gateway City: A Multi-Scalar, Multidirectional Connector

In the previous section, the links between the material manufacture of fashion and its symbolic, or design, production (spatialised, respectively, in the surroundings of the city of Milan and in the city itself) were presented. These links were also described in their multi-scalar configurations, showing that both local embeddedness and extra-local linkages play their role in the economic success of the Milanese fashion industry.

Here, we focus briefly on those institutions in Milan able to "hold down" the local economy and mobilise it globally (Amin and Thrift 1995; Raco 1998). We want to stress the importance of a system which is locally embedded, but connected globally. Hence, we briefly describe how the city of Milan (through both informal networks developed by economic actors and formal institutional bodies) engages with the hyperlocal scale. In Milan, *institutional thickness*[6] has been developed in many areas, and the city is often presented as a global one or the Italian gateway to the global arena (Magatti et al. 2005; Perulli 2016). Not only in the fashion industry, but also in many other aspects of social and economic life, the city is an important international centre: many international companies have their headquarters in Milan; the stock market is one of the most important in Europe; international theatres and exposition centres animate the urban cultural life; and the city is also one of the international centres for the design sector.

Milan is a node of the global fashion system (Jansson and Power 2010; Gilbert and Casadei 2018) and being in the city means that firms can be visible, recognised and inserted in transnational flows. Internationalisation thus includes services for small and medium-sized enterprises (information on new markets, meetings with foreign customers and suppliers, etc.), but also the availability of communication

---

[6]According to Amin and Thrift, "institutional thickness" should be understood as a way in which local-global interactions are locked together at the institutional level. Usually, a number of formal and informal institutions, based on local networks, public collective body and alliances, represent a large set of interests and are able to "hold down" global forces at the local level (Amin and Thrift 1995).

services, the presence of specialised magazines and media, and above all the organisation of trade fairs and events. Milan hosts a number of well-known exhibitions and fairs, both for the textiles industry (for instance, Milano UNICA) and the fashion industry (the women and men Milan Fashion Week, WHITE-show fair, and many more). Among them, the most important is undoubtedly the Woman Fashion Week, presenting fashion shows from the most important Italian and international designers, and positioning Milan among the main Fashion Cities in the world, together with Paris and New York (Breward and Gilbert 2006).

Therefore, a company located in Milan has the chance to operate in an international arena, and thus to benefit from goods and services provided locally that are, nevertheless, able to improve its internationalisation. Trade Fairs, and primarily the Fashion Weeks, play a central role (Jansson and Power 2010). As Perulli claims, "the crossing of fluxes and cross-fertilization between the world of domestic production and global people are made possible by the Fair infrastructure. The Fair makes it possible for small businesses located in industrial districts to move […] and develop negotiations, absorb change and exogenous shocks, survive and regenerate over the long term" (2014, p. 11). Clearly, industrial associations and collective actors offer also business-type initiatives for the internationalisation of small and medium-sized enterprises, but they must be observed in the wider framework of the many elements of the city's internationalisation. Moreover, advanced professional training is undoubtedly an important factor in Milan's urban competitiveness and a strong asset for its internalisation, because schools attract many foreign students and hire a large number of foreign instructors (Pratt et al. 2012; d'Ovidio 2015).

Discussing Milan as a Hub

The MFPS has been described as a locally integrated system that is re-territorialised in a wider global space, and that is able to move from the hyperlocal to the global in its many forms. In what Brenner notably analysed as the *scalar organisation of capital's endemic behaviour of de- and re-territorialisation* (Brenner 1999, p. 435), we observed how such spatial organisation shifts among different scales.

Inspection of the local production system through the lens of industrial districts allows us only partially to see the complex dynamics that happen. Yet, by definition, the concept of industrial district makes it possible to explore the local mechanisms of cooperation, competition and integration of an agglomerated economy, leaving aside the possible extra-local linkages.

The large literature on agglomeration economies helps us to frame the concentration of productive activities in a given space, but it is not equipped to give account of the global dynamics, for instance, the global linkages intervening in the spatialisation of creativity. As shown above, the industrial district notion refers to strong social, political and cultural embeddedness of the economy, and yields a better understanding of the role of both informal and formal institutions in creating, developing and strengthening local linkages. However, this theoretical framework does not "see" the complexity of the multi-scalar relations built by local firms (with local actors, with firms and institutions in Milan, with global players) which represent a very important asset (allowing local firms to resist global forces, enhancing cooperation with the local fashion design studios and so on).

The notion of "pipeline" has been developed to explore extra-local connections that can occur in agglomeration economies, when flows of knowledge are transferred from the outside to the inside (or the reverse). In the case of the MFPS, however, the local firms are too exposed to both local and global flows, so that pipelines cannot represent the situation adequately.

Therefore, in order to understand the spatialisation of innovation and the basic mechanisms of the local economy, the use of the notion of "hub" may be particularly helpful.

Hence, the dynamics of innovation and its spatialisation within the fashion industry in Milan can be better understood if we observe the city of Milan as a creative hub within a larger local production system. This perspective is much better able to formalise the local-global connections and flows in the fashion system.

As discussed above, the theoretical formalisation of hub identifies three main functions.

Firstly, hubs perform coordinating tasks connecting different territorial scales (local to global, global to regional, local to regional, etc.). In the case of the MFPS, Milan connects different places and coordinates the fluxes (of ideas, people, freights, creativity) among different scales (from the hyperlocal to the global).

Secondly, the hub connects different kinds of networks, not necessarily at different scales: this is the case of local productive systems (both the material and symbolic-design production of fashion in the surroundings of Milan and in the core city) which are very well connected with each other, but also the case of the connection of different networks within each system; it also refers to the strong institutional thickness of Milan (Perulli 2016).

Finally, hubs have the important task of supporting different cultural forms (Virani and Malem 2015): in the case described, the city of Milan supports a cultural form that is centred around crafts, tailoring and marketable fashion (Pratt et al. 2012), and that is able to move among different international scales; on the other hand, Milan is not really able to support particularly innovative cultural forms (d'Ovidio and Cossu 2017), so that designers looking for inspiration must travel.

Hence, we need to explore MFPS in a manner more complex than as a co-location or networking or flows. Rather than simply referring to an agglomeration economy, observing a spatial entity (the city of Milan, in this case) as a creative hub is useful for exploring the multifarious dimensions that play a part in the complex dynamics of the MFPS. We saw that co-location has a very important role, but the strength of the MFPS is not reducible to a simple geographical agglomeration of firms and research centres. It is a complex ecosystem that relies on a set of multi-scalar connections that are coordinated mainly in the city of Milan. Moreover, the agglomeration of activities is closely linked with a deep social, cultural and political embeddedness, as the empirical exploration clearly showed. Global dynamics are as crucial as they are complex, so that a coordinating hub is needed in order to compete and succeed in the global arena.

Conclusions: Hubs and Local Development Policies

In this chapter, we have described a local production system based on creativity and innovation, able to move through different places and scales, from the local to the global and the other way round.

We saw, for instance, both the strong local embeddedness and the importance of the global dimension for innovation. These are not contradictory findings; rather, they show that the local and global dimensions are complementary, and that they must be analysed as such. We also saw how fashion production is spatialised: its manufacturing is mainly concentrated in a very dense socio-spatial agglomeration in the surroundings of Milan, while symbolic and design production is mainly located in the city of Milan.

A critical focus is the "movement" of innovation and creativity that is generated, shaped and channelled by the city of Milan, which is not only connected with the global but also acts as a gateway to the global for the surrounding areas.

Focusing on the global–local dynamics on the one hand, and on the production, management and spatialisation of creativity and innovation on the other, we gave account of the fashion industry's dynamic of multi-scalar spatialisation, identifying the city of Milan as a creative hub. The notion of hub, applied to a creative industry, makes it possible to focus on the link among manufacturing, creativity and the spatial organisation of the fashion industry, as well as any other cultural creative industry. As a coordinating element, the hub enables the intersection of different spheres: very local and embedded institutions, a regional governance, and an international production chain, all of which are components that must be kept together to face global competition.

As a concluding issue, the creative hub is also a powerful concept as far as local development policies are concerned. Increasingly, policies focused on providing local creative hubs tend to consider them a kind of trigger for coordinated actions and networks per se, neglecting exploration of what kinds of local resources are already present, nor planning what kinds of actors are to be coordinated and for what purpose. The case of the MFPS showed that hubs must be embedded in the local society; therefore, as a tool of local development policies, they should become part of multifaceted, situated and carefully planned strategies.

Yet, on the one hand, local development policies are essential to face the contemporary global challenges and to drive towards an economic development which is sustainable in both sociological and environmental terms. On the other hand, the local context matters and policies must be tailored to local assets and local features. Moreover, local development policies tend to focus on strengthening or creating global connections, ignoring or neglecting the elements of local embeddedness. For instance, many resources are spent on territorial marketing policies, which are excellent for attracting foreign investments; but this should not lead to abandoning strategies aimed at local development and local roots, such as professional schools, local agencies, local infrastructures and so on. Or, again, local institutions are of crucial importance, but they have to be able to intercept both local stances and global flows. The embeddedness of the economy in social, political and cultural life is a crucial factor that must be supported by targeted political strategies. At the same time, in an era where the model of the "economy of sign and space" is accelerated, the local industrial district risks collapsing if it is isolated. We have to envisage a future when this economy will be dominated by industrial districts connected to and by creative hubs which link the local production to the global arena in many different ways. And this should also have deep consequences for local development policies.

References

Amin, A., & Thrift, N. (1995). Institutional issues for the European regions: From markets and plans to socioeconomics and powers of association. *Economy and Society, 24*(1), 41–66.

Bathelt, H., Malmberg, A., & Maskell, P. (2004). Clusters and knowledge: Local buzz, global pipelines and the process of knowledge creation. *Progress in Human Geography, 28*(1), 31–56.

Bathelt, H., & Turi, P. (2011). Local, global and virtual buzz: The importance of face-to-face contact in economic interaction and possibilities to go beyond. *Geoforum, 42*(5), 520–529.

Becattini, G. (1990). The Marshallian industrial district as a socioeconomic notion. In F. Pyke, G. Becattini, & W. Sengerberger (Eds.), *Industrial districts and inter-firm co-operation in Italy*. Geneva: International Institute for Labour Studies.

Becattini, G. (2004). *Industrial districts: A new approach to industrial change*. Cheltenham and Northampton: Edward Elgar.

Best, M. H. (1990). *The new competition: Institutions of industrial restructuring*. Harvard: Harvard University Press.

Brenner, N. (1999). Globalisation as reterritorialisation: The re-scaling of urban governance in the European Union. *Urban Studies, 36*(3), 431–451.

Breward, C., & Gilbert, D. (2006). *Fashion's world cities*. Oxford and New York: Berg.

British Council. (2016). *The creative hubs report 2016: Understanding the new economy*. London: British Council.

Brusco, S. (1982). The Emilian model: Productive decentralisation and social integration. *Cambridge Journal of Economics, 6*(2), 167–184.

Bunnell, T. G., & Coe, N. M. (2001). Spaces and scales of innovation. *Progress in Human Geography, 25*(4), 569–589.

Coe, N. M., & Yeung, H. W.-C. (2015). *Global production networks: Theorizing economic development in an interconnected world*. Oxford: Oxford University Press.

Currid, E. (2007). *The Warhol economy: How fashion, art, and music drive New York City*. Princeton: Princeton University Press.

d'Ovidio, M. (2010). Fashion and the city—Social interaction and creativity in London and Milan. In S. Vicari (Eds.), *Brand-building: The creative city. A critical look at current concepts and practices*. Firenze: Firenze University Press.

d'Ovidio, M. (2015). The field of fashion production in Milan: A theoretical discussion and an empirical investigation. *City, Culture and Society, 6*(2), 1–8.

d'Ovidio, M., & Cossu, A. (2017). Culture is reclaiming the creative city: The case of Macao in Milan, Italy. *City, Culture and Society, 8*, 7–12.

Dunford, M. (2006). Industrial districts, magic circles, and the restructuring of the Italian textiles and clothing chain. *Economic Geography, 82*(1), 27–59.

Evers, H.-D., Nordin, R., & Nienkemper, P. (2010). *Knowledge cluster formation in peninsular Malaysia: The emergence of an epistemic landscape* (SSRN

Scholarly Paper No. ID 1691008). Rochester, NY: Social Science Research Network.

Gereffi, G., & Korzeniewicz, M. (Eds.). (1994). *Commodity chains and global capitalism*. Westport, CT: Greenwood Press.

Gilbert, D., & Casadei, P. (2018). Unpicking the fashion city: Global perspectives on design, manufacturing and symbolic production in urban formations. In L. Lazzeretti & M. Vecco (Eds.), *Creative industries and entrepreneurship: Paradigms in transition from a global perspective*. Cheltenham and Northampton: Edward Elgar.

Henn, S., & Bathelt, H. (2018). Cross-local knowledge fertilization, cluster emergence, and the generation of buzz. *Industrial and Corporate Change, 27*(3), 449–466.

Jansson, J., & Power, D. (2010). Fashioning a global city: Global city brand channels in the fashion and design industries. *Regional Studies, 44*(7), 889–904.

Leslie, D., & Rantisi, N. M. (2011). Creativity and place in the evolution of a cultural industry. *Urban Studies, 48*(9), 1771–1787.

Magatti, M., Senn, L., Sapelli, G., Ranci, C., Manghi, B., Dente, B., et al. (2005). *Milano, nodo della rete globale: un itinerario di analisi e proposte*. Milano: B. Mondadori.

Markusen, A. (1996). Sticky places in slippery space: A typology of industrial districts. *Economic Geography, 72*(3), 293–313.

Martin, R., & Sunley, P. (2003). Deconstructing clusters: Chaotic concept or policy panacea? *Journal of Economic Geography, 3*(1), 5–35.

Mora, E., Rocamora, A., & Volonté, P. (2014). On the issue of sustainability in fashion studies. *International Journal of Fashion Studies, 1*(2), 139–147.

Neal, Z. P. (2014). Types of hub cities and their effects on urban creative economies. In B. Derudder, F. Witlox, S. Conventz, & A. Thierstein (Eds.), *Hub cities in the knowledge economy: Seaports, airports, brainports*. London and New York: Routledge.

Oakley, K. (2004). Not so cool Britannia. The role of the creative industries in economic development. *International Journal of Cultural Studies, 7*(1), 67–77.

Perulli, P. (2014). Milan in the age of global contract. *Glocalism: Journal of Culture, Politics and Innovation, 3*. Available at https://doi.org/10.12893/gjcpi.2014.3.4.

Perulli, P. (2016). *The urban contract: Community, governance and capitalism*. London and New York: Routledge.

Piore, M. J., & Sabel, C. F. (1984). *The second industrial divide: Possibilities for prosperity*. New York: Basic Books.

Pratt, A. C., Borrione, P., Lavanga, M., & D'Ovidio, M. (2012). International change and technological evolution in the fashion industry. In M. Agnoletti, A. Carandini, & W. Santagata (Eds.), *Studi E Ricerche*. Pontedera: Bandecchi & Vivaldi.

Pratt, A. C., & Jeffcutt, P. (Eds.). (2011). *Creativity, innovation and the cultural economy*. London and New York: Routledge.

Raco, M. (1998). Assessing 'institutional thickness' in the local context: A comparison of Cardiff and Sheffield. *Environment and Planning A, 30*(6), 975–996.

Ramella, F. (2017). The 'enterprise of innovation' in hard times: Corporate culture and performance in Italian high-tech companies. *European Planning Studies, 25*(11), 1954–1975.

Sedini, C., Vignati, A., & Zurlo, F. (2013). *Conceiving a (new) definition of hub for the development of a transnational network for creative companies*. Presented at the The Idea of Creative City/The Urban Policy Debate, Cracow.

Segre-Reinach, S. (2010). If you speak fashion you speak Italian: Notes on present day Italian fashion identity. *Critical Studies in Fashion and Beauty, 1*(2), 203–215.

Van Heur, B. (2009). The clustering of creative networks: Between myth and reality. *Urban Studies, 46*(8), 1531–1552.

Virani, T. E., & Malem, W. (2015). *Re-articulating the creative hub concept as a model for business support in the local creative economy: The case of Mare Street in Hackney* (Creativeworks London Working Paper No. 12).

White, N. (2000). *Reconstructing Italian fashion: America and the development of the Italian fashion industry*. Oxford and New York: Berg.

16

Grassroots Creative Hubs: Urban Regeneration, Recovered Industrial Factories and Cultural Production in Buenos Aires and Rio de Janeiro

Cecilia Dinardi

Introduction

This chapter examines the nature, functioning and politics of grass-roots creative hubs in refurbished industrial factories. The renewal and transformation of factories into arts and cultural venues have been a key feature of post-industrial urbanism in the last three decades. Examples abound across the world, from railway and power stations to post office buildings and chocolate factories. These recovered infrastructures have been re-signified as cultural facilities—as performing or multi-arts centres, galleries, cultural centres, creative economy laboratories, incubators and museums. These initiatives, be that they are led by local governments or community groups, are part of broader urban strategies for revitalising historical centres, revalorising cultural heritage and creating work opportunities as well as resources for tourism and business

C. Dinardi (✉)
Institute for Creative and Cultural Entrepreneurship (ICCE),
Goldsmiths, University of London, London, UK
e-mail: c.dinardi@gold.ac.uk

© The Author(s) 2019
R. Gill et al. (eds.), *Creative Hubs in Question*, Dynamics of Virtual Work,
https://doi.org/10.1007/978-3-030-10653-9_16

investment. But in the light of the compelling, widespread evidence showing how many of these initiatives lead to gentrification, do grassroots creative hubs constitute a feasible alternative to such neoliberal outcomes? Can the materiality of these urban artefacts provide a solution to the often-transient nature of ephemeral cultural urbanism with its pop-up cafes and seasonal festivals?

Refurbishing old industrial factories and warehouses for cultural use and creative production has been the subject of much investigation since the 1980s–1990s, mainly through the study of culture-led urban regeneration and gentrification (Zukin 1989; Montgomery 1995; Evans and Shaw 2004; Mommaas 2004; Pratt 2009), and more recently, creative industry clusters and districts (Evans 2009; Zukin and Braslow 2011; O'Connor and Gu 2014). These studies have pointed out the variety of problems related to the conversion of industrial structures into cultural venues: some refer to existing issues with the organisation, management and long-term sustainability of the converted sites; others shed light on the policy uses (and abuses) of these cultural projects that, more often than not, function as an instrument for real-estate development, producing further social displacement.

Drawing on insights from urban sociology and critical geography, the chapter conducts a case-study analysis of two cultural and creative economy factories in Latin America: *Fábrica Bhering* in Rio de Janeiro, Brazil, and *IMPA, la Fábrica Cultural* in Buenos Aires, Argentina. The chapter is comprised of three sections: the first discusses whether recovered industrial factories can be thought of as creative hubs in relation to ephemeral cultural urbanism; the second examines the two case studies in the context of Brazil and Argentina; and the third offers concluding remarks. Overall, the chapter contributes a Latin American perspective on culture-led urban regeneration to the study of creative hubs. Particularly, grassroots creative initiatives of urban renewal are presented as an alternative to the exclusionary gentrification processes to which creative hubs and other territorial forms of creativity are often related to, in times largely shaped by neoliberal operations driven by real-estate interests and alliances between political and economic urban elites.

Converted Factories as Creative Hubs?

Creative hubs can be approached and questioned on a number of levels: whether they have been planned or developed spontaneously; what their financial and management models are like; how creative labour is organised (including issues of class, gender and ethnicity); what their urban impact is; and how they relate to the wider socio-economic and political contexts in which they are immersed. What makes a site of cultural production or an arts centre a 'creative hub'? Are creative hubs to be defined by the activities taking place inside them, the agents who created them, or the outputs being produced (Virani and Malem 2015; Dovey et al. 2016)?

Hubs are centres of production and they are central to the making or functioning of things or activities. In its original meaning, the term hub was firstly used as an English dialect in the sixteenth century to refer to the 'hob', an antique version of modern cookers, that is, a heating device which, by the seventeenth century, had become the 'central part of a wheel' (Cresswell 2010, p. 215), an essential element of a machine. If creative hubs can be related to the idea of the city as a machine, what urban political economists might term a 'growth machine' (Molotoch 1976), we can expect to find both urban development and investment in and through the creative hubs/creative economy, as well as tensions with local residents, who might be left out from such urban processes and might oppose new uses of spaces or buildings. We will see that both converted factories, Bhering and IMPA, are constitutive parts of their cities' creative economies, providing labour force, goods, services and infrastructures, and function as 'hubs'—in the form of networks and events—within particular local cultural circuits. Equally they are contested and contestatory spaces. As a Bhering artist protested, the factory wasn't a 'cultural centre' in his view, but rather, a commercial space that was becoming increasingly market-driven by attracting a larger number of mainstream events.

Another important question relates to the changing nature and the temporality of the creative hub. Ontologically, these spaces are often 'in the process of becoming', and their material future tends to be uncertain in view of the usual lack of funding or policy support. Becoming a 'creative hub' can seem the result of a branding operation or—an equally marketable—policy strategy to orient or attract funding and investment. *When* does a venue become a hub? Does time matter in defining creative hubs? The rise of ephemeral urbanism, with its pop-up and recycled uses of buildings and spaces, gives us a sense of the larger scale on which these urban processes operate, reminding us that nothing is permanent, and constant change is the norm. Non-permanence, openness, adaptation and flexibility define the ephemeral landscapes of the new urban condition (Mehrotra et al. 2016)—a post-industrial condition that involves temporary interventions that reinvent the city, such as short-lived activities, i.e. festivals, tents and markets, informal events and one-off urban design initiatives that seem to characterise also the nature of some creative hubs. Although the materiality of large factories such as Bhering or IMPA embeds hubs in fixed space and, one might say, anchors them in a temporal dimension where history is not to be forgotten thanks to the presence of their industrial architecture, the factory's functions, aesthetics, uses and users inevitably change with time. In doing so, they create an opportunity to engage with its past in creative ways, or surrender it to oblivion.

For instance, in 'How to build a creative hub' Strauss (2010) identifies a number of factors that allegedly lead to the success of the hubs: the right fit, defined as being able to select who participates; good facilities provision—Internet, meeting spaces, kitchen, cafes and restaurants; the ability to build partnerships across members; communal working with social spaces; and affordable rents. Strikingly, this account makes no reference to the history of the area where the hubs are located, the previous and current uses of the building in question, the existing population and activities in the surrounding area, and the relation between the hubs and the wider policy context of support (or lack thereof) for the creative economy.

In short, creative hubs show how a particular type of labour gets organised in post-industrial societies and reveal the spatiality that the new economy creates. If the creative city was to be interpreted as the new style of urbanisation generated by a post-fordist economic order (Scott 2006), what do cultural spaces such as Bhering or IMPA reveal about the state of the cultural and the creative economy in Latin America and beyond? Apart from giving us clues about the governance of the cultural sector and the complex relationship between state and civil society, they reflect the decay and abandonment produced by the failure of (national policies in support of) manufacturing economies, as well as global economy shifts towards post-industrialisation. Furthermore, they allow us to observe how at the grassroots level that void is filled by spontaneous, bottom-up experiences that resort to creativity to generate jobs and workspaces. Some cases of planned creative hubs, in contrast, might reveal a type of fast-food policy where quick, easy and already processed recipes are sought to revitalise neighbourhoods by invoking culture as a panacea, that is, a universal magic cure to all urban illnesses (Dinardi 2015).

In the Latin American context, the institutional field of the creative economy is developing rapidly. Creative hubs have been understood as '*polos creativos*' (in Spanish) or '*distritos criativos*' (in Portuguese) and in the last decade they have been at the centre of public policy initiatives aimed at local economic development through an agglomeration of creative activities, tax incentives and targeted training, particularly in deprived city areas. At the same time, grassroots creative hubs have existed for long, without using the 'creative hub' label, as self-managed (*autogestionados*) or community-run cultural centres, with collaborative learning, informal networks and shared spaces for cultural production. Despite the central importance of the creative economy for the region, its contribution to employment and national economies remains, to a large extent, invisible to official measurements and the general public (Buitrago and Duque 2013).

In the case of Brazil, creative hubs can be interpreted within the so-called entrepreneurialisation of society, where policy discourses and public investment at various governmental levels have praised, since 2000s, technology-based start-up urbanism as a catalyst for local economic development and urban regeneration through neoliberal and neo-developmentalist approaches (Rossi and Di Bella 2017). Rio de Janeiro, in particular, has pioneered the production of data about the creative sector, publishing creative industry mapping documents back in 2008 (by FIRJAN, the Federation of Rio de Janeiro State Industries), and launching new specialised governmental bodies, such as the Rio Criativo Incubation Agency. The internationalisation of Rio with the hosting of mega-events (World Cup in 2014 and the Olympic Games in 2016) created a narrative of a city of events, which in turn rendered it the main beneficiary of Brazil's public initiative for creative start-ups, supported by a range of actors, institutions and interests, including banks, businesses, universities, media and NGOs (Rossi and Di Bella 2017).

Brazil's current meltdown, seen in the controversial removal of democratically elected President Dilma Rousseff by Congress members and the recent political corruption scandals and detentions of public servants, created a context of deep uncertainty, social unrest and anxiety over the future, particularly in the light of Rio de Janeiro's high levels of unemployment, social deprivation, increasing levels of violence, public funding cuts and the military control of the city, which inescapably disrupts and complicates the prospects of cultural initiatives and policies.

In the case of Argentina, a relatively similar creative industry institutional scenario has been developing, with the early creation of: the Metropolitan Design Centre (CMD) in Buenos Aires in 2001, the subsequent Creative Industries General Direction, official observatories and laboratories, the Creative Economy National Secretary and the launch of the specialised market for Argentina's creative industries (MICA), running since 2011, which has recently acquired a regional dimension with MICSUR (the creative industries market of MERCOSUR's countries). The creative districts policy at the city government level, now under the orbit of the Ministry of Modernisation, Innovation and Technology, epitomises the current (Mauricio Macri) administration's market-oriented approach towards the creative sector. This has been translated into the promotion and organisation of creative activities into geographical clusters, through the creation of five creative districts (audio-visual, technological, arts, design and sports) in the city's Northern and Southern neighbourhoods. In turn, these function as key marketing tools for urban and economic development in a national context shaped by the shrinking of the state and public spending, as well as a *tarifazo* policy (increase in basic utility fares) with negative consequences for the economically worse-off, expressing some of the contradictions of the allure of the creative economy.

Case Studies from Two Latin American Cities

Fábrica Bhering, Rio de Janeiro, Brazil

Originally a chocolate and sweets factory, Fábrica Bhering, has become one of the largest centres for arts production and creative economy in Rio de Janeiro, Brazil. Located in the neighbourhood of Santo Cristo in the city's port region, the factory provides in its 20,000 sq. metres workspace to over 70 artists and 20 small creative enterprises across a range of fields—from sculpture, visual arts and photography, to video art, design, restoration and multimedia. There is also gallery space, a book publisher, a restaurant and a café, and factory space is available for cinema and television rental and for private events.

Built in 1934, Bhering used to employ over a thousand workers in the making of sweets until 2003, when it closed down due to major economic problems. The closure of the factory reflects a wider process of industrial decline that affected the city during the 1990s and profoundly transformed its central and port areas, which witnessed both deterioration and abandonment as well as redevelopment and renewal. As factory owner Rui Barreto stated in an interview, 'The history of Bhering is the very history of the development of the occupation of Rio de Janeiro'. The revitalisation of the area involved the refurbishment of old buildings and the construction of new structures, a retail boost and the development of cultural activities, venues and institutions that decentralised the concentration of cultural infrastructures in the Southern neighbourhoods (Fessler Vaz and Silveira 1994, p. 96).

In that context, the factory owners (the Barreto family) found in the arts market a solution to the problem of economic decline. They began to let factory spaces to artists who, from 2010, started to move into the building spontaneously through word of mouth. The Barreto family had a large tax debt with the federal government, which led to a judicial auction in 2011, and an offer was made by a real-estate company which finally bought the building to the federal government. The factory owners contested the value at which the building was sold as well as the judicial auction, since they claimed they were paying back their debt. The artists-tenants, unaware of the auction, received eviction notices to leave the factory within thirty days, which they resisted by organising an online campaign to save what had become an 'arts factory'. The judge who authorised the judicial auction has been investigated in view of various irregularities in the process (Figs. 16.1 and 16.2).

Surprisingly, the municipal government announced the potential expropriation of the building in 2012 by issuing an official decree which declared it part of the city's heritage in view of its architectural value and importance for the urban landscape. Rio de Janeiro's former Mayor (2009–2017), Eduardo Paes, expressed his support in his twitter account to the fifty artists who were then occupying Bhering:

Fig. 16.1 Bhering factory

Fig. 16.2   Bhering factory 2

The eviction of various art spaces in the old Bhering Factory in the port area makes no sense, even considering the small amount for which the building was taken to auction. We will act to stop this nonsense. It is precisely that function that we want the area to perform (Paes 30 July 2012) [*original in Portuguese, author's translation*]

This is not a casual statement of support. Santo Cristo, adjacent to the Gamboa, Saúde and Caju districts in the central area of Rio de Janeiro, is part of what is termed the city's port region, which has undergone dramatic transformation since 2009 for the hosting of the 2016 Olympic Games. The municipal government's large urban operation,

Porto Maravilha (Wonderful Port), sought to revitalise Rio's decayed port region and boost its economic development through high-impact interventions in public space, transport, urban infrastructure, culture and heritage, and property development (mostly for commercial, residential and institutional use). In terms of cultural development, initiatives included the (re)development of cultural infrastructure (Museu de Arte do Rio de Janeiro, and Museu do Amanhã by star-architect Santiago Calatrava), restoration of heritage buildings, and a series of events, festivals and entrepreneurial activities. In this context, it becomes clear why the by then Mayor would support an initiative like Bhering's.

However, Porto Maravilha has been planned in line with an ideal city of spectacles created for urban branding and mediatised cultural consumption (Jaguaribe 2011). The urban renovation project, following a neoliberal entrepreneurial logic, has used public funds mainly to benefit private investors and landowners (Diniz 2014). It has also shown a lack of attention and consideration towards local residents, who have attempted to resist forced evictions and new uses of space through community mobilisation in view of the absence of adequate official mechanisms to mitigate a gentrification process in the port area (Carlos 2010) (Fig. 16.3).

Far from being an invisible underground initiative, Bhering is today one of the city's main creative hubs and appears listed on Mapa de Cultura, a state government's online platform, as well in the Time Out magazine. It is also one of the venues of the popular Rio Design Week and Art Rio festival. It is interesting to consider the relationship between Bhering artists and the local authorities. Advised by the later, the artists created a civil association and successfully applied for government funding (Porto Maravilha Cultural awards) to develop a one-off event aimed at getting closer to local residents by offering free workshops, activities and training. In this way, the factory functions indirectly as an intermediary between the local residents and the newly transformed port area, raising the question of artists'—and creative hubs'—unintentional complicity in gentrification processes. This is an issue that emerged in my conversations with Bhering artists—the difficult position in which they find themselves, being aware of, on the one hand, their powerful role in nurturing an officially promoted

Fig. 16.3 View of the urban surroundings from factory Bhering's terrace

arts-infused urban brand, and on the other, of how this can pave the way for a rise in house prices, eventually leading to changes in the aesthetic and social composition of the local neighbourhood.

IMPA Ciudad Cultural, Buenos Aires, Argentina

IMPA cultural factory was born out of Argentina's 2001 profound political, economic, social and institutional crises. The implementation of a series of neoliberal policies oriented towards a 'free', de-regulated market and major structural adjustments, particularly during the 1990s, created a context of economic instability with substantial foreign debt, the privatisation of key public services, spending cuts, long recession and increasing social exclusion with high unemployment rates and incessant strikes. In such a context, the devaluation of the national currency in a highly dollarised economy and the governmental restriction to access and withdraw personal savings in banks sparked social protests across the country, including riots and supermarket looting. Pot-banging protests took to the streets demanding to 'throw all politicians out!' and ended in the resignation of former President De La Rúa.

In the aftermath of these crises, the country witnessed the return of barter clubs and alternative currencies, the emergence of new political actors such as picket organisations and neighbourhood-based public assemblies and an emergence of the *fábricas recuperadas* (recovered factories) phenomenon, which included 170 factories between 2001 and 2003 (Micheletto 2003) and 480 nowadays (Rivas Molina 2016). IMPA was the first factory to be taken over and run by workers. Founded in 1910, it produced aluminium and plastic packaging in three industrial plants in Buenos Aires, however, only one persists today in the Almagro neighbourhood. In the 1940s, the company was nationalised and from 1961 run by a cooperative. During 1990s, widespread unemployment, labour precariousness and interrupted production led the factory administrators to declare bankruptcy due to a substantial debt. However, in 1998 the workers occupied the factory, managed to renegotiate the debt and started to work again, despite receiving little or no salary, through a self-managed cooperative (Fig. 16.4).

Fig. 16.4 IMPA's facade

Apart from producing aluminium packaging, a year later the factory started to produce cultural activities. An open cultural centre was created, IMPA Ciudad Cultural, and began to offer community workshops across different areas, ranging from popular music, theatre, puppetry and dance, to circus, capoeira, mask-making, tango and many more. There is also a theatre, a radio and a TV channel, a free health centre, a popular education college, an adults' school and a museum. In 2001, it was declared 'site of cultural interest' by the municipal government, which described it as the city's most creative and valuable experience, born out of the recent crisis (GCBA 2001). This declaration responded to the great visibility and pioneering role the factory gained in a context shaped by a deep economic crisis, by offering an innovative model of political organisation and cultural management at a grassroots level. However, this official recognition didn't crystallise in material support to the factory activities or its workers (Figs. 16.5 and 16.6).

Despite working at times with no light or electricity as a result of service-cuts, the factory cultural centre 'has managed to offer productions and expressions of great artistic quality, demonstrating that it is possible to produce valuable cultural facts without large budgets or logics ruled by commercial success' (Bokser 2010, p. 7). It runs on collaboration, voluntary work, financial contributions from workers and the self-management of technical equipment. A total of 180 people work at the factory, including 49 industrial workers, 50 cultural centre staff (teaching and administrative), 42 college teachers, 22 community radio and TV staff

Fig. 16.5   IMPA's aluminium production and cultural space

Fig. 16.6   IMPA's aluminium production and cultural space 2

and other co-op workers (Telam 2015). Bokser (2010) argues that it is precisely in the problems cultural and industrial workers face on a daily basis that bonds are strengthened among them and between them and the building. This, he notes, leads to the erasure of hierarchical distinctions between audiences, workers and artists, as each of them shares the common experience of being in a factory with very limited resources. In fact, 'notions of solidarity, mutuality, and voluntary altruism constitute prime rationales of non-profit activity' (Toepler 2003, p. 237).

After a few years of being occupied, IMPA became the target of legal disputes with the creditors. In 2005, the cultural centre and college closed down and in 2008 workers were evicted from the premises and protests were violently repressed by the police. Finally, after camping and resisting the eviction, the workers managed to occupy the factory and reopened the facilities. In 2015, the Senate passed a new law in favour of the workers and at present the IMPA cooperative awaits the definitive expropriation of the factory.

The factory workers' success in self-management led to the emergence of what has been termed the IMPA method, 'occupy, resist and produce', which has informed other social organisations' political struggles, cooperative efforts and squatting methods. Today many of the recovered factories in Argentina are experiencing harsh economic times due to the existing recession, the high increase in public utilities and the ongoing legal cases involving workers' eviction orders alongside a lack of official support to forms of self-managed industrial production.

Conclusion

This chapter has examined how derelict industrial infrastructures have been appropriated from the bottom-up and re-signified through cultural and artistic practices, leading to the emergence of 'grassroots creative hubs'. This final section reflects on the relations that constitute the everyday functioning of the hubs and provide some concluding remarks about their prospects for the future

The birth of grassroots creative hubs has been shown to be unplanned and spontaneous. We have seen that the occupation of Bhering factory was initiated by one individual visual artist who then invited her friends to join her; IMPA, in contrast, was taken over by a group of factory labourers who used to work in the premises and wanted to preserve their jobs in a context of tough economic crisis.

In terms of cultural content, we have seen that IMPA offers a diverse range of activities that could be grouped under the category of 'popular culture' in terms of their art forms, target audiences, accessible model and oppositional stance to mainstream culture and Bhering largely concentrates on the (more commercial) arts and the creative industries. While in IMPA a wide diversity of non-commercial cultural and arts activities unusually coexist in a factory setting with metallurgic workers, in Bhering artists pay rent to use the factory as workspace. IMPA attracts a mix of audiences that bring together adult students, party goers, artists, militants, local residents and members of other workers' movements and social organisations. Both Bhering and IMPA have established links with external organisations; being part of formal cultural circuits in the city helps the factories widen and diversify their audiences.

The recovered factories operate under different management and funding models. In the case of IMPA, funding is still an area of concern as workers rely on individual donations and run the cultural centre with whatever resources they manage to find. They applied for public funding without success, for not meeting the city government's safety and licensing requirements for cultural venues (Bokser 2010). Bhering artists, on the other hand, have been awarded municipal funding for a one-off initiative aimed at strengthening the relationship with local residents.

While Bhering artists have struggled to create a civil association during times of eviction threats, in IMPA cultural resistance and political contestation shape the cultural programme on offer. The potential of cultural activities to imagine more just societies through collaborative practices has been invoked by IMPA's cultural workers. In this sense, a decentralised and horizontal management of cultural activities as well an ad hoc planning and informal decision-making at IMPA allowed for cultural development based on experimentation and the creation of alternative spaces of socialisation, which widen social inclusion networks (De Felice 2007).

Considering the future prospects of creative hubs, there are different scenarios in each case. Because IMPA has pioneered the recovered factories movement in Argentina, it has accumulated several years of experience in conflict management, receiving support from other social movements and political organisations. Yet the definitive transfer of property ownership to the workers is still the object of legal processes and political struggles. Bhering, in contrast, is a fairly recent initiative and its early development reminds of traditional processes of artists-led urban regeneration contributing to gentrification, exemplified internationally in the familiar cycle of artist zones in London, Berlin, Toronto and New York (Evans and Shaw 2004, p. 17). Awareness of these processes, critical thinking and action, and a more fluid and continued relationship with the local communities might allow Bhering factory, now in its new role as a cultural institution, to be better integrated and rooted in the neighbourhood, moving away from contributing to gentrification-led interventions in a much-disputed area of Rio de Janeiro.

When researching creative hubs, how can we, as social scientists, shed light on a phenomenon that is increasingly becoming globalised, yet in the process not promote it as *the* organising mode of those working in the creative economy? McRobbie points to the need to generate greater debate about questions of method and radical reflection about the conduct of research in the field of creative labour studies, developing 'a new kind of post-industrial sociology with the university as hub' and with cross-sector knowledge-sharing and partnerships with creative workers (McRobbie 2016, p. 936). Perhaps an alternative way forward to assess creative hubs is the extent to which artists and other creative workers effectively and creatively engage with the local population, be that through collaboration or training opportunities, contributing to revitalise—rather than gentrify—the areas surrounding the hubs. Activities of public engagement and collaboration between artists, local residents and the city government might constitute a first step towards imagining forms of urban revitalisation without gentrification, where the benefits of urban renewal remain in the existing communities rather than going to real-estate developers. What is the role of the academy in this process? How can we, as academics, contribute to analyse and perhaps articulate such process of collaborative public planning?

We have seen that urban creativity interventions constitute an open-ended process with an uncertain future. Several factors currently threaten the development of grassroots creative hubs, namely, lack of resources, unpaid voluntary work, eviction threats, safety issues, limited technical infrastructure and increasing commercialisation. This signals an area where cultural policy action is needed by providing financial and legal support as well as a platform for experimentation in participatory policy design. The challenge for policy lies in going beyond a rhetorical call for participation to actually provide artists and other creative practitioners greater voice and influence over the decisions that affect their lives (Jenkins 2014, p. 271), and in so doing, contribute to enhance the sustainability and functioning of creative hubs.

Acknowledgements The author would like to thank the Urban Studies Foundation for funding the research upon which this paper is based during a postdoctoral fellowship (2013–2016) at City University London.

References

Bokser, J. (2010, November 19–20). *Tensiones de la autogestión cultural: el Centro Cultural de IMPA*. Conference Paper Presented at the II Jornadas Internacionales de Problemas Latinoamericanos, Universidad Nacional de Córdoba. Available at http://fisyp.org.ar/media/uploads/autogestion.pdf#page=5. Accessed 20 May 2016.

Buitrago, F., & Duque, I. (2013). *La economía naranja: Una oportunidad infinita*. New York: Banco Interamericano de Desarrollo.

Carlos, C. A. S. L. (2010). Um Olhar Crítico sobre a Zona Portuária da Cidade do Rio de Janeiro. *Bitacora, 17*(2), 23–54.

Cresswell, J. (Ed.). (2010). Hub. In *Oxford dictionary of word origins* (p. 215). New York: Oxford University Press.

De Felice, A. (2007). La fábrica cultural, otra forma de producción simbólica. *Reflexión Académica en Diseño y Comunicación, 8*(8), 85–94.

Dinardi, C. (2015). Unsettling the role of culture as panacea: The politics of culture-led urban regeneration in Buenos Aires. *City, Culture & Society, 6*(2), 9–18.

Diniz, N. (2014). *Porto Maravilha: antecedentes e perspectivas da revitalização da região portuária do Rio de Janeiro.* Rio de Janeiro: Editora Letra Capital.

Dovey, J., Pratt, A., Lansdowne, J., Moreton, S., Merkel, J., & Virani, T. E. (2016). *Creative hubs: Understanding the new economy.* London: British Council.

Evans, G. (2009). Creative cities, creative spaces and urban policy. *Urban Studies, 46*(5/6), 1003–1040.

Evans, G., & Shaw, P. (2004). *The contribution of culture to regeneration in the UK: A report to the DCMS.* London: London Met.

Fessler Vaz, L., & Silveira, C. B. (1994). A Área Central do Rio de Janeiro. *Cadernos IPPUR/UFRJ, Aeo VIII*(2/3), 95–105.

Gobierno de la Ciudad de Buenos Aires (GCBA). (2001). *Sitios de Interés Cultural.* Available at http://www.buenosaires.gob.ar/areas/cultura/cpphc/sitios/?menu_id=14928. Accessed 15 May 2014.

Jaguaribe, B. (2011). Imaginando a "cidade maravilhosa": modernidade, espetáculo e espaços urbanos. *Revista FAMECOS, 18*(2), 327–347.

Jenkins, H. (2014). Rethinking 'rethinking convergence/culture'. *Cultural Studies, 28*(2), 267–297.

McRobbie, A. (2016). Towards a sociology of fashion micro-enterprises: Methods for creative economy research. *Sociology, 50*(5), 934–948.

Mehrotra, R., Vera, F., & Mayoral, J. (2016). *Ephemeral urbanism: Cities in constant flux.* Venice Biennale Exhibition. Video presentation available at https://www.youtube.com/watch?v=vzEcVEFdIHs. Accessed 12 September 2017.

Micheletto, K. (2003, December 20). Rescate a puro candombe. *Pagina 12.* Available at http://www.pagina12.com.ar/diario/espectaculos/6-29498-2003-12-20.html. Accessed 15 May 2014.

Molotch, H. (1976). The city as a growth machine: Toward a political economy of place. *American Journal of Sociology, 82*(2), 309–332.

Mommaas, H. (2004). Cultural clusters and the post-industrial city: Towards the remapping of urban cultural policy. *Urban Studies, 41*(3), 507–532.

Montgomery, J. (1995). The story of temple bar: Creating Dublin's cultural quarter. *Planning Practice & Research, 10*(2), 135–172.

O'Connor, J., & Gu, X. (2014). Creative industry clusters in Shanghai: A success story? *International Journal of Cultural Policy, 20*(1), 1–20.

Pratt, A. C. (2009). Urban regeneration: From the arts 'feel good' factor to the cultural economy: A case study of Hoxton, London. *Urban Studies, 46*(5–6), 1041–1061.

Rivas Molina, F. (2016, December 16). Miles de obreros tomaron sus fábricas en 2001, la mayoría aún resiste. *Diario El País*. Available at https://elpais.com/internacional/2016/12/14/argentina/1481679343_026699.html. Accessed 12 September 2017.

Rossi, U., & Di Bella, A. (2017). Start-up urbanism: New York, Rio de Janeiro and the global urbanization of technology-based economies. *Environment and Planning A, 49*(5), 999–1018.

Scott, A. (2006). Creative cities: Conceptual issues and policy questions. *Journal of Urban Affairs, 28*(1), 1–17.

Strauss, W. (2010). How to build a creative hub. *Broadcast*, p. 24.

Telam. (2015, December 4). Exproprian el IMPA y la ceden a la cooperativa que la maneja desde 1998. *Telam*. Available at http://www.telam.com.ar/notas/201512/129083-expropiacion-impa-cooperativa.php. Accessed 12 September 2017.

Toepler, S. (2003). Grassroots associations versus larger nonprofits: New evidence from a community case study in arts and culture. *Nonprofit and Voluntary Sector Quarterly, 32*(2), 236–251.

Virani, T. E., & Malem, W. (2015). *Re-articulating the creative hub concept as a model for business support in the local creative economy: The case of Mare Street in Hackney* (Creativeworks London Working Paper Series).

Zukin, S. (1989). *Loft living: Culture and capital in urban change*. New Brunswick, NJ: Rutgers University Press.

Zukin, S., & Braslow, L. (2011). The life cycle of New York's creative districts: Reflections on the unanticipated consequences of unplanned cultural zones. *City, Culture and Society, 2*(3), 131–140.

17

Creative Hubs and the Night-Time Economy: Convergent or Divergent?

Andy C. Pratt and Tom Gill

Introduction

In recent years, the night-time economy (NTE) has become 'a thing' for the policy community. Of course, there have always been economic activities happening at night but seldom have policy makers previously made them the focus of attention, preferring to leave them metaphorically, and actually, 'in the dark'. The NTE carries with it the strong overtones of a moral economy: one that is concerned with, on the one hand, transgression and liminality; and on the other hand, with control and order. Policy makers have 'woken up' to the notion of the 24-hour city and its potential opportunities, and the fact that previously urban governance has meant by default 'daytime governance'. The popular action that has followed both plays to a promotional audience, as well as to the aspiration of effective control of the NTE, is the appointment of

A. C. Pratt (✉) · T. Gill
Department of Sociology, City, University of London, London, UK
e-mail: andy.pratt.1@city.ac.uk

© The Author(s) 2019
R. Gill et al. (eds.), *Creative Hubs in Question*, Dynamics of Virtual Work,
https://doi.org/10.1007/978-3-030-10653-9_17

a Night Czar/Mayor.[1] The aim of this chapter is to examine what we can learn about the NTE and creative hubs; specifically if, on the one hand, the notion of the NTE as used by many urban policy makers and scholars, actually corresponds more closely with the idea of a hub. On the other hand, we suggest that the unique focus of the NTE (or hub) exposes a 'one-sided' weakness in most conceptions of an urban creative field that ignores the diurnal process: most studies assume an exclusive framework of the 'daytime economy' (DTE).

The normative term NTE is concerned with entertainment activities, primarily conceived of as cultural consumption. So the NTE is the creative economy (or one part of it), just as the normative discussion about creative hubs is primarily the DTE. Hence, the notion slots into the policy field without a problem. However, one of the themes of this chapter is to explore how these two fields have failed to merge and overlap. For the most part, the actually existing governance has been twofold: bringing together a diverse set of groups or stakeholders for which a forum does not already exist and to deal with the 'externalities' of the NTE. Whilst it may have some similarities with the cultural economy, the NTE occupies a separate conceptual and policy space. This chapter seeks to bridge these debates about NTE and creative hubs more closely together, arguably to their mutual benefit.

Wandering the streets of Soho, the vibrancy and importance of the NTE are apparent as people spill on to the street enjoying a night out drinking, visiting clubs, theatres and restaurants. If the creative economy is viewed more generally as a Cinderella industrial sector, the same holds true, but more strongly, for the NTE, it has commonly be dismissed as economically relatively insignificant: in fact, it is estimated that 1 in 8 jobs in London are supported by the NTE (London First 2017). If you are still on the streets at dawn, the picture is not so pleasant; especially if you happen to live there, the noise of the night and the detritus left behind by its revellers has to be cleared up (with more

---

[1] The notion of a Mayor for the night, or a Night Mayor, suffers linguistically in pronunciation as it sounds too much like 'nightmare': clearly not a message that a city government wants to communicate, hence the use of 'Czar'. Recent converts to the Night Czar model are the cities of London, Amsterdam, Hamburg, Paris, Berlin and Zurich.

noise): for the most part, discussion of the NTE has concerned itself with issues of policing, licensing laws and the coordination of street cleansing. As will be discussed below in the case study of London's Soho, NTEs also have a daytime face: in the case of Soho, it is one of the premier creative hubs in the world, which includes digital animation, film producing and advertising hubs. Aside from the studios and editing rooms, the high price of a Soho location is all about networking and restaurants. Private clubs and bars, and related activities are the sites that constitute a significant part of the NTE. Otherwise, places like Soho can seem as if their day and night activities are part of quite separate domains. A key insight gleaned from research about the cultural industries is the internal relationship of the whole production chain: through production and to consumption. There is an apparent flaw in NTE strategies if these companion components are ignored and likewise, if the NTE components are not considered in discussions of creative hubs.

Beside from a ritualistic statement of the economic value of the NTE, most policy actions concentrate not on the economy, but on the social externalities (noise, alcohol consumption, prostitution, public disorder and street cleaning).[2] The notable exception is transportation; in London's case, this has concerned the night bus network and more recently (2016) the night tube. Whilst these transport initiatives might be seen as ways for NTE consumers to get home, arguably the most important element is getting the workers home (TUC 2015). This encapsulates the challenge of the NTE: the city has been built to serve a DTE, primarily operating between 9–5. Changes in UK trading legislation to allow Sunday opening, and relaxed pub-opening hours, have been a harbinger of a more significant demands on workers in all areas of the economy. Unions have noted concerns about workers in the NTE, just as they did about Sunday trading and as they have always

---

[2]Interestingly, the other moral concern, gambling, rarely overlaps, although logically it should be included. Regulatory policies have been directed to the strict spatial control/institutional of gambling activities. In the UK, the debates about the NTE and gambling have seldom overlapped as a result of legal codes. In contrast, in Australia casinos have been used as the anchor of urban regeneration Michael Hall, C., & Hamon, C. (1996). Casinos and urban redevelopment in Australia. *Journal of Travel Research, 34*(3), 30–36.

done back to the struggle over the length of the working day. One concern is about workers being able to get home safely (as well as to get consumers to activities) (TUC 2015). A transport infrastructure that serves the night is a prerequisite to a functioning NTE. It is interesting that these debates about the NTE are almost a mirror image of debates about the creative economy and creative hubs. Hence, this chapter poses the question: can we learn from both debates, and finally, can we explore a more holistic position encompassing the whole 24 hours?

The aim of this chapter is to explore the idea of the NTE, clustering and hubs. We begin with a definition of the NTE and its relationship to the creative economy (and hubs). Next, though a case study of London's Soho, the emergent practices and complexities of a particular hub are elaborated. We then make an exemplary case for NTE Hubs, and the following section reflects upon what we might learn in relation to 'day-time economy' hubs; moreover, what is the relationship between the two? Finally, the paper argues that it could be helpful to add the dimension of the diurnal practices of hubs to understand how hubs operate more adequately.

The Night-Time Economy

In this section, we will explore what is meant by the NTE. The NTE has seldom had a core position in urban or cultural policy, aside from it being a supporting minor concern for tourism. The NTE has clearly suffered from the normative moral judgement that it was, if not 'bad', then better not discussed at all. The focus of interest by urban policy makers and academics has clearly changed rapidly over the last 25 years, and this moral viewpoint has shifted, so much so that the NTE is now advertised as one of the city's attractions. However, as will be outlined below, this is a conditional acceptance, and one heavily skewed to control and safety. Moreover, a related and critical issue for this chapter is both the changing conceptions of the NTE and the practical metrics of its activity that are available to, and used by, the policy community.

Initial debates of the NTE were a response to the changing use of time by the population: more flexible working hours, retail opening hours and the relaxation of licensing laws. These changes co-evolved; as more people broke out of 9–5 patterns of activity, it created more demand for similar service provision and the servicing of leisure time. The initial interest was in the phenomenon of the patterns of collective night-time socialising and related entertainment which have always existed, but were delimited by closing times (Bianchini 1995; Hannigan 1998; O'Connor and Wynne 1998). To an extent, this process was a continuation of social trends that have given life to the cultural economy more generally: the increased length in participation in education and the rise in disposable income notably by the youth that has occurred since the 1960s (Smith 2014). This increase in activity and the extending spread of hours clearly began to exert new pressures on the city (Green 2001). At the same time, there was a discussion of the notion of a 24-hour city (Kreitzman 1999); whilst all-night cities exist, London, let alone provincial cities, was not even close to this.[3] However, the idea that infrastructure could be more efficiently used if the activities were spread over more hours, and that some of the social 'congestion' problems associated with pub 'closing time' might be mitigated, led to urban initiatives that sought to change drinker's attitudes to alcohol; what was felt was a more 'continental' pattern,[4] as opposed to binge drinking (Lovatt and O'Connor 1995; Roberts et al. 2006; Lovatt 2017). The physical 'opening up' of bars to be more like coffee shops was part of such a trend, as was the relaxation of licensing laws. As the shift in socialising continued to change policy-makers realised that the barrier to developing the process further was a transport system that only services 8, not 24-hour, activity patterns (for both workers and pleasure seekers).

The combination of these processes has led to the existence of, and institutional and infrastructural support for, a substantial NTE. On the one hand, it has become mainstream that the NTE was important for employment and earnings in the city, and hence, it needed to be looked after; on the other hand, the growth in night-time activities generated

---

[3]Cairo has been ranked the 'most 24-hour' of all cities, followed by Montevideo, Beirut, six Spanish cities (Malaga, Zaragoza, Madrid, Barcelona, Valencia and Seville) and Buenos Aires. London was ranked 17th. Sood, S. (2012). The cities that never sleep, *BBC*.

[4]At a time when European and Continental were viewed as positive and aspirational attributes.

more social disturbance. The latter highlighted the stress on policing, health workers and sanitation services that previously did not have such night-time pressures. As we have noted below, the new (governance) concern was to create a coordinated approach to managing this (Roberts and Eldridge 2012). Less attention has been paid to the economic governance, aside from providing a positive counter to the costs of 'clearing up' afterwards (Hadfield and Davis 2015).

Analytically, it is a real challenge to measure the NTE. Only by using a very strict definition has the case been made. However, it has also created some problems. There is no official or commercial data collected and divided along lines of day and night activity. The statistics that have been used are drawn from one source, the Trends Business Research (TBR) Night Mix Index (NMI), which is based on commercial private business data provided by Dun and Bradstreet, and classified by TBR. Specifically, the data refer to the evening and night-time economy (ENTE): the core is 'a business activity that provides a direct leisure related service to a member of the public and its main activity and its service profile must be mainly evening or night time related'; the non-core 'will not include businesses that in fact mainly depend on any form of daytime trade', so, for example, TBR put overnight accommodation in non-core as most of its activity is daytime, likewise retailing (except liquor retailing).

It is interesting that the technical definition of the E/NTE does not mention definitions of the creative industries (CI), which have been extant for more or less the same period (DCMS 1998). There are clearly strategic differences in the objectives of policy makers in this decision, on how to best make their point. The definers of the E/NTE clearly want to include not just the related activities, but associated ones too. The critical differences in definitions are that the focus begins with production, and definitions have developed to track the whole production chain from ideation to consumption, implicitly including the 'core' E/NTE. The CI definitions have not included police, social and sanitary services that the E/NTE definition has chosen to include. The important point here is that E/NTE definitions have been developed with a specific objective in mind: to separate out the costs and benefits of the immediate activities. The NTE works with a limited notion of consumption (that ignores production for the most part). The CI definitions began with a likewise limited basis (direct production activities), but developed using an industrial logic to encompass the production chain (including the social and economic aspects). As we note elsewhere in this collection, research and policy about creative hubs generally work with such a wider, inclusive, definition. Accordingly, it is difficult to marry up the concerns of the NTE and creative hubs, as the very economic or social linkages (or spillovers) would demonstrate the connection and interaction of excluded from the conventional NTE definition. In the overview of the NTE in London's Soho, we point to the rich codependency of activities between the creative hub and the NTE.

Soho: Hubs, the DTE and NTE

Soho in London is one of the obvious examples that come to mind when the NTE is mentioned. Like many, but not all, NTE hubs, Soho has a long history; this marks it and shapes it in particular ways that are different to 'de novo' NTE places. Located in central London, Soho lies between Bloomsbury in the North, St James in the South, Mayfair in the West and Covent Garden in the East; it is bounded by more or less a triangle described by Oxford Circus, Piccadilly and Tottenham Court Road Tube stations. As with many NTE places where they are *not*, or what they are adjacent to, can be important in their success. Soho has been shaped by its location and its liminality in both spatial and social terms.

The area has an historic building stock dating from the eighteenth and nineteenth centuries, and for much of the twentieth century, it was in poor condition. Not surprisingly, it became a popular location for migrants from wars, expulsions and famine. The twentieth century saw significant communities of French, Italians, Eastern European Jews and Chinese established (in that order); these communities established both restaurants and retail establishments which gave the area a cosmopolitan character and added to which in the post-World War II period many ex-service people lived in the area due to the low rents and central location. In the 1950s, Soho gained a particular reputation for drunkenness, art and sex (and not necessarily confined to the night hours). Artists such as Francis Bacon and his circle, and the many others were closely linked through the regular use of the Colony Room (Richardson 2000). The Colony Room Club, managed by Muriel Belcher, lasted nearly 50 years and had a licence running from 3 to 11 pm, bridging the extant licensing laws and allowing clientele to decant to the neighbouring Gargoyle club when it opened. It was a drinking hole for what became major British artistic talent of the period all the way through to 'Young British Artists' such as Tracey Emin and Damien Hirst (Speiser 2017).

As with many cities, the location adjacent to the formal districts of the City has always made a popular site for entertainment (see Pratt 2009). In Soho's case, the area has a long history of prostitution, private clubs and bars, and later sex shops. Much of this activity operated at the edge of legality and to which the police formerly operated an uncomfortable coexistence. Up to 1968,[5] Victorian laws regarding the theatre were sidestepped by the Windmill Theatre by performing 'Tableaux vivant'.[6] However, 'membership clubs' had always had a different legal position—an opportunity famously exploited by the Raymond Review Bar from the early 1960s onwards (the Raymond Review Bar eventually took over the Windmill).

In the mid-1970s, as a result of both community pressure and wider political moral imperatives, a high-profile series of steps were undertaken by the police and regulators which was presented as a clampdown and led to the 'red light' district being formalised (i.e. shops and clubs were brought within legal control and regulation), and more closely monitored and prosecuted (Summers 1989). A legacy of this period is the domination of land ownership by former club owners such as 'Raymond Review Bar', who would as a result of the property boom in the 1980s onward be 'gifted' an alternative business model (based on the property market).

---

[5]The Theatres Act, 1968.

[6]A technicality of the law at the time was that nudity was permitted as long as there was no movement: hence the inventive living nude statues.

Within this, more or less, square mile has developed a burgeoning economy catering (in Old Compton Street in particular) to the LGBTQ community. Soho's once hidden, illegal,[7] and persecuted gay scene took on a new official identity (Avery and Graham 2016), when even 'Visit Britain' listed it as a key attraction (Houlbrook 2006). More generally, many bars and restaurants, and a significant number of private clubs (often frequented by those in the entertainment industries), formed a substantial NTE often lionised as an example of the power of the 'pink pound' (Hicklin 2012).[8] Moreover, there has been a dawning recognition of the cultural and social benefits of a diverse and inclusive nightlife. Talbot (2004, 2016; Talbot and Böse 2007), in a comprehensive review of the multiple social exclusions of the NTE, refers to this as the 'mainstreaming of subcultural expression at night'. However, there exist parallel concerns that 'mainstreaming' could lead to the 'whitewashing' of diversity (Gill 2016), and that the economic 'successes' of Soho may threaten to force out the very communities that create the diversity that is apparently valued.

Clearly, such a densely concentrated locale that has 'everything' also has its negative sides: due to both the informal and illegality of some activities, as well as the 'normal' spillovers associated with over-consumption of alcohol (noise, violence, rubbish and general public nuisance). In a series of papers, Roberts (2015; Roberts and Turner 2005; Roberts and Eldridge 2012) has comprehensively detailed these issues. Recently, an alliance of stakeholders has emerged, which was eventually been corralled by the Greater London Authority in 2017 under the auspices of the 'London Night Time Commission', and a 'Night Czar' was appointed, that seeks to coordinate and mediate between these diverse activities in Soho and other areas (Association 2016; Greater London Authority 2017; London First 2017). However, despite the economic headlines '11,000 pubs, bars, restaurants and nightclubs employ more than 200,000 people and contribute around £5 Bn to London's economy each

---

[7]The 1967 Sexual Offences act decriminalised homosexuality.

[8]A sobering reminder of the hate crimes against the LGBTQ community was the 1999 nail-bombing of the Admiral Duncan Pub in Old Compton Street which left 3 dead and 80 or more injured.

year' (Greater London Authority 2017), the actual focus is firmly on regulation, control and mitigation of public nuisance (and an inclusion agenda).[9] Similar moves have taken place, with a comparable focus in many other world cities. In a newly planned and zoned city, many of these problems would not exist, but the historical development in Soho presents a complex picture of proximate and incompatible residents and land uses. Moreover, NTE initiatives are suggestive of the fact that cities have been planned and governed as if the NTE did not exist. Moreover, many of the institutions and regulations that policy makers and residents have to deal with were devised with 'industrial' activities in mind. Soho really presents us with an example of an extreme case, as the DTE is as, if not more, vibrant that the NTE, albeit in a different way; however, in this sense, it represents the cutting edge of challenges that will surely affect other NTE districts.

On the one hand, there are the residents of the area (there has traditionally been significant social housing in the area), and in the early 2000's up-market, 'loft developments' have attracted more residents (from higher socio-economic groups). This has not played out in the normal gentrification mode (Pratt 2018a) that of the exclusion of artists (who in this case are digital post-production companies, who are more able to pay the inflated rents) and/or poorer residents (who, in this case, are in protected social housing).[10] As has already been noted, London's Night Time Commission correctly identifies the nuisance to both rich and poor residential dwellers (which of course impacts on loss of value and amenity). However, on the other hand, there are the daytime users of Soho: most significant amongst them are the music, film and advertising industries. These residents have tended to be underrepresented, or missing, from debates. Soho's current mix of actives slowly emerged as a result of a long chain of developments in the cultural economy in the

---

[9]The London NTE policy covers all 'entertainment zones' in the city, whilst Soho is the dominant centre; efforts are being made to spread benefits more widely and to manage NTE zones in outer boroughs. Recently, there have been significant debates in Hackney. The chapter is only focused on Soho.

[10]In a recent twist, previous NTE centres in London, such as Shoreditch and Hackney, have attracted gentrifiers who are now petitioning the council to restrict night-time uses.

twentieth century: both in London, and in the world; emerging at the end of the century to be the definitive 'cultural hub' (Nachum and Keeble 2003), the development of Skiffle, and Rock and Roll in places like the '2is' club, and later at the Marquee, and jazz at Ronnie Scott's Club, made Soho a place where new trends we made; there quickly grew up a number of recording studios in the area and some of the most important musical instrument retailers (stocking the new electric guitars); co-located in Denmark Street was London's 'tin-pan' Alley where songwriters plied their trade, recording studios offer innovative facilities, and the music press had their headquarters (Burrows 2015).[11] There is clear evidence here of how in the early 1960s the nascent popular music industry relied upon a supportive 'industrial' ecosystem to develop.

The film industry had always had its UK head offices, editing and review suites in Wardour Street; however, it was the digitisation of film in the early 2000s that saw London emerged as a centre for film post-production work and special effects (Pratt et al. 2007; Pratt 2011). The digital film and TV post-production companies of Soho[12] joined together to finance the private construction of world-leading high-capacity broadband infrastructure to enable both inter-working within the district and a direct connection to Burbank, the technical core of the Los Angeles film industry. These are the high-value, high-cost elements of film, items that 'sell' a film (to its financial backers, as well as the audience) as much as the talent. Two world leaders in this field of special effects—The Mill and Framestore—were located in the same street of Soho. It is characteristic that in this the most digitally focused activity is also one where the values and qualities of an image are the difference between success and failure. In interviews, we heard from editor

---

[11]As Burrows' (2015) paper notes, Denmark Street is currently being redeveloped as part of the Tottenham Court Road underground station rebuilding. The area had declined from the Late 1990s and now looks set for 'museumification'.

[12]The regulatory changes in the television industry from the mid-1980s onward led to a boom in small independent production companies who became increasingly dominant source of UK TV output Darlow, M. (2004). *Independents struggle*. London: Quartet; Pratt, A. C., & Gornostaeva, G. (2009). The governance of innovation in the film and television industry: A case study of London, UK. In A. C. Pratt & P. Jeffcutt (Eds.), *Creativity, innovation and the cultural economy* (pp. 119–136). London: Routledge.

and producers who chose London to Los Angeles because you could 'walk across the street' to see a collaborator rather than drive across the city (typically, in Los Angeles the journey between Burbank and Santa Monica, which is a 25-mile trip, takes on average an hour each way). The, even in the 'digital world' (Pratt 2000), face-to-face meetings are critical in creative decision-making to resolve subtle and fine-drawn differences in the 'look and feel' of the media being produced: such micro-value judgements represent the gap between success and failure in these industries.

The advertising industry has also been a critically important neighbour for film and television (see Pratt 2006). In the 1960s, the 'creative revolution' leveraged by disposable income growth, and colour Sunday newspaper supplements and colour television as the new canvas on which the creative messages could be displayed. Creative advertising was developed by companies such as DBB[13] to use creative skills of writing, sound and images to sell via an emotional engagement of consumers, not to simply compete on price. It was very successful and the production budgets were huge, which allowed innovative experimentation. In Soho, this was both a platform and a calling card, for many who went on to work in film and TV (e.g. David Putnam, Alan Parker and Ridley Scott[14]).

The cross-pollination of talent, technologies and ideas backed by significant investment pushed Soho to the cutting edge of the relevant creative fields. Arguably, it is the combination of production and consumption, as well as the mix of skills and artistic disciplines, and the sense of an insider 'community of practice' (Wenger 1998) that has underpinned the success of Soho. Co-location in Soho made it easier for career 'hops' between employers, but the existence of an overlapping

---

[13]In 1959, DBB (Doyle Dane Bernbach) delivered a seminal change in advertising focusing on image and desire, not information, for the Volkswagen Beetle in the USA: see the 'Think Small' campaign Fox, S. R. (1984). *The mirror makers: A history of American advertising and its creators.* Champaign: University of Illinois Press. A memoir by the 'father of advertising', Ogilvy, D., & Horgan, P. (1963). *Confessions of an advertising man.* New York: Atheneum, was a million seller.

[14]Both originally worked for innovative UK creative advertising company CDP known for its bold surrealistic images; both went on to become film producers; Putnam eventually up running Columbia Studios in the USA.

creative community is more important. Within such a milieu, regular meeting and the sharing of cutting-edge ideas take place every day in pitches, professional meetings and over lunches. The emergent collective talent, technology and creative capacity of Soho, linked with a creative audience, have enabled it to secure a leading role across converging media fields. It is the audience that brings us back to the NTE and the interface between it at the DTE.

Reflection on NTE Clusters and Hubs

The selective history of Soho presented above illustrates both the connections, and gaps, within and between the NTE and the DTE. Analytically, this might be more clearly stated as a connection between production and consumption of culture, a gap that has always been artificial and contingent upon particular technologies. Convergence of cultural forms, and the production and consumption of culture, constitutes a new field of scholarship—one that has long been visible, albeit not generally appreciated.

The notion of hubs has been used in a general manner by policy makers. The example of the NTE and hubs raises the question of how temporality and indeed spatial extent, as well as specifically which activities, are carried out there. The instrumental use of both the NTE and NTE hubs has been to designate and signpost a zone that enables a more efficient governance and policing. Moreover, it can also represent a rational means of 'protecting' the rest of the city from its moral challenges or simply separating it from the nuisance of noise and disturbance—a process that carries overtones of ghettoisation (Hannerz 1969). There has been considerably less discussion of the social and cultural practices supported and sustained in the NTE: they are important themes of sexuality and race that have only intersected with the NTE policy debate in a tangential manner. In most cases, the notion of a NTE hub is defined by cultural consumption. A step further from the norm is the relationship to cultural production that we can witness in Soho. A key point emerging from the review of Soho is that some NTEs are also significant DTE: that the DTE may be 'under-recognised, but moreover, that the relationship with the NTE and vice versa is overlooked. It is a logical next step to recognise that we should recognise the temporalities of all hubs, as well as the range of activities that support and sustain forms of social interaction.

The DTE of creative hubs was initially underpinned by reference to the cost-saving interactions of trust and proximity as with manufacturing. More recent research has been based on an understanding of the 'social infrastructure' of complex and fluid social and economic relations of creativity and its governance associated with a wider appreciation of the operation of the cultural economy. Within these debates, issues of scale, intermediation and 'intelligent' governance have come to the fore. Arguably, debates about the NTE have some way to go to escape the instrumental framing of the moral economy. Critically, for both the NTE and the DTE, there is the further issue of their interrelationships and interdependencies.

The case of music demonstrates the co-evolution of audiences and producers, and how experimental spaces 'break out' new styles and fashions. The participation of other producers at events generates lateral innovation, and the existence of an audience brings 'style leaders' and 'interpreters' (journalists) to the party. We can recognise these interactions in other cultural forms from fine art, to theatre and literature. However, the development of new technologies has regularly reconfigured the forms and practices deployed. This relationship had generally been explored (albeit partially) within the literature on scenes (Straw 2001) and sub-cultures (Hebdige 1979). However, the linkage to production has generally been outside the conceptual frame of such writing. The discussion of Soho demonstrates multiple interrelationships between the monolithic notions of production and consumption/day and night economies.

Both popular music and film, as with fashion, thrive on celebrity and the scene; this has two aspects. First, we can identify the staging and infrastructure of private members' clubs such as the Colony Club, Soho House and the Groucho that allows celebrities to distance themselves from their public. However, at the same time, this affords the 'paparazzi' a regular photo call when celebrities leave such venues looking 'tired and emotional'. The private members' club provides a setting that is only open to the initiates and insiders a prime site for the exchange of information about volatile markets, trends and techniques—who's 'up' and who's 'down', and which deals are to be made. In an industry character-ised by very strong competition and cooperation, comprised of multiple small producers, such an informal forum further increases the value of face-to-face interaction afforded by (but not reducible to) proximity.

Second, Soho is about display 'on the street' beyond the liminal 'doorstepping' by journalists. The spaces in and between bars, clubs and restaurants are places to see and to be seen. Whilst it had only a short-lived period, Carnaby Street constituted such a location in the mid-1960s (before moving westwards to the King's Road, and north-wards to Camden Market). In this case, the synergies between clothing and music, notably the mod and then hippy scene, were co-constitutive of fashion, music and place (Breward and Gilbert 2006). Moreover, authors have also pointed out that the rapidly changing sexual and gen-der stereotypes were being re-negotiated within the cultural industries (Mort 1998; Nixon 2003). In recent years, despite the discussion of (the hopes for) 'pro-sumption' (Ritzer and Jurgenson 2010), its contrast to the reality of practices such as 'cool hunting' (Quart 2003) and 'fashion vlogging' (Luvaas 2016) provides a vital conduit of 'in situ' and 'tacit' knowledge within contemporary fashion-driven markets.[15]

Whilst the lively discussion of the NTE has undoubtedly broad-ened an agenda, this chapter carries with it the warning that it would be better viewed as a continuity, rather than a dualism, with respect to the DTE or regular creative hubs. The argument here is that the appar-ent and real contrast between day and night activities is underpinned by many connections. The pursuit of thinking about, and making pol-icy for, hubs in isolation risks undervaluing these connections as well as the character of their social embedding. Elsewhere in this collection, authors have noted the importance of the not reducing hubs to eco-nomics or to co-location. The discussion of the NTE in effect suffers from these shortcomings. However, we can also see that most discussion

---

[15]That is all of the cultural industries with a 'product turnover' or 'short innovation' character measured in days and weeks, not months or years as in traditional industries Pratt, A. C., & P. Jeffcutt. (2009). Creativity, innovation and the cultural economy: Snake oil for the 21st cen-tury? In A. C. Pratt & P. Jeffcutt (Eds.), *Creativity, innovation in the cultural economy* (pp. 1–20). London: Routledge.

of creative hubs fails to explore the relationships with consumption and with 'the night-time'. Based on the Soho case study, there is a fruitful line of study to explore further here.

Conclusions

The aim of this chapter has been to examine the recent debates about the NTE and to explore what their relationship might be with the parallel discussion about creative hubs and furthermore, to plot out any commonalities and linkages. The practical definitions, particularly the classificatory definitions upon which metrics are produced, separate our practical understandings of the NTE and creative hubs. Creative hubs, whilst adopting a more systematic production chain notion of the CI and a more socio-economic perspective on 'spillovers', have tended to ignore consumption activities.[16] Clearly, this chapter has pointed to a rich field to explore here, not simply to look more closely at consumption, but to explore the codependencies across the whole production chain and to be aware of the timing of activities. There is already a strong strand of research on the 'all hours' working practices of those in the CI; it is a small step to weave the approaches together more closely.

However, there are practical barriers to such an academic logic. The debates about the NTE are situated within a particular institution and a specific moment in the evolution of cities and the CI. The NTE has developed a database and metrics that have served local planning authorities reasonably well: they have unlocked more resources for 'support' for the NTE from transport to policing and social mediation. However, this definition has the effect of re-enforcing the binaries of production and consumption (echoed by the use of day/night economies). Such a conception, and policy approach, makes it difficult to 'see', or address, the linkages such as those that have been pointed up in the Soho case study and in urban cultural policies and creative

---

[16]Arguably, as the initial stress studies on production sought to differentiate the CI from previous approaches that had focused on consumption.

industry policies. This highlights another issue, namely whether a functional separation of urban policy making has outlived its utility (Pratt 2018b). With particular regard to the NTE, we can note that whilst the rhetoric of 'economy' is placed at the forefront of generally instrumental reports, little attention is paid to the articulation of that economy and issues such as the ownership and control of the NTE and its position in the city: the politics, despite discussions of stakeholders and community issues of power—such as the narrow base of ownership of NTE industries and production chains—escape attention (Chatterton and Hollands 2003). There is a reminder here with an older debate that sought to critically explore the dominance (and the attendant control of policy objectives) that retailing and hotels achieved in political coalitions in US cities: urban 'growth machines' (Molotch 1976). The current configuration of NTE debates leaves such a relationship hidden and, for the moment, unaddressed.

There is a case for considering the social embedding of the NTE, as much as the DTE/hubs and clusters debate are engaged with it, that is extending beyond the services to explore the quality of services offered to workers and to residents (Gill 2016). This should inevitably lead us to explore the interrelationships—social, economic and political—between the creative cluster and the NTE. Viewing the NTE in both a wider context of the changing cultural economy, and through the conceptual lens of the cultural economy, might compensate for the blind spots and provide a joint platform for debate. Furthermore, it might contribute to breaking down the dualisms of production and consumption, and day and night, a field that has yielded insights in cluster research: namely that of boundaries between formal and informal activities (Mbaye and Dinardi 2018). Analyses of informality would surely illustrate the practical transfer of knowledge between participants in clusters and NTEs. Generally speaking, it is clear that the 'affordance' of both locations, social and economic networks, the formal and the informal, is already being practised and exploited by those in clusters and NTE zones (Fayard and Weeks 2007). Policy makers perhaps could be excused a degree of functional separation and instrumentalist, but academic research should be exploring these interstices of the urban cultural economy; hopefully, this chapter will contribute to that initiative.

Bibliography

Association, N. T. I. (2016). *Forward into the night.* London: NTIA.

Avery, S., & Graham, K. M. (2016). *Sex, time and place: Queer histories of London, C. 1850 to the present.* London: Bloomsbury Publishing.

Bianchini, F. (1995). Night cultures, night economies. *Planning Practice and Research, 10*(2), 121–126.

Breward, C., & Gilbert, D. (2006). *Fashion's world cities.* Oxford: Berg.

Burrows, M. (2015). Why London's music scene has been rocked by the death of Denmark street. *The Guardian.* London.

Chatterton, P., & Hollands, R. (2003). *Urban nightscapes: Youth cultures, pleasure spaces and corporate power.* London: Routledge.

Darlow, M. (2004). *Independents struggle.* London: Quartet.

Department of Culture, Media and Sport (DCMS). (1998). *Creative industries mapping document.* London, UK: Department of Culture, Media and Sport.

Fayard, A.-L., & Weeks, J. (2007). Photocopiers and water-coolers: The affordances of informal interaction. *Organization Studies, 28*(5), 605–634.

Fox, S. R. (1984). *The mirror makers: A history of American advertising and its creators.* Champaign: University of Illinois Press.

Gill, T. (2016). 'The lid is on the pot, but every now and then the lid bounces off…and that needs to be managed': Exploring the impact of the night time economy on a London Borough* (MSc Social Policy and Planning). London School of Economics.

Greater London Authority. (2017). *Rewrite the night: The future of London's night time economy.* London: GLA.

Green, F. (2001). It's been a hard day's night: The concentration and intensification of work in late twentieth century Britain. *British Journal of Industrial Relations, 39*(1), 53–80.

Hadfield, P., & Davis, P. (2015). *Westminster evening and night time economy: A cost benefit study for Westminster City Council.* London: Westminster City Council.

Hannerz, U. (1969). *Soulside: Inquiries into ghetto culture and community.* New York: Columbia University Press.

Hannigan, J. (1998). *Fantasy city: Pleasure and profit in the postmodern metropolis.* London: Routledge.

Hebdige, D. (1979). *Subculture: The meaning of style.* London: Methuen.

Hicklin, A. (2012). Power of the pink pound. *Financial Times Wealth Magazine.*

Houlbrook, M. (2006). *Queer London: Perils and pleasures in the sexual metropolis, 1918–1957*. Chicago: University of Chicago Press.

Kreitzman, L. (1999). *24 hour society*. London: Profile.

London First. (2017). *London's 24 hour economy*. London: London First and EY.

Lovatt, A. (2017). The ecstasy of urban regeneration: Regulation of the night-time economy in the transition to a post-Fordist city. In *From the margins to the centre* (pp. 141–168). London: Routledge.

Lovatt, A., & O'Connor, J. (1995). Cities and the night-time economy. *Planning Practice Research, 10*(2), 127–134.

Luvaas, B. (2016). *Street style: An ethnography of fashion blogging*. London, UK: Bloomsbury Publishing.

Mbaye, J., & Dinardi, C. (2018). Ins and outs of the cultural polis: Informality, culture and governance in the global South. *Urban Studies*. Available at https://doi.org/10.1177/0042098017744168.

Michael Hall, C., & Hamon, C. (1996). Casinos and urban redevelopment in Australia. *Journal of Travel Research, 34*(3), 30–36.

Molotch, H. (1976). The city as a growth machine: Toward a political economy of place. *American Journal of Sociology, 82*, 309–332.

Mort, F. (1998). Cityscapes: Consumption, masculinities and the mapping of London since 1950. *Urban Studies, 35*(5), 889–907.

Nachum, L., & Keeble, D. (2003). Neo-Marshallian clusters and global networks—The linkages of media firms in central London. *Long Range Planning, 36*(5), 459–480.

Nixon, S. (2003). *Advertising cultures: Gender, commerce, creativity*. London: Sage.

O'Connor, J., & Wynne, D. (1998). Consumption and the post-modern city. *Urban Studies, 35*, 841–864.

Ogilvy, D., & Horgan, P. (1963). *Confessions of an advertising man*. New York: Atheneum.

Pratt, A. C. (2000). New media, the new economy and new spaces. *Geoforum, 31*(4), 425–436.

Pratt, A. C. (2006). Advertising and creativity, a governance approach: A case study of creative agencies in London. *Environment and Planning A, 38*(10), 1883–1899.

Pratt, A. C. (2009). Urban regeneration: From the arts 'feel good' factor to the cultural economy. A case study of Hoxton, London. *Urban Studies, 46*(5–6), 1041–1061.

Pratt, A. C. (2011). Microclustering of the media industries in London. In C. Karlsson & R. G. Picard (Eds.), *Media clusters* (pp. 120–135). Cheltenham: Edward Elgar.

Pratt, A. C. (2018a). Gentrification, artists and the cultural economy. In L. Lees & M. Philips (Eds.), *Handbook of gentrification studies* (pp. 346–362). Cheltenham: Edward Elgar.

Pratt, A. C. (2018b). Making space for culture and well-being in the city. In C. Boyko & R. Cooper (Eds.), *Designing future cities for well-being*. London: Routledge.

Pratt, A. C., & Gornostaeva, G. (2009). The governance of innovation in the film and television industry: A case study of London, UK. In A. C. Pratt & P. Jeffcutt (Eds.), *Creativity, innovation and the cultural economy* (pp. 119–136). London: Routledge.

Pratt, A. C., & Jeffcutt, P. (2009). Creativity, innovation and the cultural economy: Snake oil for the 21st century? In A. C. Pratt & P. Jeffcutt (Eds.), *Creativity, innovation in the cultural economy* (pp. 1–20). London: Routledge.

Pratt, A. C., Gill, R. C., & Spelthann, V. (2007). Work and the city in the e-society: A critical investigation of the socio-spatially situated character of economic production in the digital content industries, UK. *Information, Communication Society, 10*(6), 921–941.

Quart, A. (2003). *Branded: The buying and selling of teenagers*. Cambridge, MA: Perseus Publishing.

Richardson, N. (2000). *Dog days in Soho: One man's adventures in 1950s*. Bohemia: Gollancz.

Ritzer, G., & Jurgenson, N. (2010). Production, consumption, prosumption: The nature of capitalism in the age of the digital 'prosumer'. *Journal of Consumer Culture, 10*(1), 13–36.

Roberts, M. (2015). 'A big night out': Young people's drinking, social practice and spatial experience in the 'liminoid' zones of English night-time cities. *Urban Studies, 52*(3), 571–588.

Roberts, M., & Eldridge, A. (2012). *Planning the night-time city*. London: Routledge.

Roberts, M., & Turner, C. (2005). Conflicts of liveability in the 24-hour city: Learning from 48 hours in the life of London's Soho. *Journal of Urban Design, 10*, 171–193.

Roberts, M., Turner, C., Greenfield, S., & Osborn, G. (2006). A continental ambience? Lessons in managing alcohol-related evening and night-time entertainment from four European capitals. *Urban Studies, 43*(7), 1105–1125.

Smith, O. (2014). *Contemporary adulthood and the night-time economy.* London: Springer.

Sood, S. (2012). The cities that never sleep. *BBC.*

Speiser, P. (2017). *Soho: The heart of Bohemian London.* London: British Library Publishing.

Straw, W. (2001). Scenes and sensibilities. *Public, 22–23,* 245–257.

Summers, J. (1989). *Soho: A history of London's most colourful neighbourhood.* London: Bloomsbury Publishing.

Talbot, D. (2004). Regulation and racial differentiation in the construction of night-time economies: A London case study. *Urban Studies, 41*(4), 887–901.

Talbot, D. (2016). *Regulating the night: Race, culture and exclusion in the making of the night-time economy.* London: Routledge.

Talbot, D., & Böse, M. (2007). Racism, criminalization and the development of night-time economies: Two case studies in London and Manchester. *Ethnic and Racial Studies, 30*(1), 95–118.

TUC. (2015). *A hard day's night: The effect of night shift work on work/life balance.* London: TUC.

Wenger, E. (1998). *Communities of practice: Learning, meaning, and identity.* Cambridge: Cambridge University Press.

18

Exploring the Relationship Between Creative Hubs and Urban Policy in East London

Tarek E. Virani

Introduction

Much of the literature on creative hubs describes them as physical manifestations that range from hyperlocal co-working and creative workspaces to neighbourhoods to entire cities and in some cases countries (Virani and Malem 2015; Dovey et al. 2016). This is further proof that understanding creative hubs through their physical and scalar properties alone provides an incomplete picture of their importance to the creative and cultural economy—especially locally. This chapter argues that much more can be learned by examining what they actually do, how they support creative people as well as creative communities. One way of doing this is by uncoupling the term 'creative hub' from that of the 'creative cluster' where both have been used synonymously by a number

T. E. Virani (✉)
School of Business and Management,
Queen Mary University of London, London, UK
e-mail: t.virani@qmul.ac.uk

© The Author(s) 2019
R. Gill et al. (eds.), *Creative Hubs in Question*, Dynamics of Virtual Work,
https://doi.org/10.1007/978-3-030-10653-9_18

of scholars and policymakers regarding regeneration and local development. This chapter argues that there is a distinction between creative clusters and neighbourhood-scale creative hubs, and that urban policy aimed at (re)producing creative clusters can have a detrimental effect on areas that might be better understood as creative hubs. This is because clusters-oriented policy, in this context, prioritises market forces based on consumption (exemplified by the work of Richard Florida 2002) thereby missing and, in this particular case, delegitimising the many intangible characteristics that make an area and its development, over time, unique. This chapter illustrates this through an analysis of secondary sources and participant observation of/in Hackney Wick and Fish Island (HWFI) in London's east end. Specifically, it argues that by failing to fully acknowledge the importance of Live/Workspaces, by elevating housing policy that benefits property developers, by failing to anticipate the detrimental effects of slow planning approval processes, and by not stemming the misuse of Section 106[1] agreements, policymakers have had a damaging effect on HWFI. This chapter argues that places like HWFI are not being protected from the market forces that clusters-oriented regeneration policies influence. These are primarily developer-led and consumption-based policies leading to unsustainable increases in property and land values placing affordable workspace out of reach. Instead, urban policy aimed at such areas must be tailored to their unique characteristics and must assist in providing protection from market forces, especially development-led pressure, as opposed to opening them up to them. Interestingly, very recently (in fact during the proofing stage of this volume) HWFI has been named as one of six Creative Enterprise Zones (CEZ) in London, whether this will result in measures that will protect it from the forces that will be discussed in this chapter is yet to be seen. A discussion of the CEZ will not be undertaken in this chapter, however, please see Virani et al. (2018) for a report conducted as part of HWFI's application for CEZ status.

---

[1]Planning obligations, also known as Section 106 agreements (based on that section of The 1990 Town and Country Planning Act) are private agreements made between local authorities and developers and can be attached to a planning permission to make acceptable development which would otherwise be unacceptable in planning terms. The land itself, rather than the person or organisation that develops the land, is bound by a Section 106 Agreement, something any future owners will need to take into account. This is discussed later in the chapter.

Creative Clusters, Creative Hubs and Urban Policy

The most influential work that champions the role of creativity in regeneration and development policy is by Richard Florida (2002). Florida's work advocates the importance of attracting and retaining the creative class who act as engines of local economic growth through the provision of spaces and places that they can utilise and/or consume—usually provided through regeneration policy. Florida's theory is one of agglomeration economics and thus borrows heavily from clusters theory (Porter 1990). It is this discourse that gave birth to the 'creative cluster' as a concept as well as a regeneration tool. Although suffering a number of hefty critiques (Peck 2005), Florida's cluster influenced policy is still influential today despite any tangible evidence that can substantiate his claims. Policymakers the world over are convinced that creative clusters policy is the cure for de-industrialisation. In a similar vein, the creative hub concept emerged as part of this narrative surrounding creative clusters and the notion of 'culture-led' and/ or 'arts-led' regeneration policy (Evans 2009). The emergence of the creative hub, as a concept in the economic development of regions, speaks to the elevation by government and policymakers of the creative economy as a critical part of the economic development portfolio of many deindustrialising countries and regions (Dovey et al. 2016; Shiach et al. 2017; Shiach and Virani 2017). The term began to emerge in regeneration policy documents in London in 2003 and was criticised at the time for having no commonly accepted definition (City Fringe Partnership 2005).

There are currently three overarching conceptualisations of the creative hub as it pertains to regional economic development and specifically its utilisation as a regeneration tool—although all three are also heavily informed by the clusters concept. The first, and perhaps the most comprehensive, views them as hyperlocal entities of creative and cultural production that are synonymous with emergent new and flexible workspace (both real and virtual) that cater to specifically creative MSMEs (micro, small and medium-sized enterprises) and start-ups (Virani and Malem 2015; Dovey et al. 2016).

They are varied organisationally and might be identified as: co-working spaces, incubators, training institutions, service centres for businesses, virtual forums, fab labs, artists' studios, Live/Workspaces and a mix of all or some of the above. This understanding of them views them as small and medium scale cultural production centres located in specific parts of cities—usually within or very close to creative districts. This is underpinned by the discourse on hubs more generally including primarily the recent emergence of innovation hubs, knowledge hubs and other more policy-oriented and policy-designed hyperlocal production centres. The second articulation understands them as local areas of agglomerative economic activity closely aligned to or synonymous with creative clusters which posits that creative economic activity tends to agglomerate in specific parts of cities such as creative districts, quarters and zones (Evans 2009; Pratt 2004). As such, much of this work tends to either position creative hubs under the same rubric as creative clusters or understand them as identical. The third articulation views them as part of the Global City discourse (Currid 2006) demarcating entire cities, and sometimes entire countries, as creative hubs. This way of understanding them speaks to reputational economies built through historic creative economic activity thereby branding a city a hub for specific subsectors—examples would include Hollywood for film, Nashville for music, Paris and London for fashion. These three articulations of the creative hub overlap in many ways most significantly by being underpinned by a focus on agglomeration and by extension clustering.

In policy discourse, hubs and clusters are used synonymously regarding the regeneration of de-industrialised parts of cities. For example, Oakley understands creative hubs as synonymous with cultural quarters in her critique of UK economic development policy (2004, p. 68). Specifically, while criticising creative industries led economic development policy, she identifies creative hubs as a spatial ingredient, including others like incubators and universities, meant to enhance a city regions creative economic capacity (2004, p. 73). Accordingly, she views hubs as places where creative economic activity 'clusters'. Similarly, Bagwell (2008) discusses the importance of the City Fringe area of North London where a large portion of creative economic activity seems to be concentrated. Bagwell describes the geographic area as a hub due to this concentration of activity and its spread over a geographical area. Thus for Bagwell a hub is a cluster of activity where the urban spatial parameters are bounded, aligning closely to the creative district or cultural quarter. Evans understands creative hubs as 'new- industrial clusters' however he does not view them as synonymous with creative or cultural quarters (2009, p. 1003). While not explicitly laid out, he seems to propose that they are a result of top-down policy interventions and/or public–private investment usually located in 'sub-regional' sites—similar to science parks. Again this assumes the agglomeration of economic activity albeit purely as a result of policy and primarily as a way to pursue economic development. Montgomery (2007), similar to Oakley and Evans, also views them as clustered districts within parts of cities.

The challenge is that understanding hubs and clusters as synonymous, or at least not problematising creative hubs, misses what they do. While the hub concept might have emerged through policy, it has taken on a life of its own because it represents something else, something more nuanced—it acknowledges processes that clusters do not and cannot explain. Thus regardless of their spatial manifestation creative hubs provide important 'creative services' to the creative sector and within a localised creative economy (Virani and Malem 2015). This alternative is what we could call a 'process-oriented' view of hubs and thus distinguishes them quite significantly from creative clusters which are primarily output driven. At its core, the creative hub is about the facilitation of knowledge sharing and exchange (and all the micro-processes that are enmeshed in this such as the role of mediation and governance praxis), and since proximity has a role to play here it might be worth acknowledging that while the hub construct can exist at multiple scales it might be at the hyper-local scale that knowledge exchange is the most effective. This however does not mean that proximity automatically results in 'patents pending' which is seen by many as the gold standard regarding industrial clusters, what they produce, and how they innovate. In fact, many critiques of the cluster concept have found that the results of clusters are mixed at best (Baptista and Swann 1998; Spencer et al. 2010). Moreover, the cluster concept has only ever been examined when applied to traditional industrial activity where the product is usually material (Porter 1990).

Applying the concept to the creative sector, where the product is usually immaterial, has implications that have not been properly considered, assessed or examined. Andy Pratt rightly critiques creative cluster policy for this very reason by saying it misses important intangible elements that are intrinsic to the creative industries (2004). Furthermore, the creative cluster concept does not engage with the importance of communities of practice (Lave and Wenger 1991) within creative communities where huge investments in social, cultural and economic capital happen over a given timescale by its inhabitants. In other words, it does not engage with the lived and co-habiting experience and nature of creative communities as they evolve and as they learn to sustain themselves. The cluster concept as an influence on regeneration policy focuses on the economic outputs of consumption and thus misses these aspects that must exist in order to perpetuate and support cultural production. Lastly, creative clusters do not engage with the fact that often times it is the market that these places need protection from as opposed to being exposed to—which is the exact opposite to what Florida espouses. The story of the cultural quarter since as far back as the 1970s, and the advent of de-industrialisation, has always been tied to displacement and gentrification which is a direct result of exposure to the market—thus any belief that the market will somehow sustain a sector with a notoriously high 'failure' rate is folly. Thus we need to move beyond clusters when we think about policy, the creative sector, and the importance of sustaining cultural production—and problematising 'the hub' concept might be one way forward.

Regarding the neighbourhood-scale creative hub, and following Bontje and Musterd (2009, p. 844), it can be suggested that while many regions market themselves as vibrant centres of creativity and knowledge in order to catalyse regional growth, through city branding and/or place branding strategies and the like, and have taken actions to strengthen that profile, not all will be able to have such a profile (see Sasaki 2010). There is a clear distinction between those regions that do creativity and innovation and those that do it at a level where they can be identified as 'creative hubs'. Thus the hub idea is also that of a process of evolution and delivery as well as reputation building, as opposed to something that can simply be created and then quickly branded as such. Moreover what happens at the hyperlocal scale directly affects the local and national scale thereby contributing to reputation economies of scale, and subsequently the branding of a place, space, region as a creative hub—although this needs further research. Thus the creative hub, again, is about how the processes of knowledge exchange create, sustain, and then magnify centres of cultural production. In fact, the term 'scene' might be a useful way to think of hubs as has been argued elsewhere (Seman, this volume; Virani 2016). Nevertheless, the point here is that urban policy continues to be informed by how the physical manifestation and 'design' of place draw in the market thereby making it less effective at maintaining community building and retaining creative workers. Moreover, conflating hubs and clusters is a symptom of this, where the more cultural and social mechanisms that are evident and vital to the survival of creative communities, and which are potentially acknowledged through the construct of the creative hub, are lost in the conversation around creative clusters in order to cater to the real estate market. The following section exemplifies how these issues materialise in a locality.

Case Study: Hackney Wick and Fish Island (HWFI)

The creative community in HWFI represents an organic neighbourhood-scale creative hub that is hugely dependent on the types of creative workspace provided by the once empty warehouses that exist in the area. This section illustrates how policy has contributed to the disappearance of affordable creative workspace in HWFI.

Background

HWFI is a small area that straddles the northeast part of the London Borough of Tower Hamlets (LBTH) and the southeast part of the London Borough of Hackney (LBH). It is characterised by many distinct warehouses used during the existence of the London Docks. The London Legacy Development Corporation (LLDC), who are the Mayor of London's appointed Olympic legacy caretakers, have planning and regeneration responsibilities for Hackney Wick and Fish Island due to it being part of the Olympic Legacy area including Queen Elizabeth Olympic Park. The London Borough of Tower Hamlets has divided the Fish Island area specifically into precincts; the artists cluster is located in the central precinct inhabiting the warehouses and factories as well as what are known as Live/Work developments.

Live/Work as Catalyst

Live/Workspaces are essentially warehouses that have been converted to suit the needs of the tenants themselves in order for practitioners to live and work—this includes fine artists, sculptors, film-makers, musicians, designers, event professionals and more which represent the breadth of artistic activity in HWFI. The official definition in the 1996 Live/ Work Development Supplementary Planning Guidance produced by the London Borough of Hackney is as follows: Live/Work development is the provision of integrated living and working accommodation within a single self-contained unit. Importantly, when it comes to their use by the creative sector, they are primarily spaces of production, but they also represent a 'sharing economy' in many ways as artist communities often share equipment as well as each other's space as a mechanism of sustainability (see Virani et al. 2018). Live/Workspaces are a point of contention with regard to local authorities as they do not meet the minimum threshold of what might constitute legal residences—although this is being re-examined as part of creative industries policy-led urban regeneration. Nevertheless, one can easily see how abandoned and disused warehouse space might easily be unofficially converted into Live/ Work units—which is exactly the reason why so many artists began to descend on HWFI in the early 2000s. It is not unlikely that the area had a healthy number of creative people there before the early 2000s since the first studios in the area date back to 1980 (Acme 2011). Where there is consensus it shows that, the real accumulation of artists happened in and around the mid-1990s. The first Hackney Wicked Art Festival took place in 2008 so the build-up towards a critical mass of artists able to organise and stage the event must have happened in the years prior to that, from the mid-1990s. Space Studios, Decima Gallery, Mother Studios, Schwartz Gallery, Elevator Gallery, Residence Gallery, Liquid Studios, Cell Studios, Main Yard Gallery, Oslo House all took part. Fish Island afforded artists, and would be new Live/Work residents, ample space, attractive space, the 'feel good factor', and a general level of understanding and tolerance regarding the types of artistic activities being undertaken. Arts and crafts artists could begin work on their next project whenever inspiration arrived without the worry of having to abide to any rules or regulations or worries about noise complaints and the like—and because of this a community spirit and ethos evolved which exists to this very day. Therefore, a sense of community, shared activity, a healthy sharing economy and a communal atmosphere resulted in what was once called the largest agglomeration of artists in Europe—although this is changing. In 2009, Muf architects land use survey found 624 studios with an estimate of 1500 artists at that time.

Delegitimising Live/Work

Local government's encouragement of Live/Work was formally published in 2006 with the London Borough of Tower Hamlets Live/Work Report. The report recognised it as valuably linked to the creative and cultural sector, including the quickly growing tech scene. Importantly, while the report advocated the importance of Live/Work arrangements, LBTH has maintained policy restrictions on units on industrial land since November 2005. In 2005, the London Development Agency began its compulsory purchase orders (CPOs) of the site that was to become the Olympic Park. At the same time, LBTH began a policy of refusal to grant planning permission to artists who were occupying the warehouses in the area in order to convert them into Live/Workspaces. Artists in this cluster were made aware by the LDA, LBTH, and later the LLDC, that they could be asked to leave with one month's notice and that the buildings they were occupying were in fact only available for temporary use. This effectively had a direct impact on how artists treated their living space where they essentially saw their living arrangement, or their Live/Work arrangement, as temporary. In some cases, this was viewed as attractive by those who began occupying the warehouses of Fish Island. However, as time passed the artistic community began viewing the area as a viable and attractive long-term place to live mainly as a result of what they had created. The reasons are evident: 24-hour access to studios, 24-hour access to artistic practice, no need to comply with noise laws or deal with complaints, the right amount of space and light, belonging to a like-minded creative community, participating in a sharing economy, and the list goes on. This shift has proven to be problematic for policymakers as it poses a challenge to delivering parts of the Olympic Legacy Plan in the Lower Lea Valley[2] (legacy master plan) and by extension the Legacy Communities Scheme.[3] Specifically, it affects how both the legacy master plan and the LCS deliver on housing-led policy promises and the construction of new housing estates adjacent to HWFI as well as access points. Alongside these estates, which have been part of the plan since 2011, a number of planning policies have been put forth in order to grant the new housing complexes access to the Olympic Park as well as the creative community across the canal. This includes the building of access points and bridges across the canal which are causing upheaval and tensions in the area as they essentially mean the destruction of buildings where artistic communities have already

---

[2]According to Shirai (2014, p. 109), The Olympic and legacy master plan in the Lower Lea Valley was published by the London Development Agency (LDA) in May 2004. While the report was issued under the name of the LDA, a number of other organisations were the master planners. The 'legacy masterplan' as it came to be known is an in-depth spatial strategy for the post-Olympic period and came to represent various spatial aspirations including the Legacy Communities Scheme. Regarding this spatial strategy, the abovementioned diverse visions were to be integrated in the post-Olympic master plan. Thus, in order to examine the relationship with various prior spatial strategies, the legacy master plan came to be the one which would represent the various spatial aspirations.

[3]The Legacy Communities Scheme (LCS) is an important document which sets out plans by the LLDC for the development of new neighbourhoods across the Olympic Park. They submitted this for planning approval in September 2011, and it has guided all of their work since it was approved in September 2012. The plans are for developing five new neighbourhoods—Chobham Manor, East Wick, Sweetwater, Marshgate Wharf and Pudding Mill. The LCS sets out a master plan for development across the Park, covering building heights, land uses, open space, access plans, street layout, development of infrastructure and more for all five neighbourhoods. For more go to: http://www.queenelizabetholympicpark.co.uk/our-story/transforming-east-london/legacy-communities-scheme.

established themselves. Specifically, this issue pertains to the construction of two bridges known as H14 and H16 which will affect warehouses that have been converted into Live/Workspaces, studios and other types of creative workspace.[4] Interestingly, a recent survey conducted by Queen Mary University of London found that 37% of the creative community in HWFI live in Live/Workspaces (Virani et al. 2018).

The Planning Process

Delivering the spatial strategies outlined by various master plans means that planning approval must be given for any building works being done in the legacy zone, which is a slow process. Regarding the construction of access points mentioned above, many of the planning proposals were placed a number of years ago (some as far back as ten years ago) only receiving approval now (2018). Thus, while planning proposals go through the process of being approved things evolve. This can be understood as 'planning blight' in reverse, in this particular case things have developed over time as opposed to deteriorating. Enforcing spatial strategies means that as the plan slowly becomes reality it must contend with the changing and morphing environments for artists as they grow in HWFI primarily—this is not unique to east London, but also occurring in South London outside of the Olympic legacy context highlighting a need for constant consultation. The provision of access points to and from the Olympic Park in this case is part of a larger regeneration plan for the area and of course translates into dramatic increases in rent as landlords in HWFI are made aware of the opportunities being developed outside of their front door. This means that property developers offered large sums of money to landlords who owned freeholds in Fish Island primarily—in fact property developers already own most of it; those who did not want to sell are increasing their rental rates exponentially. All of this is pushing the prices of affordable creative workspace higher and higher (London Assembly 2017).

---

[4]For more on bridges H14 and H16 please see the work done by Save Hackney Wick or visit: https://savehackneywick.org/save-vittoria-wharf.

Mixed Use

These issues have resulted in a push by policymakers for what are called Section 106 provisions to be used in such a way in order to sustain and create workspace for artists since around 2010. Section 106 (S106) Agreements are legal agreements between local authorities and developers; they are drafted when it is considered that a development will have significant impacts on the local area that cannot be moderated by means of conditions attached to a planning decision. Thus the provision of social housing in a new housing development usually comes under the rubric of an S106 provision. In the case of artists' workspace, S106 is being used as the mechanism to create affordable space for artists in housing developments. This however has not been the solution that policymakers have envisaged. S106 provisions for artist space have resulted in 'mixed use policy' which essentially creates residential units/flats in the top half of a building where the ground floor is given over for 'artist use'. These factors have resulted in rising rents in the artist's quarter due to the development of new homes as well as the advent of new ground floor commercial space (and renovated commercial buildings like 99 Wallis Rd, White Building) beneath new residential units valued at £30–40 per square foot. The result has been that many of these ground floors have been empty for years as they are viewed as a poor substitute for what the warehouses provide. They also essentially remove many of the affordances that warehouses provide by bringing developer-led residential space into an artistic area. The result is the wholesale removal of creative workspace.

Discussion

This section illustrates how policy has contributed to the disappearance of affordable workspace in HWFI due to the assumption that somehow opening it up to developer-led market forces and stubbornly sticking to outdated spatial strategies in a legacy framework will have a positive effect. What has also happened, although there is no scope to discuss this in this chapter, is that clusters-oriented policy is being developed across the canal in Queen Elizabeth Park including large cultural and educational institutions such as University College London, the Victoria and Albert Museum, the London College of Fashion and more. This policy-driven and policy-designed cluster has also had an effect on elevating property values in the immediate vicinity—especially due to the amount of student accommodation that might need to be built in and around this area; again the focus is on consumption.

Thus the prevalent theme in HWFI has been the loss, and placing out of reach, of affordable creative workspace—as well as living space. As of 2018, HWFI has lost half of Vittoria Wharf, Things Fashions, and Mother Studios but gained new workspace through the construction of Fish Island Village, Here East Gantry, 9294 Main Yard. Even though new buildings have been constructed aimed at 'retaining' the creative community questions surrounding affordability are front and centre with rates of £25–30 per square foot being discussed as 'low cost studios'. Most artists know that affordable space in this part of London means between £8–15 per square foot which if not delivered translates into displacement. This is a complicated situation which provides a perfect example of how urban policy affects and changes creative districts. By not acknowledging the importance of Live/Workspaces, by elevating housing policy that benefits property developers, by not addressing the slow planning approval process, and by not stemming the misuse of Section 106 provisions policymakers have had a negative effect on HWFI. As a result so-called culture-led regeneration has been criticised. According to the London Assembly (2017, p. 6):

> It can lead to rapid gentrification and have negative impacts on long-term residents and the very artists, shop keepers and activists whose energies attracted regeneration. It is also seen as a process whereby government 'does to an area' rather than as something organic which better reflects local interests and needs.

Conclusion

The view of the London Assembly on the current state of affairs is chastening, the wrong results apparently happened for the 'right initiatives'; sadly, an all too common outcome. This chapter has tried to explain why; it argues that (re)producing creative clusters can have a detrimental effect on areas that might be better understood as neighbourhood-scale creative hubs. This is because clusters-oriented policy in this context prioritises market forces based on consumption thereby missing and, in this case, delegitimising the many intangible characteristics that make an area and its development, over time, unique. That by the normative application of regeneration policies policymakers can actually have a negative effect, rather than a positive one, assumes place and context matters here. By looking at the case of HWFI, much of the context revolves around affordable workspace. It is evident that affordable workspace is not only critical to the existence of the creative community but represents how clusters-oriented policy is affecting HWFI as a 'creative hub'—understood by what it grants the creative community. First, as a hub HWFI perpetuates and sustains a creative community that in turn invests it social, financial and cultural capital into the area. HWFI's unique history and evolution are tied to the provision and the malleability of its warehouse space and the lifestyle that Live/Workspaces symbolise. This means that while the physical characteristics of the neighbourhood and indeed the warehouses were an attractive and integral part of developing a creative community in HWFI, it is the interconnections implied by living and working here that is the real catalyser. This is exemplified by the 'making' of Live/Workspaces. Importantly, Live/Work implies the existence of a co-habiting artistic community at a local level—Live/Work artists therefore invest their cultural, economic and social capital into the places where they live, which is the essence of community building and by extension 'placemaking' and which contributes significantly to the type of creative district that might evolve into a creative hub. Moreover, this investment by Live/Workers and others from the artistic community has contributed to the development of reputation economies of scale. As a consequence, the creative community in HWFI became elevated to that of an idealised 'creative district' which in turn became a neighbourhood-scale creative hub due to the apparatus and networks that have been provided to ensure and facilitate knowledge sharing and exchange—all based on ensuring cultural production. This is exactly the reason why HWFI became the largest concentration of artists in Europe. As a result, governance structures emerge and become the de facto glue that holds the hub together but perhaps most importantly, they emerge due to the fact that a community lives here. This implies quite strongly that hyperlocal creative hubs can act as conduits for strategies of defiance (which is already evident in HWFI) and (again) knowledge sharing. Creative clusters policy does not speak to these types of attributes and as a result of missing them delegitimises them by not including them as part of a portfolio of interventions for regeneration. Thus, to reiterate, treating Live/Work as a barrier to regeneration in HWFI, elevating housing policy and sticking to outdated legacy plans that benefit property developers and not the creative community, allowing the slow planning approval process to displace people, and not putting in place extra provisions to stop the misuse of Section 106 is emblematic of this disconnect between top-down policy and what is happening on the ground, but also why hubs and clusters need to be distilled from each other. They represent two completely different vantage points.

Second, Live/Work also implies the elevation of cultural production which translates into the preservation of, and indeed the magnification of, a creative place. This can mean that a concentration of Live/Workspaces constitutes an increase in cultural production and thus an increase in the amount of capital being invested in an area. Thus the issue of scale is closely tied to cultural production, levels of social and cultural capital, and their role in the creation of reputation economies of scale. These characteristics are, it can be argued, contingent on the sharing of knowledge—which is at the heart of what hubs do and not what clusters do. This is because clusters are based on the premise/promise of competitiveness as the route to wealth and growth (Porter 1990).

Third, the instrumentalisation of creative industries led urban regeneration policy does not work because the premise that underpins it is based on viewing clusters as engines of local economic growth for industries whose product is for the most part immaterial. This is why, if the evidence is examined, that the connection between creative industries led regeneration policy and actual development is tenuous at best and why most policy-led creative quarters become sites of consumption—slipping into tourist hot spots peppered by 'Box Parks'.

References

Acme Studios. (2011). *Unearthed, the creative history of a brownfield site.*

Bagwell, S. (2008). Creative clusters and city growth. *Creative Industries Journal, 1*(1), 31–46.

Baptista, R., & Swann, P. (1998). Do firms in clusters innovate more? *Research Policy, 27*(5), 525–540.

Bontje, M., & Musterd, S. (2009). Creative industries, creative class and competitiveness: Expert opinions critically appraised. *Geoforum, 40*(5), 843–852.

City Fringe Creative Partnership. (2005). *A creative hub for the city fringe area.* Final Report. Available at http://www.integreatplus.com/sites/default/files/creative_hub_for_city_fringe_area.pdf.

Currid, E. (2006). New York as a global creative hub: A competitive analysis of four theories on world cities. *Economic Development Quarterly, 20*(4), 330–350.

Dovey, J., Pratt, A. C., Moreton, S., Virani, T. E., Merkel, J., & Lansdowne, J. (2016). *The Creative Hubs Report: 2016.* British Council.

Evans, G. (2009). Creative cities, creative spaces and urban policy. *Urban Studies, 46*(5–6), 1003–1040.

Florida, R. (2002). *The rise of the creative class: And how it's transforming work, leisure, community and everyday life.* New York: Basic Books.

Lave, J., & Wenger, E. (1991). *Situated learning: Legitimate peripheral participation* (Vol. 521423740). Cambridge: Cambridge University Press.

London Assembly. (2017). *Creative tension: Optimising the benefits of culture through regeneration.* The Regeneration Committee.

Montgomery, J. (2007). Creative industry business incubators and managed workspaces: A review of best practice. *Planning, Practice & Research, 22*(4), 601–617.

Oakley, K. (2004). Not so cool Britannia the role of the creative industries in economic development. *International Journal of Cultural Studies, 7*(1), 67–77.

Peck, J. (2005). Struggling with the creative class. *International Journal of Urban and Regional Research, 29*(4), 740–770.

Porter, M. E. (1990). *The competitive advantage of nations.* New York, NY: Free Press.

Pratt, A. C. (2004). Creative clusters: Towards the governance of the creative industries production system? *Media International Australia, 112,* 50–66.

Sasaki, M. (2010). Urban regeneration through cultural creativity and social inclusion: Rethinking creative city theory through a Japanese case study. *Cities, 27,* S3–S9.

Shiach, M., Virani, T. E. (2017). *Creative economy in perspective: Creativeworks London and understanding creative hubs.* In Proceedings of the ABRAPCORP Conference. ediPUCRS.

Shiach, M. E., Nakano, D., Virani, T., & Poli, K. (2017). *Report on creative hubs and urban development goals (UK/Brazil).* UK and Brazil: Creative Hubs and Urban Development Goals.

Shirai, H. (2014). *The evolving vision of the Olympic legacy: The development of the mixed-use Olympic Parks of Sydney and London* (PhD thesis submitted to Department of Sociology). Cities Programme of the London School of Economics and Political Science.

Spencer, G. M., Vinodrai, T., Gertler, M. S., & Wolfe, D. A. (2010). Do clusters make a difference? Defining and assessing their economic performance. *Regional Studies, 44*(6), 697–715.

Virani, T. E. (2016). The resilience of a local music scene in Dalston, London. *The Production and Consumption of Music in the Digital Age, 58,* 101.

Virani, T. E., & Malem, W. (2015). *Re-articulating the creative hub concept as a model for business support in the local creative economy: The case of Mare Street in Hackney* (Creativeworks London Working Paper Series).

Virani, T. E., Piza, A., & Shiach, M. E. (2018). *Creative clusters, social inclusion, and sustainability: The case of Hackney Wick and Fish Island.* A Report for the London Borough of Tower Hamlets, the London Borough of Hackney, and the London Legacy Development Corporation.

19

Universities as Creative Hubs: Modes and Practices in the UK Context

Daniel Ashton and Roberta Comunian

Introduction

The chapter critically reflects on the notion of 'Creative Hubs' from a higher education perspective. In recent years, many universities in the UK have initiated projects to interact and connect with the creative economy locally and regionally. Firstly, this chapter reviews the literature on universities engagement with creative hubs. Secondly, drawing on an extensive desktop mapping of practices in the UK, it develops a framework to understand the modes and practice of engagement of higher education institutions in the establishment and management of 'creative hubs' within or attached to their institutions.

D. Ashton (✉)
Winchester School of Art, University of Southampton,
Southampton, UK
e-mail: d.k.ashton@soton.ac.uk

R. Comunian
King's College London, London, UK
e-mail: Roberta.Comunian@kcl.ac.uk

© The Author(s) 2019
R. Gill et al. (eds.), *Creative Hubs in Question*, Dynamics of Virtual Work,
https://doi.org/10.1007/978-3-030-10653-9_19

This includes outlining seven types of university creative hubs, reflecting on different dimensions, and exploring the distribution and institutional aims. Thirdly, a common approach around 'managed interventions' is highlighted to raise some of the tensions and areas for further debate and discussion. These include the relationship with existing research and teaching agendas, the extent to which they connect with existing forms of creative (hub) activity, and issues of inclusivity and accessibility.

Introducing Universities as Creative Hubs

As Dovey et al. (2016, p. 2) note in the introduction to the British Council report, *Creative Hubs: Understanding the New Economy*, 'the word "hub" has become a universal but slippery term to label centres of creative enterprise, representing many different shapes, sizes and agendas'. This report includes a number of case studies and a scoping of hubs in key UK cities. Our focus in this chapter is on universities and/as creative hubs. This includes both a mapping of how universities intersect with the concept of creative hubs and reflections on the specific opportunities and tensions associated with this intersection.

While it is acknowledged that universities have been long-term supporters of artistic and cultural development in cities and regions throughout the UK (Chatterton and Goddard 2000), their engagement with the creative economy is a more recent phenomenon that has been intensifying in the last decade both at national (Evans 2009; Comunian et al. 2014; Benneworth 2016) and international levels (Comunian and Ooi 2016). Comunian and Gilmore (2015) have identified three nested levels of engagement. The first level is linked to the basic co-presence of the university in its creative and cultural context and often coincides with the presence and development of venues, facilities and cultural spaces within universities. The second level considers the importance of creative knowledge generated by universities and at the boundaries between universities and the creative economy. Here it is important to consider the role of 'third spaces' that facilitate opportunities for shared research and innovation. The third and final level is at the core of this engagement and focuses on the creative human capital itself—the academics, graduates and practitioners that interact within and across these spaces.

When we talk about universities as hubs for the creative economy, the centrality of creative human capital cannot be ignored. While physical and virtual infrastructures are important, Comunian et al. (2015) describe the role played by academics and graduates on one side and researchers and practitioners on the other, in creating local networks and opportunities. Creative human capital is seen here as a permeable and hybrid concept, which tries to capture the importance of education with creative disciplines but also the value of knowledge and experience within the creative sector (Comunian et al. 2011). This concept connects with teaching and learning practices in relation to higher education and the creative economy (discussed in the next section), but also highlights the emergence of new practitioners within academia and the creative sector that are able to work at the boundaries of these sectors (Research and Enterprise in Arts Creative Technology [REACT] 2016).

Within the general trends and frameworks identified by Comunian and Gilmore (2015), there has been a recent trend for universities to establish 'creative hubs' to develop their connection with the creative economy and their provision to students in this subject area. The concept of 'creative hubs' has of course been used for a long time to refer to 'creative clusters' (Virani and Malem 2015) and more broadly capture the opportunities that are generated when a critical mass of creative ideas and people concentrate in a specific locale (physical or virtual). These can be established with a range of objectives and formats (that will be explored later in the chapter) but all respond to the objective of pushing universities in their 'third mission' to engage beyond teaching and research and general connections and impact within their locale (Benneworth 2016).

In reporting on the activities of REACT, the 2016 report noted that 'creative economy hubs as an idea have historical roots stretching back at least 30 years' and 'are part of a long game, [and] will not work as randomly spaced short-term projects' (REACT 2016, p. 13). One of the main recommendations is that 'universities should establish long-term relationships with these delivery partners based around "third spaces" that offer neutral ground for collaboration' (REACT 2016, p. 8). The concept of the 'third space' is also explored by Comunian and Gilmore (2015, p. 18) as, 'spaces which are neither solely academic spaces nor solely creative and cultural production spaces but an open, creative and generative combination of the two'. These approaches help for establishing the importance of creative hub initiatives as co-constructed and collaborative. In addition to this broad conceptualisation or ethos, there are important steps to take in differentiating different modes and practices. In his analysis of the 'creative hub' concept, Virani and Malem (2015) identify five types of creative hub and services for creative sector SMEs. In this chapter, we undertake an extensive mapping exercise to unpack the various interpretations that the term 'creative hubs' takes within the higher education context.

Mapping University Creative Hubs

Creative Hubs Types

The chapter is based on an in-depth desktop research conducted over 2017 that targeted all UK universities to explore any activities or infrastructure that could be loosely associated with the term 'creative hub'. Through this research, we identified a total of 128 hubs unevenly distributed across 86 institutions with most institutions having one such hub but others including up to 4 hubs. The nature of this exploratory research does not mean to be exhaustive and there might a number of hubs that might not have been captured by our mapping (due to the lack of visibility or because being project-based they had already ceased when the research took place). Reviewing the range of creative hubs present across UK universities, we have identified 7 types of hubs according to their objectives and focus, but also articulated by the type of investment and infrastructure on which they are based. It is important to clarify with some notes how we proceeded with data collection. Although a few institutions presented exhibitions, galleries and art spaces as 'hubs', we have not included this kind of infrastructure if there was no reference to other forms of engagement (with research, teaching or external creative practitioners) beyond exhibiting.

We have also excluded projects which were not university-led (e.g. a creative hub owned and run by a local authority but where the university might have been mentioned). We then mapped some projects that have already ended (under the type 1 creative hub) when extensive web resources were still available. This is because we believed it was important to capture the temporary nature of some of these infrastructures. Finally, we focused on universities as hubs, so some of the projects where multiple universities were involved have been counted as individual projects and associated with each institution as we tried to map the connection between creative hubs and institutional type.[1]

In our research, we have identified seven types of creative hubs. Of course, many included a range of activities and objectives and could have been considered under more than one of our categories. However, we looked at the main focus of the hub to define a single type for each of the hub identified in our online research.

1. Creative hub as temporary infrastructure
   Our mapping reveals a number of projects, which we could identify with the term 'creative hub' but that were temporary in framework and have now ended. We still think it is important to include these in our reflection as they highlight two key aspects of the nature of creative hub. In one respect, they are often linked to temporary funding and therefore need to end. However, this is not always an issue as they are also based on the idea that stimulating networks and interaction can create long-term self-sustaining ecologies. For example, the four Knowledge Exchange Hubs for the creative economy funded by

---

[1]We grouped HEIs under 4 commonly used categories: 1. Russell group universities (24 research-intensive universities who receive the majority of research grant and contract income); 2. Other 'old' universities (including institutions who used to belong to the 1994 group); 3. New universities (or post-1992 established as part of the abolition of the binary divide in 1992); 4. Higher Education/ Further education colleges also known as specialist colleges as in this case they include institutions that only teach creative subjects (such as Royal College of Music). The Russell group universities followed by the other old universities are generally considered to be more prestigious.

the AHRC which are now closed projects have been included in this category.[2]

2. Creative hubs as rented workspaces/incubator

Many universities have themselves started/renovated spaces to rent out to professionals on a temporary basis or are involved in other external projects of these nature as partners. There are a range of advantages both in bringing in professionals (whether giving them access also to students and research within the university) and in creating spaces that alumni and ex-students can also benefit from, often with the view to locally retaining talent. Some examples of these kinds of incubators and rented workspaces are: the Creative Studios Project supported by Aberystwyth University (targeting mainly external practitioners as renters) and Marketplace Studios supported by Manchester Metropolitan University specifically for its graduates from the Manchester School of Art.

3. Creative hub as research (impact/ industry-based) unit or brokering unit

Many universities interpret a creative hub as meeting space for industry and academic research, where academics and research can focus on 'impact driven research' or commissions delivered for the benefit of outside partners and customers. Often these kinds of hubs are centrally driven by the institutions to engage with the industry as well as showcase current research project and activities. Examples of this type of hubs are the Digital Creativity Labs at the University of York or the CoAST Research Group at Canterbury Christ Church. They can vary in size and infrastructure as sometimes they can be centrally managed by the university or affiliated and created by an individual department.

4. Creative hub as shared/open lab

This interpretation of the creative hub is quite flexible and influenced by the emergence of the FabLab movement that connects

---

[2]Further information http://www.ahrc.ac.uk/innovation/knowledgeexchange/hubsforthecreative economy/.

with the idea of seeing a hub as an open space (Walter-Herrmann and Büching 2014). The infrastructure is used for knowledge exchange, Research and Development support, and access to university networks, students and researchers. Often depending on the nature of the subjects involved, this can be seen as a gallery space or recording studios. The main characteristic of these types of hubs is the fluidity and flexibility that these labs provide, involving a range of stakeholders (internal and external) for different activities. An example of this type of hub is FACTLab based at Liverpool John Moores University.

5. Creative hub as student shared workspace/student-base service provider

In this format of the creative hub, students are key in the delivery of content and services to outside partners. This approach closely resonates with Virani and Malem's (2015, p. 8) discussion of the 'Training Institution': 'This can be a college or university or course or programme. Training institutions in the creative sector primarily use apprenticeship-type learning. Fashion colleges with studio provision are a prime example of this type of hub'. As Virani and Malem's analysis shows, there are multiple configurations and aims associated with university initiatives operating with/as businesses. There were two examples from our analysis that have also featured in extant scholarship. Artswork Media at Bath Spa University is a creative industries simulated work-based learning environment. Students on a specific degree programme work together as part of 'a creative agency'—moving off-campus to a dedicated facility located at the Paintworks creative quarter in Bristol (Ashton 2016). As part of this, students aim to position themselves as industry professionals and develop industry identities in working on 'real world' projects for external 'clients' (Ashton 2013). A similar initiative at Bournemouth University, Red Balloon, sees students also working for external clients. In distinction to Artswork Media, this activity is not assessed as part of a degree programme and the overall Red Balloon producer is a University staff member who acts as a gatekeeper and overseas students working in a freelance capacity on different projects. In both examples, the emphasis is on student employability and enterprise.

6. Creative hub as talent event / competition / festival
Rather than a physical or virtual space, some universities use talent events and competitions as a way to bring together students, current research and specific industry sectors. For example, 'Tranzfuser' is a talent programme led UK Games Talent with the aim 'to provide an annual shot of top talent into the UK development ecosystem' and is hosted and supported by a range of universities throughout the UK. This can prove a cost-effective way to broker relationships with the industry without long-term financial commitments.

7. Creative hub as business support network
Some universities or specific departments engage with outside partners through the creation of a business support network, inviting external companies to events and opportunities and offering them support in relation to specific university expertise. This type of activity requires less infrastructure and investment. An example of this type of network is the Design Knowledge Network (DKN) at Birmingham City University. However, it is important to note that many other hubs (especially of type 2 and 5) also include business support networks activities.

Creative Hubs Dimensions

While these 7 types are present in many universities across the UK and, in many cases, some of the hubs perform more than one role, distinguishing precisely between types of hubs is problematic. However, we think it is important to place them all in a continuum, which tends to stretch across two axes.

- Physical vs. virtual spaces
Some hubs are just events, opportunities or web platform while others are much more based on the physical infrastructure of a studio or gallery. These two extremes often also coincide with the level of investment and commitment that an institution intended to make in its own hub, or the level of partnership and co-funding that some university can take part into in order to develop physical premises.

The hub as a 'third space' can be further interpreted by shifting the emphasis on space away from physical locations to the activities that happen in the space created between/by universities and a range of key players that includes 'higher education, creative industries and arts and cultural sector, public policy, and community' as illustrated in Comunian and Gilmore's 'Who's Who?' (2015, p. 8). For example, Virani and Malem (2015, p. 6) cite the concerns of the City Fringe Partnership (2005, p. 12) on the 'placeness' of hubs and their association with 'a single organisation' or a building, rather as a 'focus on activities or processes'. Our approach of examining universities *as* creative hubs similarly puts the emphasis on the activities, events and initiatives that are developed and facilitated by universities. Of course, there are highly visible manifestations established as buildings and organisational identities that form part of the public communication and construction concerning what universities are. For example, universities as organisations skilled in marketing are highly attentive to how they reach out to students, alumni, partners and so on (see Pettinger et al. 2016). As Virani and Malem (2015) argue in reviewing different articulations of the concept of hubs, seeing them as buildings or spaces only gives a partial account. Bringing together the different articulations, Virani and Malem (2015, p. 7) argue that, 'newer articulations of creative hubs view them as a combination of physical/virtual spaces that provide and facilitate important business support activities and processes like networking, research opportunities, collaborations and the like'. For the university then, this is an important combination which highlights the situatedness within a particular region and accounts for the diverse range of activities and contributions. As Virani and Malem (2015, p. 8) summarise, 'creative hubs, arguably, become important nodes for creative SMEs partly because they provide these services, but also because they provide the spaces and places for these services to exist and coalesce around'.

- Internal and externally facing communities
  The other axis addresses the hub in relation to specific communities it aims to serve. On one side, there are hubs which are mainly there to support students or academic research. On the opposite, there

are hubs that do not aim to serve the academic community but to bring on campus companies and start-ups and engage them in the kind of services the university can provide. There is however a degree of mutuality when it comes to shared priorities around employability, the development of 'industry ready' graduates and the development and retention of local talent. An important distinction then is between creative hubs which provide support, resources, etc. for creative businesses, and student enterprise units in which students work as business for clients on their projects and briefs.

The student enterprise unit can be situated within a broader pedagogical approach to employability which values flexibility and authenticity in student engagement with employers. The student enterprise unit is the focus of Jackson et al.'s (2014) report into university business services and is firmly connected with a creative economy vocational agenda that has been evaluated by a number of commentators (Ashton 2011, 2015; Bridgstock and Cunningham 2016). There have been a number of reports that focus on employability and educational initiatives that provide students with 'real-world' experiences (see Ashton 2014). For Shreeve and Smith (2012), within the creative arts there are a range of ways of providing 'authentic' learning experiences, including industry practitioners setting briefs, students undertaking work placements and the replication of conditions of working in studio or workshop structure. As Ashton (2016, p. 27) suggests, 'enterprise education, as with other models of work-based learning, places a premium on "real-world", situated learning, and the formation of professional competencies and identities'. Pettinger et al. (2016, p. 10) show how this approach manifests globally in their research on the 'industry' approach of Limkokwing University: 'as a teaching philosophy, industry was made manifest through pedagogical strategies where the classroom mimics the corporate world: such as working on "multidisciplinary teams on assigned projects based upon the world of work which will be group assessed" (Global Classroom)'. This idea of the 'real world' will be returned to in our discussion section when we reflect on notions of 'managed interventions'. As part of the range of learning and teaching approaches to embedding employability and encouraging entrepreneurship (see Ashton 2013; Naudin 2013; Pettinger et al. 2016), the student enterprise unit presents a distinctive offering around proximity to and in-betweenness with industry.

On the opposite side, there are hubs where the aim is not concerned with serving the academic community but rather bringing to campus companies and start-ups and engaging them in the kind of services the university can provide. Here we have for example creative hubs that offer workspace specifically to external companies or research unit that are able to provide consultancy or other services to local industries and policy bodies (type 3). The recent push for universities to be engaged more with this external impact agenda is recognised in the literature as an extension of both the civic role of the universities but also of their regional economic impact (Comunian et al. 2014). However, as discussed in the conclusions of this chapter, it is important to question of how much these opportunities can be 'engineered' by institutional policies.

Creative Hubs Distribution and Institutional Missions

In our data analysis we consider, firstly, the frequency of different types of hubs and, secondly, the connection between the nature of the institution and the type of hub. The first table below shows the numbers of 'creative hubs' mapped per each type. As it could be expected, the largest number of hubs belongs to the *creative hub as temporary infrastructure* type. Of course, this often requires limited financial and infrastructural commitments but also the projects are more numerous as we were able to map both some current projects and some that had recently concluded. The second most common type of hub (although the number differences between the overall count of hubs type 2–3 and 4 are very similar) is the *creative hub as 'shared/open lab'*. It was surprising to find such a large number of these types of hubs, especially as 'FabLab' style infrastructures are a recent phenomenon. However, we see that these kinds of hubs offer a great degree of flexibility as they cater flexibly for students, new research and external partners or commercial operations, so we see them as a growing trend in academia (as they are outside academia). The third type of hub by popularity is the *creative hub as rented workspaces/incubator*. We expected this to be a common option as the attention towards affordable workspace for both young graduates and local creatives has been a concern in the literature and policy field for the past decades. Many universities who see their mission in supporting and regenerating the local context use this kind of intervention to benefit students but also to work with local authorities and partners. Fourth is the *creative hub as research (impact/industry-based) unit or brokering unit*. We expected this kind of hub to be even more common as impact has become very high on universities' research agendas. This needs to be facilitated and demonstrated to benefit external partners, but also to help with research funding and university ranking. The last three types of hubs are certainly more specific and less popular but still important. *Creative hub as student shared workspace/student-base service* provider is certainly a type of hub which applies to specific type of institutions (we discuss this later) as not all institutions aim to give professional level training to their arts/creative graduates. Similarly, *creative hub as talent event/competition/festival* would benefit more institutions with arts/creative graduates. Finally, the *creative hub as business support network* was very limited in presence but was often embedded in other projects (specifically in the type 2 and type 4 hubs) integrating physical with virtual/event-based support and infrastructure for practitioners (Table 19.1).

We are now interested in discussing how the presence of these hubs connects to the institutional types (and different mission and students/subjects they present) as illustrated in Table 19.2. As we can notice, *Creative hubs as temporary infrastructure* are very popular for both Russell group universities and other old universities. This seems to connect with the strength and ability of these institutions to attract temporary research funding and activities to establish creative hubs. *Creative hubs as rented workspaces/incubator* are specifically important for post-1992 institutions (and specialised institutions) as these include universities with many creative subjects and courses with a larger student population interested in these incubators and start-up opportunities. This is the

Table 19.1   Creative hubs types and their distribution

Creative hub type	Number of hubs
1. Creative hub as temporary infrastructure	32
2. Creative hub as rented workspaces/incubator	24
3. Creative hub as research (impact industry-based) unit or brokering unit	22
4. Creative hub as shared/open lab	27
5. Creative hub as student shared workspace/student-base service provider	11
6. Creative hub as talent event/competition/festival	9
7. Creative hub as business support network	3
	128

Table 19.2   Creative hubs and institutional types

Institutional types (in brackets number of HEIs mapped in each category)					
Creative hub type	Russell group (13)	Other old (and former 1994 group) (22)	Post-1992 (42)	Specialist (8)	Total
1	9	16	4	3	32
2	1	5	14	4	24
3	6	3	8	5	22
4	4	8	13	2	27
5	1	1	9	0	11
6	0	0	8	1	9
7	0	1	2	0	3
Total	21	34	58	15	128

case also *for creative hub as student shared workspace/student-base service provider. Creative hub as research (impact/industry-based) unit or brokering unit* has a strong presence in Russell group universities as well as in post-1992 and specialised institutions. *Creative hubs as shared/open lab* are instead more popular with other old universities and post-1992 institutions capturing a mix of student-focused initiatives and need for engagement with innovation and research. The last two types of hubs—*creative hub as talent event/competition/festival and creative hub as business support network-* remain more popular with post-1992 institutions again because of their activities and student-focused initiatives.

Debating Universities as Creative Hubs

The chapter has highlighted the extensive range of ideas and activities captured by the expression 'creative hub' across UK universities. Following Dovey et al. (2016, p. 14) and their analysis of creative hubs, this is less about 'enumerating the various types or instances of creative hubs, but rather in understanding the types of processes and values that shape and govern their day to day activities'. By focusing on universities as creative hubs, this chapter contributes to understanding how hubs emerge from 'particular histories and circumstances', take on 'emergent properties' and 'are forged in the experience of practice' (Dovey et al. 2016, p. 14). We also highlighted the connections of the hubs with the institutional type and focus. While all these initiatives have different objectives and structures, there are certain commonalities in considering them as 'managed interventions' that function as conduit between academia and the outside creative sector. Comunian and Gilmore (2015, p. 19) identify that many of the higher education interventions associated with the creative economy 'push for more managed interventions and business structures'. This point around 'managed interventions' helps to raise a number of further points for discussion and debate.

Firstly, an important question remains as to how many of these creative hubs end up serving established institutional teaching and research agendas, rather than offering a space for a range of unexpected and emergent practices to emerge across academia and the creative economy. While there is no 'one-size-fits-all approach' (Dovey et al. 2016, p. 6), the earlier emphasised core ethos of co-construction and collaboration was not always visible in the examples we reviewed. This was especially the case of *creative hubs as student shared workspace/student-base service provider*. While there were indications that students could seek to take ownership of an initiative and contribute to the structure and vision for the hub (Ashton 2016), the overall impression was that the processes and ways of working were set in place. The possibilities for emergent practices to develop spontaneously seem to be limited in the light of the established aims and infrastructure. A related point may be made in looking at the Centre for Fashion Enterprise (CFE) started by London College of Fashion. In reviewing the CFE, Virani and Malem (2015) note the funding from the European Regional Development Fund, the incubator status and the ways in which it uses targeted interventions. While the CFE is tied to extant teaching agendas like the examples of the student shared workspace/student-base service provider, there remains a question of balance between exploring emergent possibilities and engaging with an established approach to fulfilling a set remit (i.e. developing a business through a programme of content including business advice, finance, sales, legal and brand building).

This point has wider resonances with discussions on the role of universities in societies in ensuring measurable contributions to the creative economy and/or as spaces of experimentation (De Lissovoy 2015). The possibilities for experimentation associated with universities have a longer history that precedes current attention on creative economy hubs. For example, Banks and Oakley (2016, p. 48) consider review critical perspectives on the art school, notably by Frith and Horne (1987), and argue that it is 'less as a conveyor belt or production line for fully-formed creative industry "talent", and more as an indeterminate context for the cultivation of a type – the creative or artistic personality – whose "career path", was regarded as an extrinsic and external matter'. It is clear that there are significant differences in looking to art schools in the 1980s and creative hubs in the 2010s—not least in the fate of arts schools and the ways in which they are positioned within universities (Beck and Cornford 2012). That said, an emphasis on university creative hubs within the 'developmental pathways between HE and creative industry' (Banks and Oakley 2016, p. 49) raises this question around hubs as spaces of experimentation. This is not to overlook a number of examples of serendipitous meetings and spontaneous encounters leading to unexpected productive exchanges (see Virani and Malem 2015; Crogan 2015). Rather, an avenue to pursue here is the mix of the established and the emergent. Hubs as having a clear enough established set of aims and approaches to be coherent and compelling to those that it might engage, yet open and flexible enough to be emergent, co-constructed and collaborative.

Secondly, in some cases, it seems important to question whether the cultural milieu of the university and the other associated elements such as the Student Unions (see Long 2011) can remain at the heart of these interventions or if the pressure for these hubs to become successful marketing or sponsorship interventions might be stronger (Comunian and Gilmore 2015). The focus of type 3 creative hubs for example seems very much about externalising university research for the benefit of the industry/society rather than facilitating organic developments. Banks and Oakley (2016, p. 51) highlight the 'informal links between art school and the cultural sector, that sustained a relatively porous and indeterminate relationship between HE and the wider world' and how this has been replaced 'with a more formal "knowledge transfer" model'. We can certainly see that some types of hubs have taken forward an agenda for knowledge transfer and are used as a formal output and impact activity rather than an informal activity.

Thirdly, there is an important next step to address in more detail around the practices, processes and politics of access. As Virani and Malem (2015) identify in relation to The Trampery, there is a curatorship element in accepting entry to and bringing people together within creative hubs. Connecting with analysis of access and equality in relation to art schools (Burke and McManus 2011; Banks and Oakley 2016), work placements and internships (Allen 2013; Ashton 2014; Lee 2013) and the creative and cultural industries more broadly (Allen et al. 2017), we would ask how practices of curatorship operate in relation to university creative hubs. Given the importance of creative hubs as nodes (Virani and Malem 2015), an examination of how issues of access are managed is vital. Three of the five recommendations by Crogan (2015, pp. 7–8) for the *Good Hubbing Guide* for indie games development address openness and inclusivity:

> Be open to new people and new talent: hubs need a regular refresh of the beneficiaries; Operate as a hub for the surrounding community of game and creative makers via events, social media and collaboration with other groups; Create open and accessible opportunities for 'non-members' in the local community to engage and exchange.

These issues of access and diversity also feature in the Birmingham Open Media case study discussed by Dovey et al. (2016, pp. 50–51): 'BOM explores how to use the language of innovation and creativity to be accessible to a wide range people, e.g. BAME, LGBT+, precarious communities like refugees'. This approach is further elaborated on: 'rather than an "engagement plan" this is understood as establishing open access spaces' (Dovey et al. 2016, p. 52). Noting the idea of 'third spaces', further research into universities as creative hubs should address who can access and shape these spaces.

Conclusion: Communities of Practice

Creative hubs continue to grow in importance as ways of organising creative economy innovation (Dovey et al. 2016). This is a priority for universities too as they engage 'beyond the campus' (Comunian and Gilmore 2015). While there are definitional and mapping challenges, it remains productive to understand how creative hubs operate. As part of this broader examination of creative hubs, this chapter has focused on how universities have connected with the concept of creative hubs and make it happen in different ways. While there are again definitional and mapping challenges and a range of contextual factors, the mapping presented here contributes both to understanding creative hubs and how universities can seek to engage with the creative economy.

The question of how creative hubs operate within a university context underpinned all the points raised in the section above on Debating Universities as Creative Hubs responding to hubs as 'managed interventions': How do they align with or have the capacity to reshape existing research and teaching agendas?; how do they build on, replicate or hinder existing forms of creative (hub) activity?; how do they work towards accessibility? A further way to unite these questions is through the concept of communities of practice as defined by Wenger as a: 'special kind of community in which the bond is the shared interest in a specific subject or topic' (cited in Comunian and Gilmore 2015, p. 7). As Comunian and Gilmore (2016, p. 6) suggest, 'communities of practice are specifically relevant for the creative industries, as they build networks of knowledge and support among practitioners in specialised fields'. Across the seven types of hub we identified, there is a shared, core element of 'networks of knowledge and support'. However, as Comunian (2017) notes, with networks and collaboration it is also important to consider issue of power and institutional policy. Similarly, as England and Comunian (2016) highlight, while universities interventions in local creative ecosystems might aim to support local creative industries, it can sometimes create dynamics of competition and hinder the development of local small creative businesses. Across the three questions we raise in the final section there is a shared concern around the creation of and connection between communities. Bringing together our analysis of hubs with some of the tensions around 'managed interventions' leads us to three conclusions which we frame as questions for continued investigation. Firstly, how do creative hub communities of practice overlap and intersect with research and teaching communities? Secondly, how do creative hub communities of practice overlap and intersect with existing creative communities of practice within a local milieu? Thirdly, what are the mechanisms for ensuring accessibility for the creative hub as a community of practice?

Across the different types of hubs we identify, there was a recurring theme around the balance between connecting communities of practice and creating communities of practice. A balance between the extant and the emergent. How established is the knowledge and how open are the networks? As universities, practitioners and policymakers continue to explore the modes and practices of creative hubs within a university context, exploring this balance will remain of great significance.

References

Allen, K. (2013). 'What do you need to make it as a woman in this industry? Balls!': Work placements, gender and the cultural industries. In D. Ashton & C. Noonan (Eds.), *Cultural work and higher education* (pp. 232–253). Basingstoke: Palgrave Macmillan.

Allen, K., Friedman, S., O'Brien, D., & Saha, A. (2017). Producing and consuming inequality: A cultural sociology of the cultural industries. *Cultural Sociology, 11*(3), 271–282.

Ashton, D. (2011). Media work and the creative industries: Identity work, professionalism and employability. *Education and Training, 53*(6), 546–560.

Ashton, D. (2013). Cultural workers in-the-making. *European Journal of Cultural Studies, 16*(4), 368–388.

Ashton, D. (2014). Creative contexts: Work placement subjectivities for the creative industries. *British Journal of Sociology of Education, 38*(2), 268–287.

Ashton, D. (2015). Creative workers and career trajectories: Pathways and portfolios for the creative economy. *Journal of Education and Work, 28*(4), 388–406.

Ashton, D. (2016). From campus to creative quarter: Constructing industry identities in creative places. In R. Comunian & A. Gilmore (Eds.), *Beyond the campus: Higher education & creative economy* (pp. 21–40). London: Routledge.

Banks, M., & Oakley, K. (2016). The dance goes on forever? Art schools, class and UK higher education. *International Journal of Cultural Policy, 22*(1), 41–57.

Beck, J., & Cornford, M. (2012). The arts school in ruins. *Journal of Visual Culture, 11*(1), 58–83.

Benneworth, P. (2016). Tensions in university-community engagement: Creative economy, urban regeneration and social justice. In R. Comunian & A. Gilmore (Eds.), *Beyond the campus: Higher education & creative economy* (pp. 223–241). London: Routledge.

Bridgstock, R., & Cunningham, S. (2016). Creative labour and graduate outcomes: Implications for higher education and cultural policy. *International Journal of Cultural Policy, 22*(1), 10–26.

Burke, P. J., & McManus, J. (2011). Art for a few: Exclusions and misrecognitions in higher education admissions practices. *Discourse: Studies in the Cultural Politics of Education, 32*(5), 699–712.

Chatterton, P., & Goddard, J. (2000). The response of higher education institutions to regional needs. *European Journal of Education, 35*(4), 475–496.

Comunian, R. (2017). Creative collaborations: The role of networks, power and policy. In M. Shiach & T. E. Virani (Eds.), *Cultural policy, innovation and the creative economy* (pp. 231–244). London: Palgrave Macmillan.

Comunian, R., & Gilmore, A. (2015). *Beyond the creative campus: Reflections on the evolving relationship between higher education and the creative economy.* Published by King's College London, London, UK. Available at www.creative-campus.org.uk.

Comunian, R., & Gilmore, A. (2016). Higher education and the creative economy. In R. Comunian & A. Gilmore (Eds.), *Higher education and the creative economy: Beyond the campus* (pp. 3–18). London: Routledge.

Comunian, R., & Ooi, C. S. (2016). Global aspirations and local talent: The development of creative higher education in Singapore. *International Journal of Cultural Policy, 22*(1), 58–79.

Comunian, R., Faggian, A., & Jewell, S. (2011). Winning and losing in the creative industries: An analysis of creative graduates' career opportunities across creative disciplines. *Cultural Trends, 20*(3/4), 291–308.

Comunian, R., Taylor, C., & Smith, D. N. (2014). The role of universities in the regional creative economies of the UK: Hidden protagonists and the challenge of knowledge transfer. *European Planning Studies, 22*(12), 2456–2476.

Comunian, R., Gilmore, A., & Jacobi, S. (2015). Higher education and the creative economy: Creative graduates, knowledge transfer and regional impact debates. *Geography Compass, 9*(7), 371–383.

Crogan, P. (2015). *Good hubbing guide*. Arts and Humanities Research Council. Available at https://dcrc.org.uk/wp-content/uploads/2015/06/Good%20Hubbing%20Guide.pdf. Accessed 22 October 2017.

De Lissovoy, N. (2015). *Education and emancipation in the neoliberal era: Being, teaching, and power*. Basingstoke and New York: Palgrave Macmillan.

Dovey, J., Pratt, A. C., Moreton, S., Virani, T. E., Merkel, J., & Lansdowne, J. (2016). *Creative hubs: Understanding the new economy*. London: British Council.

England, L., & Comunian, R. (2016). Support or competition? Assessing the role of HEIs in professional networks and local creative communities. In R. Comunian & A. Gilmore (Eds.), *Beyond the campus: Higher education & creative economy* (pp. 145–163). London: Routledge.

Evans, G. (2009). Creative cities, creative spaces and urban policy. *Urban Studies, 46*(5–6), 1003–1040.

Frith, S., & Horne, H. (1987). *Art into pop*. London: Metheun.

Jackson, D., Molesworth, M., & Goode, G. (2014). *Students and knowledge exchange in university business services*. Bournemouth: Bournemouth University. Available at https://microsites.bournemouth.ac.uk/cmc/files/2014/07/BU-Students-and-knowledge-exchange-in-university-business-services.pdf. Accessed 30 March 2015.

Lee, D. (2013). Creative networks and social capital. In D. Ashton & C. Noonan (Eds.), *Cultural work and higher education* (pp. 195–213). Basingstoke: Palgrave Macmillan.

Long, P. (2011). Student music. *Art Marketing: An International Journal, 1*(2), 121–135.

Naudin, A. (2013). Media enterprise in higher education: A laboratory for learning. In D. Ashton & C. Noonan (Eds.), *Cultural work and higher education* (pp. 110–130). Basingstoke: Palgrave Macmillan.

Pettinger, L., Forkert, K., & Goffey, A. (2016). The promises of creative industry higher education: An analysis of university prospectuses in Malaysia. *International Journal of Cultural Policy.* Online first, http://dx.doi.org/10.10 80/10286632.2016.1223644.

REACT. (2016). *REACT report 2012–2016.* Available at http://www.react-hub.org.uk/sites/default/files/publications/REACT%20Report%20low%20 res_2.pdf. Accessed 20 September 2017.

Shreeve, A., & Smith, C. (2012). Multi-directional creative transfer between practice-based arts education and work. *British Educational Research Journal, 38*(4), 539–556.

Transfuzer. (n.d.). *About us.* Available at http://tranzfuser.com/about/. Accessed 20 September 2017.

Virani, T. E., & Malem, W. (2015). *Re-articulating the creative hub concept as a model for business support in the local creative economy: The case of Mare Street in Hackney* (Creativeworks London Working Paper Series Number 12). Available at http://www.creativeworkslondon.org.uk/wp-content/ uploads/2013/11/PWK-Working-Paper-12.pdf.

Walter-Herrmann, J., & Büching, C. (2014). *FabLab: Of machines, makers and inventors.* Bielefeld: transcript Verlag.

Index

© The Editor(s) (if applicable) and The Author(s) 2019   **381**
R. Gill et al. (eds.), *Creative Hubs in Question*, Dynamics of Virtual Work,
https://doi.org/10.1007/978-3-030-10653-9

Printed by Printforce, the Netherlands